New Perspectives on

MICROSOFT® WORD 2002

Introductory

COURSE TECHNOLOGY

THOMSON LEARNING ™

New Perspectives on Microsoft® Word 2002—Introductory
is published by Course Technology.

Managing Editor:
Greg Donald

Senior Editor:
Donna Gridley

Senior Product Manager:
Kathy Finnegan

Product Manager:
Melissa Hathaway

Technology Product Manager:
Amanda Young

Editorial Assistant:
Jessica Engstrom

Marketing Manager:
Sean Teare

Developmental Editor:
Lisa Ruffolo

Production Editor:
Elena Montillo

Composition:
GEX Publishing Services

Text Designer:
Meral Dabcovich

Cover Designer:
Efrat Reis

New Perspectives on

MICROSOFT® WORD 2002

Introductory

S. SCOTT ZIMMERMAN
Brigham Young University

BEVERLY B. ZIMMERMAN
Brigham Young University

ANN SHAFFER

COURSE TECHNOLOGY

THOMSON LEARNING™

Australia • Canada • Mexico • Singapore • Spain • United Kingdom • United States

APPROVED COURSEWARE

What does this logo mean?

It means this courseware has been approved by the Microsoft Office User Specialist Program to be among the finest available for learning Microsoft® Word 2002. It also means that upon completion of this courseware, you may be prepared to become a Microsoft Office User Specialist.

What is a Microsoft Office User Specialist?

A Microsoft Office User Specialist is an individual who has certified his or her skills in one or more of the Microsoft Office desktop applications of Microsoft Word, Microsoft Excel, Microsoft PowerPoint, Microsoft Outlook or Microsoft Access, or in Microsoft Project. The Microsoft Office User Specialist Program typically offers certification exams at the "Core" and "Expert" skill levels*. The Microsoft Office User Specialist Program is the only Microsoft approved program in the world for certifying proficiency in Microsoft Office desktop applications and Microsoft Project. This certification can be a valuable asset in any job search or career advancement.

More Information:

To learn more about becoming a Microsoft Office User Specialist, visit www.mous.net

To purchase a Microsoft Office User Specialist certification exam, visit www.DesktopIQ.com

To learn about other Microsoft Office User Specialist approved courseware from Course Technology, visit www.course.com/NewPerspectives/TeachersLounge/mous.cfm

Preface

Course Technology is the world leader in information technology education. The New Perspectives Series is an integral part of Course Technology's success. Visit our Web site to see a whole new perspective on teaching and learning solutions.

New Perspectives—Building Computer Skills Has Never Been This Real

Why New Perspectives will work for you.

Critical thinking and **problem solving**—without them, computer skills are learned but soon forgotten. With its **case-based** approach, the New Perspectives Series challenges students to apply what they've learned to real-life situations. Become a member of the New Perspectives community and watch your students not only **master** computer skills, but also **retain** and carry this **knowledge** into the world.

New Perspectives catalog
Our online catalog is never out of date! Go to the Catalog button on our Web site to check out our available titles, request a desk copy, download a book preview, or locate online files.

Complete system of offerings
Whether you're looking for a Brief book, an Advanced book, or something in between, we've got you covered. Go to the Catalog button on our Web site to find the level of coverage that's right for you.

Instructor materials
We have all the tools you need—data files, solution files, figure files, a sample syllabus, and ExamView, our powerful testing software package.

How well do your students know Microsoft Office?
Find out with performance-based testing software that measures your students' proficiency in the application. Click the Tech Center button to learn more.

Get certified
If you want to get certified, we have the titles for you. Find out more by clicking the Teacher's Lounge button.

Interested in online learning?
Enhance your course with any one of our online learning platforms. Go to the Teacher's Lounge to find the platform that's right for you.

Your link to the future is at
www.course.com/NewPerspectives

What you need to know about this book.

- Student Online Companion takes students to the Web for additional work.

- ExamView testing software gives you the option of generating a printed test, LAN-based test, or test over the Internet.

- New Perspectives Labs provide students with self-paced practice on computer-related topics.

- All cases are NEW to this edition!

- Contemporary case stories draw on the latest high-tech scenarios, including a network consulting business and an electronic graphic design firm. Other case stories involve more traditional businesses (such as a landscape design company) that have adapted to modern business demands.

- Students will appreciate how the concepts of desktop publishing are presented and compared to Web page design.

- Our coverage of mail merge explains how to complete a merge using both the new Mail Merge Task Pane and the toolbar buttons. Students use mail merge techniques to create merged letters, a telephone directory, and envelopes—and even to send e-mail.

- The tutorial on sharing documents begins by having students compare and merge three documents. The tutorial clearly explains the issues related to sharing documents in printed form, via e-mail, and as a Web page. Then students prepare three versions of the same document—one to print, one to e-mail, and one to publish as a Web page.

- This book is certified at the MOUS Core level for Word 2002!

CASE	TROUBLE?	SESSION 1.1	QUICK CHECK	RW
Tutorial Case Each tutorial begins with a problem presented in a case that is meaningful to students. The case sets the scene to help students understand what they will do in the tutorial.	**TROUBLE? Paragraphs** These paragraphs anticipate the mistakes or problems that students may have and help them continue with the tutorial.	**Sessions** Each tutorial is divided into sessions designed to be completed in about 45 minutes each. Students should take as much time as they need and take a break between sessions.	**Quick Check Questions** Each session concludes with conceptual Quick Check questions that test students' understanding of what they learned in the session.	**Reference Windows** Reference Windows are succinct summaries of the most important tasks covered in a tutorial. They preview actions students will perform in the steps to follow.

BRIEF CONTENTS

TABLE OF CONTENTS

Microsoft Word 2002—

Level II Tutorials **WD 5.01**

Read This Before You Begin **WD 5.02**

Tutorial 5   WD 5.03

Creating Styles, Outlines, Tables and Tables of Contents

Writing a Business Plan for Sate Site Inc.

Tutorial 6   WD 6.01

Creating Form Letters and Mailing Labels

Writing a Form Letter for Palm Tree Athletic Club

Tutorial 7 — WD 7.01

Collaborating with Others and Creating Web Pages

Writing a Grant Proposal for Space Station Education

Acknowledgments

I'm extremely grateful to the following reviewers for their detailed comments and suggestions, which were very helpful. Reviewing a manuscript is hard work, and they did a great job: Anne Burchardt, Jackson Community College; Michael Feiler, Merritt College; Eric Johnston, Vatterott College; Carol Milliken, Kellogg Community College; and Barbara Williams, Wisconsin Indianhead Technical College.

Many thanks to the following members of the Quality Assurance team at Course Technology for verifying the technical accuracy of every step: John Bosco, Quality Assurance Project Leader; Marianne Broughey, Harris Bierhoff, Serge Palladino, and John Freitas, Quality Assurance Testers.

Thank you to the smart, friendly, helpful people on the New Perspectives Team, including Greg Donald, Donna Gridley, Jessica Engstrom and Rachel Crapser. Special thanks to Kathy Finnegan, Senior Product Manager, who cheerfully kept track of a thousand details and deadlines and who always managed to provide encouragement at exactly the right moment. Sincere thanks to the amazing Lisa Ruffolo, of The Software Resource; a writer couldn't hope for a better editor or a kinder friend. Thank you, also, to Elena Montillo, Production Editor, for patiently managing a very complicated production process, transforming the manuscript into a published book. I owe a great debt to Beverly and Scott Zimmerman, writers and teachers extraordinaire, for giving me the opportunity to be a part of their team. Finally, this book is dedicated to Dean, Joe, and Jerome, three of the nicest wise guys I could ever hope to meet.

— Ann Shaffer

We likewise want to thank all those who made this book possible. We specifically thank Ann Shaffer, our co-author, for her hard work and creative talents in bringing this new edition to fruition.

— Beverly and Scott Zimmerman

New Perspectives

Preface

Course Technology is the world leader in information technology education. The New Perspectives Series is an integral part of Course Technology's success. Visit our Web site to see a whole new perspective on teaching and learning solutions.

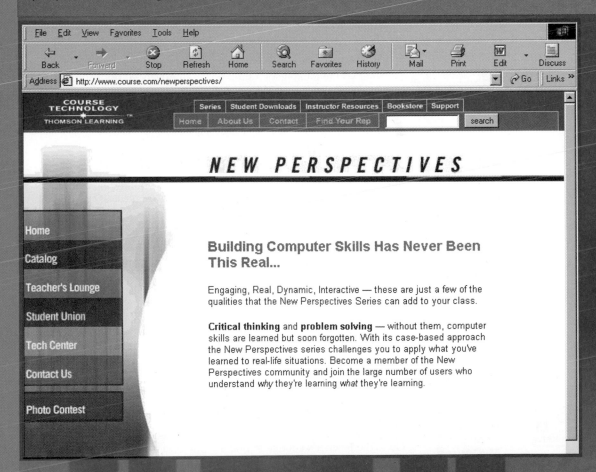

New Perspectives—Building Computer Skills Has Never Been This Real

Why New Perspectives will work for you.

Critical thinking and **problem solving**—without them, computer skills are learned but soon forgotten. With its **case-based** approach, the New Perspectives Series challenges students to apply what they've learned to real-life situations. Become a member of the New Perspectives community and watch your students not only **master** computer skills, but also **retain** and carry this **knowledge** into the world.

New Perspectives catalog
Our online catalog is never out of date! Go to the Catalog button on our Web site to check out our available titles, request a desk copy, download a book preview, or locate online files.

Complete system of offerings
Whether you're looking for a Brief book, an Advanced book, or something in between, we've got you covered. Go to the Catalog button on our Web site to find the level of coverage that's right for you.

Instructor materials
We have all the tools you need—data files, solution files, figure files, a sample syllabus, and ExamView, our powerful testing software package.

How well do your students know Microsoft Office?
Find out with performance-based testing software that measures your students' proficiency in the application. Click the Tech Center button to learn more.

Get certified
If you want to get certified, we have the titles for you. Find out more by clicking the Teacher's Lounge button.

Interested in online learning?
Enhance your course with any one of our online learning platforms. Go to the Teacher's Lounge to find the platform that's right for you.

Your link to the future is at
www.course.com/NewPerspectives

New Perspectives on

MICROSOFT®
OFFICE XP

Read This Before You Begin

To the Student

Data Disks

To complete this tutorial and the Review Assignments, you need one Data Disk. Your instructor will either provide you with the Data Disk or ask you to make your own.

If you are making your own Data Disk, you will need **one** blank, formatted high-density disk. You will need to copy a set of files and/or folders from a file server, standalone computer, or the Web onto your disk. Your instructor will tell you which computer, drive letter, and folder contain the files you need. You could also download the files by going to www.course.com and following the instructions on the screen.

The information below shows you which folder goes on your disk, so that you will have enough disk space to complete the tutorial and Review Assignments:

Data Disk 1

Write this on the disk label:
Data Disk 1: Introducing Office XP

Put this folder on the disk:
Tutorial.01

When you begin the tutorial, be sure you are using the correct Data Disk. Refer to the "File Finder" chart at the back of this text for more detailed information on which files are used in the tutorial. See the inside front or inside back cover of this book for more information on Data Disk files, or ask your instructor or technical support person for assistance.

Using Your Own Computer

If you are going to work through this tutorial using your own computer, you need:

- **Computer System** Microsoft Windows 98, NT, 2000 Professional, or higher must be installed on your computer. This book assumes a typical installation of Microsoft Office XP.

- **Data Disk** You will not be able to complete this tutorial or Review Assignments using your own computer until you have your Data Disk.

Visit Our World Wide Web Site

Additional materials designed especially for you are available on the World Wide Web.
Go to www.course.com/NewPerspectives.

To the Instructor

The Data Disk Files are available on the Instructor's Resource Kit for this title. Follow the instructions in the Help file on the CD-ROM to install the programs to your network or standalone computer. For information on creating the Data Disk, see the "To the Student" section above.

You are granted a license to copy the Data Disk Files to any computer or computer network used by students who have purchased this book.

In this tutorial you will:

- Explore the programs that comprise Microsoft Office

- Explore the benefits of integrating data between programs

- Start programs and switch between them

- Use personalized menus and toolbars

- Save and close a file

- Open an existing file

- Print a file

- Get Help

- Close files and exit programs

INTRODUCING MICROSOFT OFFICE XP

Preparing Promotional Materials for Delmar Office Supplies

CASE

Delmar Office Supplies

Delmar Office Supplies, a company in Wisconsin founded by Nicole Delmar in 1996, sells recycled office supplies to businesses and home-based offices around the world. The demand for quality recycled papers, reconditioned toner cartridges, and renovated office furniture has been growing each year. Nicole and all her employees use Microsoft Office XP, which provides everyone in the company the power and flexibility to store a variety of information, create consistent documents, and share data. In this tutorial, you'll review some of the latest documents the company's employees have created using Microsoft Office XP.

Exploring Microsoft Office XP

Microsoft Office XP, or simply **Office**, is a collection of the most popular Microsoft programs: Word, Excel, PowerPoint, Access, and Outlook. Each Office program contains valuable tools to help you accomplish many tasks, such as composing reports, analyzing data, preparing presentations, and compiling information.

Microsoft Word 2002, or simply **Word**, is a **word processing program** you use to create text documents. The files you create in Word are called **documents**. Word offers many special features that help you compose and update all types of documents, ranging from letters and newsletters to reports, fliers, faxes, and even books—all in attractive and readable formats. You also can use Word to create, insert, and position figures, tables, and other graphics to enhance the look of your documents. Figure 1 shows a business letter that a sales representative composed with Word.

Figure 1   **LETTER COMPOSED IN A WORD DOCUMENT**

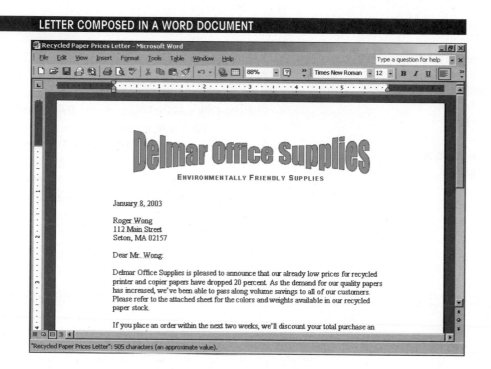

Microsoft Excel 2002, or simply **Excel**, is a **spreadsheet program** you use to display, organize, and analyze numerical information. You can do some of this in Word with tables, but Excel provides many more tools for performing calculations than Word does. Its graphics capabilities also enable you to display data visually. You might, for example, generate a pie chart or bar chart to help readers quickly see the significance of and the connections between information. The files you create in Excel are called **workbooks**. Figure 2 shows an Excel workbook with a line chart that the Operations Department uses to track the company's financial performance.

Figure 2	FINANCIAL DATA IN AN EXCEL WORKBOOK

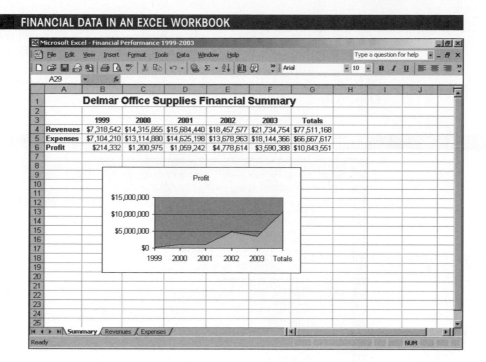

Microsoft PowerPoint 2002, or simply **PowerPoint**, is a **presentation graphics program** you use to create a collection of "slides" that can contain text, charts, pictures, and so on. The files you create in PowerPoint are called **presentations**. You can show these presentations on your computer monitor, project them onto a screen as a slide show, print them, share them over the Internet, or display them on the World Wide Web. You also can use PowerPoint to generate presentation-related documents such as audience handouts, outlines, and speakers' notes. Figure 3 shows an effective slide presentation the Sales Department created with PowerPoint to promote the latest product line.

Figure 3	SLIDE PRESENTATION CREATED IN POWERPOINT

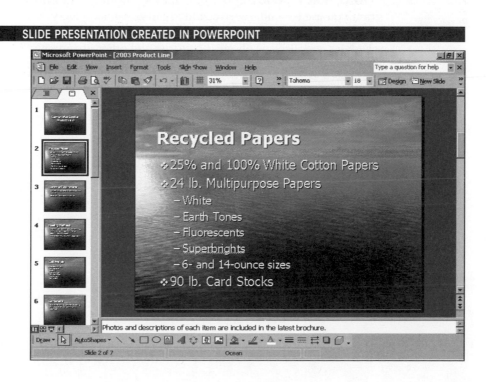

Microsoft Access 2002, or simply **Access**, is a **database program** you use to enter, organize, display, and retrieve related information. The files you create in Access are called **databases**. With Access you can create data entry forms to make data entry easier, and you can create professional reports to improve the readability of your data. Figure 4 shows a table in an Access database with customer names and addresses compiled by the Sales Department.

Figure 4   CUSTOMER ADDRESSES COMPILED IN AN ACCESS DATABASE

Customer Num	Name	Street	City	State/Prov	Postal Code
201	Wonder Supplies	5499 Alpine Lane	Gardner	MA	01440
285	The Best Supplies	2837 Commonwealth Avenue	Cambridge	MA	02142
129	Office World	95 North Bay Boulevard	Warwick	RI	02287
135	Supplies Plus	2840 Cascade Road	Laconia	NH	03246
104	American Office	Pond Hill Road	Millinocket	ME	04462
515	Pens and Paper	8200 Baldwin Boulevard	Burlington	VT	05406
165	Pen and Ink	1935 Snow Street	Nagatuck	CT	06770
423	Wonderful World of Work	H 1055	Budapest	Hungary	1/A
83	Sophia's Supplies	87 Weeping Willow Road	Brooklyn	NY	11201
17	Supplies and More	132-A Old Country Road	Bellport	NY	11763
322	Supply Closet	114 Lexington	Plattsburgh	NY	12901
302	Blackburg's Stationers	4489 Perlman Avenue	Blacksburg	VA	24060
136	Home Office Needs	4090 Division Stret NW	Fort Lauderdale	FL	33302
131	Supplies 4 U	14832 Old Bedford Trail	Mishawaka	IN	46544
122	VIP Stationery	8401 E. Fletcher Road	Clare	MI	48617
164	Supply Depot	1355 39th Street	Roscommon	MI	48653
325	Max Office Supplies	56 Four Mile Road	Grand Rapids	MI	49505
133	Supply Your Office	2874 Western Avenue	Sioux Falls	SD	57057
107	A+ Supplies	82 Mix Avenue	Bonners Ferry	ID	83805
203	Discount Supplies	28320 Fruitland Street	Studio City	CA	94106
536	One Stop Shop	31 Union Street	San Francisco	CA	94123
82	Supply Stop	2159 Causewayside	Edinburgh	Scotland	EH9 1PH
202	Office Products	3130 Edgwood Parkway	Thunder Bay	Ontario	L5B 1X2
407	Paper and More	44 Tower Lane	Leeds	England	LS12 3SD
394	The Office Store	397 Pine Road	Toronto	Ontario	M4J1B5

Microsoft Outlook 2002, or simply **Outlook**, is an **information management program** you use to send, receive, and organize e-mail; plan your schedule; arrange meetings; organize contacts; create a to-do list; and jot down notes. You also can use Outlook to print schedules, task lists, or phone directories and other documents. Figure 5 shows how Nicole Delmar uses Outlook to plan her schedule and create a to-do list.

Figure 5   **CALENDAR AND TASKS IN OUTLOOK**

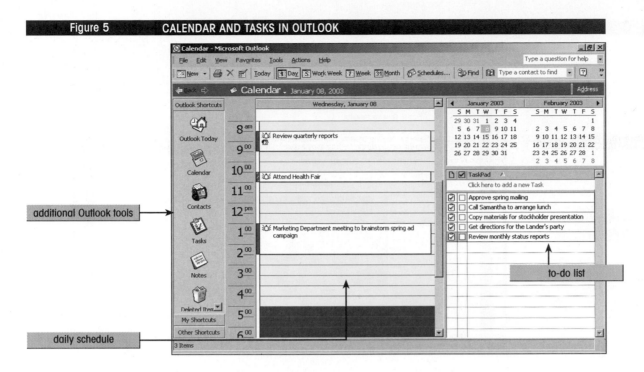

additional Outlook tools

to-do list

daily schedule

Although each Office program individually is a strong tool, their potential is even greater when used together.

Integrating Programs

One of the main advantages of Office is **integration**, the ability to share information between programs. Integration ensures consistency and accuracy, and it saves time because you don't have to re-enter the same information in several Office programs. The staff at Delmar Office Supplies uses the integration features of Office daily, including the following examples:

- The Accounting Department created an Excel bar chart on the last two years' fourth-quarter results, which they inserted into the quarterly financial report, created in Word. They added a hyperlink to the Word report that employees can click to open the Excel workbook and view the original data. See Figure 6.

Figure 6   WORD DOCUMENT WITH AN EXCEL CHART

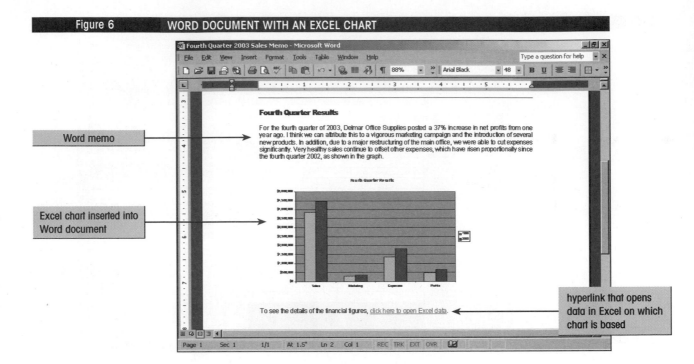

An Excel pie chart of sales percentages by divisions of Delmar Office Supplies can be duplicated on a PowerPoint slide. The slide is part of the Operations Department's presentation to stockholders. See Figure 7.

Figure 7   POWERPOINT PRESENTATION WITH AN EXCEL CHART

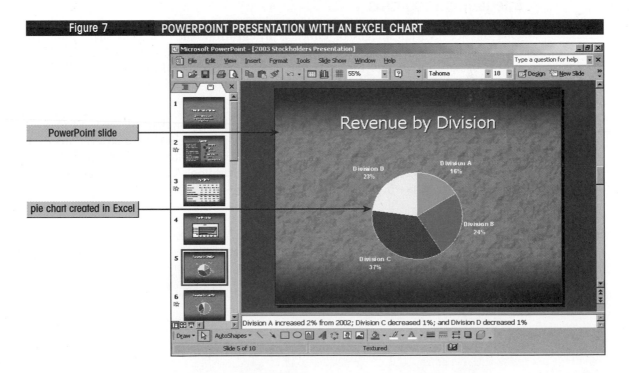

An Access database or an Outlook contact list that stores the names and addresses of customers can be combined with a form letter that the Marketing Department created in Word, to produce a mailing promoting the company's newest products. See Figure 8.

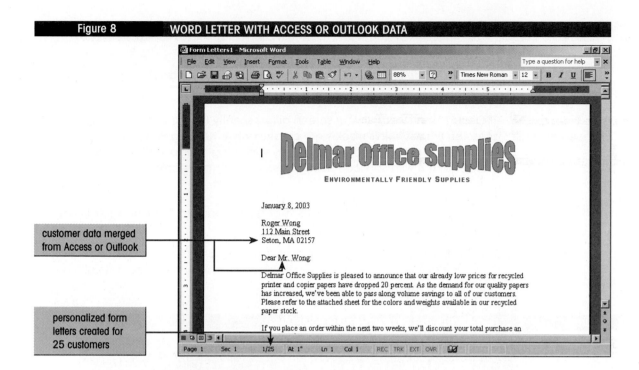

| Figure 8 | WORD LETTER WITH ACCESS OR OUTLOOK DATA |

customer data merged from Access or Outlook

personalized form letters created for 25 customers

These are just a few examples of how you can take information from one Office program and integrate it into another.

Starting **Office Programs**

All Office programs start the same way—from the Programs menu on the Start button. You select the program you want, and then the program starts so you can immediately begin to create new files or work with existing ones.

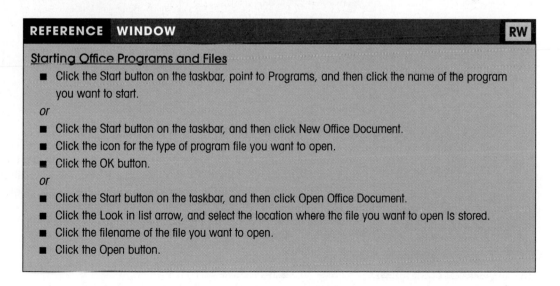

REFERENCE WINDOW   RW

Starting Office Programs and Files
- Click the Start button on the taskbar, point to Programs, and then click the name of the program you want to start.

or
- Click the Start button on the taskbar, and then click New Office Document.
- Click the icon for the type of program file you want to open.
- Click the OK button.

or
- Click the Start button on the taskbar, and then click Open Office Document.
- Click the Look in list arrow, and select the location where the file you want to open is stored.
- Click the filename of the file you want to open.
- Click the Open button.

You'll start Excel using the Start button.

*To start Excel and open a new, blank workbook from the
Start menu:*

1. Make sure your computer is on and the Windows desktop appears on your
   screen.

   TROUBLE? Don't worry if your screen differs slightly from those shown in the figures. The figures in this book were created while running Windows 2000 in its
   default settings, but Office runs equally well using Windows 98 or later or
   Windows NT 4 with Service Pack 5. These operating systems share the same
   basic user interface.

2. Click the **Start** button on the taskbar, and then point to **Programs** to display the
   Programs menu.

3. Point to **Microsoft Excel** on the Programs menu. See Figure 9. Depending on
   how your computer is set up, your desktop and menu might contain different
   icons and commands.

Figure 9   START MENU WITH PROGRAMS MENU DISPLAYED

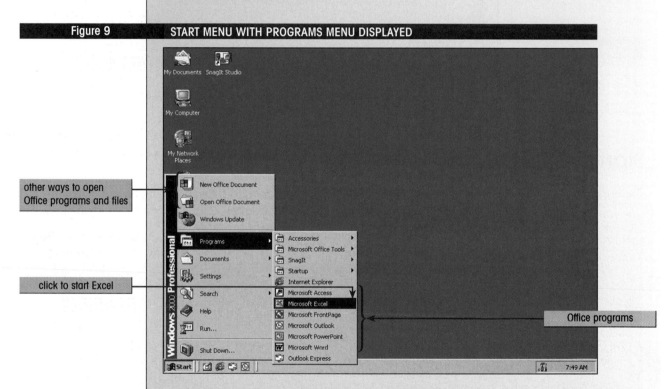

other ways to open
Office programs and files

click to start Excel

Office programs

TROUBLE? If you don't see Microsoft Excel on the Programs menu, point to
Microsoft Office, and then point to Microsoft Excel. If you still don't see Microsoft
Excel, ask your instructor or technical support person for help.

4. Click **Microsoft Excel** to start Excel and open a new, blank workbook. See
   Figure 10.

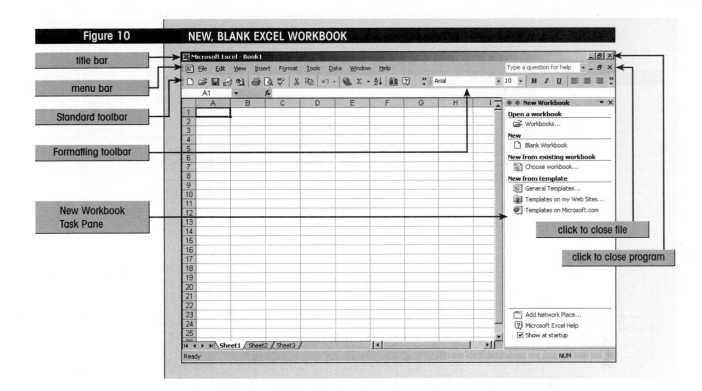

Figure 10 — **NEW, BLANK EXCEL WORKBOOK**

title bar

menu bar

Standard toolbar

Formatting toolbar

New Workbook Task Pane

click to close file

click to close program

An alternate method for starting programs with a blank file is to click the New Office Document command on the Start menu; the kind of file you choose determines which program opens. You'll use this method to start Word and open a new, blank document.

To start Word and open a new, blank document with the New Office Document command:

1. Leaving Excel open, click the **Start** button on the taskbar, and then click **New Office Document**. The New Office Document dialog box opens, providing another way to start Office programs. See Figure 11.

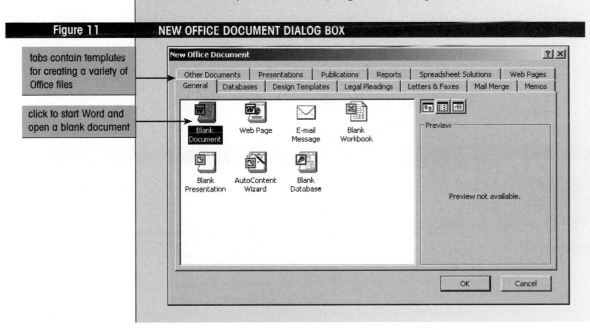

Figure 11 — **NEW OFFICE DOCUMENT DIALOG BOX**

tabs contain templates for creating a variety of Office files

click to start Word and open a blank document

2. If necessary, click the **General** tab, click the **Blank Document** icon, and then click the **OK** button. Word opens with a new, blank document. See Figure 12.

Figure 12	NEW, BLANK DOCUMENT IN WORD

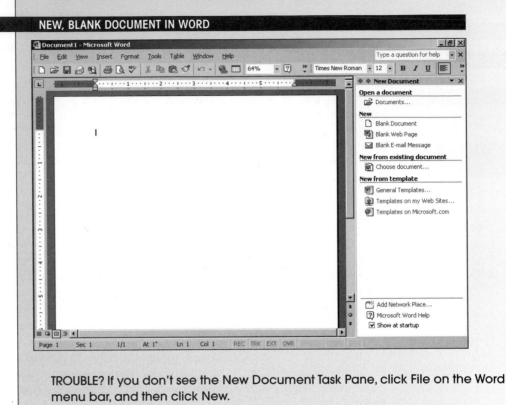

TROUBLE? If you don't see the New Document Task Pane, click File on the Word menu bar, and then click New.

You've tried two ways to start a program. There are several methods for performing most tasks in Office. This flexibility enables you to use Office in the way that fits how you like to work.

Switching Between Open Programs and Files

Two programs are running at the same time—Excel and Word. The taskbar contains buttons for both programs. When you have two or more programs running, or two files within the same program open, you can use the taskbar buttons to switch from one program or file to another. The employees at Delmar Office Supplies often work in several programs at once.

To switch between Word and Excel:

1. Click the **Microsoft Excel – Book1** button on the taskbar to switch from Word to Excel. See Figure 13.

Figure 13	EXCEL AND WORD PROGRAMS OPENED

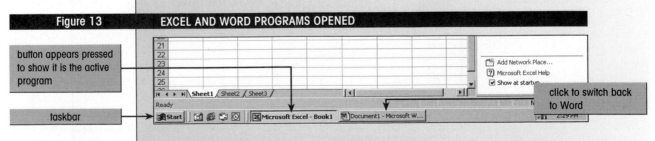

button appears pressed to show it is the active program

click to switch back to Word

taskbar

2. Click the **Document1 – Microsoft Word** button on the taskbar to return to Word.

As you can see, you can start multiple programs and switch between them in seconds.

The Office programs also share many features, so once you've learned one program, it's easy to learn the others. One of the most visible similarities among all the programs is the "personalized" menus and toolbars.

Using **Personalized Menus and Toolbars**

In each Office program, you perform tasks using a menu command, a toolbar button, or a keyboard shortcut. A **menu command** is a word on a menu that you click to execute a task; a **menu** is a group of related commands. For example, the File menu contains commands for managing files, such as the Open command and the Save command. A **toolbar** is a collection of **buttons** that correspond to commonly used menu commands. For example, the Standard toolbar contains an Open button and a Save button. **Keyboard shortcuts** are combinations of keys you press to perform a command. For example, Ctrl+S is the keyboard shortcut for the Save command (you hold down the Ctrl key while you press the S key). Keyboard shortcuts are displayed to the right of many menu commands.

When you first use a newly installed Office program, the menus and toolbars display only the basic and most commonly used commands and buttons, streamlining the program window. The other commands and buttons are available, but you have to click an extra button to see them (the double-arrow button on a menu and the Toolbar Options button on a toolbar). As you select commands and click buttons, the ones you use often are put on the short, personalized menu and on the visible part of the toolbars. The ones you don't use remain available on the full menus and toolbars. This means that the Office menus and toolbars might display different commands and buttons on each person's computer.

To view a personalized and full menu:

1. Click **Insert** on the Word menu bar to display the short, personalized menu. See Figure 14. The Bookmark command, for example, does not appear on the short menu.

| Figure 14 | SHORT, PERSONALIZED MENU |

double-arrow button

TROUBLE? If the Insert menu displays different commands than shown in Figure 14, you need to reset the menus. Click Tools on the menu bar, click Customize (you might need to pause until the full menu appears to see that command), and then click the Options tab in the Customize dialog box. Click the Always show full menus check box to remove the check mark if necessary, and then click the Show full menus after a short delay check box to insert a check mark if necessary. Click the Reset my usage data button, and then click the Yes button to confirm that you want to reset the commands. Click the Close button. Repeat Step 1.

You can display the full menu in one of three ways: (1) pause until the full menu appears, which might happen as you read this; (2) click the double-arrow button at the bottom of the menu; or (3) double-click the menu name on the menu bar.

2. Pause until the full Insert menu appears, as shown in Figure 15. The Bookmark command and other commands are now visible.

| Figure 15 | EXPANDED, FULL MENU |

commands with light border appear on short menu

commands with dark border appear only on full menu

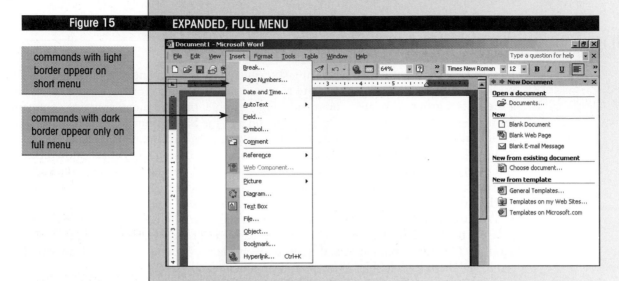

3. Click the **Bookmark** command. A dialog box opens when you click a command whose name is followed by an ellipsis (...). In this case, the Bookmark dialog box opens.

4. Click the **Cancel** button to close the Bookmark dialog box.

5. Click **Insert** on the menu bar again to display the short, personalized menu. The Bookmark command appears on the short, personalized menu because you used it.

6. Press the **Esc** key to close the menu.

As you can see, the menu changed based on your actions. Over time, only the commands you use frequently will appear on the personalized menu. The toolbars work similarly.

To use the personalized toolbars:

1. Observe that the Standard and Formatting toolbars appear side by side below the menu bar.

TROUBLE? If the toolbars appear on two rows, you need to reset them. Click Tools on the menu bar, click Customize, and then click the Options tab in the Customize dialog box. Click the Show Standard and Formatting toolbars on two rows check box to remove the check mark. Click the Reset my data usage button, and then click the Yes button to confirm you want to reset the commands. Click the Close button. Repeat Step 1.

The Formatting toolbar sits to the right of the Standard toolbar. You can see most of the Standard toolbar buttons, but only a few Formatting toolbar buttons.

2. Click the **Toolbar Options** button ⊞ at the right side of the Standard toolbar. See Figure 16.

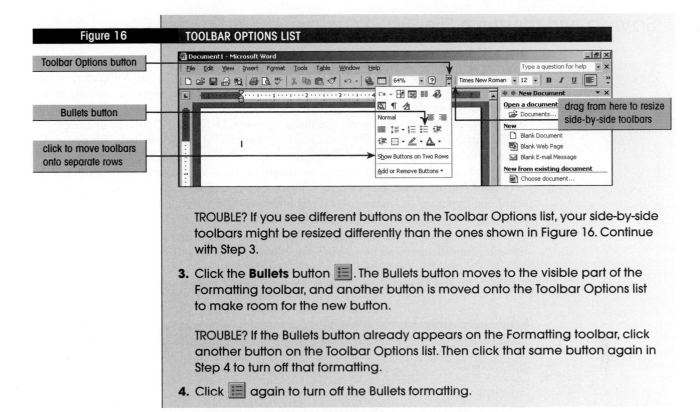

Figure 16   TOOLBAR OPTIONS LIST

Toolbar Options button

Bullets button

click to move toolbars onto separate rows

drag from here to resize side-by-side toolbars

TROUBLE? If you see different buttons on the Toolbar Options list, your side-by-side toolbars might be resized differently than the ones shown in Figure 16. Continue with Step 3.

3. Click the **Bullets** button . The Bullets button moves to the visible part of the Formatting toolbar, and another button is moved onto the Toolbar Options list to make room for the new button.

   TROUBLE? If the Bullets button already appears on the Formatting toolbar, click another button on the Toolbar Options list. Then click that same button again in Step 4 to turn off that formatting.

4. Click again to turn off the Bullets formatting.

Some people like that the menus and toolbars change to meet their work habits. Others prefer to see all the menu commands or to display the toolbars on different rows so that all the buttons are always visible. You'll change the toolbar setting now.

To turn off the personalized toolbars:

1. Click the **Toolbar Options** button at the right side of the Standard toolbar.

2. Click the **Show Buttons on Two Rows command**. The toolbars move to separate rows (the Standard toolbar on top) and you can see all the buttons on each toolbar.

You can easily access any button on the toolbars with one mouse click. The drawback is that the toolbars take up more space in the program window.

Using Speech Recognition

Another way to perform tasks in Office is with your voice. Office's **speech recognition technology** enables you to say the names of the toolbar buttons, menus, menu commands, dialog box items, and so forth, rather than clicking the mouse or pressing keys to select them. The Language toolbar includes the Speech Balloon, which displays the voice command equivalents of a selected button or command. If you switch from Voice mode to Dictation mode, you can dictate the contents of your files rather than typing the text or numbers. For better accuracy, complete the Training Wizard, which helps Office learn your vocal quality, rate of talking, and speech patterns. To start using speech recognition, click Tools on the menu bar in any Office program, and then click Speech. The first time you start this feature, the Training Wizard guides you through the setup process.

Saving and Closing a File

As you create and modify Office files, your work is stored only in the computer's temporary memory, not on disk. If you were to exit the programs, turn off your computer, or experience a power failure, your work would be lost. To prevent losing work, frequently save your file to a disk—at least every ten minutes. You can save files to the hard disk located inside your computer or to portable storage disks, such as CD-ROMs, Zip disks, or floppy disks.

The first time you save a file, you need to name it. This name is called a **filename**. When you choose a filename, select a descriptive one that accurately reflects the content of the document, workbook, presentation, or database, such as "Shipping Options Letter" or "Fourth Quarter Financial Analysis." Filenames can include a maximum of 255 letters, numbers, hyphens, or spaces in any combination. Office appends a **file extension** to the filename, which identifies the program in which that file was created. The file extensions are .doc for Word, .xls for Excel, .ppt for PowerPoint, and .mdb for Access. Whether you see file extensions depends on how Windows is set up for your computer.

You also need to decide where you'll save the file—on which disk and in what folder. Choose a logical location that you'll remember whenever you want to use the file again.

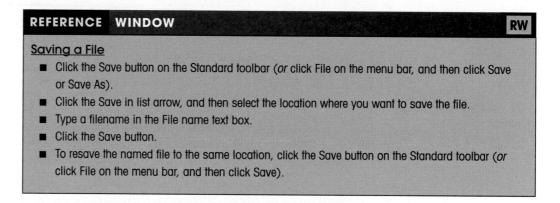

REFERENCE WINDOW   RW

Saving a File

- Click the Save button on the Standard toolbar (*or* click File on the menu bar, and then click Save or Save As).
- Click the Save in list arrow, and then select the location where you want to save the file.
- Type a filename in the File name text box.
- Click the Save button.
- To resave the named file to the same location, click the Save button on the Standard toolbar (*or* click File on the menu bar, and then click Save).

Nicole has asked you to start working on the agenda for the stockholder meeting. You enter text in a Word document by typing. After you type some text, you'll save the file.

To enter text in a document:

1. Type **Delmar Office Supplies**, and then press the **Enter** key. The text you typed appears on one line in the Word document.

   TROUBLE? If you make a typing error, press the Backspace key to delete the incorrect letters, and then retype the text.

2. Type **Stockholder Meeting Agenda**, and then press the **Enter** key. The text you typed appears on the second line.

The two lines of text you typed are not yet saved on disk. You'll do that now.

To save a file for the first time:

1. Insert your Data Disk in the appropriate drive.

TROUBLE? If you don't have a Data Disk, you need to get one before you can proceed. Your instructor or technical support person will either give you one or ask you to make your own by following the instructions on the "Read This Before You Begin" page at the beginning of this tutorial. See your instructor or technical support person for more information.

2. Click the **Save** button 🖫 on the Standard toolbar. The Save As dialog box opens. See Figure 17. The first few words of the first line appear in the File name text box, as a suggested filename. You'll replace this with a more descriptive filename.

Figure 17	SAVE AS DIALOG BOX

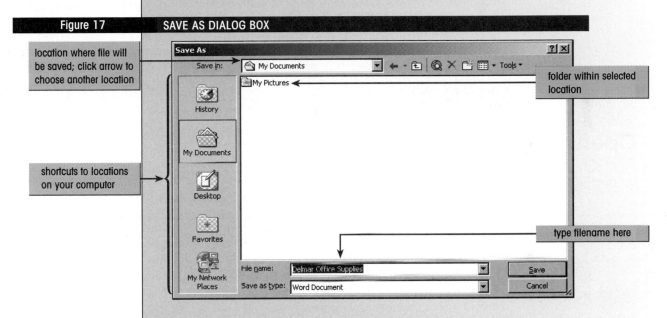

location where file will be saved; click arrow to choose another location

folder within selected location

shortcuts to locations on your computer

type filename here

TROUBLE? If the .doc file extension appears after the filename, then your computer is configured to show file extensions. Just continue with Step 3.

3. Type **Stockholder Meeting Agenda** in the File name text box.

4. Click the **Save in** list arrow, and then click the drive that contains your Data Disk.

5. Double-click the **Tutorial.01** folder in the list box, and then double-click the **Tutorial** folder. This is the location where you want to save the document.

6. Click the **Save** button. The Save As dialog box closes, and the name of your file appears in the program window title bar.

The saved file includes everything in the document at the time you saved. Any edits or additions you then make to the document exist only in the computer's memory and are not saved in the file on the disk. As you work, remember to save frequently so that the file is updated to reflect the latest content of the document.

Because you already named the document and selected a storage location, the second and subsequent times you save, the Save As dialog box doesn't open. If you wanted to save a copy of the file with a different filename or to a different location, you would reopen the Save As dialog box by clicking File on the menu bar, and then clicking Save As. The previous version of the file remains on your disk as well.

You need to add your name to the agenda. Then you'll save your changes and close the file. You can close a file by clicking the Close command on the File menu or by clicking the Close Window button in the upper-right corner of the menu bar.

To modify, save, and close a file:

1. Type your name, and then press the **Enter** key. The text you typed appears on the next line.

2. Click the **Save** button on the Standard toolbar.

   The updated document is saved to the file. When you're done with a file, you can close it. Although you can keep multiple files open at one time, you should close any file you are no longer working on to conserve system resources.

3. Click the **Close Window** button ☒ on the Word menu bar to close the document. Word is still running, but no documents are open.

   TROUBLE? If a dialog box opens and asks whether you want to save the changes you made to the document, you modified the document since you last saved. Click the Yes button to save the current version and close it.

Opening a File

Once you have a program open, you can create additional new files for the open programs or you can open previously created and saved files. You can do both of these from the New Task Pane. The New Task Pane enables you to create new files and open existing ones. The name of the Task Pane varies, depending on the program you are using: Word has the New Document Task Pane, Excel has the New Workbook Task Pane, PowerPoint has the New Presentation Task Pane, and Access has the New File Task Pane.

When you want to work on a previously created file, you must open it first. Opening a file transfers a copy of the file from the storage disk (either a hard disk or a portable disk) to the computer's memory and displays it on your screen. The file is then in your computer's memory and on the disk.

REFERENCE WINDOW   **RW**

Opening an Existing or New File

- Click File on the menu bar, click New, and then (depending on the program) click the More documents, More workbooks, More presentations, or More files link in the New Task Pane (*or* click the Open button on the Standard toolbar *or* click File on the menu bar, and then click Open).
- Click the Look in list arrow, and then select the storage location of the file you want to open.
- Click the filename of the file you want to open.
- Click the Open button.

or

- Click File on the menu bar, click New, and then (depending on the program) click the Blank Document, Blank Workbook, Blank Presentation, or Blank Database link in the New Task Pane (*or* click the New button on the Standard toolbar).

Nicole asks you to print the agenda. To do that, you'll reopen the file. Because Word is still open, you'll use the New Document Task Pane.

To open an existing file:

1. If necessary, click **File** on the menu bar, and then click **New** to display the New Document Task Pane. See Figure 18.

| Figure 18 | NEW DOCUMENT TASK PANE |

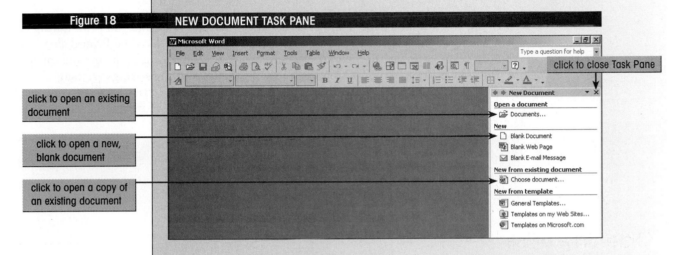

click to open an existing document

click to open a new, blank document

click to open a copy of an existing document

click to close Task Pane

2. Click the **Documents** link in the Open a document area of the New Document Task Pane. The Open dialog box, which works similarly to the Save As dialog box, opens.

   TROUBLE? If you don't see the Documents link, look for a More Documents link below a list of recently opened files. The link name changes from Documents to More Documents after you have opened a file.

3. Click the **Look in** list arrow, and then select the **Tutorial** folder within the **Tutorial.01** folder on your Data Disk. This is the location where you saved the agenda document.

4. Click **Stockholder Meeting Agenda** in the file list. See Figure 19.

| Figure 19 | OPEN DIALOG BOX |

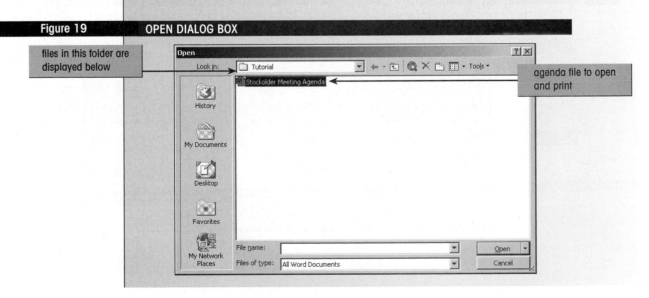

files in this folder are displayed below

agenda file to open and print

5. Click the **Open** button. The file you saved earlier reopens in the Word program window, and the New Document Task Pane closes.

After the file is open, you can view, edit, print, or resave it.

Printing a File

At times, you'll want a paper copy of your Office file. The first time you print during each computer session, you should use the Print menu command to open the Print dialog box so you can verify or adjust the printing settings. You can select a printer, the number of copies to print, the portion of the file to print, and so forth; the printing settings vary slightly from program to program. For subsequent print jobs you can use the Print button to print without opening the dialog box, if you want to use the same default settings.

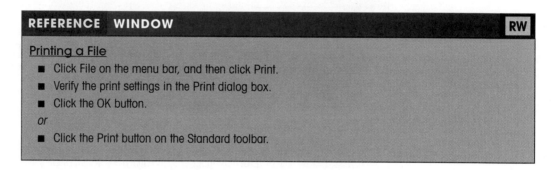

REFERENCE WINDOW   **RW**

Printing a File
- Click File on the menu bar, and then click Print.
- Verify the print settings in the Print dialog box.
- Click the OK button.

or

- Click the Print button on the Standard toolbar.

You'll print the agenda document.

To print a file:

1. Make sure your printer is turned on and contains paper.

2. Click **File** on the menu bar, and then click **Print**. The Print dialog box opens. See Figure 20.

Figure 20   PRINT DIALOG BOX

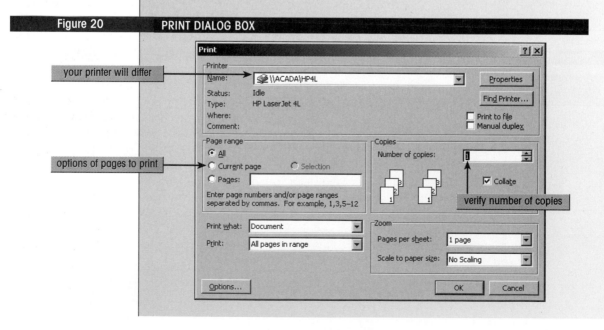

3. Verify that the correct printer appears in the Name list box. If the wrong printer appears, click the **Name** list arrow, and then click the correct printer from the list of available printers.

4. Verify that **1** appears in the Number of copies text box.

5. Click the **OK** button to print the document. See Figure 21.

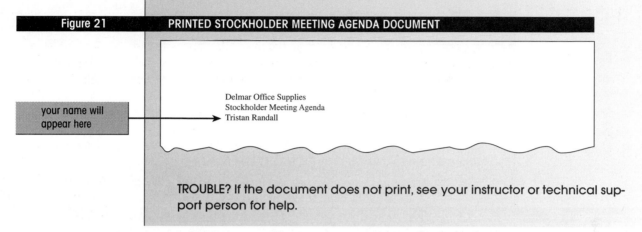

| Figure 21 | PRINTED STOCKHOLDER MEETING AGENDA DOCUMENT |

your name will appear here

Delmar Office Supplies
Stockholder Meeting Agenda
Tristan Randall

TROUBLE? If the document does not print, see your instructor or technical support person for help.

Another important aspect of Office is the ability to get help right from your computer.

Getting Help

If you don't know how to perform a task or want more information about a feature, you can turn to Office itself for information on how to use it. This information, referred to simply as **Help**, is like a huge encyclopedia stored on your computer. You can access it in a variety of ways.

There are two fast and simple methods you can use to get Help about objects you see on the screen. First, you can position the mouse pointer over a toolbar button to view its **ScreenTip**, a yellow box with the button's name. Second, you can click the **What's This?** command on the Help menu to change the pointer to ☖**?**, which you can click on any toolbar button, menu command, dialog box option, worksheet cell, or anything else you can see on your screen to view a brief description of that item.

For more in-depth help, you can use the **Ask a Question** box, located on the menu bar of every Office program, to find information in the Help system. You simply type a question using everyday language about a task you want to perform or a topic you need help with, and then press the Enter key to search the Help system. The Ask a Question box expands to show Help topics related to your query. You click a topic to open a Help window with step-by-step instructions that guide you through a specific procedure and explanations of difficult concepts in clear, easy-to-understand language. For example, you might ask how to format a cell in an Excel worksheet; a list of Help topics related to the words you typed will appear. The Help window also has Contents, Answer Wizard, and Index tabs, which you can use to look up information directly from the Help window.

If you prefer, you can ask questions of the **Office Assistant**, an interactive guide to finding information from the Help system. In addition, the Office Assistant can provide Help topics and tips on tasks as you work. For example, it might offer a tip when you select a menu command instead of clicking the corresponding toolbar button. You can turn on or off the tips, depending on your personal preference.

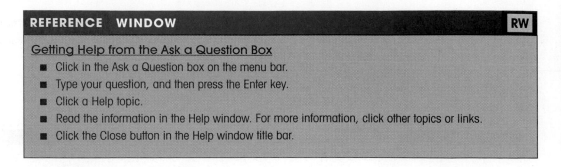

REFERENCE   WINDOW   RW

Getting Help from the Ask a Question Box
- Click in the Ask a Question box on the menu bar.
- Type your question, and then press the Enter key.
- Click a Help topic.
- Read the information in the Help window. For more information, click other topics or links.
- Click the Close button in the Help window title bar.

You'll use the Ask a Question box to obtain more information about Help.

To use the Ask a Question box:

1. Click in the **Ask a Question** box on the menu bar, and then type **How do I search help?**.

2. Press the **Enter** key to retrieve a list of topics, as shown in Figure 22.

Figure 22   ASK A QUESTION BOX WITH HELP TOPICS

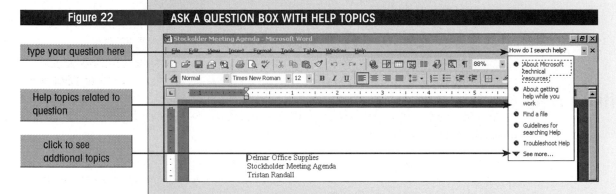

type your question here

Help topics related to question

click to see addtional topics

3. Click the **See more** link, review the additional Help topics, and then click the **See previous** link.

4. Click **About getting help while you work** to open the Help window and learn more about the various ways to obtain assistance in Office. See Figure 23.

Figure 23   HELP WINDOW

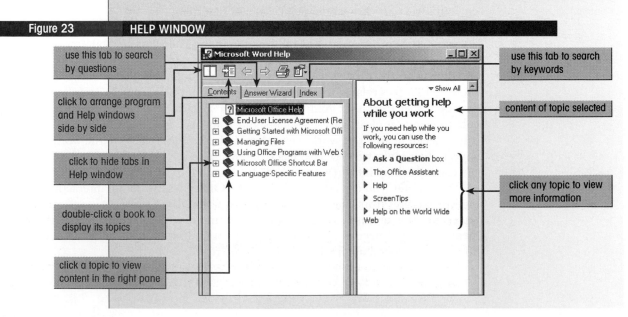

use this tab to search by questions

click to arrange program and Help windows side by side

click to hide tabs in Help window

double-click a book to display its topics

click a topic to view content in the right pane

use this tab to search by keywords

content of topic selected

click any topic to view more information

5. Click **Help** in the right pane to display information about that topic.

6. Click the other links about Help features and read the information.

7. When you're done, click the **Close** button ☒ in the Help window title bar to return to the Word window.

The Help features enable the staff at Delmar Office Supplies to get answers to questions they have about any task or procedure when they need it. The more you practice getting information from the Help system, the more effective you will be at using Office to its full potential.

Exiting **Programs**

Whenever you finish working with a program, you should exit it. As with many other aspects of Office, you can exit programs with a button or from a menu. You'll use both methods to close Word and Excel.

To exit a program:

1. Click the **Close** button ☒ in the upper-right corner of the screen to exit Word. Word exits, and the Excel window is visible again on your screen.

TROUBLE? If a dialog box opens, asking whether you want to save the document, you may have inadvertently made a change to the document. Click the No button.

2. Click **File** on the menu bar, and then click **Exit**. The Excel program exits.

Exiting programs after you are done using them keeps your Windows desktop uncluttered for the next person using the computer, frees up your system's resources, and prevents data from being lost accidentally.

QUICK CHECK

1. Which Office program would you use to write a letter?
2. Which Office programs could you use to store customer names and addresses?
3. What is integration?
4. Explain the difference between Save As and Save.
5. What is the purpose of the New Task Pane?
6. When would you use the Ask a Question box?

REVIEW ASSIGNMENTS

Before the stockholders meeting at Delmar Office Supplies, you'll open and print documents for the upcoming presentation.

1. Start PowerPoint using the Start button and the Programs menu.

2. Use the Ask a Question box to learn how to change the toolbar buttons from small to large, and then do it. Use the same procedure to change the buttons back to regular size. Close the Help window when you're done.

3. Open a blank Excel workbook using the New Office Document command on the Start menu.

Explore   4. Switch to the PowerPoint window using the taskbar, and then close the presentation but leave open the PowerPoint program. (*Hint:* Click the Close Window button in the menu bar.)

Explore   5. Open a new, blank PowerPoint presentation from the New Presentation Task Pane. (*Hint:* Click Blank Presentation in the New area of the New Presentation Task Pane.)

6. Close the PowerPoint presentation and program using the Close button in the PowerPoint title bar; do not save changes if asked.

Explore   7. Open a copy of the Excel **Finances** workbook located in the **Review** folder within the **Tutorial.01** folder on your Data Disk using the New Workbook Task Pane. (*Hint:* Click File on the Excel menu bar and then click New to open the Task Pane. Click Choose Workbook in the New from existing workbook area of the New Workbook Task Pane; the dialog box functions similarly to the Open dialog box.)

8. Type your name, and then press the Enter key to insert your name at the top of the worksheet.

9. Save the worksheet as **Delmar Finances** in the **Review** folder within the **Tutorial.01** folder on your Data Disk.

10. Print one copy of the worksheet using the Print command on the File menu.

11. Exit Excel using the File menu.

Explore   12. Open the **Letter** document located in the **Review** folder within the **Tutorial.01** folder on your Data Disk using the Open Office Document command on the Start menu.

13. Use the Save As command to save the document with the filename **Delmar Letter** in the **Review** folder within the **Tutorial.01** folder on your Data Disk.

Explore   14. Press and hold the Ctrl key, press the End key, and then release both keys to move the insertion point to the end of the letter, and then type your name.

15. Use the Save button on the Standard toolbar to save the change to the Delmar Letter document.

16. Print one copy of the document, and then close the document.

17. Exit the Word program using the Close button on the title bar.

QUICK | CHECK ANSWERS

1. Word
2. Access or Outlook
3. the ability to share information between programs
4. Save As enables you to change the filename and save location of a file. Save updates a file to reflect its latest contents using its current filename and location.
5. enables you to create new files and open existing files
6. when you don't know how to perform a task or want more information about a feature

New Perspectives on

MICROSOFT®
WORD 2002

Read This Before You Begin

To the Student

Data Disks

To complete the Level I tutorials, Review Assignments, and Case Problems, you need one Data Disk. Your instructor will either provide you with the Data Disk or ask you to make your own.

If you are making your own Data Disk, you will need **one** blank, formatted high-density disk. You will need to copy a set of files and/or folders from a file server, standalone computer, or the Web onto your disk. Your instructor will tell you which computer, drive letter, and folders contain the files you need. You could also download the files by going to **www.course.com** and following the instructions on the screen.

The information below shows you which folders go on your disk, so that you will have enough disk space to complete all the tutorials, Review Assignments, and Case Problems:

Data Disk 1

Write this on the disk label:

Data Disk 1: Word 2002 Tutorials 1-4

Put these folders on the disk:

Tutorial.01, Tutorial.02, Tutorial.03, Tutorial.04

When you begin each tutorial, be sure you are using the correct Data Disk. Refer to the File Finder chart at the back of this text for more detailed information on which files are used in which tutorials. See the inside front or inside back cover of this book for more information on Data Disk files, or ask your instructor or technical support person for assistance.

Course Labs

The Word Level I tutorials feature an interactive Course Lab to help you understand word processing concepts.

There are Lab Assignments at the end of Tutorial 1 that relate to this Lab.

To start a Lab, click the **Start** button on the Windows taskbar, point to **Programs**, point to **Course Labs**, point to **New Perspectives Course Labs**, and then click the name of the Lab you want to use.

Using Your Own Computer

If you are going to work through this book using your own computer, you need:

- **Computer System** Microsoft Windows 98, NT, 2000 Professional, or higher must be installed on your computer. This book assumes a typical installation of Microsoft Word.

- **Data Disk** You will not be able to complete the tutorials or exercises in this book using your own computer until you have your Data Disk.

- **Course Labs** See your instructor or technical support person to obtain the Course Lab software for use on your own computer.

Visit Our World Wide Web Site

Additional materials designed especially for you are available on the World Wide Web.

Go to **www.course.com/NewPerspectives**.

To the Instructor

The Data Disk Files and Course Labs are available on the Instructor's Resource Kit for this title. Follow the instructions in the Help file on the CD-ROM to install the programs to your network or standalone computer. For information on creating Data Disks or the Course Labs, see the "To the Student" section above.

You are granted a license to copy the Data Files and Course Labs to any computer or computer network used by students who have purchased this book.

LAB

Word Processing

CREATING A DOCUMENT

Writing a Business Letter for Art4U Inc.

CASE

Creating a Contract Letter for Art4U Inc.

Megan Grahs is the owner and manager of Art4U Inc., a graphics design firm in Tucson, Arizona. When Megan founded Art4U in the early 1980s, the company drew most of its revenue from design projects for local magazines, newspapers, advertising circulars, and other print publications. The artists at Art4U laboriously created logos, diagrams, and other illustrations by hand, using watercolors, ink, pastels, and a variety of other media. Since the advent of the Internet, however, Art4U has become one of the Southwest's leading creators of electronic artwork. The firm's artists now work exclusively on computers, saving each piece of art as an electronic file that they can e-mail to a client in a matter of minutes.

Thanks to e-mail, Art4U is no longer limited to the local Tucson market. As a result, Art4U has nearly doubled in size over the past few years. Most of the increase in business has come from Web page designers, who continually need fresh and innovative graphics to use in their Web pages. In fact, Megan has just signed a contract with Web Time Productions agreeing to create a series of logos for a high-profile Web site. She needs to return the signed contract to Web Time's office in Chicago.

In this tutorial, you will create the cover letter that will accompany the contract. You will create the letter using Microsoft Word 2002, a popular word-processing program. Before you begin typing the letter, you will learn to start the Word program, identify and use the elements of the Word screen, and adjust some Word settings. Next you will create a new Word document, type the text of the cover letter, save the letter, and then print the letter for Megan. In the process of entering the text, you'll learn several ways to correct typing errors.

SESSION 1.1

In this session you will learn how to start Word, identify and use the parts of the Word window, and adjust some Word settings. With the skills you learn in this session, you'll be prepared to use Word to create a variety of documents, such as letters, reports, and memos.

Four Steps to a Professional Document

Word helps you produce quality work in minimal time. Not only can you type a document in Word, but you can also quickly make revisions and corrections, adjust margins and spacing, create columns and tables, and add graphics to your documents. The most efficient way to produce a document is to follow these four steps: (1) planning and creating, (2) editing, (3) formatting, and (4) printing.

In the long run, *planning* saves time and effort. First, you should determine what you want to say. State your purpose clearly and include enough information to achieve that purpose without overwhelming or boring your reader. Be sure to *organize* your ideas logically. Decide how you want your document to look as well. In this case, your letter to Web Time Productions will take the form of a standard business letter. It should be addressed to Web Time's president, Nicholas Brower. Megan has given you a handwritten note indicating what she would like you to say in the letter. This note is shown in Figure 1-1.

Figure 1-1	MEGAN'S NOTES FOR CONTRACT LETTER

Please write a cover letter for the Web Time Productions contract. In the letter please include the following questions:

- When will we receive a complete schedule for the project?
- How many preliminary designs do you require?
- Will you be available to discuss the project with our artists via a conference call next week?

Send the letter to Web Time's president, Nicholas Brower. The address is: 2210 West Sycamore Avenue, Chicago, IL 60025.

After you plan your document, you can go ahead and *create* it using Word. This generally means typing the text of your document. The next step, *editing*, consists of reading the document you've created, correcting your errors, and, finally, adding or deleting text to make the document easy to read.

Once your document is error-free, you can *format* it to make it visually appealing. Formatting features, such as adjusting margins to create white space (blank areas of a page), setting line spacing, and using boldface and italics, can help make your document easier to read. *Printing* is the final phase in creating an effective document. In this tutorial, you will preview your document before you spend time and resources to print it.

Exploring the Word Window

Before you can apply these four steps to produce a letter in Word, you need to start Word and learn about the general organization of the Word window. You'll do that now.

To start Microsoft Word:

1. Make sure Windows is running on your computer and that you can see the Windows desktop on your screen.

2. Click the **Start** button on the taskbar to display the Start menu, and then point to **Programs** to display the Programs menu.

3. Point to **Microsoft Word** on the Programs menu. Depending on how your computer is set up, you might see a small yellow box (called a ScreenTip) containing an explanation of some common uses for Microsoft Word. See Figure 1-2.

Figure 1-2	STARTING MICROSOFT WORD

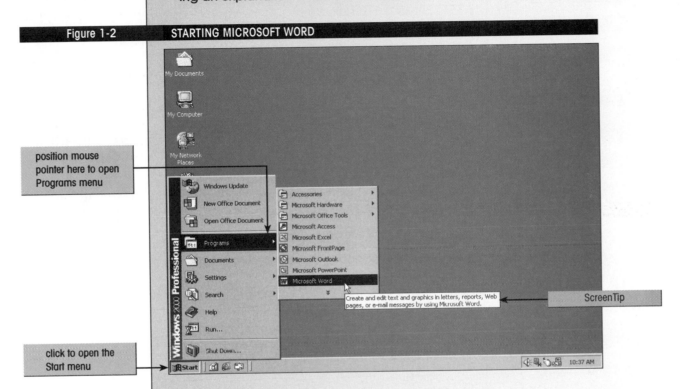

position mouse pointer here to open Programs menu

click to open the Start menu

ScreenTip

TROUBLE? Don't worry if your screen differs slightly from Figure 1-2. Although the figures in this book were created while running Windows 2000 in its default settings, Microsoft Word should run equally well using Windows 98, Windows 2000, Windows Millennium Edition, or Windows NT 4 (with Service Pack 6 installed).

TROUBLE? If you don't see the Microsoft Word option on the Programs menu, ask your instructor or technical support person for help.

TROUBLE? If the Office Shortcut Bar appears on your screen, your system is set up to display it. Because the Office Shortcut Bar is not required to complete these tutorials, it has been omitted from the figures in this text. You can close it or simply ignore it.

4. Click **Microsoft Word**. After a short pause, the Microsoft Word copyright information appears in a message box and remains on the screen until the Word program window opens. See Figure 1-3.

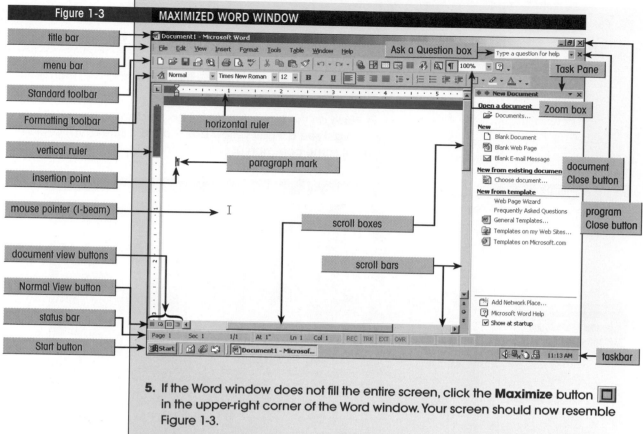

Figure 1-3   MAXIMIZED WORD WINDOW

5. If the Word window does not fill the entire screen, click the **Maximize** button ▢ in the upper-right corner of the Word window. Your screen should now resemble Figure 1-3.

TROUBLE? If your screen looks slightly different from Figure 1-3, just continue with the steps. You will learn how to change the appearance of the Word window shortly.

TROUBLE? If you see the Language Bar (a toolbar with buttons such as correction and microphone), click its Minimize button, and then click OK.

Word is now running and ready to use.

The Word window is made up of a number of elements which are described in Figure 1-4. You are already familiar with some of these elements, such as the menu bar, title bar, and status bar, because they are common to all Windows programs. Don't be concerned if you don't see everything shown in Figure 1-3. You'll learn how to adjust the appearance of the Word window soon.

Figure 1-4   PARTS OF THE WORD WINDOW

SCREEN ELEMENT	DESCRIPTION
Ask a Question box	Allows you to type a question for Word Help
Document Close button	Closes the current document
Document view buttons	Switches the document between four different views: Normal view, Web Layout view, Print Layout view, and Outline view
Document window	Area where you enter text and graphics
Formatting toolbar	Contains buttons to activate common font and paragraph formatting commands

Figure 1-4	PARTS OF THE WORD WINDOW (CONTINUED)
SCREEN ELEMENT	**DESCRIPTION**
Horizontal ruler	Adjusts margins, tabs, and column widths; vertical ruler appears in Print Layout view
Insertion point	Indicates location where characters will be inserted or deleted
Menu bar	Contains lists or menus of all the Word commands. When you first display a menu, you see a short list of the most frequently used commands. To see the full list of commands in the menu, you can either click the menu and then wait a few seconds for the remaining commands to appear, or click the menu and then click or point to the downward-facing double-arrow at the bottom of the menu.
Mouse pointer	Changes shape depending on its location on the screen (i.e., I-beam pointer in text area; arrow in nontext areas)
Paragraph mark	Marks the end of a paragraph
Program Close button	Closes the current document if more than one document is open; closes Word if one or no document is open
Scroll bars	Shift text vertically and horizontally on the screen so you can see different parts of the document
Scroll box	Helps you move quickly to other pages of your document
Standard toolbar	Contains buttons to activate frequently used commands
Start button	Starts a program, opens a document, provides quick access to Windows Help
Status bar	Provides information regarding the location of the insertion point
Taskbar	Shows programs that are running and allows you to switch quickly from one program to another
Task Pane	Contains buttons and options for common tasks
Title bar	Identifies the current application (i.e., Microsoft Word); shows the filename of the current document
Zoom box	Changes the document window magnification

If at any time you would like to check the name of a Word toolbar button, position the mouse pointer over the button without clicking. A **ScreenTip**, a small yellow box with the name of the button, will appear. (If you don't see ScreenTips on your computer, click Tools on the Word menu bar, click Options, click the View tab, click the ScreenTips check box to insert a check, and then click OK.)

Keep in mind that the commands on the menu bars initially display the commands that are used most frequently on your particular computer. When you leave the menu open for a few seconds or point to the double-arrow, a complete list of commands appears. Throughout these tutorials, you should point to the double-arrow on a menu if you do not see the command you need.

Setting Up the Window Before You Begin Each Tutorial

Word provides a set of standard settings, called **default settings**, that control how the screen is set up, and how a document looks when you first start typing. These settings are appropriate for most situations. However, these settings are easily changed, and most people begin a work session by adjusting Word to make sure it is set up the way they want it.

When you become more comfortable using Word, you will learn how to customize Word to suit your needs. But to make it easier to follow the steps in these tutorials, you should take care to arrange your window to match the tutorial figures. The rest of this section explains what your window should look like and how to make it match those in the tutorials. Depending on how many people use your computer (and how much they adjust Word's appearance), you might have to set up the window to match the figures each time you start Word.

Closing the Task Pane

The **Task Pane** is part of the Word window that you can use to perform common chores, such as sending e-mail. By default, the Task Pane appears on the right side of the Word window (as in Figure 1-5) when you start Word.

Figure 1-5	TASK PANE IN THE WORD WINDOW

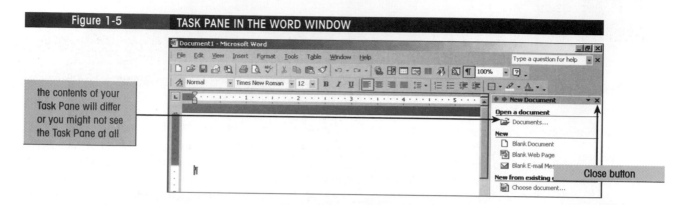

the contents of your Task Pane will differ or you might not see the Task Pane at all

Close button

Depending on how your computer is currently set up, your Task Pane might look different from the one in Figure 1-5, or you might not see the Task Pane at all. When you become a more experienced Word user, you will learn how to take advantage of the Task Pane to work more efficiently. But for now you will close it, using the Close button shown in Figure 1-5.

To close the Task Pane:

1. If the Task Pane is open on your computer, click its **Close** button ⊠. The Document window expands to fill the space left by the Task Pane.

Setting the Document View to Normal

You can view your document in one of four ways—Normal, Web Layout, Print Layout, or Outline. **Web Layout view** and **Outline view** are designed for special situations that you don't need to worry about now. You will learn more about **Print Layout view**—which allows you to see a page's overall design and format—in later tutorials. In Print Layout view, Word displays both a horizontal ruler (below the toolbars) and a vertical ruler (along the left side of the Document window). For this tutorial you will use **Normal view**, which allows you to see more of the document than Print Layout view. By default, Word often displays the document in Print Layout view, just as it is in Figure 1-5. For this tutorial, you need to display the document in Normal view.

To make sure the Document window is in Normal view:

1. Click the **Normal View** button ▤ to the left of the horizontal scroll bar. See Figure 1-6. If your Document window was not in Normal view, it changes to Normal view now. The Normal View button is outlined, indicating that it is selected.

Figure 1-6	CHANGING TO NORMAL VIEW

Outline View button
Print Layout button
Web Layout button
Normal View button

status bar

Page 1   Sec 1   1/1   At 1"   Ln 1   Col 1   REC TRK EXT OVR

Start   Document1 - Microsof...   11:15 AM

Displaying the Toolbars and Ruler

The Word toolbars allow you to perform common tasks quickly by clicking a button. In the Word tutorials, you will most often use the Standard toolbar and the Formatting toolbar. While working through these tutorials, you should check to make sure that only the Formatting and Standard toolbars appear on your screen. The Standard toolbar should be positioned on top of the Formatting toolbar, just as they are in Figure 1-7.

Figure 1-7	STANDARD TOOLBAR ON TOP OF FORMATTING TOOLBAR

Standard toolbar

Formatting toolbar

Depending on the settings specified by the last person to use your computer, you may not see both toolbars or your toolbars may all appear on one row. You also may see additional toolbars, such as the Drawing toolbar. In the following steps, you will make sure that your Word window shows only the Standard and Formatting toolbars. Later you will make sure that they are stacked on top of each other.

To verify that your Word window shows the correct toolbars:

1. Position the pointer over any toolbar and click the right mouse button. A shortcut menu appears. The menu lists all available toolbars with a check mark next to those currently displayed. If the Standard and Formatting toolbars are currently displayed on your computer, you should see check marks next to their names.

   TROUBLE? If you don't see any toolbars on your screen, click Tools on the menu bar, click Customize, and then click the Toolbars tab. Click the Standard and Formatting check boxes to insert a check in each, and then click Close. To gain practice using a shortcut menu, begin again with Step 1, above.

2. Verify that you see a check mark next to the word "Standard" in the shortcut menu. If you do not see a check mark, click **Standard** now. (Clicking any item on the shortcut menu closes the menu, so you will need to re-open it in the next step.)

3. Redisplay the shortcut menu, if necessary, and look for a check mark next to the word "Formatting."

4. Redisplay the shortcut menu, if necessary. If any toolbars besides the Formatting and Standard toolbars have check marks, click each one to remove the check mark and hide the toolbar. When you are finished, only the Standard and Formatting toolbars should have check marks.

If the toolbars appear on one row, perform the next steps to arrange the toolbars on two rows.

To arrange the Standard toolbar and the Formatting toolbar on two rows:

1. Click **Tools** on the menu bar, and then click **Customize**. The Customize dialog box opens.

TROUBLE? If you don't see the Customize command on the Tools menu, point to the double arrow, as explained earlier in this tutorial, to show the full list of commands.

2. Click the **Options** tab, and then click the **Show Standard and Formatting toolbars on two rows** check box to select it (that is, to insert a check).

3. Click **Close**. The Customize dialog box closes. The toolbars on your screen should now match those shown earlier in Figure 1-7.

Displaying the Horizontal Ruler

In Normal view, you can use the **Horizontal ruler** to position text on the page. As you complete these tutorials, the ruler should be visible to help you place items precisely. If the ruler is not displayed on your screen as it is in Figure 1-8, you need to perform the following steps.

Figure 1-8	HORIZONTAL RULER DISPLAYED IN NORMAL VIEW

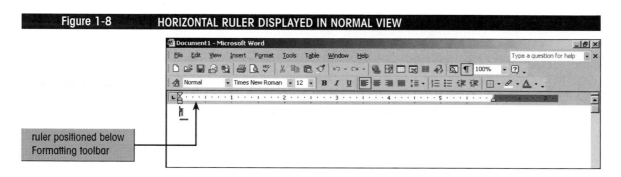

ruler positioned below Formatting toolbar

To display the ruler:

1. Click **View** on the menu bar, and then point to the **double-arrow** at the bottom of the menu to display the hidden menu commands.

2. If "Ruler" does not have a check mark next to it, click **Ruler**. The horizontal ruler should now be displayed, as shown earlier in Figure 1-8.

Selecting a Zoom Setting

You can use the **Zoom box** on the Standard toolbar to change the magnification of the Document window. (The Zoom box is shown in Figure 1-9.) This is useful when you need a close-up view of a document—especially if you have difficulty reading small print on a computer screen. You will learn how to use the Zoom box later. For now you just need to know how to make the Zoom setting match the figures in these tutorials. By default, the Zoom setting is 100% when you first start Word (as it is in Figure 1-9). But the Zoom setting you see now depends on the setting used by the last person to work with Word on your computer. If your Zoom setting is not 100%, you need to perform the following steps.

Figure 1-9	ZOOM BOX IN STANDARD TOOLBAR

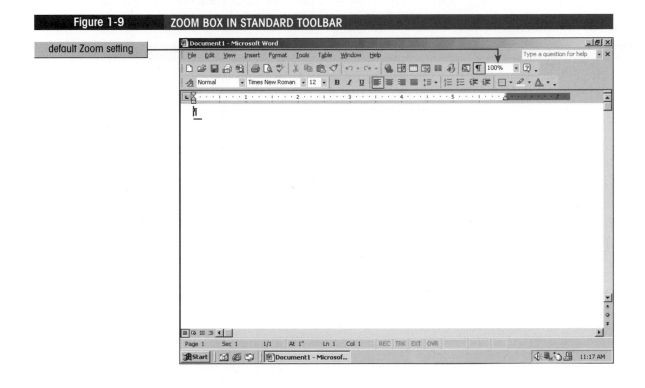

default Zoom setting

To adjust the Zoom setting:

1. Click the **list arrow** in the Zoom box. A list of settings appears.

2. Click **100%**. The list box closes, and 100% appears in the Zoom box, as shown in Figure 1-9.

Setting the Font and Font Size

A **font** is a set of characters that has a certain design, shape, and appearance. Each font has a name, such as Courier, Times New Roman, or Arial. The **font size** is the actual height of a character, measured in points, where one point equals 1/72 of an inch in height. You'll learn more about fonts and font sizes later, but for now keep in mind that most documents you create will use the Times New Roman font in a font size of 12 points. Word usually uses a default setting of Times New Roman 12 point, but someone else might have changed the setting after Word was installed on your computer. You can see your computer's current settings in the Font list box and the Font Size list box in the Formatting toolbar, as shown in Figure 1-10.

Figure 1-10	DEFAULT FONT AND FONT SIZE SETTINGS

default font

default font size

If your font setting is not Times New Roman 12 point, you should change the default setting now. You'll use the menu bar to choose the commands.

To change the default font and font size:

1. Click **Format** on the menu bar, and then click **Font**. The Font dialog box opens. If necessary, click the **Font** tab. See Figure 1-11.

| Figure 1-11 | FONT DIALOG BOX |

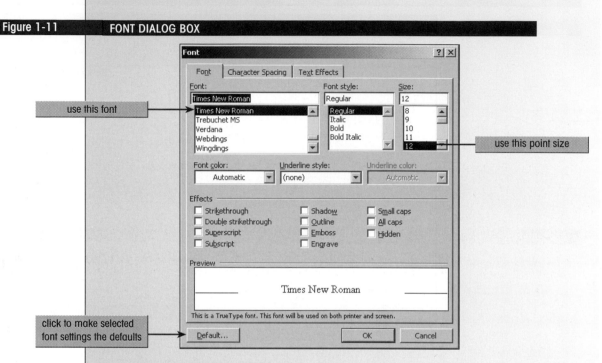

use this font

use this point size

click to make selected
font settings the defaults

2. In the Font text box, click **Times New Roman**.

3. In the Size list box, click **12**.

4. Click the **Default** button to make Times New Roman and 12 point the default settings. Word displays a message asking you to verify that you want to make 12 point Times New Roman the default font.

5. Click **Yes**.

Displaying Nonprinting Characters

Nonprinting characters are symbols that can appear on the screen but do not show up when you print a document. You can display nonprinting characters when you are working on the appearance, or **format**, of your document. For example, one nonprinting character marks the end of a paragraph (¶), and another marks the space between words (•). It's helpful to display nonprinting characters so you can see whether you've typed an extra space, ended a paragraph, and so on.

Depending on how your computer is set up, nonprinting characters might have been displayed automatically when you started Word. In Figure 1-12, you can see the paragraph symbol (¶) in the blank Document window. Also, the Show/Hide ¶ button is outlined in the Standard toolbar. Both of these indicate that nonprinting characters are displayed. If they are not displayed on your screen, you need to perform the following steps.

Figure 1-12	NONPRINTING CHARACTERS DISPLAYED

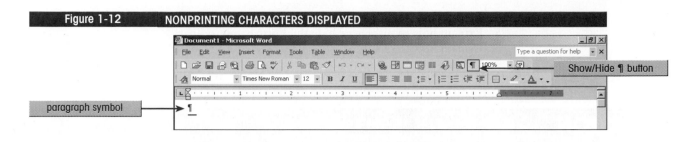

To display nonprinting characters:

1. Click the **Show/Hide ¶** button ¶ on the Standard toolbar. A paragraph mark (¶) appears at the top of the Document window. Your screen should now match Figure 1-12. To make sure your window always matches the figures in these tutorials, remember to complete the checklist in Figure 1-13 each time you sit down at the computer.

   TROUBLE? If the Show/Hide ¶ button was already highlighted before you clicked it, you have now deactivated it. Click the Show/Hide ¶ button a second time to select it.

Figure 1-13	WORD WINDOW CHECKLIST

SCREEN ELEMENT	SETTING	CHECK
Document view	Normal view	☐
Word window	Maximized	☐
Standard toolbar	Displayed, below the menu bar	☐
Formatting toolbar	Displayed, below the Standard toolbar	☐
Other toolbars	Hidden	☐
Nonprinting characters	Displayed	☐
Font	Times New Roman	☐
Point size	12 point	☐
Ruler	Displayed	☐
Task Pane	Closed	☐
Zoom box	100%	☐

Now that you have planned your letter, opened Word, identified screen elements, and adjusted settings, you are ready to begin typing a letter. In the next session, you will create Megan's letter to Web Time Productions.

Session 1.1 QUICK | CHECK

1. In your own words, list the steps in creating a document.
2. How do you start Word from the Windows desktop?
3. Define each of the following in your own words:
   a. nonprinting characters   c. font size
   b. document view buttons   d. default settings

4. Explain how to change the default font size.
5. Explain how to display or hide the Formatting toolbar.
6. Explain how to change the document view to Normal view.
7. To close the Task Pane, you need to use a command on the menu bar. True or False?

SESSION 1.2

In this session you will create a one-page document using Word. You'll correct errors and scroll through your document. You'll also name, save, preview, and print the document. Finally, you will create an envelope for the letter.

Beginning a Letter

Word Processing

You're ready to begin typing Megan's letter to Nicholas Brower at Web Time Productions. Figure 1-14 shows the completed letter printed on company letterhead. You'll begin by opening a new blank page (in case you accidentally typed something in the current page). Then you'll move the insertion point to about 2.5 inches from the top margin of the paper to allow space for the Art4U letterhead.

Figure 1-14	COMPLETED LETTER

Art4U, Inc.
1921 Sedona Avenue
Tucson, AZ 85701
Art4U@WorldNet.com

February 21, 2003

Nicholas Brower, President
Web Time Productions
2210 West Sycamore Avenue
Chicago, IL 60025

Dear Nicholas:

Enclosed you will find the signed contract. As you can see, I am returning all three pages, with my signature on each.

Now that we have finalized the contract, I have a few questions: When will we receive a complete schedule for the project? Also, how many preliminary designs do you require? Finally, will you be available to discuss the project with our artists via a conference call some afternoon next week?

Thanks again for choosing Art4U. We look forward to working with you.

Sincerely yours,

Megan Grahs

To open a new document:

1. If you took a break after the previous session, make sure the Word program is running, that nonprinting characters are displayed, and that the font settings in the Formatting toolbar are set to 12 point Times New Roman. Also verify that the toolbars and the ruler are displayed. Currently, you have one document open in Word. This document is named Document1. If you have the taskbar displayed at the bottom of your screen, it should contain a button named Document1. If for some reason you need to switch between Word and another Windows program, you could click this taskbar button to redisplay the Word window. In the next steps, you'll try using this button, just for practice.

2. Click the **Minimize** button ▬ in the Word title bar. The Word window minimizes, revealing the Windows desktop. (If you couldn't see the taskbar earlier, you should see it now.)

3. Click the **Document1** button in the taskbar. The Word window maximizes again. Now you can open a new document where you can type Megan's letter.

4. Click the **New Blank Document** button ▯ on the Standard toolbar. A new document, named Document2, opens, as shown in Figure 1-15.

| Figure 1-15 | NEWLY OPENED DOCUMENT |

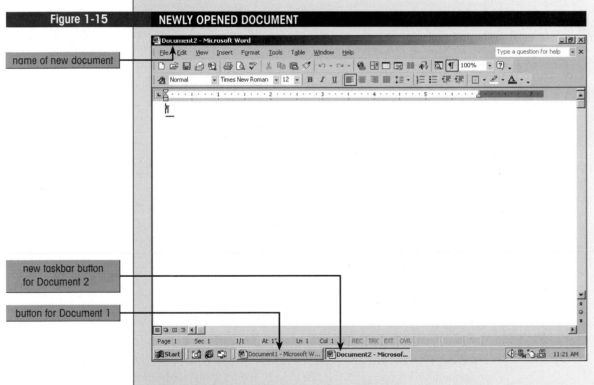

name of new document

new taskbar button for Document 2

button for Document 1

If you have the taskbar displayed at the bottom of your screen, you see an additional button for the new document. If you wanted to switch back to Document1, you could click its button on the taskbar.

Now that you have opened a new document, you need to insert some blank lines in the document so you leave enough room for the company letterhead.

To insert blank lines in the document:

1. Press the **Enter** key eight times. Each time you press the Enter key, a nonprinting paragraph mark appears. In the status bar (at the bottom of the Document window), you should see the setting "At 2.5"," indicating that the insertion point is approximately 2.5 inches from the top of the page. Another setting in the status bar should read "Ln 9," indicating the insertion point is in line 9 of the document. See Figure 1-16. (Your settings may be slightly different.)

Figure 1-16	DOCUMENT WINDOW AFTER INSERTING BLANK LINES

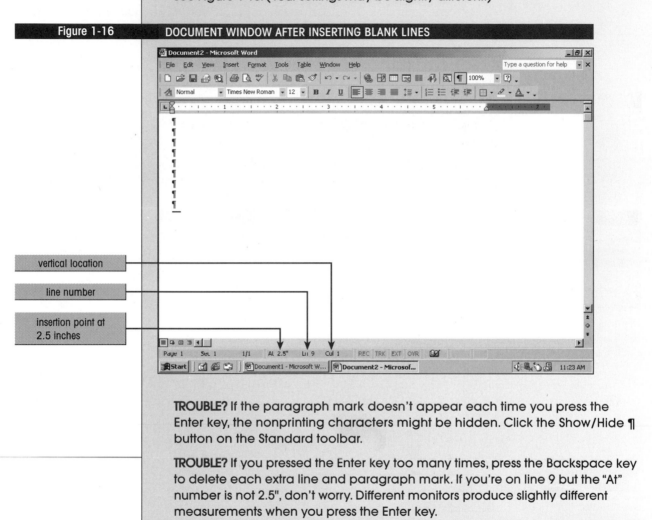

vertical location

line number

insertion point at
2.5 inches

TROUBLE? If the paragraph mark doesn't appear each time you press the Enter key, the nonprinting characters might be hidden. Click the Show/Hide ¶ button on the Standard toolbar.

TROUBLE? If you pressed the Enter key too many times, press the Backspace key to delete each extra line and paragraph mark. If you're on line 9 but the "At" number is not 2.5", don't worry. Different monitors produce slightly different measurements when you press the Enter key.

Pressing Enter is a simple, fast way to insert space in a document. When you are a more experienced Word user, you'll learn how to insert space without using the Enter key.

Entering Text

Normally, you begin typing a letter by entering the date. However, Megan tells you that she's not sure whether the contract will be ready to send today or tomorrow. So she asks you to skip the date for now and begin with the inside address. Making changes to documents is easy in Word, so you can easily add the date later.

In the following steps, you'll type the inside address (shown on Megan's note, in Figure 1-1). If you type a wrong character, press the Backspace key to delete the mistake and then retype the correct character.

To type the inside address:

1. Type **Nicholas Brower, President** and then press the **Enter** key. As you type, the nonprinting character (•) appears between words to indicate a space. Depending on how your computer is set up, you may also see a dotted underline beneath the name, Nicholas Brower, as shown in Figure 1-17. You'll learn the meaning of this underline later in this tutorial, when you type the date. For now you can just ignore it and concentrate on typing the letter.

Figure 1-17	FIRST LINE OF INSIDE ADDRESS

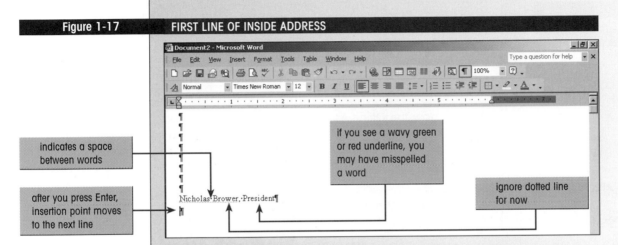

indicates a space between words

after you press Enter, insertion point moves to the next line

if you see a wavy green or red underline, you may have misspelled a word

ignore dotted line for now

Nicholas Brower, President¶

TROUBLE? If a wavy line (as opposed to a dotted line) appears beneath a word, check to make sure you typed the text correctly. If you did not, use the Backspace key to remove the error, and then retype the text correctly.

2. Type the following text, pressing the **Enter** key after each line to complete the inside address:
   Web Time Productions
   2210 West Sycamore Avenue
   Chicago, IL 60025

   Ignore the dotted underline below the street address. As mentioned earlier, you'll learn the meaning of this type of underline later in this tutorial.

3. Press the **Enter** key again to add a blank line after the inside address. (You should see a total of two paragraph marks below the inside address.) Now you can type the salutation.

4. Type **Dear Nicholas:** and press the **Enter** key twice to double space between the salutation and the body of the letter. When you press the Enter key the first time, the Office Assistant might appear, asking if you would like help writing your letter, as in Figure 1-18. (Depending on the settings on your computer, you might see a different Office Assistant.)

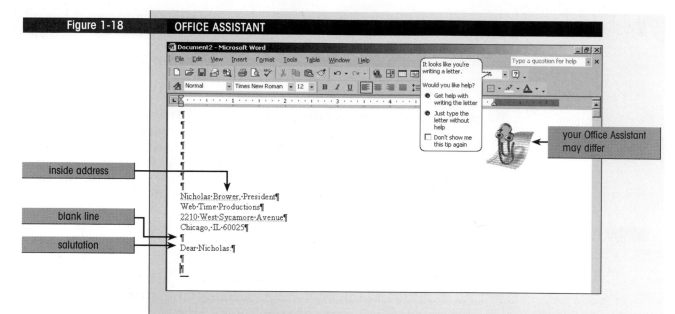

Figure 1-18   OFFICE ASSISTANT

inside address

blank line

salutation

your Office Assistant may differ

As you know, the Office Assistant is an interactive feature that sometimes appears to offer help on routine tasks. In this case, you could click "Get help with writing the letter" and have the Office Assistant lead you through a series of dialog boxes designed to set up the basic elements of a letter. For now, though, you'll close the Office Assistant and continue writing your letter.

5. Click **Just type the letter without help**. The Office Assistant closes.

   TROUBLE? If the Office Assistant remains open, right-click the Office Assistant, and then click Hide.

Before you continue with the rest of the letter, you should save what you have typed so far.

To save the document:

1. Place your Data Disk in the appropriate disk drive.

   TROUBLE? If you don't have a Data Disk, see the "Read This Before You Begin" page at the beginning of this tutorial.

2. Click the **Save** button 🖫 on the Standard toolbar. The Save As dialog box opens, similar to Figure 1-19. (Your Save As dialog box might be larger than the one shown in Figure 1-19.) Note that Word suggests using the first few words of the letter ("Nicholas Brower") as the filename. You will first replace the suggested filename with something more descriptive.

| Figure 1-19 | SAVE AS DIALOG BOX |

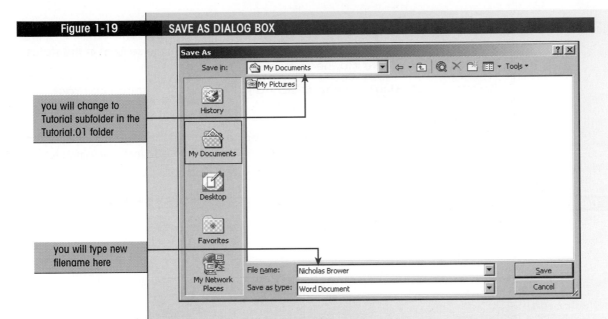

you will change to Tutorial subfolder in the Tutorial.01 folder

you will type new filename here

3. Type **Web Time Contract Letter** in the File name text box. Next, you need to tell Word where you want to save the document. In this case, you want to use the Tutorial subfolder in the Tutorial.01 folder on your Data Disk.

4. Click the **Save in** list arrow, click the drive containing your Data Disk, double-click the **Tutorial.01** folder, and then double-click the **Tutorial** folder. The word "Tutorial" is now displayed in the Save in box, indicating that the Tutorial folder is open and ready for you to save the document.

   TROUBLE? If Word automatically adds the .doc extension to your filename, your computer is configured to show filename extensions. Just continue with the tutorial.

5. Click the **Save** button In the Save As dialog box. The dialog box closes, and you return to the Document window. The new document name (Web Time Contract Letter) appears in the title bar.

Note that Word automatically appends the .doc extension to the filename to identify the file as a Microsoft Word document. However, unless your computer is set up to display file extensions, you won't see the .doc extension in any of the Word dialog boxes or in the title bar. These tutorials assume that filename extensions are hidden.

Taking **Advantage of Word Wrap**

Now that you have saved your document, you're ready to continue working on Megan's letter. As you type the body of the letter, you do not have to press the Enter key at the end of each line. Instead, when you type a word that extends into the right margin, both the insertion point and the word moves automatically to the next line. This automatic line breaking is called **word wrap.** You'll see how word wrap works as you type the body of the letter.

To observe word wrap while typing a paragraph:

1. Make sure the insertion point is at Ln 16 (according to the settings in the status bar). If it's not, move it to line 16 by pressing the arrow keys.

2. Type the following sentence: **Enclosed you will find the signed contract.**

3. Press the **spacebar**.

4. Type the following sentence: **As you can see, I am returning all three pages, with my signature on each.** Notice how Word moves the last few words to a new line when the preceding line is full. See Figure 1-20.

Figure 1-20	WORD WRAPPING TEXT

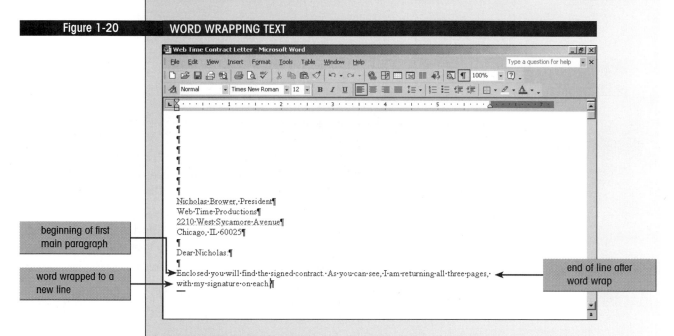

beginning of first main paragraph

word wrapped to a new line

end of line after word wrap

TROUBLE? If your screen does not match Figure 1-20 exactly, don't be concerned. The Times New Roman font can have varying letter widths and produce slightly different measurements on different monitors. As a result, the word or letter where the line wraps in your document might be different from the one shown in Figure 1-20. Continue with Step 5.

5. Press the **Enter** key to end the first paragraph, and then press the **Enter** key again to double space between the first and second paragraphs.

6. Type the following text:

   Now that we have finalized the contract, I have a few questions: When will we receive a complete schedule for the project? Also, how many preliminary designs do you require?

   When you are finished, your screen should look similar to Figure 1-21, although the line breaks on your screen might be slightly different.

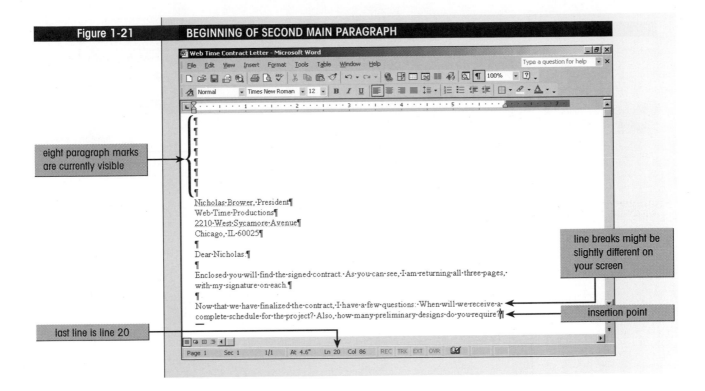

Figure 1-21   BEGINNING OF SECOND MAIN PARAGRAPH

eight paragraph marks are currently visible

line breaks might be slightly different on your screen

insertion point

last line is line 20

Scrolling a Document

After you finish the last set of steps, the insertion point should be near the bottom of the Document window. It looks like there's not enough room to type the rest of Megan's letter. However, as you continue to add text at the end of your document, the text that you typed earlier will **scroll** (or shift up) and disappear from the top of the Document window. You'll see how scrolling works as you enter the rest of the second paragraph.

To observe scrolling while you're entering text:

1. Make sure the insertion point is positioned to the right of the question mark after the word "require" in the second main paragraph. In other words, the insertion point should be positioned at the end of line 20. (See Figure 1-21 above.)

   TROUBLE? If you are using a very large monitor, your insertion point may still be some distance from the bottom of the screen. In that case, you may not be able to perform the scrolling steps that follow. Read the steps to familiarize yourself with the process of scrolling. You'll have a chance to scroll longer documents later.

2. Press the **spacebar**, and then type the following text:

   Finally, will you be available to discuss the project with our artists via a conference call some afternoon next week?

   Notice that as you begin to type the text, Word moves the insertion point to a new line. Also, the first paragraph mark at the top of the letter scrolls off the top of the Document window to make room for the end of the question. When you are finished typing, your screen should look like Figure 1-22. (Don't worry if you make a mistake in your typing. You'll learn a number of ways to correct errors in the next section.)

Figure 1-22   PARAGRAPH MARK SCROLLED OFF THE SCREEN

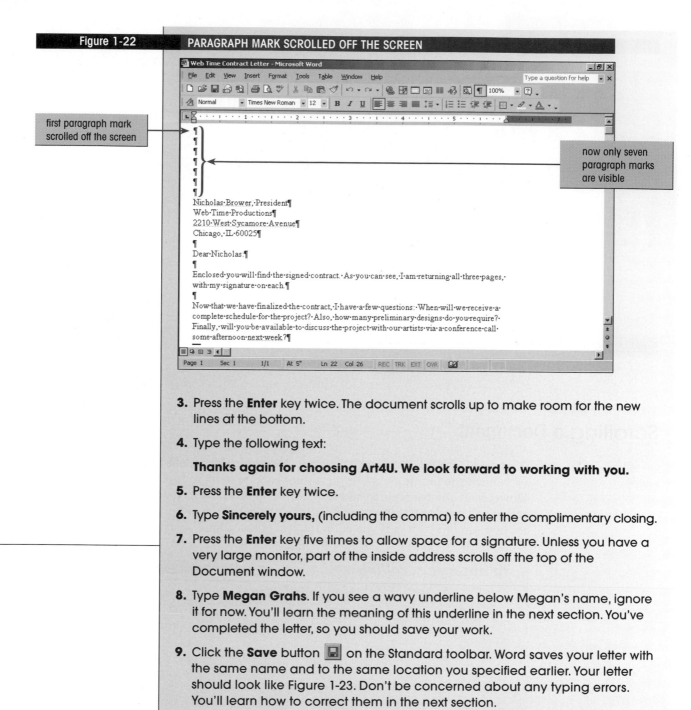

first paragraph mark scrolled off the screen

now only seven paragraph marks are visible

Nicholas·Brower,·President¶
Web·Time·Productions¶
2210·West·Sycamore·Avenue¶
Chicago,·IL·60025¶
¶
Dear·Nicholas:¶
¶
Enclosed·you·will·find·the·signed·contract.·As·you·can·see,·I·am·returning·all·three·pages,·
with·my·signature·on·each.¶
¶
Now·that·we·have·finalized·the·contract,·I·have·a·few·questions.·When·will·we·receive·a·
complete·schedule·for·the·project?·Also,·how·many·preliminary·designs·do·you·require?·
Finally,·will·you·be·available·to·discuss·the·project·with·our·artists·via·a·conference·call·
some·afternoon·next·week?¶

3. Press the **Enter** key twice. The document scrolls up to make room for the new lines at the bottom.

4. Type the following text:

   Thanks again for choosing Art4U. We look forward to working with you.

5. Press the **Enter** key twice.

6. Type **Sincerely yours,** (including the comma) to enter the complimentary closing.

7. Press the **Enter** key five times to allow space for a signature. Unless you have a very large monitor, part of the inside address scrolls off the top of the Document window.

8. Type **Megan Grahs**. If you see a wavy underline below Megan's name, ignore it for now. You'll learn the meaning of this underline in the next section. You've completed the letter, so you should save your work.

9. Click the **Save** button 🖫 on the Standard toolbar. Word saves your letter with the same name and to the same location you specified earlier. Your letter should look like Figure 1-23. Don't be concerned about any typing errors. You'll learn how to correct them in the next section.

Figure 1-23   SIGNATURE PORTION OF LETTER

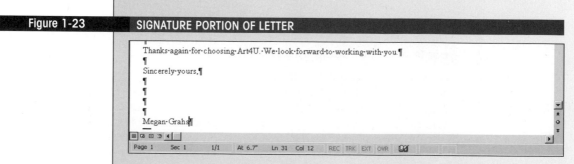

Thanks·again·for·choosing·Art4U.·We·look·forward·to·working·with·you.¶
¶
Sincerely·yours,¶
¶
¶
¶
¶
Megan·Grahs¶

In the last set of steps, you watched the text at the top of your document move off your screen. You can scroll this hidden text back into view so you can read the beginning of the letter. When you do, the text at the bottom of the screen will scroll out of view. To scroll the Document window, you can click the up or down arrows in the vertical scroll bar, click anywhere in the vertical scroll bar, or drag the scroll box. Figure 1-24 summarizes these options.

Figure 1-24	SCROLLING THE DOCUMENT WINDOW

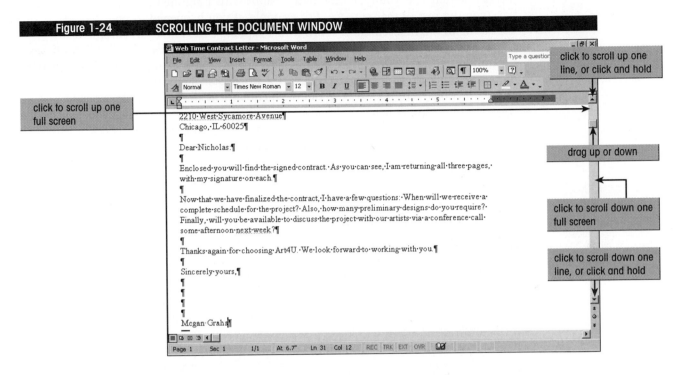

In the next set of steps, you will practice using the vertical scroll bar.

To scroll the document using the vertical scroll bar:

1. Position the mouse pointer on the up arrow at the top of the vertical scroll bar. Press and hold the mouse button to scroll the text. When the text stops scrolling, you have reached the top of the document and can see the beginning of the letter. Note that scrolling does not change the location of the insertion point in the document.

2. Click the down arrow on the vertical scroll bar. The document scrolls down one line.

3. Click anywhere in the vertical scroll bar, below the scroll box. The document scrolls down one full screen.

4. Drag the scroll box up until the first line of the inside address ("Nicholas Brower, President") is positioned at the top of the Document window.

Correcting Errors

If you discover a typing error as soon as you make it, you can press the Backspace key to erase the characters and spaces to the left of the insertion point one at a time. Backspacing erases both printing and nonprinting characters. After you erase the error, you can type the correct characters. (You can also press the Delete key to delete characters to the right of the insertion point.)

In many cases, however, Word's **AutoCorrect** feature will do the work for you. This helpful feature automatically corrects common typing errors, such as entering "adn" for "and." You might have noticed AutoCorrect at work if you forgot to capitalize the first letter in a sentence as you typed the letter. AutoCorrect automatically corrects this error as you type the rest of the sentence. For example, if you happened to type "enclosed" at the beginning of the first sentence, Word would capitalize the initial "e" automatically.

In the case of more complicated errors, you can take advantage of Word's **Spelling and Grammar** checker. This feature continually checks your document against Word's built-in dictionary and a set of grammar rules. If a word is spelled differently from how it is in Word's dictionary, or if a word isn't in the dictionary at all (for example, a person's name), a wavy *red* line appears beneath the word. A wavy red line also appears if you type duplicate words (such as "the the"). If you accidentally type an extra space between words or make a grammatical error (such as typing "He walk to the store." instead of "He walks to the store."), a wavy *green* line appears beneath the error. The easiest way to see how these features work is to make some intentional typing errors.

To correct intentional typing errors:

1. Click the **Document1** button in the taskbar.

   TROUBLE? If you closed Document1 earlier, click the New Blank Document button in the Standard toolbar to open a blank document.

2. Carefully and slowly type the following sentence exactly as it is shown, including the spelling errors and the extra space between the last two words: **microsoft Word corects teh commen typing misTakes you make.** Press the **Enter** key when you are finished typing. Notice that as you press the spacebar after the word "commen," a wavy red line appears beneath it, indicating that the word might be misspelled. Notice also that when you pressed the spacebar after the words "corects," "teh," and "misTakes," Word automatically corrected the spelling. After you pressed the Enter key, a wavy green line appeared under the last two words, alerting you to the extra space. See Figure 1-25.

| Figure 1-25 | DOCUMENT WITH INTENTIONAL TYPING ERRORS |

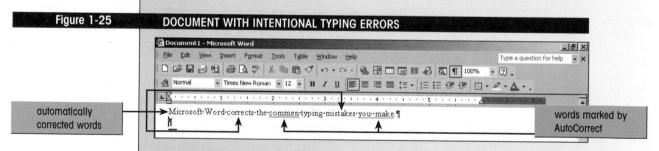

automatically corrected words

words marked by AutoCorrect

TROUBLE? If red and green wavy lines do not appear beneath mistakes, Word is probably not set to check spelling and grammar automatically as you type. Click Tools on the menu bar, and then click Options to open the Options dialog box. Click the Spelling & Grammar tab. If necessary, insert check marks in the "Check spelling as you type" and the "Check grammar as you type" check boxes, and click OK. If Word does not automatically correct the incorrect spelling of "the," click Tools on the menu bar, click AutoCorrect Options, and make sure that all seven boxes at the top of the AutoCorrect tab have check marks. Then scroll down the AutoCorrect list to make sure that there is an entry that changes "teh" to "the," and click OK.

Working with AutoCorrect

Whenever AutoCorrect makes a change, Word inserts an **AutoCorrect Options button** in the document. You can use this button to undo a change, or to prevent AutoCorrect from making the same change in the future. To see an AutoCorrect Options button, you position the mouse pointer over a word that has been changed by AutoCorrect.

To display the AutoCorrect Options buttons:

1. Position the mouse pointer over the word "corrects." A small blue rectangle appears below the first few letters of the word, as in Figure 1-26.

   TROUBLE? If you see a blue button with a lightning bolt, you pointed to the blue rectangle after it appeared. Move the pointer so that only the rectangle is visible, and continue with the next step.

Figure 1-26	WORD CHANGED BY AUTOCORRECT

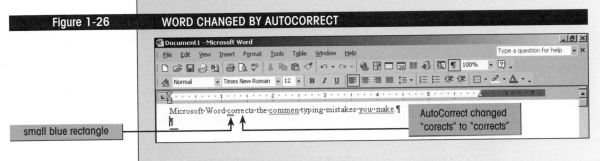

small blue rectangle

AutoCorrect changed "corects" to "corrects"

2. Point to the **blue rectangle** below "corrects". The blue rectangle is replaced by the AutoCorrect Options button.

3. Click the **AutoCorrect Options** button. A menu with commands related to AutoCorrect appears. You could choose to change "corrects" back to "corects". You could also tell AutoCorrect to stop automatically correcting "corects".

4. Click anywhere in the document. The AutoCorrect menu closes.

Correcting Spelling and Grammar Errors

After you verify that AutoCorrect made changes you want, you should scan your document for wavy underlines. Again, the red underlines indicate potential spelling errors, while the green underlines indicate potential grammar or punctuation problems. In the following steps, you will learn a quick way to correct such errors.

To correct spelling and grammar errors:

1. Position the I-Beam pointer I over the word "commen" and click the right mouse button. A shortcut menu appears with suggested spellings. See Figure 1-27.

Figure 1-27	SHORTCUT MENU WITH SUGGESTED SPELLINGS

click to replace
misspelled word

TROUBLE? If the shortcut menu doesn't appear, repeat Step 1, making sure you click the right mouse button, not the left one. If you see a different menu from the one shown in Figure 1-27, you didn't right-click exactly on the underlined word. Press the Esc key to close the menu, and then repeat Step 1.

2. Click **common** in the shortcut menu. The menu disappears, and the correct spelling appears in your document. Notice that the wavy red line disappears after you correct the error.

3. Click to the right of the letter "u" in the word "you". Press the **Delete** key to delete the extra space.

You can see how quick and easy it is to correct common typing errors with AutoCorrect and the Spelling and Grammar checker. Remember, however, to thoroughly proofread each document you create. AutoCorrect will not catch words that are spelled correctly, but used improperly (such as "your" for "you're").

Proofreading the Letter

Before you can proofread your letter, you need to close the document with the practice sentence. You don't need to save this document, because you only created it to practice correcting errors.

To close the practice document:

1. Click the **Document Close** button ☒ (on the right end of the menu bar). You see a dialog box asking if you want to save your changes to the document.

2. Click **No**. You return to the document named Web Time Contract Letter.

Now you can proofread the letter for any typos. You can also get rid of the wavy red underline below Megan's last name.

To respond to possible spelling errors:

1. Scroll down until the signature line is visible. Because Word doesn't recognize "Grahs" as a word, it marked it as a potential error. You need to tell Word to ignore this name wherever it occurs in the letter.

2. Right-click **Grahs**. A shortcut menu opens.

3. Click **Ignore All**. The wavy red underline disappears from below "Grahs".

4. Scroll up to the beginning of the letter, and proofread it for typos. If a word has a wavy red or green underline, right-click it and choose an option in the shortcut menu. To correct other errors, click to the right or left of the error, use the Backspace or Delete key to remove it, and then type a correction.

Inserting a Date with AutoComplete

The beauty of using a word processing program such as Microsoft Word is that you can easily make changes to text you have already typed. In this case, you need to insert the current date at the beginning of the letter. Megan tells you that she wants to send the contract to Web Time Productions on February 21, so you need to insert that date into the letter now.

Before you can enter the date, you need to move the insertion point to the right location. In a standard business letter, the date belongs approximately 2.5 inches from the top. (As you recall, this is where you started the inside address earlier.) You also need to insert some blank lines to allow enough space between the date and the inside address.

To move the insertion point and add some blank lines:

1. Scroll up to display the top of the document.

2. Click to the left of the "N" in "Nicholas Brower," in the inside address. The status bar indicates that the insertion point is on line 9, 2.5 inches from the top. (Your status bar might show slightly different measurements.) You might see a square with a lowercase "i" displayed just above the name. Ignore this for now. You'll learn about this special button (called a Smart Tag Actions button) later in this tutorial.

3. Press **Enter** four times, and then press the ↑ key four times. Now the insertion point is positioned at line 9, with three blank lines between the inside address and the line where you will insert the date. See Figure 1-28.

Figure 1-28 POSITION OF INSERTION POINT

insert date here

three blank lines between date and inside address

```
Nicholas·Brower,·President¶
Web·Time·Productions¶
2210·West·Sycamore·Avenue¶
Chicago,·IL·60025¶
```

You're ready to insert the date. To do this you can take advantage of Word's **AutoComplete** feature, which automatically inserts dates and other regularly used items for you. In this case, you can type the first few characters of the month, and let Word insert the rest. (This only works for long month names like February.)

To insert the date:

1. Type **Febr** (the first four letters of February). A small yellow box, called an AutoComplete suggestion, appears above the line, as shown in Figure 1-29. If you wanted to type something other than February, you could continue typing to complete the word. In this case, though, you want to accept the AutoComplete tip, so you will press the Enter key in the next step.

Figure 1-29 AUTOCOMPLETE SUGGESTION

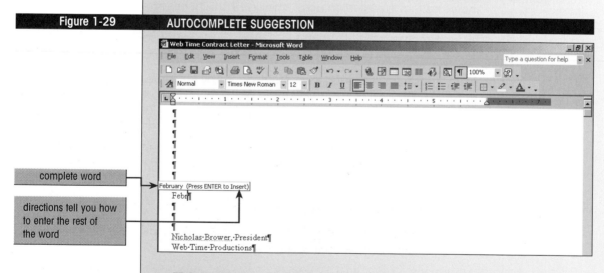

complete word

directions tell you how to enter the rest of the word

TROUBLE? If the AutoComplete tip doesn't appear, this feature may not be active. Click Tools on the menu bar, click AutoCorrect Options, click the AutoText tab, click the "Show AutoComplete suggestions" check box to insert a check, and then click OK.

2. Press **Enter**. The rest of the word "February" is inserted in the document.

3. Press the **spacebar** and then type **21, 2003**.

TROUBLE? If February happens to be the current month, you will see an AutoComplete suggestion displaying the current date after you press the spacebar. To accept that AutoComplete tip, press Enter. Otherwise type the rest of the date as instructed in Step 3.

4. Click one of the blank lines below the date. Depending on how your computer is set up, you may see a dotted underline below the date. (You will learn the meaning of this underline in the next section.) You have finished entering the date. See Figure 1-30.

Figure 1-30	DATE ENTERED IN THE DOCUMENT

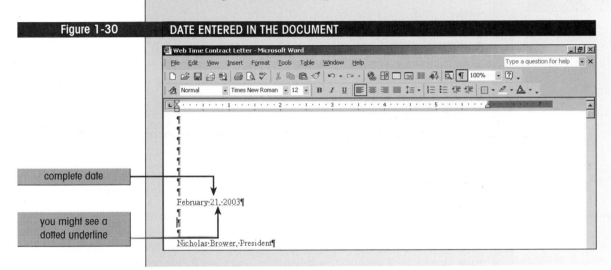

complete date

you might see a dotted underline

Removing Smart Tags

A dotted underline below a date, name, or address indicates that Word has inserted a Smart Tag in the document. A **Smart Tag** is a feature that that allows you to perform actions (such as sending e-mail or scheduling a meeting) that would normally require a completely different program. Word attaches Smart Tag Action buttons to certain kinds of text, including dates and names. You can click this button to open a menu (similar to a shortcut menu) where you can select commands related to that item. (For example, you might click a Smart Tag on a name to add that name to your e-mail address book.) You don't really need Smart Tags in this document, though, so you will delete them. (Your computer may not be set up to show Smart Tags at all, or it might show them on dates and addresses, but not names. If you do not see any Smart Tags in your document, simply read the following steps.)

To remove the Smart Tags from the document:

1. If you see a dotted underline below the date, position the mouse pointer over the date. A Smart Tag Icon 🔘 appears over the date.

2. Move the mouse pointer over the Smart Tag icon. The Smart Tag Actions button 🔘▾ appears, as shown in Figure 1-31.

Figure 1-31 | DISPLAYING THE SMART TAG ACTIONS BUTTON

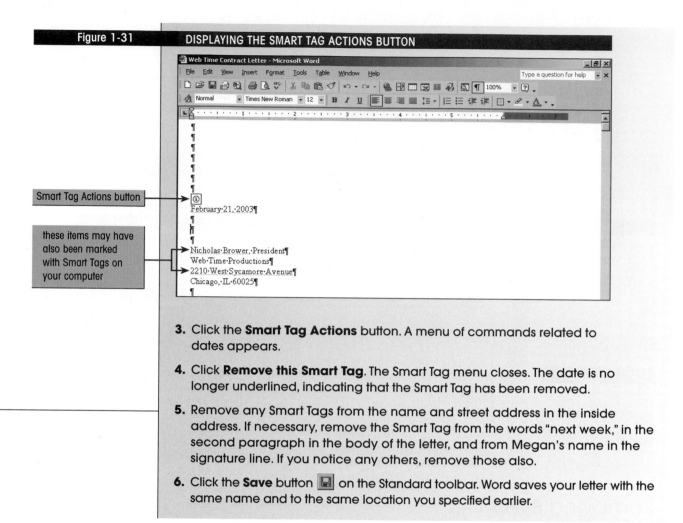

Smart Tag Actions button

these items may have also been marked with Smart Tags on your computer

3. Click the **Smart Tag Actions** button. A menu of commands related to dates appears.

4. Click **Remove this Smart Tag**. The Smart Tag menu closes. The date is no longer underlined, indicating that the Smart Tag has been removed.

5. Remove any Smart Tags from the name and street address in the inside address. If necessary, remove the Smart Tag from the words "next week," in the second paragraph in the body of the letter, and from Megan's name in the signature line. If you notice any others, remove those also.

6. Click the **Save** button 🖫 on the Standard toolbar. Word saves your letter with the same name and to the same location you specified earlier.

Previewing and Printing a Document

Do you think the letter is ready to print? You could find out by clicking the Print button on the Standard toolbar and then reviewing the printed page. In doing so, however, you risk wasting paper and printer time. For example, if you failed to insert enough space for the company letterhead, you would have to add more space, and then print the letter all over again. To avoid wasting paper and time, you should first display the document in the Print Preview window. By default, the Print Preview window shows you the full page; there's no need to scroll through the document.

To preview the document:

1. Click the **Print Preview** button 🔍 on the Standard toolbar. The Print Preview window opens and displays a full-page version of your letter, as shown in Figure 1-32. This shows how the letter will fit on the printed page. The Print Preview toolbar includes a number of buttons that are useful for making changes that affect the way the printed page will look.

Figure 1-32	FULL PAGE DISPLAYED IN PRINT PREVIEW WINDOW

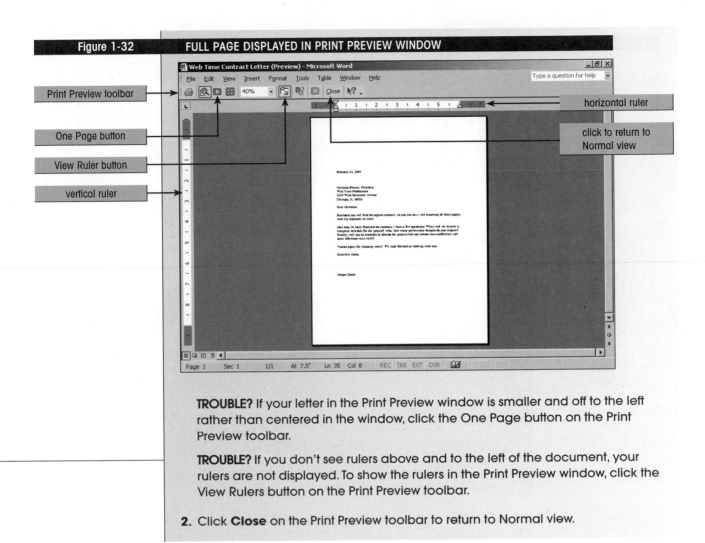

Print Preview toolbar

One Page button

View Ruler button

vertical ruler

horizontal ruler

click to return to Normal view

TROUBLE? If your letter in the Print Preview window is smaller and off to the left rather than centered in the window, click the One Page button on the Print Preview toolbar.

TROUBLE? If you don't see rulers above and to the left of the document, your rulers are not displayed. To show the rulers in the Print Preview window, click the View Rulers button on the Print Preview toolbar.

2. Click **Close** on the Print Preview toolbar to return to Normal view.

Note that it is especially important to preview documents if your computer is connected to a network so that you don't keep a shared printer tied up with unnecessary printing. In this case, the text looks well spaced and the letterhead will fit at the top of the page. You're ready to print the letter.

When printing a document, you have two choices. You can use the Print command on the File menu, which opens the Print dialog box in which you can adjust some printer settings. Or, if you prefer, you can use the Print button on the Standard toolbar, which prints the document using default settings, without opening a dialog box. In these tutorials, the first time you print from a shared computer, you should check the settings in the Print dialog box and make sure the number of copies is set to one. After that, you can use the Print button.

To print a document:

1. Make sure your printer is turned on and contains paper.

2. Click **File** on the menu bar, and then click **Print**. The Print dialog box opens. See Figure 1-33.

Figure 1-33   PRINT DIALOG BOX

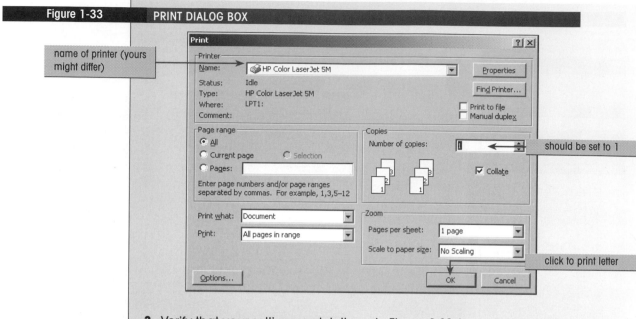

name of printer (yours
might differ)

should be set to 1

click to print letter

3. Verify that your settings match those in Figure 1-33. In particular make sure the number of copies is set to 1. Also make sure the Printer section of the dialog box shows the correct printer. If you're not sure what the correct printer is, check with your instructor or technical support person.

TROUBLE? If the Print dialog box shows the wrong printer, click the Name list arrow, and then select the correct printer from the list of available printers.

4. Click **OK**. Assuming your computer is attached to a printer, the letter prints.

Your printed letter should look similar to Figure 1-14, but without the Art4U letterhead. The word wraps, or line breaks, might not appear in the same places on your letter because the size and spacing of characters vary slightly from one printer to the next.

Creating an Envelope

After you print the letter, Megan stops by your desk and asks you to print an envelope in which to mail the contracts. Creating an envelope is a simple process because Word automatically uses the inside address from the letter as the address on the envelope.

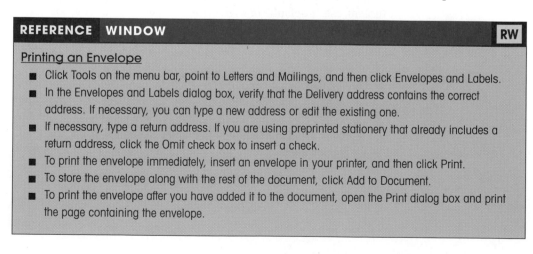

REFERENCE WINDOW   **RW**

Printing an Envelope
- Click Tools on the menu bar, point to Letters and Mailings, and then click Envelopes and Labels.
- In the Envelopes and Labels dialog box, verify that the Delivery address contains the correct address. If necessary, you can type a new address or edit the existing one.
- If necessary, type a return address. If you are using preprinted stationery that already includes a return address, click the Omit check box to insert a check.
- To print the envelope immediately, insert an envelope in your printer, and then click Print.
- To store the envelope along with the rest of the document, click Add to Document.
- To print the envelope after you have added it to the document, open the Print dialog box and print the page containing the envelope.

Megan tells you that your printer is not currently stocked with envelopes. She asks you to create the envelope and add it to the document. Then she will print the envelope later, when she is ready to mail the contracts to Web Time Productions.

To create an envelope:

1. Click **Tools** on the menu bar, point to **Letters and Mailings**, and then click **Envelopes and Labels**. The Envelopes and Labels dialog box opens, as shown in Figure 1-34. By default, Word uses the inside address from the letter as the delivery address. Depending on how your computer is set up, you might see an address in the Return address box. Since you will be using Art4U's printed envelopes, you don't need to include a return address on this envelope.

Figure 1-34	ENVELOPES AND LABELS DIALOG BOX

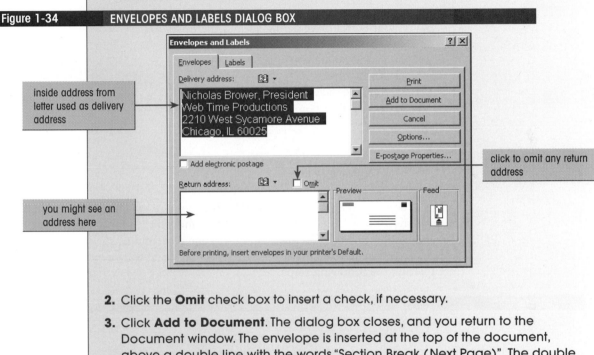

inside address from letter used as delivery address

click to omit any return address

you might see an address here

2. Click the **Omit** check box to insert a check, if necessary.

3. Click **Add to Document**. The dialog box closes, and you return to the Document window. The envelope is inserted at the top of the document, above a double line with the words "Section Break (Next Page)". The double line indicates that the envelope and the letter are two separate parts of the document. The envelope will print in the standard business envelope format. The letter will still print on standard 8.5 × 11-inch paper. (You'll have a chance to actually print an envelope in the exercises at the end of this tutorial.)

4. Click the **Save** button 🖫 on the Standard toolbar.

Congratulations on creating your first letter in Microsoft Word. Since you are finished with the letter and the envelope, you can close the document and exit Word.

To close the document and exit Word:

1. Click the **Close** button ✕ in the menu bar. The Web Time Contract Letter closes.

   TROUBLE? If you see a dialog box with the message "Do you want to save the changes to 'Web Time Contract Letter?', you didn't save your most recent changes. Click Yes.

2. If necessary, close other open documents without saving them.

3. Click the **Close** button ☒ in the upper-right corner of the Word window. Word closes, and you return to the Windows desktop.

Session 1.2 QUICK | CHECK

1. Explain how to save a document for the first time.
2. Explain how to enter the name of a month using AutoCorrect.
3. Explain how word wrap works in a Word document.
4. List the steps required to print an envelope.
5. In your own words, define each of the following:
    a. Scrolling
    b. AutoComplete
    c. AutoCorrect
    d. Print Preview
    e. Smart Tag

REVIEW ASSIGNMENTS

Megan received an e-mail from Nicholas Brower at Web Time Productions, confirming their plans for a conference call. Megan has e-mailed the graphic artists at Art4U, informing them about the call. To make sure everyone remembers, she would like you to post a memo on the bulletin board in the break room. Create the memo shown in Figure 1-35 by completing the following steps.

Figure 1-35

Art4U, Inc.
1921 Sedona Avenue
Tucson, AZ 85701
Art4U@WorldNet.com

TO: Art4U Staff Artists

FROM: Megan Grahs

DATE: February 27, 2003

SUBJECT: Conference Call

Please plan to join us for a conference call at 3 P.M. on Friday, March 1. Nicholas Brower, president of Web Time Productions, will be taking part, as will five of the company's most experienced Web page designers. This will be your chance to ask the designers some important questions.

You will be able to join the call from your desk by dialing an 800 number and a special access code. You'll receive both of these numbers via e-mail the day of the call.

1. If necessary, start Word and make sure your Data Disk is in the appropriate disk drive, and then check your screen to make sure your settings match those in the tutorials. In particular, make sure that nonprinting characters are displayed.

2. If the Office Assistant is open, hide it.

3. Click the New Blank Document button on the Standard toolbar to open a new document.

4. Press the Enter key eight times to insert enough space for the company letterhead.

5. Press the Caps Lock key, and then type "TO:" in capital letters.

Explore ▸ 6. You can use the Tab key to align text as a column. In this case, you want to align the To, From, Date, and Subject information. To begin, press the Tab key three times. Word inserts three nonprinting characters (right-pointing arrows), one for each time you pressed the Tab key.

7. Press the Caps Lock key to turn off capitalization, and then type "Art4U Staff Artists".

8. Press the Enter key twice, type "FROM:", press the Tab key twice, and then type your name in lowercase. Throughout the rest of this exercise, use the Caps Lock key as necessary to turn capitalization on and off.

9. Press the Enter key twice, type "DATE:", and then press the Tab key two times.

Explore ▸ 10. You can take advantage of AutoCorrect to type the current date. To try it now, type the name of the current month. If an AutoCorrect suggestion appears, press Enter to complete the name of the month; otherwise, continue typing. Press the spacebar. After you press the spacebar, an AutoCorrect suggestion appears with the current date. Press Enter to accept the suggestion.

11. Press the Enter key twice, type "SUBJECT:" and then press the Tab key two times. Type "Conference Call" and then press the Enter key twice.

12. Continue typing the rest of the memo as shown in Figure 1-35. (You will have a chance to correct any typing errors later.) Ignore any AutoCorrect suggestions that are not relevant to the text you are typing.

13. Save your work as **Conference Call Memo** in the Review folder for Tutorial 1.

14. Scroll to the beginning of the document and proofread your work.

15. Correct any misspelled words marked by wavy red lines. If the correct spelling of a word does not appear in the list box, press the Escape key to close the list, and then make the correction yourself. Remove any red wavy lines below words that are actually spelled correctly. Then correct any grammatical or other errors indicated by wavy green lines. Use the Backspace or Delete key to delete any extra words or spaces.

16. Remove any Smart Tags.

17. Save your most recent changes.

18. Preview and print the memo.

19. Close the document. Save any changes if necessary.

Explore ▸ 20. If you will be sending mail to someone regularly, it's helpful to add an envelope to a blank document, and then save the document, so that you can print the envelope in the future, whenever you need it. Open a new, blank document. Create an envelope for Nicholas Brower at Web Time Productions. Use the address you used as the inside address in the tutorial. For the return address, type your own address. Add the envelope to the document. If you are asked if you want to save the return address as the new default return address, click No. If your computer is connected to a printer that is stocked with envelopes, click File on the menu bar, click Print, click the Pages option button, type 1 in the Pages text box, and then click OK.

21. Save the document as **Web Time Envelope** in the Review folder for Tutorial 1.

22. Close any open documents and then exit Word.

CASE PROBLEMS

Case 1. Letter to Request Information about a Field Trip to Roaring Rapids Water Park
You are a teacher at Luis Sotelo Elementary School. Your students have been raising money all year for a trip to Roaring Rapids Water Park. Before you can plan the outing, you need to write for some information. Create the letter by doing the following:

1. If necessary, start Word, make sure your Data Disk is in the appropriate disk drive, and check your screen to make sure your settings match those in the tutorials.

2. Open a new blank document.

3. Type your name, press Enter, and then type the following address:

   Luis Sotelo Elementary School

   1521 First Avenue

   Durham, North Carolina 27701

Explore

4. Press the Enter key four times, and then type the name of the current month. (If an AutoCorrect suggestion appears, press Enter to complete the name of the month.) Press the spacebar. After you press the spacebar, an AutoCorrect suggestion appears with the current date. Press Enter to accept the suggestion.

5. Press the Enter key four times after the date, and, using the proper business letter format, type the inside address: "Scott Rowland, Roaring Rapids Water Park, 2344 West Prairie Street, Durham, North Carolina 27704".

6. Double space after the inside address (that is, press the Enter Key twice), type the salutation "Dear Mr. Rowland:" and then insert another blank line. Close the Office Assistant if it opens.

7. Type the first paragraph as follows: "I'd like some information about a class field trip to Roaring Rapids Water Park. Please answer the following questions:"

8. Save your work as **Water Park Information Letter** in the Cases folder for Tutorial 1.

9. Insert one blank line, and then type these questions on separate lines with one blank line between each:
   How much is a day pass for a 10-year-old child?
   How much is a day pass for an adult?
   Can you offer a discount for a group of 25 children and 5 adults?
   Are lockers available for storing clothes and other belongings?

10. Correct any typing errors indicated by wavy lines. (*Hint*: Because "Sotelo" is spelled correctly, click Ignore All on the shortcut menu to remove the wavy red line under the word "Sotelo" and prevent Word from marking the word as a misspelling.)

11. Insert another blank line at the end of the letter, and type the complimentary closing "Sincerely," (include the comma).

12. Press the Enter key four times to leave room for the signature, and type your full name. Then press the Enter key and type "Luis Sotelo Elementary School". Notice that "Sotelo" is not marked as a spelling error this time.

13. Scroll up to the beginning of the document, and then remove any Smart Tags in the letter.

14. Save your changes to the letter, and then preview it using the Print Preview button.

15. Print the letter, close the document, and exit Word.

Case 2. Letter to Confirm Food Service During the National Purchasing Management Association Conference As catering director for the Madison Convention and Visitors Bureau, you are responsible for managing food service at the city's convention center. The National Physical Therapy Association has scheduled a daily breakfast buffet during its annual convention (which runs July 6–10, 2003). You need to write a letter confirming plans for the daily buffet.

Create the letter using the skills you learned in the tutorial. Remember to include today's date, the inside address, the salutation, the date of the reservation, the complimentary closing, and your name and title. If the instructions show quotation marks around text you type, do not include the quotation marks in your letter. To complete the letter, do the following:

1. If necessary, start Word, make sure your Data Disk is in the appropriate disk drive, and check your screen to make sure your settings match those in the tutorials.

2. Open a new, blank document and press the Enter key until the insertion point is positioned about 2 inches from the top of the page. (Remember that you can see the exact position of the insertion point, in inches, in the status bar.)

3. Enter "June 6, 2003" as the date.

4. Press the Enter key four times after the date, and, using the proper business letter format, type the inside address: "Charles Quade, National Physical Therapy Association, 222 Sydney Street, Whitewater, WI 57332".

5. Double space after the inside address (that is, press the Enter key twice), type the salutation "Dear Mr. Quade:", and then double space again. If the Office Assistant opens, close it.

6. Write one paragraph confirming the daily breakfast buffets for July 6–10, 2003.

7. Insert a blank line and type the complimentary closing "Sincerely,".

8. Press the Enter key four times to leave room for the signature, and then type your name and title.

9. Save the letter as **Confirmation Letter** in the Cases folder for Tutorial 1.

10. Remove any Smart Tags. Reread your letter carefully, and correct any errors.

11. Save any new changes, and then preview and print the letter.

Explore 12. Create an envelope for the letter, and add it to the document. For the return address, type your own address. Add the envelope to the document. If you are asked if you want to save the return address as the new default return address, click No. If your computer is connected to a printer that is stocked with envelopes, click File on the menu bar, click Print, click the Pages option button, type 1 in the Pages text box, and then click OK.

13. Save your work and close the document, then exit Word.

Case 3. *Letter Congratulating a Professor* Liza Morgan, a professor of e-commerce at Kentucky State University, was recently honored by the Southern Business Council for her series of free public seminars on developing Web sites for nonprofit agencies. She also was recently named Teacher of the Year by a national organization called Woman in Technology. As one of her former students, you need to write a letter congratulating her on these honors. To write this letter, do the following:

1. If necessary, start Word, make sure your Data Disk is in the appropriate disk drive, and check your screen to make sure your settings match those in the tutorials.

2. Write a brief letter congratulating Professor Morgan on her awards. Remember to use the four-part planning process. You should plan the content, organization, and style of the letter, and use a standard letter format. For the inside address, use the following: Professor Liza Morgan, Department of Business Administration, Kentucky State University, 1010 College Drive, Frankfort, Kentucky 40601.

3. Save the document as **Liza Morgan Letter** in the Cases folder for Tutorial 1.

4. Correct any typing errors, remove any Smart Tags, and then preview and print the memo.

Explore 5. Create an envelope for the letter, and add it to the document. For the return address, type your own address. Add the envelope to the document. If you are asked if you want to save the return address as the new default return address, click No. If your computer is connected to a printer that is stocked with envelopes, click File on the menu bar, click Print, click the Pages option button, type 1 in the Pages text box, and then click OK.

6. Save the document and close it, and then exit Word.

Case 4. Memo Created With a Template You are the office manager for Head for the Hills, a small company that sells hiking equipment over the Internet. The company has just moved to a new building which requires a special security key card after hours. Some employees have had trouble getting the key cards to work properly. You decide to hold a meeting to explain the security policies for the new building and to demonstrate the key cards. But first you need to post a memo announcing the meeting. The recently ordered letterhead (with the company's new address) has not yet arrived, so you will use a Word template to create the memo. Word provides templates—that is, models with predefined formatting—to help you create complete documents (including a professional-looking letterhead) quickly. To create the memo, do the following:

1. If necessary, start Word, make sure your Data Disk is in the appropriate disk drive, and check your screen to make sure your settings match those in the tutorials.

Explore

2. If the Task Pane is not displayed, click View on the menu bar, and then click Task Pane. The Task Pane is displayed on the right side of the Word window. You see a number of options related to creating new documents.

Explore

3. Under "New from template," click General Templates. The Templates dialog box opens.

Explore

4. Click the Memos tab, click Professional Memo, and then click the OK button. A memo template opens containing generic, placeholder text that you can replace with your own information.

5. Make sure the template is displayed in Normal View. Click at the end of the line "Company Name Here" (at the top of the document), press Backspace to delete the text, and type "Head for the Hills".

6. Click the text "Click here and type name," and in the To: line, type "All Employees". After "From," replace the current text with your name.

7. Click after "CC:" and then press Delete to delete the placeholder text. Use the Backspace key to delete the entire "CC" line. Note that Word inserts the current date automatically after the heading "Date."

8. After "Re:" type "Meeting to discuss building security".

9. Delete the placeholder text in the body of the letter, and replace it with a paragraph announcing the meeting, which is scheduled for tomorrow at 2 P.M. in the Central Conference Room.

10. Save the letter as **Meeting Memo** (in the Cases folder for Tutorial 1).

Explore

11. The memo text is in a small font, which is hard to read. To make it easier to review your work, you can change the Zoom setting in Normal view. Click the Zoom list arrow in the Standard toolbar, and then click 150%.

12. Review the memo. Correct any typos and delete any Smart Tags. Save the memo again, preview it, and then print it.

13. Close the document and exit Word.

LAB ASSIGNMENTS

Word Processing

The New Perspectives Labs are designed to help you master some of the key computer concepts and skills presented in each chapter of the text. If you are using your school's lab computers, your instructor or technical support person should have installed the Labs software for you. If you want to use the Labs on your home computer, ask your instructor for the appropriate software. See the Read This Before You Begin page for more information on installing and starting the Lab.

Each Lab has two parts: Steps and Explore. Use Steps first to learn and review concepts. Read the information on each page and do the numbered steps. As you work through the Lab, you will be asked to answer Quick Check questions about what you have learned. At the end of the Lab, you will see a Summary Report of your answers to the Quick Checks. If your instructor wants you to turn in this Summary Report, click the Print button on the Summary Report screen.

When you have completed the Steps, you can click the Explore button to complete the Lab Assignments. You also can use Explore to practice the skills you learned and to explore concepts on your own.

Word Processing Word-processing software is the most popular computerized productivity tool. In this Lab you will learn how word-processing software works. When you have completed this Lab, you should be able to apply the general concepts you learned to any word-processing package you use at home, at work, or in your school lab.

1. Click the Steps button to learn how word-processing software works. As you proceed through the Steps, answer all of the Quick Check questions that appear. After you complete the Steps, you will see a Quick Check Summary Report. Follow the instructions on the screen to print this report.

2. Click the Explore button to begin. Click File, and then click Open to display the Open dialog box. Click the file **Timber.tex**, and then press the Enter key to open the letter to Northern Timber Company. Make the following modifications to the letter, and then print it. You do not need to save the letter.
   a. In the first and last lines of the letter, change "Jason Kidder" to your name.
   b. Change the date to today's date.
   c. The second paragraph begins "Your proposal did not include…". Move this paragraph so it is the last paragraph in the text of the letter.
   d. Change the cost of a permanent bridge to $20,000.
   e. Spell check the letter.

3. In Explore, open the file **Stars.tex**. Make the following modifications to the document and then print it. You do not need to save the document.
   a. Center and boldface the title.
   b. Change the title font to size —16-point Arial.
   c. Boldface the DATE, SHOWER, and LOCATION.
   d. Move the January 2–3 line to the top of the list.
   e. Double-space the entire document.

4. In Explore, compose a one-page double-spaced letter to your parents or to a friend. Make sure you date the letter and check your spelling. Print the letter and sign it. You do not need to save your letter.

INTERNET ASSIGNMENTS

Student Union

The purpose of the Internet Assignments is to challenge you to find information on the Internet that you can use to create effective documents. The actual assignments are updated and maintained on the Course Technology Web site. Log on to the Internet and use your Web browser to go to the Student Union on the New Perspectives Series site at **www.course.com/NewPerspectives/studentunion**. Click the Online Companions link, and then click the link for this text.

QUICK | CHECK ANSWERS

Session 1.1

1. (1) Plan the content, purpose, organization, and look of your document. (2) Create and then edit the document. (3) Format the document to make it visually appealing. (4) Preview and then print the document.

2. Click the Start button, point to Programs, and then click Microsoft Word.

3. **a.** symbols you can display on-screen but that don't print
   b. buttons to the left of the horizontal status bar that switch the document to Normal view, Web Layout view, Print Layout view, or Outline view
   c. actual height of a character measured in points
   d. standard settings

4. Click Format on the menu bar, click Font, select the font size in the Size list box, click the Default button, and then click Yes.

5. Right-click a toolbar, and then click Formatting on the shortcut menu.

6. Click the Normal View button.

7. False

Session 1.2

1. Click the Save button on the Standard toolbar, switch to the drive and folder where you want to save the document, enter a filename in the File name text box, and then click the Save button.

2. Type the first few characters of the month. When an AutoCorrect suggestion appears, press the Enter key.

3. When you type a word that extends into the right margin, Word moves that word and the insertion point to the next line.

4. Click Tools on the menu bar, point to Letters and Mailings, and then click Envelopes and Labels. In the Envelopes and Labels dialog box, verify that the Delivery address contains the correct address. If necessary, you can type a new address or edit the existing one. If necessary, type a return address. If you are using preprinted stationery that already includes a return address, click the Omit check box to insert a check. To print the envelope immediately, insert an envelope in your printer, and click Print. To store the envelope along with the rest of the document, click Add to Document. To print the envelope after you have added it to the document, open the Print dialog box and print the page containing the envelope.

5. **a.** The means by which text at the bottom of the document shifts out of view when you display the top of the document, and text at the top shifts out of view when you display the bottom of the document.
   b. A feature that automatically enters dates and other regularly used items.
   c. A feature that fixes common typing errors automatically.
   d. A window in which you can see how the document will look when printed.
   e. A feature that that allows you to perform actions (such as sending e-mail or scheduling a meeting) that would normally require a completely different program. Word attaches Smart Tag Action buttons to certain kinds of text, including dates and names.

In this tutorial you will:

- Check spelling and grammar

- Move the insertion point around the document

- Select and delete text

- Reverse edits using the Undo and Redo buttons

- Move text within the document

- Find and replace text

- Change margins, line spacing, alignment, and paragraph indents

- Copy formatting with the Format Painter

- Change fonts and adjust font sizes

- Emphasize points with bullets, numbering, boldface, underlining, and italics

- Add a comment to a document

EDITING AND FORMATTING A DOCUMENT

Preparing a FAQ Document for Long Meadow Gardens

CASE

Long Meadow Gardens

Marilee Brigham is the owner of Long Meadow Gardens, a landscape and gardening supply company. The firm's large nursery provides shrubs and trees to professional landscape contractors throughout the Minneapolis/St. Paul area. At the same time, Long Meadow's retail store caters to home gardeners, who often call the store with questions about planting and caring for their purchases.

Marilee has noticed that retail customers tend to ask the same set of questions. To save time in answering these questions, she would like a series of handouts designed to answer these common questions. (Such a document is sometimes known as a FAQ—which is short for "frequently asked questions.") The company's chief horticulturist, Peter Chi, has just finished creating a FAQ containing information on planting trees. Now that Marilee has commented on and corrected the draft, Peter asks you to make the necessary changes and print the document.

In this tutorial, you will edit the FAQ according to Marilee's comments. You will open a draft of the document, resave it, and edit it. You will check the document's grammar and spelling, and then move text using two different methods. You will also find and replace one version of the company name with another.

Next, you will change the overall look of the document by changing margins and line spacing, indenting and justifying paragraphs, and copying formatting from one paragraph to another. You'll create a bulleted list to emphasize the species of water-tolerant trees and a numbered list for the steps involved in removing the burlap from around the base of a tree. Then you'll make the title more prominent by centering it, changing its font, and enlarging it. You'll add boldface to the questions to set them off from the rest of the text and underline an added note about how to get further information. Finally, you will add a comment, and then print the FAQ document.

SESSION 2.1

In this session you will learn how to use the Spelling and Grammar checker to correct any errors in your document. You will also learn how to undo and redo changes in a document. Then you will edit the draft of the FAQ document by deleting words and moving text. Finally, you'll find and replace text throughout the document.

Reviewing the Document

Marilee's editing marks and notes on the first draft are shown in Figure 2-1. You'll begin by opening the first draft of the document, which has the filename FAQ.

Figure 2-1   DRAFT OF FAQ WITH MARILEE'S EDITS (PAGE 1)

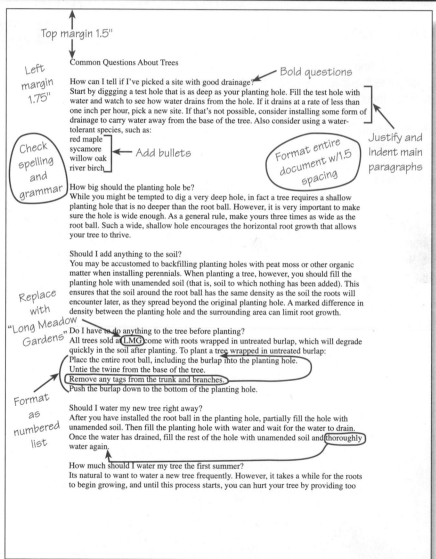

Figure 2-1 DRAFT OF FAQ WITH MARILEE'S EDITS (PAGE 2)

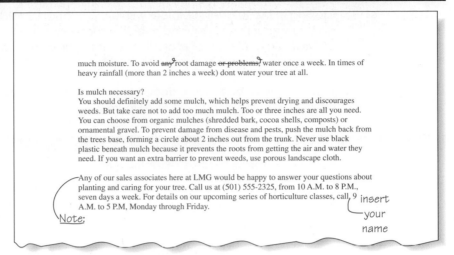

To open the document:

1. Place your Data Disk into the appropriate disk drive.

2. Start Word as usual.

3. Click the **Open** button on the Standard toolbar to display the Open dialog box, shown in Figure 2-2.

Figure 2-2 OPEN DIALOG BOX

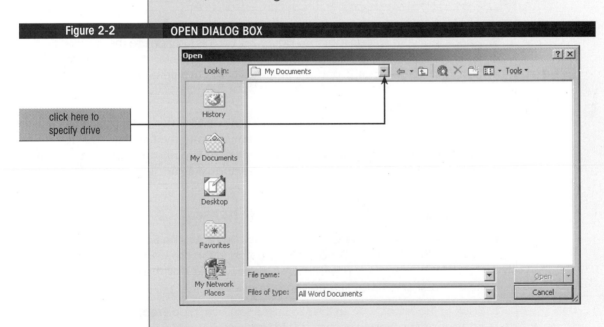

click here to specify drive

4. Click the **Look in** list arrow. The list of drives and files appears.

5. Click the drive that contains your Data Disk.

6. Double-click the **Tutorial.02** folder, and then double-click the **Tutorial** folder.

7. Click **FAQ** to select the file, if necessary.

TROUBLE? If you see "FAQ.doc" in the folder, Windows might be configured to display filename extensions. Click FAQ.doc and continue with Step 8. If you can't find the file with or without the filename extension, make sure you're looking in the Tutorial subfolder within the Tutorial.02 folder on the drive that contains your Data Disk, and check to make sure the Files of type text box displays All Word Documents or All Files. If you still can't locate the file, ask your instructor or technical support person for help.

8. Click the **Open** button. The document opens with the insertion point at the beginning of the document. See Figure 2-3.

Figure 2-3   OPEN DOCUMENT

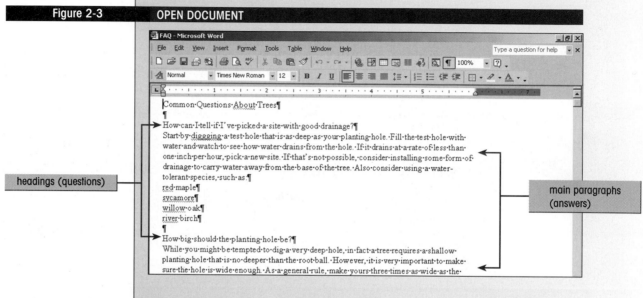

headings (questions)

main paragraphs (answers)

9. Check that your screen matches Figure 2-3. For this tutorial, use the Show/Hide ¶ button to display nonprinting characters. This will make formatting elements (tabs, paragraph marks, and so forth) visible and easier to change.

Now that you've opened the document, you can save it with a new name. To avoid altering the original file, FAQ, you will save the document using the filename Tree FAQ. Saving the document with another filename creates a copy of the file and leaves the original file unchanged in case you want to work through the tutorial again.

To save the document with a new name:

1. Click **File** on the menu bar, and then click **Save As**. The Save As dialog box opens with the current filename highlighted in the File name text box. You could type an entirely new filename, or you could edit the current one. In the next step, you will practice editing a filename.

2. Click to the left of "FAQ" in the File name text box, type **Tree**, and then press the **spacebar**. The filename changes to "Tree FAQ."

3. Verify that the Tutorial folder for Tutorial 2 is selected in the Save in box.

4. Click the **Save** button. The document is saved with the new filename.

Now you're ready to begin working with the document. First, you will check it for spelling and grammatical errors.

Using the Spelling and Grammar Checker

When typing a document, you can check for spelling and grammatical errors by looking for words underlined in red (for spelling errors) or green (for grammatical errors). But when you're working on a document that someone else typed, it's a good idea to start by using the Spelling and Grammar checker. This feature automatically checks a document word by word for a variety of errors. Among other things, the Spelling and Grammar checker can sometimes find words that, though spelled correctly, are not used properly. For example, it highlights the word "their" when it is mistakenly used instead of the word "there."

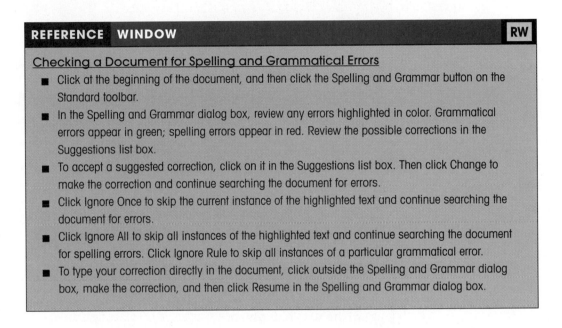

REFERENCE   WINDOW   **RW**

Checking a Document for Spelling and Grammatical Errors
- Click at the beginning of the document, and then click the Spelling and Grammar button on the Standard toolbar.
- In the Spelling and Grammar dialog box, review any errors highlighted in color. Grammatical errors appear in green; spelling errors appear in red. Review the possible corrections in the Suggestions list box.
- To accept a suggested correction, click on it in the Suggestions list box. Then click Change to make the correction and continue searching the document for errors.
- Click Ignore Once to skip the current instance of the highlighted text and continue searching the document for errors.
- Click Ignore All to skip all instances of the highlighted text and continue searching the document for spelling errors. Click Ignore Rule to skip all instances of a particular grammatical error.
- To type your correction directly in the document, click outside the Spelling and Grammar dialog box, make the correction, and then click Resume in the Spelling and Grammar dialog box.

You'll see how the Spelling and Grammar checker works as you check the FAQ document for mistakes.

To check the FAQ document for spelling and grammatical errors:

1. Verify that the insertion point is located at the beginning of the document, to the left of the "C" in "Common Questions."

2. Click the **Spelling and Grammar** button on the Standard toolbar. The Spelling and Grammar dialog box opens with the word "About" highlighted in green, indicating a possible grammatical error. The word "about" (with a lowercase "a") is suggested as a possible replacement. The line immediately under the title bar indicates the type of possible problem, in this case, Capitalization. See Figure 2-4. Normally, prepositions of fewer than six letters are not capitalized in titles. But Marilee prefers to keep this word capitalized because she thinks it makes the title look better.

TROUBLE? If you see the word "diggging" selected instead of "About", your computer is not set up to check grammar. Click the Check grammar check box to insert a check, and then click Cancel to close the Spelling and Grammar dialog box. Next, click at the beginning of the document, and then repeat Step 2.

Figure 2-4   SPELLING AND GRAMMAR DIALOG BOX

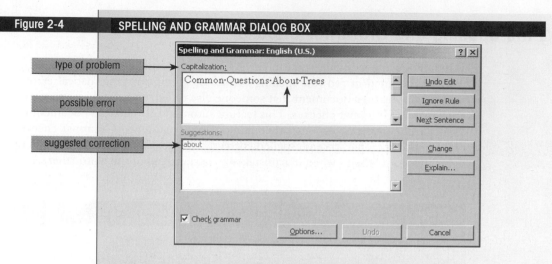

type of problem

possible error

suggested correction

3. Click the **Ignore Rule** button. The word "diggging" is highlighted in red, with "digging" and "diggings" listed as possible corrections.

4. Verify that "digging" is highlighted in the Suggestions list box, and then click the **Change** button. "Digging" is inserted into the document.

At this point the word "composts" is highlighted in green, with "and composts" listed as a possible correction. It's not clear why Word suggests this change, so you need to request an explanation.

To ask the Spelling and Grammar Checker for an explanation:

1. Click the **Explain** button. The Office Assistant opens, showing an explanation of the rule in question.

2. Read the explanation, and then click the **Ignore Rule** button. The last sentence of the document is highlighted in green. The Office Assistant indicates that the highlighted text is a sentence fragment. In this case, Word is correct. The word "call" lacks a direct object—that is, you need to indicate whom the reader should call. You'll fix this problem later, when you insert your name in this sentence.

3. Click **Ignore Once**. The Office Assistant closes, and you see a message indicating that the spelling and grammar check is complete.

4. Click the **OK** button. The Spelling and Grammar dialog box and the Office Assistant close. You return to the FAQ document.

Although the Spelling and Grammar checker is a useful tool, remember that there is no substitute for careful proofreading. Always take the time to read through your document to check for errors the Spelling and Grammar checker might have missed. Keep in mind that the Spelling and Grammar checker probably won't catch *all* instances of words that are spelled correctly but used improperly. And of course, the Spelling and Grammar checker cannot pinpoint phrases that are confusing or inaccurate. To produce a professional document, you must read it carefully several times, and, if necessary, ask a co-worker to read it, too.

To proofread the FAQ document:

1. Scroll to the beginning of the document and begin proofreading. When you get near the bottom of the document, notice that the word "Too" is used instead of the word "Two" in the paragraph on mulch. See Figure 2-5. You will correct this error later in this tutorial, after you learn how to move the insertion point in a document.

Figure 2-5	WORD "TOO" USED INCORRECTLY

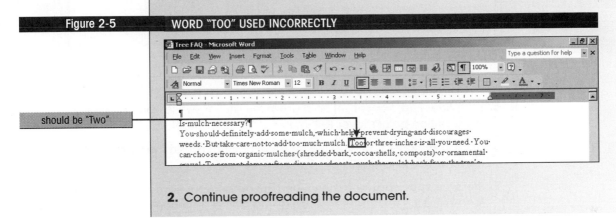

should be "Two"

2. Continue proofreading the document.

To make the proofreading corrections, and to make all of Marilee's changes, you need to learn how to move the insertion point quickly to any location in the document.

Moving the Insertion Point Around a Document

The arrow keys on your keyboard, ↑, ↓, ←, and →, allow you to move the insertion point one character at a time to the left or right, or one line at a time up or down. If you want to move more than one character or one line at a time, you can point and click in other parts of a line or the document. You also can press a combination of keys to move the insertion point. As you become more experienced with Word, you'll decide which method you prefer.

To see how quickly you can move through the document, you'll use keystrokes to move the insertion point to the beginning of the second page and to the end of the document.

To move the insertion point with keystrokes:

1. Press the **Ctrl** key and hold it down while you press the **Home** key. The insertion point moves to the beginning of the document.

2. Press the **Page Down** key to move the insertion point down to the next screen.

3. Press the **Page Down** key again to move the insertion point down to the next screen. Notice that the status bar indicates the location of the insertion point.

4. Press the ↑ or ↓ key to move the insertion point to just below the dotted line that spans the width of the page. The insertion point is now at the beginning of page 2, as shown in Figure 2-6. The dotted line is an **automatic page break** that Word inserts to mark the beginning of the new page. As you insert and delete text or change formatting in a document, the location of the automatic page breaks in your document continually adjust.

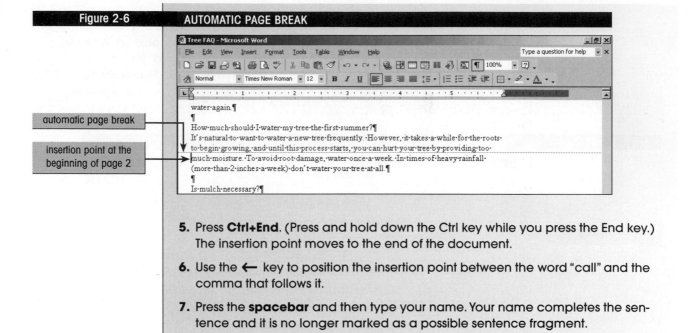

automatic page break

insertion point at the beginning of page 2

5. Press **Ctrl+End**. (Press and hold down the Ctrl key while you press the End key.) The insertion point moves to the end of the document.

6. Use the ← key to position the insertion point between the word "call" and the comma that follows it.

7. Press the **spacebar** and then type your name. Your name completes the sentence and it is no longer marked as a possible sentence fragment.

8. Move the insertion point back to the beginning of the document.

Figure 2-7 summarizes the keystrokes you can use to move the insertion point around the document. When you simply need to display a part of a document, you'll probably want to use the vertical scroll bar. But when you actually need to move the insertion point to a specific spot, it's helpful to use these special keystrokes.

Figure 2-7	KEYSTROKES FOR MOVING THE INSERTION POINT
PRESS	**TO MOVE INSERTION POINT**
← or →	Left or right one character at a time
↑ or ↓	Up or down one line at a time
Ctrl+← or Ctrl+→	Left or right one word at a time
Ctrl+↑ or Ctrl+↓	Up or down one paragraph at a time
Home or End	To the beginning or to the end of the current line
Ctrl+Home or Ctrl+End	To the beginning or to the end of the document
PageUp or PageDown	To the previous screen or to the next screen
Alt+Ctrl+PageUp or Alt+Ctrl+PageDown	To the top or to the bottom of the document window

Selecting **Parts of a Document**

Before you can do anything to text (such as deleting, moving, or formatting it), you often need to highlight, or **select** it. You can select text by using the mouse or the keyboard, although the mouse is usually easier and more efficient. With the mouse you can quickly select a line or paragraph by clicking the **selection bar** (the blank space in the left margin area of the Document window). You can also select text using various combinations of keys.

Figure 2-8 summarizes methods for selecting text with the mouse and the keyboard. The notation "Ctrl+Shift" means you press and hold the two keys at the same time. Note that you will use the methods described in Figure 2-8 as you work on the FAQ document.

Figure 2-8	METHODS FOR SELECTING TEXT		
TO SELECT	**MOUSE**	**KEYBOARD**	**MOUSE AND KEYBOARD**
A word	Double-click the word.	Move the insertion point to the beginning of the word, hold down Ctrl+Shift, and then press →.	
A line	Click in the selection bar next to the line.	Move the insertion point to the beginning of the line, hold down Ctrl+Shift, and then press → until the line is selected.	
A sentence			Press and hold down the Ctrl key, and click within the sentence.
Multiple lines	Click and drag in the selection bar next to the lines.	Move the insertion point to the beginning of the first line, hold down Ctrl+Shift, and then press → until all the lines are selected.	
A paragraph	Double-click in the selection bar next to the paragraph, or triple-click within the paragraph.	Move the insertion point to the beginning of the paragraph, hold down Ctrl+Shift, and then press ↓.	
Multiple paragraphs	Click and drag in the selection bar next to the paragraphs, or triple-click within the first paragraph and drag.	Move the insertion point to the beginning of the first paragraph, hold down Ctrl+Shift, and then press ↓ until all the paragraphs are selected.	
Entire document	Triple-click in the selection bar.	Press Ctrl+A.	Press and hold down the Ctrl key and click in the selection bar.
A block of text	Click at the beginning of the block, then drag the pointer until the entire block is selected.		Click at the beginning of the block, press and hold down the Shift key, and then click at the end of the block.
Multiple blocks of text	Press and hold the Ctrl key, then drag the mouse pointer to select multiple blocks of nonadjacent text.		

Deleting Text

When editing a document, you frequently need to delete text. You already have experience using the Backspace and Delete keys to delete a few characters. When you need to delete an entire word or multiple words, it's faster to select the text. After you select the text, you can either replace it with something else by typing over it, or by pressing the Delete key. You need to delete the word "Too" and replace it with "Two," so you'll use the first method now.

To replace "Too" with "Two":

1. Press **Ctrl+End**. The insertion point moves to the end of the document.

2. Press and hold the **Ctrl** key while you press ↑ three times. The insertion point is now positioned at the beginning of the paragraph that begins "You should definitely add some mulch." (The status bar indicates that this is line 5 of page 2.)

3. In the second line of the paragraph, double-click the word **Too**. The entire word is highlighted.

4. Type **Two**. The selected word is replaced with the correction. The sentence now correctly reads: "Two or three inches are all you need."

Next, Marilee wants you to delete the phrase "or problems" and the word "any" in the paragraph before the one you've just corrected. Peter explains that you can do this quickly by selecting multiple items and then pressing Delete. As you'll see in the following steps, selecting parts of a document by clicking and dragging takes a little practice, so don't be concerned if you don't get it right the first time. You can always try again.

To select and delete multiple items:

1. Press ↑ five times. As shown in Figure 2-9, the insertion point is now located in the sentence that begins "To avoid any root damage or problems." The status bar indicates that this is line 1 of page 2.

Figure 2-9	TEXT TO BE DELETED

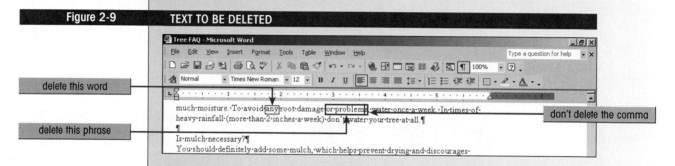

delete this word

delete this phrase

don't delete the comma

2. Double-click the word **any**. The word and the space following it are selected.

3. Press and hold the **Ctrl** key, and then click and drag to select the phrase "or problems." Do not select the comma after the word "problems". At this point the word "any" and the phrase "or problems" should be selected.

   TROUBLE? If you don't get Step 3 right the first time (for instance, if you accidentally selected the word "damage"), click anywhere in the document and then repeat Steps 2 and 3.

4. Press the **Delete** key. The selected items disappear and the words around them move in to fill the space. As you can see in Figure 2-10, you need to delete the extra space before the comma.

   TROUBLE? If you deleted the wrong text, click the Undo button (not the Redo button) on the Standard toolbar to reverse your mistake.

Figure 2-10	PARAGRAPH AFTER DELETING PHRASE

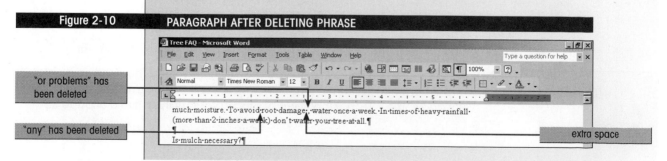

"or problems" has been deleted

"any" has been deleted

extra space

> **TROUBLE?** If your screen looks slightly different than Figure 2-10, don't be concerned. The text may wrap differently on your monitor. Just make sure the text has been deleted.
>
> 5. Click to the right of the word "damage", and then press the **Delete** key. The extra space is removed.

After rereading the paragraph, Peter wonders if perhaps the text shouldn't have been deleted after all. You can retype the text, but there's an easier way to restore the phrase.

Using the Undo and Redo Commands

To undo (or reverse) the very last thing you did, click the **Undo button** on the Standard toolbar. If you want to restore your original change, the **Redo button** reverses the action of the Undo button (or redoes the undo). To undo more than your last action, you can click the Undo list arrow on the Standard toolbar. This list shows your most recent actions. Undo reverses the action only at its original location. You can't delete a word or phrase, move the surrounding text, and then undo the deletion at a different location.

You decide to undo the deletion to see how the sentence reads. Rather than retype the phrase, you will reverse the edit using the Undo button.

To undo the deletion:

1. Place the mouse pointer over the Undo button 🔄 on the Standard toolbar. The label "Undo Clear" appears in a ScreenTip, indicating that your most recent action involved deleting (or clearing) something from the document (in this case, a space).

2. Click the **Undo** button 🔄. The space after the word "damage" reappears.

   TROUBLE? If the space doesn't reappear and something else changes in your document, you probably made another edit or change to the document between the deletion and the undo. Click the Undo button on the Standard toolbar until the space reappears in your document. If a list of possible changes appears under the Undo button, you clicked the list arrow next to the Undo button rather than the Undo button itself. Click the Undo button to restore the deleted phrase and close the list box.

3. Click 🔄 again. The deleted text reappears highlighted within the sentence.

4. Click in the paragraph to deselect the phrase.

   As you read the sentence, you decide that it reads better without the word "any" and the phrase "or problems". Instead of deleting these items again, you'll redo the undo. As you place the pointer over the Redo button, notice that its ScreenTip indicates the action you want to redo.

5. Place the mouse pointer over the Redo button 🔄 on the Standard toolbar and observe the "Redo Clear" label.

6. Click the **Redo** button 🔄. The text disappears from the document again.

7. Click 🔄 again. The extra space after "damage" disappears again.

8. Click the **Save** button 💾 on the Standard toolbar to save your changes to the document.

You have edited the document by replacing "Too" with "Two", and by removing the text that Marilee marked for deletion. Now you are ready to make the rest of the edits she suggested.

Moving Text Within a Document

One of the most useful features of a word-processing program is the ability to move text. For example, Marilee wants to reorder the four points Peter made in the section "Do I have to do anything to the tree before planting?" on page 1 of his draft. You could reorder the list by deleting the item and then retyping it at a new location, but it's easier to select and then move the text. Word provides several ways to move text: drag and drop, cut and paste, and copy and paste.

Dragging and Dropping Text

One way to move text within a document is called drag and drop. With **drag and drop**, you select the text you want to move, press and hold down the mouse button while you drag the selected text to a new location, and then release the mouse button.

REFERENCE WINDOW   **RW**

Dragging and Dropping Text
- Select the text you want to move.
- Press and hold down the mouse button until the drag-and-drop pointer appears, and then drag the selected text to its new location.
- Use the dotted insertion point as a guide to determine exactly where the text will be inserted.
- Release the mouse button to drop the text at the insertion point.

Marilee wants you to change the order of the items in the list on page 1 of the document. You'll use the drag-and-drop method to reorder these items. At the same time, you'll practice using the selection bar to highlight a line of text.

To move text using drag and drop:

1. Scroll up until you see "Do I have to do anything to the tree before planting?" (line 29 of page 1). In the list of steps involved in planting a tree, Marilee wants you to move the third step ("Remove any tags from the trunk and branches.") to the top of the list.

2. Move the pointer to the selection bar to the left of the line "Remove any tags from the trunk and branches." The pointer changes from an I-beam I to a right-facing arrow ⤸.

3. Click to the left of the line "Remove any tags from the trunk and branches." The line is selected. Notice that the paragraph mark at the end of the line is also selected. See Figure 2-11.

Figure 2-11   **SELECTED TEXT TO DRAG AND DROP**

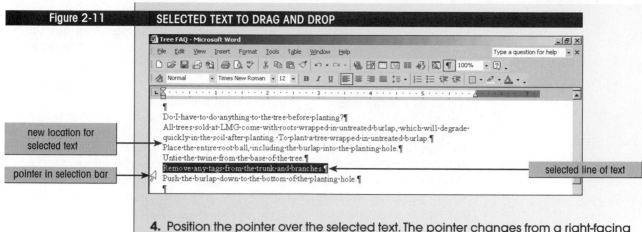

new location for
selected text

pointer in selection bar

selected line of text

4. Position the pointer over the selected text. The pointer changes from a right-facing arrow to a left-facing arrow.

5. Press and hold down the mouse button until the drag-and-drop pointer appears. Note that a dotted insertion point appears within the selected text.

6. Drag the selected text up three lines until the dotted insertion point appears to the left of the word "Place". Make sure you use the dotted insertion point, rather than the mouse pointer, to guide the text to its new location. The dotted insertion point indicates exactly where the text will appear when you release the mouse button. See Figure 2-12.

Figure 2-12   **MOVING TEXT WITH THE DRAG-AND-DROP POINTER**

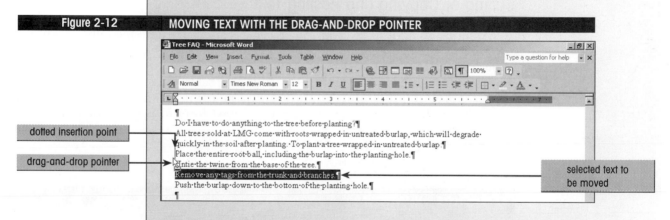

dotted insertion point

drag-and-drop pointer

selected text to
be moved

7. Release the mouse button. The selected text moves to its new location as the first step in the list. A Paste Options button appears near the newly moved text, as shown in Figure 2-13.

Figure 2-13   **PASTE OPTIONS BUTTON**

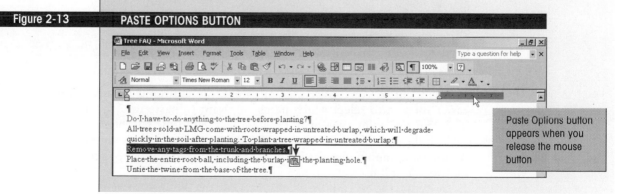

Paste Options button
appears when you
release the mouse
button

TROUBLE? If the selected text moves to the wrong location, click the Undo button on the Standard toolbar, and then repeat Steps 2 through 7. Be sure you hold the mouse button until the dotted insertion point appears to the left of the word "Place".

TROUBLE? If you don't see the Paste Options button, your computer is not set up to display it. Read Step 7, and then continue with Step 8.

8. Click the **Paste Options** 🗐 button. A menu of text-moving commands appears. These commands are useful when you are inserting text that looks different from the surrounding text. For instance, suppose you selected text formatted in Times New Roman and then dragged it to a paragraph formatted in Arial. You could then use the Match Destination Formatting command to format the moved text in Arial.

9. Deselect the highlighted text by clicking anywhere in the document. The Paste Options menu closes, but the button remains visible. It will disappear as soon as you perform another task.

Dragging and dropping works well if you're moving text a short distance in a document. However, Word provides another method, called cut and paste, that works well for moving text both long and short distances.

Cutting or Copying and Pasting Text

To **cut** means to remove text from the document and place it on the **Office Clipboard**, a feature that temporarily stores text or graphics until you need them later. To **paste** means to transfer a copy of the text from the Clipboard into the document at the insertion point. To perform a **cut-and-paste** action, you select the text you want to move, cut (or remove) it from the document, and then paste (or insert) it into the document in a new location. If you don't want to remove the text from its original location, you can copy it (rather than cutting it) and then paste the copy in a new location. This procedure is known as **copy and paste**.

REFERENCE WINDOW | **RW**

Cutting or Copying and Pasting Text
- Select the text you want to cut or copy.
- To remove the text, click the Cut button on the Standard toolbar.
- To make a copy of the text, click the Copy button.
- Move the insertion point to the target location in the document.
- Click the Paste button on the Standard toolbar.

If you cut or copy more than one item, the **Clipboard Task Pane** opens, making it easier for you to select which items you want to paste into the document. This special Task Pane contains a list of all the items copied to the Clipboard.

As indicated earlier in Figure 2-1, Marilee suggested moving the word "thoroughly" (in the paragraph under the heading "Should I water my new tree right away?") to a new location. You'll use cut and paste to move this word.

To move text using cut and paste:

1. If necessary, scroll down until you can see the paragraph below the heading "Should I water my new tree right away?" near the bottom of page 1.

2. Double-click the word **thoroughly**. As you can see in Figure 2-14, you need to move this word to the end of the sentence.

Figure 2-14	TEXT TO MOVE USING CUT AND PASTE

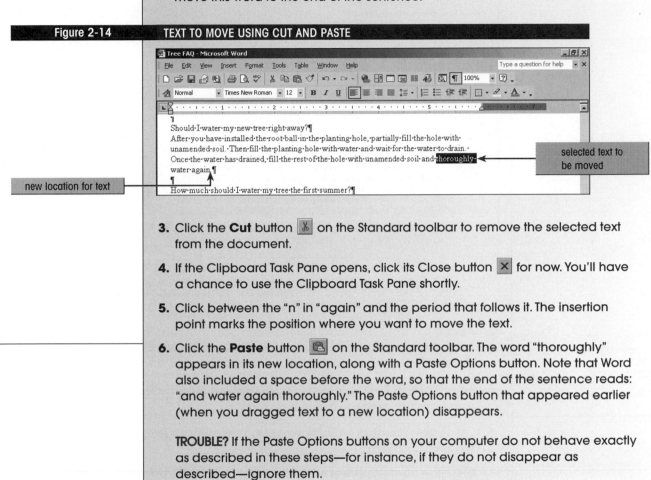

new location for text

selected text to be moved

3. Click the **Cut** button on the Standard toolbar to remove the selected text from the document.

4. If the Clipboard Task Pane opens, click its Close button for now. You'll have a chance to use the Clipboard Task Pane shortly.

5. Click between the "n" in "again" and the period that follows it. The insertion point marks the position where you want to move the text.

6. Click the **Paste** button on the Standard toolbar. The word "thoroughly" appears in its new location, along with a Paste Options button. Note that Word also included a space before the word, so that the end of the sentence reads: "and water again thoroughly." The Paste Options button that appeared earlier (when you dragged text to a new location) disappears.

   TROUBLE? If the Paste Options buttons on your computer do not behave exactly as described in these steps—for instance, if they do not disappear as described—ignore them.

Peter stops by your desk and mentions that he'll be using the paragraph on mulch and the paragraph on watering for the FAQ he plans to write on flowering shrubs. He asks you to copy that information and paste it in a new document that he can use as the basis for the new FAQ. You can do this using copy and paste. This technique is similar to cut and paste. In the process you'll have a chance to use the Clipboard Task Pane.

To copy and paste text:

1. Click **Edit** on the menu bar, and then click **Office Clipboard**. The Office Clipboard Task Pane opens on the right side of the Document window. It contains the message "Clipboard empty. Copy or cut to collect items." See Figure 2-15.

Figure 2-15   CLIPBOARD TASK PANE

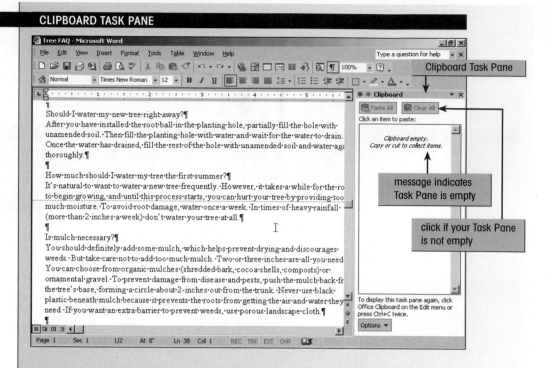

TROUBLE? If your Clipboard Task Pane does not show this message, click the Clear All button.

2. Move the mouse pointer to the selection bar and double-click next to the paragraph you edited in the last section (the paragraph that begins "After you have installed the root ball"). The entire paragraph is selected.

3. Click the **Copy** button on the Standard toolbar. The first part of the paragraph appears in the Task Pane.

4. If necessary, scroll down until you can see the paragraph below the heading "Is mulch necessary?"

5. Select the paragraph below the heading (the paragraph that begins "You should definitely add . . . ").

6. Click . The first part of the paragraph appears in the Task Pane, as shown in Figure 2-16. An icon appears in the Windows taskbar indicating that the Clipboard Task Pane is currently active.

Figure 2-16	ITEMS IN THE CLIPBOARD TASK PANE

7. Click the **New Blank Document** button ⬜ on the Standard toolbar. A new, blank document opens. The icon in the Windows taskbar indicates that although the Clipboard is no longer visible, it is still active.

8. Double-click the **Clipboard** button in the taskbar. The Clipboard Task Pane is now visible.

Now you can use the Clipboard Task Pane to insert the copied text into the new document.

To insert the copied text into the new document:

1. In the Clipboard Task Pane, click the item that begins "You should definitely add . . . " The text is inserted in the document.

2. Press **Enter** to insert a blank line, and then click the item that begins "After you have installed the root ball . . . " in the Task Pane. The text is inserted in the document.

3. Save the document as **Flowering Shrub FAQ** in the Tutorial folder for Tutorial 2, and then close the document. You return to the Tree FAQ document, where the Clipboard Task Pane is still open. You are finished using the Clipboard Task Pane, so you will delete its contents.

4. Click the **Clear All** button on the Clipboard Task Pane. The copied items are removed from the Clipboard Task Pane.

5. Click the **Close** button ✕ on the Clipboard Task Pane. The Clipboard Task Pane disappears.

6. Click anywhere in the document to deselect the highlighted paragraph.

7. Save the document.

Finding and Replacing Text

When you're working with a longer document, the quickest and easiest way to locate a particular word or phrase is to use the **Find command**. If you want to replace characters or a phrase with something else, you can use the **Replace command**, which combines the Find command with a substitution feature. The Replace command searches through a document and substitutes the text you're searching for with the replacement text you specify. As you perform the search, Word stops and highlights each occurrence of the search text. You must determine whether or not to substitute the replacement text, and do so by clicking the Replace button.

If you want to substitute every occurrence of the search text with the replacement text, you can click the Replace All button. When using the Replace All button with single words, keep in mind that the search text might be found within other words. To prevent Word from making incorrect substitutions in such cases, it's a good idea to select the Find whole words only check box along with the Replace All button. For example, suppose you want to replace the word "figure" with "illustration". Unless you select the Find whole words only check box, Word would replace "configure" with "conillustration."

As you search through a document, you can search from the current location of the insertion point down to the end of the document, from the insertion point up to the beginning of the document, or throughout the document.

REFERENCE WINDOW **RW**

Finding and Replacing Text

- Click Edit on the menu bar, and then click either Find or Replace.
- To find text, click the Find tab. To find and replace text, click the Replace tab.
- Click the More button to expand the dialog box to display additional options (including the Find whole words only option). If you see the Less button, the additional options are already displayed.
- In the Search list box, select Down if you want to search from the insertion point to the end of the document, select Up if you want to search from the insertion point to the beginning of the document, or select All to search the entire document.
- Type the characters you want to find in the Find what text box.
- If you are replacing text, type the replacement text in the Replace with text box.
- Click the Find whole words only check box to search for complete words.
- Click the Match case check box to insert the replacement text just as you specified in the Replace with text box.
- Click the Find Next button.
- Click the Replace button to substitute the found text with the replacement text and find the next occurrence.
- Click the Replace All button to substitute all occurrences of the found text with the replacement text.

Marilee wants the company initials, LMG, to be spelled out as "Long Meadow Gardens" each time they appear in the text.

To replace "LMG" with "Long Meadow Gardens":

1. Press **Ctrl+Home** to move the insertion point to the beginning of the document.

2. Click **Edit** on the menu bar, and then click **Replace**. The Find and Replace dialog box opens.

3. If you see a **More** button, click it to display the additional search options. (If you see a Less button, the additional options are already displayed.) Also, if necessary, click the **Search** list arrow, and then click **All**.

4. Click the **Find what** text box, type **LMG**, press the **Tab** key, and then type **Long Meadow Gardens** in the Replace with text box.

   TROUBLE? If you already see the text "LMG" and "Long Meadow Gardens" in your Find and Replace dialog box, someone has already performed these steps on your computer. Continue with Step 7.

5. Click the **Find whole words only** check box to insert a check.

6. Click the **Match case** check box to insert a check. This ensures that Word will insert the replacement text using initial capital letters, as you specified in the Replace with text box. Your Find and Replace dialog box should now look like Figure 2-17.

Figure 2-17	FIND AND REPLACE DIALOG BOX

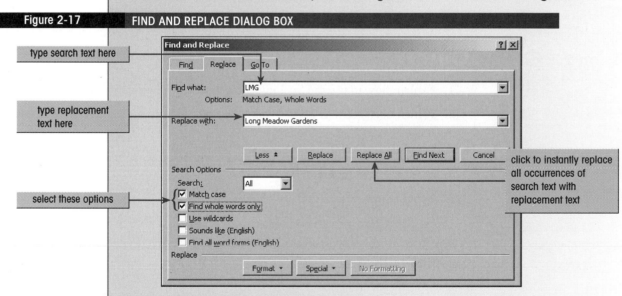

type search text here

type replacement text here

select these options

click to instantly replace all occurrences of search text with replacement text

7. Click the **Replace All** button to replace all occurrences of the search text with the replacement text. When Word finishes making the replacements, you see a dialog box telling you that two replacements were made.

8. Click the **OK** button to close the dialog box, and then click the **Close** button in the Find and Replace dialog box to return to the document. The full company name has been inserted into the document, as shown in Figure 2-18. (You may have to scroll down to see this section.)

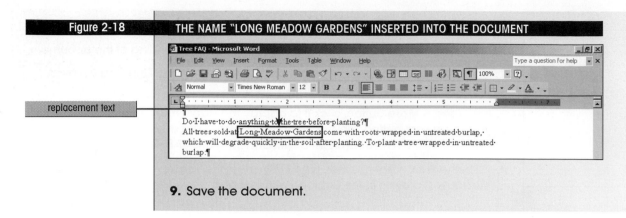

Figure 2-18 THE NAME "LONG MEADOW GARDENS" INSERTED INTO THE DOCUMENT

9. Save the document.

Note that you can also search for and replace formatting, such as bold, and special characters in the Find and Replace dialog box. Click in the Find what text box or the Replace with text box, enter any text if necessary, click the Format button, click Font to open the Font dialog box, and then select the formatting you want to find or replace. Complete the search or replace as usual.

You have completed the content changes Marilee requested. In the next session, you will make some changes that will affect the document's appearance.

Session 2.1 QUICK CHECK

1. Explain how to use the Spelling and Grammar Checker.

2. Which key(s) do you press to move the insertion point to the following places:
   a. **down one line**
   b. to the end of the document
   c. to the next screen

3. Explain how to select the following items using the mouse:
   a. one word
   b. a block of text
   c. one paragraph

4. Define the following terms in your own words:
   a. selection bar
   b. Redo button
   c. drag and drop

5. Describe a situation in which you would use the Undo button and then the Redo button.

6. True or False: You can use the Redo command to restore deleted text at a new location in your document.

7. What is the difference between cut and paste, and copy and paste?

8. List the steps involved in finding and replacing text in a document.

SESSION 2.2

In this session you will make the formatting changes Marilee suggested. You'll use a variety of formatting commands to change the margins, line spacing, text alignment, and paragraph indents. You'll also learn how to use the Format Painter, how to create bulleted and numbered lists, and how to change fonts, font sizes, and emphasis. Finally, you will add a comment to the document.

Changing the Margins

In general, it's best to begin formatting by making the changes that affect the document's overall appearance. Then you can make changes that affect only selected text. In this case, you need to adjust the document's margin settings.

Word uses default margins of 1.25 inches for the left and right margins and 1 inch for the top and bottom margins. The numbers on the ruler (displayed below the Formatting toolbar) indicate the distance in inches from the left margin, not from the left edge of the paper. Unless you specify otherwise, changes you make to the margins affect the entire document, not just the current paragraph or page.

REFERENCE   WINDOW   **RW**

__Changing Margins for the Entire Document__
- With the insertion point anywhere in your document and no text selected, click File on the menu bar, and then click Page Setup.
- If necessary, click the Margins tab to display the margin settings.
- Use the arrows to change the settings in the Top, Bottom, Left, or Right text boxes, or type a new margin value in each text box.
- Make sure the Apply to list box displays Whole document.
- Click the OK button.

You need to change the top margin to 1.5 inches and the left margin to 1.75 inches, per Marilee's request. The left margin needs to be wider than usual to allow space for making holes so that the document can be inserted in a three-ring binder. In the next set of steps, you'll change the margins with the Page Setup command. You also can change margins in Print Layout view by dragging an icon on the horizontal ruler. You'll have a chance to practice this technique in the Review Assignments at the end of this tutorial.

To change the margins in the Tree FAQ document:

1. If you took a break after the previous session, make sure Word is running, the Tree FAQ document is open, and nonprinting characters are displayed.

2. Press **Ctrl+Home** to move the insertion point to the top of the document. This should also ensure that no text is selected in the document.

3. Click **File** on the menu bar, and then click **Page Setup** to open the Page Setup dialog box.

4. If necessary, click the **Margins** tab to display the margin settings. The Top margin setting is selected. See Figure 2-19. As you complete the following steps, keep an eye on the document preview, which will change to reflect any changes you make to the margins.

Figure 2-19 PAGE SETUP DIALOG BOX

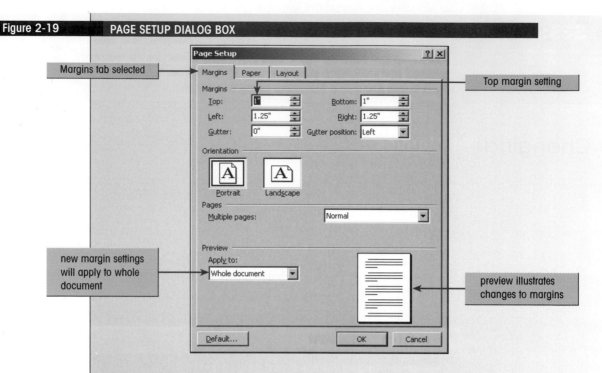

Margins tab selected

Top margin setting

new margin settings will apply to whole document

preview illustrates changes to margins

5. Type **1.5** to change the Top margin setting. (You do not have to type the inches symbol.)

6. Press the **Tab** key twice to select the Left text box and highlight the current margin setting. Notice how the text area in the Preview box moves down to reflect the larger top margin.

7. Type **1.75** and then press the **Tab** key. Watch the Preview box to see how the margin increases.

8. Make sure the **Whole document** option is selected in the Apply to list box, and then click the **OK** button to return to your document. Notice that the right margin on the ruler has changed to reflect the larger margins and the resulting reduced page area. The document text is now 5.5 inches wide. See Figure 2-20.

Figure 2-20 RULER AFTER SETTING LEFT MARGIN TO 1.75 INCHES

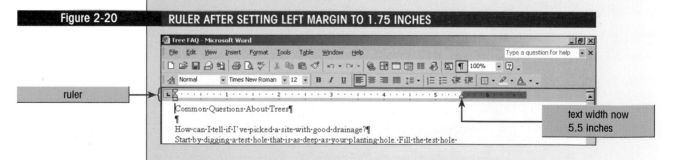

ruler

text width now 5.5 inches

TROUBLE? If a double dotted line and the words "Section Break" appear in your document, Whole document wasn't specified in the Apply to list box. If this occurs, click the Undo button on the Standard toolbar and then repeat Steps 1 through 8, making sure you select the Whole document option in the Apply to list box.

Next, you will change the amount of space between lines of text.

Changing Line Spacing

The line spacing in a document determines the amount of vertical space between lines of text. In most situations, you will want to choose from three basic types of line spacing: **single spacing** (which allows for the largest character in a particular line as well as a small amount of extra space); **1.5 line spacing** (which allows for one and one-half times the space of single spacing); and **double spacing** (which allows for twice the space of single spacing). The FAQ document is currently single-spaced because Word uses single spacing by default. Before changing the line-spacing setting, you should select the text you want to change. The easiest way to change line spacing is to use the Line Spacing button on the Formatting toolbar. You can also use the keyboard to apply single, double, and 1.5 line spacing.

REFERENCE   WINDOW   **RW**

Changing Line Spacing in a Document
- Select the text you want to change.
- Click the list arrow next to the Line Spacing button on the Formatting toolbar, and then click the line spacing you want.
- Now that you have selected a line spacing, apply it by selecting a block of text, and then clicking the Line Spacing button.

or

- Select the text you want to change.
- Press Ctrl+1 for single spacing, Ctrl+5 for 1.5 line spacing, or Ctrl+2 for double spacing.

Marilee has asked you to change the line spacing for the entire FAQ document to 1.5 line spacing. You will begin by selecting the entire document.

To change the document's line spacing:

1. Triple-click in the selection bar to select the entire document.

2. Move the mouse pointer over the Line Spacing button 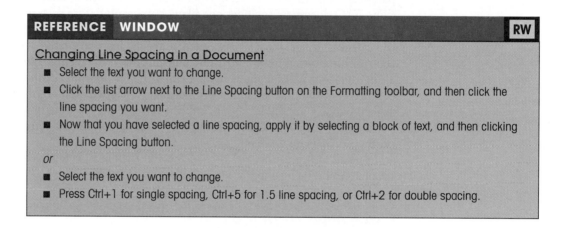 to display its ScreenTip. You see the text "Line Spacing (1)", indicating that single spacing is currently selected.

3. Click the **Line Spacing** list arrow. A list of line spacing options appears, as shown in Figure 2-21. To double-space the document, you click 2, while to triple-space it, you click 3. In this case, you need to apply 1.5 line spacing.

Figure 2-21   **LINE SPACING LIST BOX**

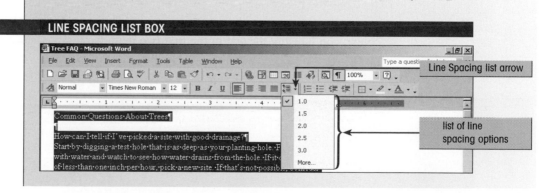

4. Click **1.5**. Notice the additional space between every line of text in the document.

5. Move the mouse pointer over 📋 to display its ScreenTip. You see the text "Line Spacing (1.5)", indicating that 1.5 spacing is currently selected.

Now you are ready to make formatting changes that affect individual paragraphs.

Aligning Text

As you begin formatting individual paragraphs in the FAQ document, keep in mind that in Word, a **paragraph** is defined as any text that ends with a paragraph mark symbol (¶). A paragraph can also be blank, in which case you see a paragraph mark alone on a single line. (The FAQ document includes one blank paragraph before each question heading.)

The term **alignment** refers to how the text of a paragraph lines up horizontally between the margins. By default, text is aligned along the left margin but is **ragged**, or uneven, along the right margin. This is called **left alignment**. With **right alignment**, the text is aligned along the right margin and is ragged along the left margin. With **center alignment**, text is centered between the left and right margins. With **justified alignment**, full lines of text are spaced between or aligned along both the left and the right margins. The paragraph you are reading now is justified. The easiest way to apply alignment settings is by clicking buttons on the Formatting toolbar.

Marilee indicates that the title of the FAQ should be centered and that the main paragraphs should be justified. First, you'll center the title.

To center-align the title:

1. Click anywhere in the title "Common Questions About Trees" at the beginning of the document.

2. Click the **Center** button 📄 on the Formatting toolbar. The text centers between the left and right margins. See Figure 2-22.

Figure 2-22	CENTERED TITLE

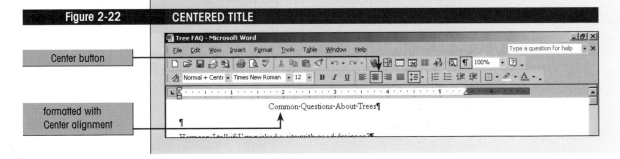

Center button

formatted with Center alignment

Next, you'll justify the text in the first two main paragraphs.

To justify the first two paragraphs using the Formatting toolbar:

1. Click anywhere in the first main paragraph, which begins "Start by digging a test hole . . . "

2. Click the **Justify** button ▤ on the Formatting toolbar. The paragraph text spreads out, so that it lines up evenly along the left and right margins.

3. Move the insertion point to anywhere in the second main paragraph, which begins "While you might be tempted . . . "

4. Click ▤ again. The text is evenly spaced between the left and right margins. See Figure 2-23.

Figure 2-23	JUSTIFIED PARAGRAPHS

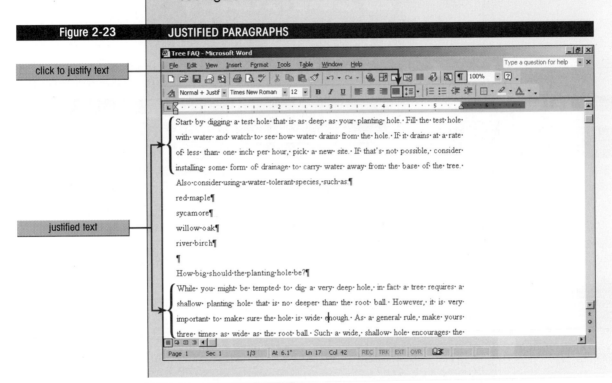

click to justify text

justified text

You'll justify the other paragraphs later. Now that you've learned how to change the paragraph alignment, you can turn your attention to indenting a paragraph.

Indenting a Paragraph

When you become a more experienced Word user, you might want to do some paragraph formatting, such as a **hanging indent** (where all lines except the first line of the paragraph are indented from the left margin) or a **right indent** (where all lines of the paragraph are indented from the right margin). You can select these types of indents on the Indents and Spacing tab of the Paragraph dialog box. (To open this dialog box, you click Format on the menu bar and then click Paragraph.)

In this document, though, you need to indent only the main paragraphs 0.5 inches from the left margin. This left indent is a simple paragraph indent, which requires only a quick click on the Formatting toolbar's Increase Indent button. According to Marilee's notes, you need to indent all of the main paragraphs.

To indent a paragraph using the Increase Indent button:

1. Click anywhere in the first main paragraph, which begins "Start by digging a test hole . . . "

2. Click the **Increase Indent** button ⊞ on the Formatting toolbar twice. (Don't click the Decrease Indent button by mistake.) The entire paragraph moves right 0.5 inches each time you click the Increase Indent button. The paragraph is indented 1 inch, 0.5 inches more than Marilee wants.

3. Click the **Decrease Indent** button ⊞ on the Formatting toolbar to move the paragraph left 0.5 inches. The paragraph is now indented 0.5 inches from the left margin. Don't be concerned about the list of tree species. You will indent it later, when you format it as a bulleted list.

4. Move the insertion point to anywhere in the second main paragraph, which begins "While you might be tempted . . . "

5. Click ⊞. The paragraph is indented 0.5 inches. See Figure 2-24.

Figure 2-24   INDENTED PARAGRAPH

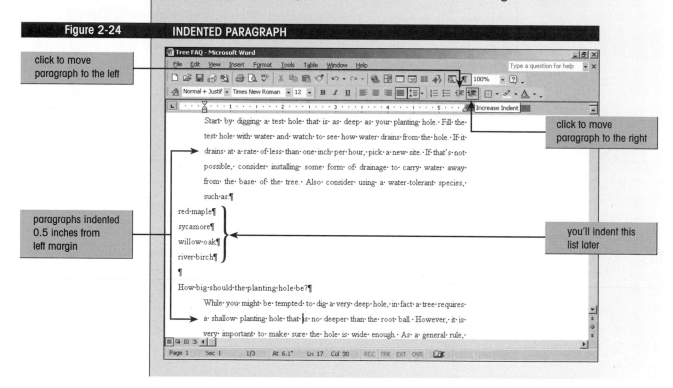

click to move paragraph to the left

click to move paragraph to the right

paragraphs indented 0.5 inches from left margin

you'll indent this list later

You can continue to indent and then justify each paragraph, or simply use the Format Painter command. The Format Painter allows you to copy both the indentation and alignment changes to all paragraphs in the document.

Using Format Painter

The **Format Painter** makes it easy to copy all the formatting features of one paragraph to other paragraphs. You can use this button to copy formatting to one or multiple items.

REFERENCE WINDOW   **RW**

Using the Format Painter Button

- Select the item whose formatting you want to copy.
- To copy formatting to one item, click the Format Painter button and then drag the mouse pointer to select the item you want to format.
- To copy formatting to multiple items, double-click the Format Painter button and then drag the mouse pointer to each item you want to format. When you are finished, click the Format Painter button again to deselect it.

Use the Format Painter now to copy the formatting of the second paragraph to other main paragraphs. Begin by moving the insertion point to the paragraph whose format you want to copy.

To copy paragraph formatting with the Format Painter:

1. Verify that the insertion point is located in the second main paragraph, which begins "While you might be tempted . . . "

2. Double-click the **Format Painter** button on the Standard toolbar. The Format Painter button will stay highlighted until you click the button again. When you move the pointer over text, the pointer changes to to indicate that the format of the selected paragraph can be painted (or copied) onto another paragraph.

3. Scroll down, and then click anywhere in the third main paragraph, which begins "You may be accustomed . . . " The format of the third paragraph shifts to match the format of the first two main paragraphs. See Figure 2-25. Both paragraphs are now indented and justified. The Format Painter pointer is still visible.

Figure 2-25   **FORMATS COPIED WITH FORMAT PAINTER**

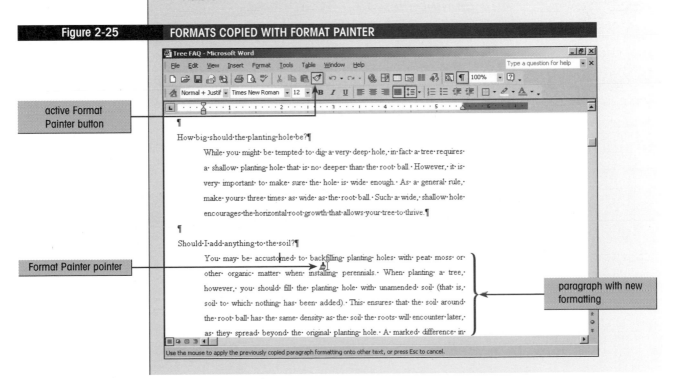

4. Click the remaining paragraphs that are preceded by a question heading. Take care to click only the paragraphs below the question headings. Do not click the document title, the one-line questions, the lists, or the last paragraph in the document.

TROUBLE? If you click a paragraph and the formatting doesn't change to match the second paragraph, you single-clicked the Format Painter button rather than double-clicked it. Select a paragraph that has the desired format, double-click the Format Painter button, and then repeat Step 4.

TROUBLE? If you accidentally click a title or one line of a list, click the Undo button on the Standard toolbar to return the line to its original formatting. Then select a paragraph that has the desired format, double-click the Format Painter button, and finish copying the format to the desired paragraphs.

5. After you are finished formatting paragraphs with the Format Painter pointer, click to turn off the feature.

6. Save the document.

All the main paragraphs in the document are formatted with the correct indentation and alignment. Your next job is to make the lists easier to read by adding bullets and numbers.

Adding Bullets and Numbers

You can emphasize a list of items by adding a heavy dot, or **bullet**, before each item in the list. For consecutive items, you can use numbers instead of bullets. Marilee requests that you add bullets to the list of tree species on page 1 to make them stand out.

To apply bullets to a list of items:

1. Scroll to the top of the document until you see the list of tree species below the text "Also consider using a water-tolerant species such as:".

2. Select the four items in the list (from "red maple" to "river birch").

3. Click the **Bullets** button on the Formatting toolbar. A bullet, a dark circle, appears in front of each item. Each line indents to make room for the bullet.

4. In order to make the bullets align with the first paragraph, make sure the list is still selected, and then click the **Increase Indent** button on the Formatting toolbar. The bulleted list moves to the right.

5. Click anywhere within the document window to deselect the text. Figure 2-26 shows the indented bulleted list.

Figure 2-26	INDENTED BULLETED LIST

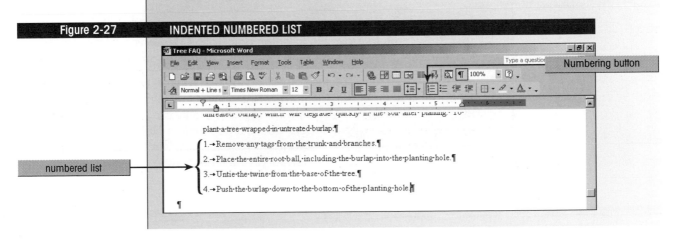

bulleted list

Next, you need to format the list of steps involved in planting a tree. Marilee asks you to format this information as a numbered list, an easy task thanks to the Numbering button, which automatically numbers selected paragraphs with consecutive numbers. If you insert a new paragraph, delete a paragraph, or reorder the paragraphs, Word automatically adjusts the numbers to make sure they remain consecutive.

To apply numbers to the list of items:

1. Scroll down until you see the list that begins "Remove any tags . . . " and ends with "of the planting hole."

2. Select the entire list.

3. Click the **Numbering** button ▦ on the Formatting toolbar. Consecutive numbers appear in front of each item in the indented list. The list is indented, similar to the bulleted list. The list would look better if it was indented to align with the paragraph.

4. Click the **Increase Indent** button ▦ on the Formatting toolbar. The list moves to the right, so that the numbers align with the preceding paragraph.

5. Click anywhere in the document to deselect the text. Figure 2-27 shows the indented and numbered list.

Figure 2-27	INDENTED NUMBERED LIST

numbered list

The text of the document is now properly aligned and indented. The bullets and numbers make the lists easy to read and give readers visual clues about the type of information they contain. Next, you need to adjust the formatting of individual words.

Changing the Font and Font Size

All of Marilee's remaining changes concern changing fonts, adjusting font sizes, and emphasizing text with font styles. The first step is to change the font of the title from 12-point Times New Roman to 14-point Arial. This will make the title stand out from the rest of the text.

REFERENCE WINDOW **RW**

Changing the Font and Font Size
- Select the text you want to change.
- Click the Font list arrow on the Formatting toolbar to display the list of fonts.
- Click the font you want to use.
- Click the Font Size list arrow, and click the font size you want to use.

or
- Select the text that you want to change.
- Click Format on the menu bar, and then click Font.
- In the Font tab of the Font dialog box, select the font and font size you want to use.
- Click the OK button.

Marilee wants you to change the font of the title as well as its size and style. To do this, you'll use the Formatting toolbar. Marilee wants you to use a **sans serif** font, which is a font that does not have the small horizontal lines (called serifs) at the tops and bottoms of the letters. Sans serif fonts are often used in titles so they contrast with the body text. Times New Roman is a serif font, and Arial is a sans serif font. The text you are reading now is a serif font, and the text in the following steps is a sans serif font.

To change the font of the title:

1. Press **Ctrl+Home** to move the insertion point to the beginning of the document, and then select the title **Common Questions About Trees**.

2. Click the **Font** list arrow on the Formatting toolbar. A list of available fonts appears in alphabetical order, with the name of the current font in the Font text box. See Figure 2-28. (Your list of fonts might be different from those shown.) Fonts that have been used recently might appear above a double line. Note that each name in the list is formatted with the relevant font. For example, "Arial" appears in the Arial font, and "Times New Roman" appears in the Times New Roman font.

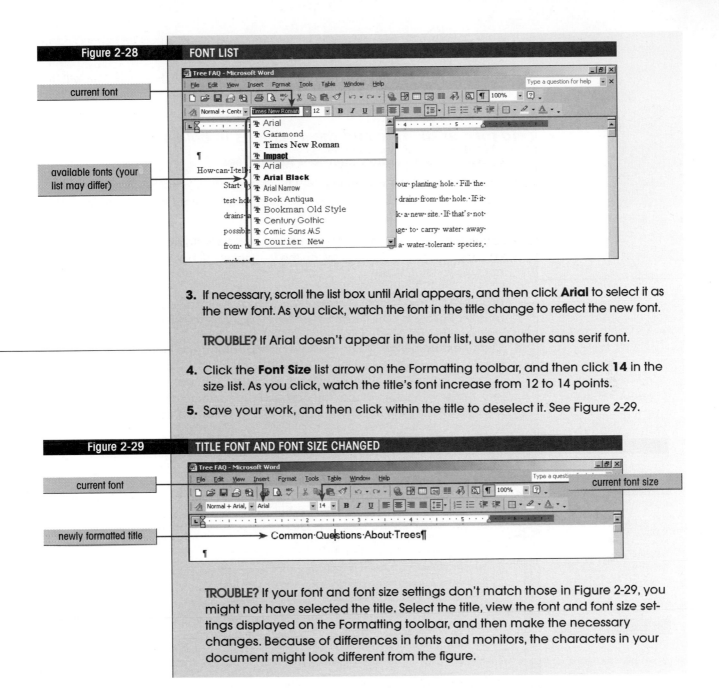

Figure 2-28 FONT LIST

current font

available fonts (your list may differ)

3. If necessary, scroll the list box until Arial appears, and then click **Arial** to select it as the new font. As you click, watch the font in the title change to reflect the new font.

TROUBLE? If Arial doesn't appear in the font list, use another sans serif font.

4. Click the **Font Size** list arrow on the Formatting toolbar, and then click **14** in the size list. As you click, watch the title's font increase from 12 to 14 points.

5. Save your work, and then click within the title to deselect it. See Figure 2-29.

Figure 2-29 TITLE FONT AND FONT SIZE CHANGED

current font

current font size

newly formatted title

Common·Questions·About·Trees¶

TROUBLE? If your font and font size settings don't match those in Figure 2-29, you might not have selected the title. Select the title, view the font and font size settings displayed on the Formatting toolbar, and then make the necessary changes. Because of differences in fonts and monitors, the characters in your document might look different from the figure.

Emphasizing **Text with Boldface, Underlining, and Italics**

You can emphasize words in your document with boldface, underlining, or italics. These styles help make specific thoughts, ideas, words, or phrases stand out. (You can also add special effects such as shadows to characters.) Marilee marked a few words on the document draft (shown in Figure 2-1) that need this kind of special emphasis. You add boldface, underlining, or italics by using the relevant buttons on the Formatting toolbar. These buttons are **toggle buttons**, which means you can click them once to format the selected text, and then click again to remove the formatting from the selected text.

Bolding Text

Marilee wants to draw attention to the title and all of the question headings. You will do this by bolding them.

To format the title and the questions in boldface:

1. Select the title **Common Questions About Trees**.

2. Press and hold **Ctrl**, and then select the first question in the document ("How can I tell if I've picked a site with good drainage?"). Both the title and the first question are now selected.

3. Hold down **Ctrl** and select the remaining questions. To display more of the document, use the down arrow on the vertical scroll bar while you continue to hold down the Ctrl key.

   TROUBLE? If you accidentally select something other than a question, keep Ctrl pressed while you click the incorrect item. This should deselect the incorrect item.

4. Click the **Bold** button **B** on the Formatting toolbar, and then click anywhere in the document to deselect the text. The title and the questions appear in bold, as shown in Figure 2-30. After reviewing this change, you wonder if the title would look better without boldface. You can easily remove boldface by selecting the text and clicking the Bold button again to turn, or toggle, off boldfacing.

Figure 2-30   TEXT IN BOLDFACE

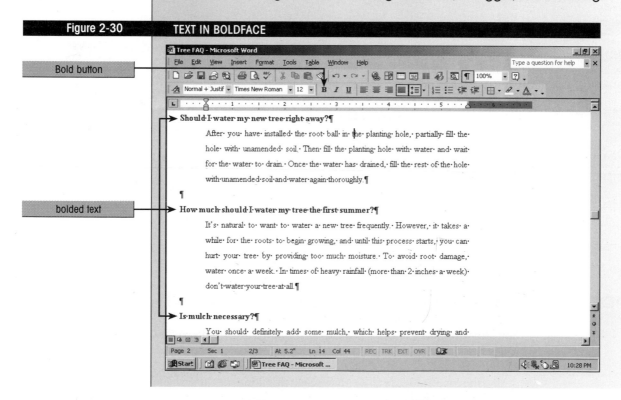

Bold button

bolded text

5. To remove the boldface, select the title, and then click **B** . The title now appears without boldface. You decide you prefer to emphasize the title with boldface after all.

6. Verify that the title is still selected, and then click **B** . The title appears in boldface again.

Underlining Text

The Underline button works in the same way as the Bold button. Marilee's edits indicate that the word "Note" should be inserted and underlined at the beginning of the final paragraph. Using the Underline button, you'll make both of these changes at the same time.

To underline text:

1. Press **Ctrl+End** to move the insertion point to the end of the document. Then move the insertion point to the left of the word "Any" in the first line of the final paragraph.

2. Click the **Underline** button **U** on the Formatting toolbar to turn on underlining. The Underline button remains highlighted. Whatever text you type now will be underlined on your screen and in your printed document.

3. Type **Note:** and then click **U** to turn off underlining. See how the Underline button is no longer pressed, and "Note:" is now underlined.

4. Press the **spacebar**. See Figure 2-31.

Figure 2-31	WORD TYPED WITH UNDERLINE

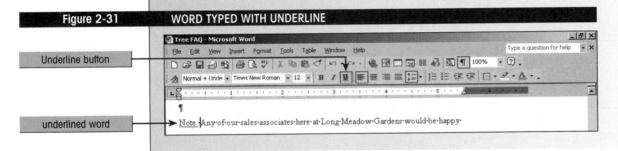

Underline button

underlined word

Italicizing Text

Next, you'll format each instance of "Long Meadow Gardens" in italics. This helps draw attention to the company name.

To italicize the company name:

1. Scroll up to the third to last question on the first page ("Do I have to do anything to the tree before planting?").

2. In the first line below the question, select **Long Meadow Gardens**.

3. Click the **Italic** button **I** on the Formatting toolbar. The company name changes from regular to italic text. In the next step, you'll learn a useful method for repeating the task you just performed.

4. Scroll down to the last paragraph of the document, select the company name, and then press the **F4** key. Keep in mind that you can use the F4 key to repeat your most recent action. It is especially helpful when formatting parts of a document.

5. Save the document.

Adding Comments

Peter stops by your desk to review your work. He's happy with the document's appearance, but wonders if he should add some information about fertilizing new trees. He asks you to insert a note to Marilee about this using Word's Comment feature. A **comment** is an electronic version of an adhesive note that you might attach to a piece of paper. To attach a comment to a Word document, select a block of text, click Comment on the Insert menu, and then type your comment in the Reviewing Pane. To display the comment, place the mouse pointer over text to which a comment has been attached. Comments are very useful when you are exchanging Word documents with co-workers electronically, either via e-mail or on floppies, because they allow you to make notes or queries without affecting the document itself.

You'll attach Peter's comment to the document title so that Marilee will be sure to see it as soon as she opens the document.

To attach a comment:

1. Scroll up to the top of the document, and then select the title **Common Questions About Trees**.

2. Click **Insert** on the menu bar, and then click **Comment**. The Reviewing Pane opens at the bottom of the document window. Depending on how your computer is set up, you might see your name, as well as the current date and time in the Reviewing Pane. The insertion point is positioned in the Reviewing Pane, ready for you to type the comment. Also, the Reviewing toolbar is displayed below the Formatting toolbar. Finally, notice that the title is enclosed in brackets. See Figure 2-32.

Figure 2-32   INSERTING A COMMENT

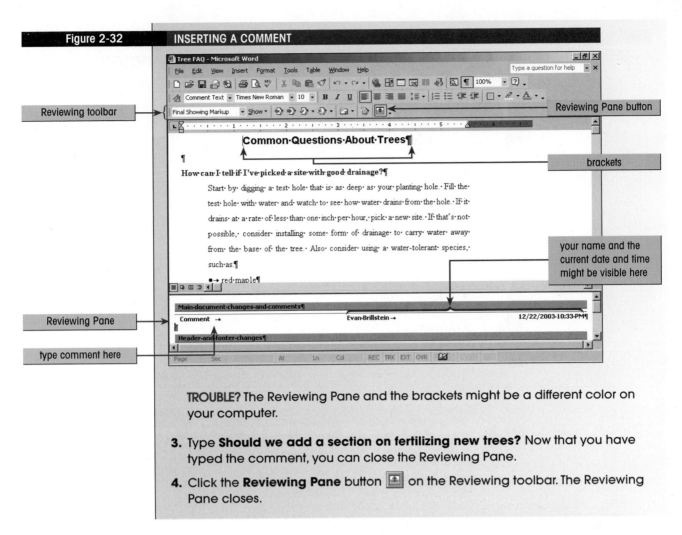

Reviewing toolbar

Reviewing Pane button

brackets

your name and the current date and time might be visible here

Reviewing Pane

type comment here

TROUBLE? The Reviewing Pane and the brackets might be a different color on your computer.

3. Type **Should we add a section on fertilizing new trees?** Now that you have typed the comment, you can close the Reviewing Pane.

4. Click the **Reviewing Pane** button on the Reviewing toolbar. The Reviewing Pane closes.

After you insert a comment, you should display it once to make sure you included all the necessary information.

To display a comment:

1. Move the mouse pointer over the title. The comment is displayed in a box over the title. Depending on how your computer is set up, you might see your name in the comment, as well as the date and time the comment was attached. See Figure 2-33.

Figure 2-33   **VIEWING A COMMENT**

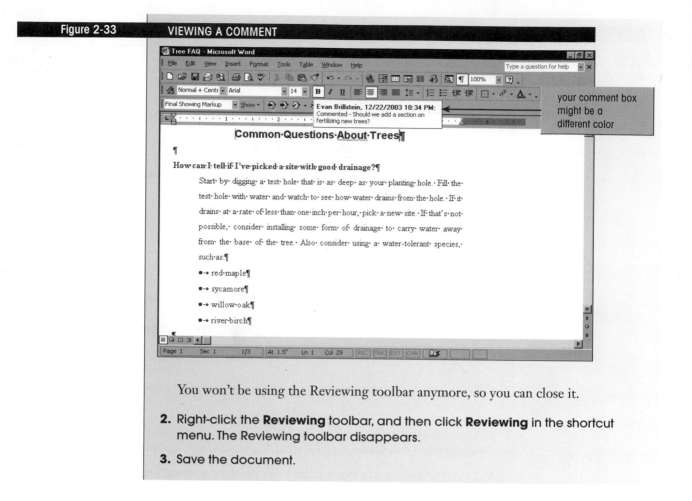

You won't be using the Reviewing toolbar anymore, so you can close it.

2. Right-click the **Reviewing** toolbar, and then click **Reviewing** in the shortcut menu. The Reviewing toolbar disappears.

3. Save the document.

Previewing Formatted Text

You have made all the editing and formatting changes that Marilee requested for the FAQ. It's helpful to preview a document after formatting it, because the Print Preview window makes it easy to spot text that is not aligned correctly.

To preview and print the document:

1. Click the **Print Preview** button 🔍 on the Standard toolbar and examine the first page of the document. Notice the box in the right margin of the document, indicating that a comment has been attached to the document title. Use the vertical scroll bar to display the second page. (If you notice any formatting errors, click the Close button on the Print Preview toolbar, correct the errors in Normal view, save your changes, and then return to the Print Preview window.)

2. Click the **Print** button 🖨 on the Print Preview toolbar. After a pause, the document prints. Note that the comment you inserted into the document earlier is not printed.

3. Click the **Close** button on the Print Preview toolbar.

4. Close the document and then close Word.

You now have a hard copy of the final FAQ, as shown in Figure 2-34.

Figure 2-34   FINAL VERSION OF TREE FAQ DOCUMENT

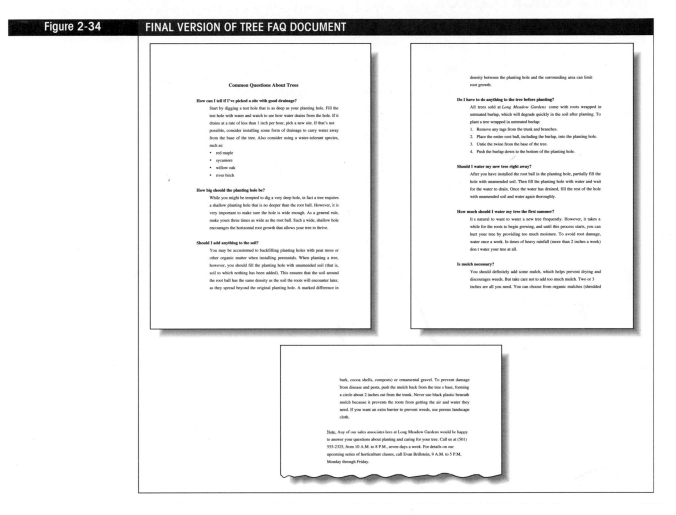

In this tutorial, you have helped Peter edit and format the FAQ that will be handed out to all customers purchasing a tree at Long Meadow Gardens. Peter will e-mail the file to Marilee later so that she can review your work and read the comment you attached.

Session 2.2 QUICK CHECK

1. What are Word's default margins for the left and right margins? For the top and bottom margins?

2. Describe the four types of text alignment.

3. Explain how to indent a paragraph 1 inch or more from the left margin.

4. Describe a situation in which you would use the Format Painter.

5. Explain how to add underlining to a word as you type it.

6. Explain how to transform a series of short paragraphs into a numbered list.

7. Explain how to format a title in 14-point Arial.

8. Describe the steps involved in changing the line spacing in a document.

REVIEW ASSIGNMENTS

Now that you have completed the FAQ, Marilee asks you to help her create a statement summarizing customer accounts for the Long Meadow Garden's wholesale nursery. She would also like you to create a document that contains contact information for Long Meadow Gardens. Remember to use the Undo and Redo buttons as you work to correct any errors.

1. If necessary, start Word, make sure your Data Disk is in the appropriate disk drive, and check your screen to make sure your settings match those in the tutorial.

2. Open the file **Statmnt** from the Review folder for Tutorial 2 on your Data Disk, and save the document as **Monthly Statement** in the same folder.

3. Use the Spelling and Grammar checker to correct any spelling or grammatical errors. If the Suggestions list box does not include the correct replacement, click outside the Spelling and Grammar dialog box, type the correction yourself, click Resume in the Spelling and Grammar dialog box, and continue checking the document.

4. Proofread the document carefully to check for any additional errors. Look for two words that are spelled correctly but used improperly.

5. Change the right margin to 2 inches using the Page Setup dialog box.

Explore

6. Change the left margin using the ruler in Print Layout view, as follows:
   a. Select the entire document.
   b. Position the pointer on the small gray square on the ruler at the left margin. A ScreenTip with the words "Left Indent" appears.
   c. Press and hold down the mouse button. A vertical dotted line appears in the document window, indicating the current left margin. Drag the margin left to the 0.5-inch mark on the ruler, and then release the mouse button.

7. Make all edits and formatting changes shown in Figure 2-35, and save your work.

Figure 2-35

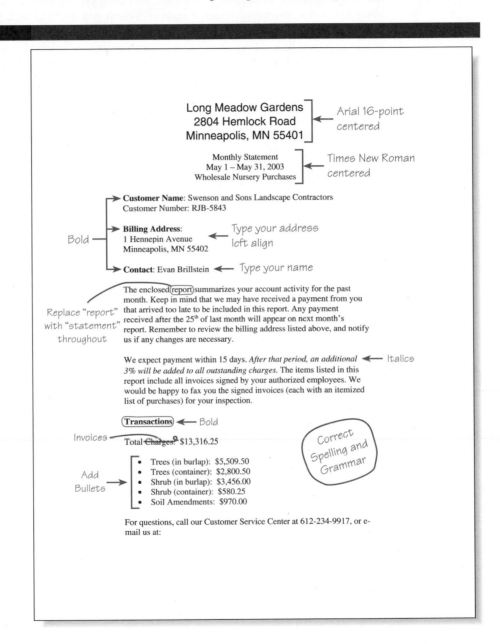

8. Remove any Smart Tags in the document.

Explore   9. When you type Web addresses or e-mail addresses in a document, Word automatically formats them as links. When you click a Web address formatted as a link, Windows automatically opens a Web browser (such as Microsoft Internet Explorer) and, if your computer is connected to the Internet, displays that Web page. If you click an e-mail address formatted as a link, Windows opens a program where you can type an e-mail message. The address you clicked is automatically included as the recipient of the e-mail. You'll see how this works as you add a Web address and e-mail address to the statement. In the address centered at the top of the document, click at the end of the ZIP code, add a new line, and then type the address for the company's Web site: www.longmeadowgardens.com. When you are finished, press Enter. Notice that as soon as you press Enter, Word formats the address in blue with an underline, marking it as a link. Move the mouse pointer over the link and read the ScreenTip. Because this Web address is fictitious, clicking it will not actually display a Web page.

Explore   10. Move the insertion point to the end of the document, press the spacebar, type long_meadow_gardens@worldlink.com and then press Enter. Word formats the e-mail address as a link. Press and hold the Ctrl button and then click the link. (If you see a message asking if you want to make Outlook Express your default mail client, click No.) You see a window where you could type an e-mail message to Long Meadow Gardens. (If your computer is not set up for e-mail, close any error messages that open.) Close the e-mail window without saving any changes. The link is now formatted in purple, indicating that the link has been clicked.

11 Move the last sentence of the document (which begins "For questions, call . . . ") to a new paragraph, just above the heading "Transactions".

12. Select the last Transactions portion of the document, from the heading "Transactions" down to the end of the document. Indent the selected text 1 inch by clicking the Increase Indent button twice.

13. Open the Clipboard Task Pane. Select the company name, address, and Web address at the top of the document and copy it to the Clipboard, and then copy the company e-mail address to the Clipboard.

Explore   14. Open a new, blank document and display the Clipboard Task Pane. In the Clipboard Task Pane, click the company address to insert this information at the top of the document. Insert two blank lines, type "Send all e-mail correspondence to YOUR NAME:" (replace YOUR NAME with your first and last name). Type a space and then, in the Clipboard Task Pane, click the company e-mail address. Type a period at the end of the e-mail address.

15. Clear the contents of the Clipboard Task Pane and then close the Task Pane.

Explore   16. If necessary, switch to Print Layout view. Then attach the following comment to the company name: "Marilee, please let me know how you want this document formatted." Notice that in Print Layout view you type the comment in a small comment window directly in the margin. Switch to Normal view, and display the comment by positioning the pointer over the company name.

              17. Save the document as **LMG Contact Information** in the Review folder for Tutorial 2. Print and close the document.

              18. Save the Monthly Statement document, preview and print it, and then close it. Also close the Clipboard Task Pane, if necessary. Then exit Word.

CASE PROBLEMS

Case 1. Authorization Form for Gygs and Bytes   Melissa Martinez is the purchasing manager for Gygs and Bytes, a wholesale distributor of computer parts based in Portland, Oregon. Most of the company's business is conducted via catalog or through the company's Web site, but local customers sometimes drop by to pick up small orders. In the past Melissa has had problems determining which of her customers' employees were authorized to sign credit invoices. To avoid confusion, she has asked all local customers to complete a form listing employees who are authorized to sign invoices. She plans to place the completed forms in a binder at the main desk, so the receptionist at Gygs and Bytes can find the information quickly.

       1. Open the file **Form** from the Cases folder for Tutorial 2 on your Data Disk, and save the file as **Authorization Form** in the same folder.

Explore   2. Correct any spelling or grammar errors. Ignore any words that are spelled correctly, but that are not included in Word's dictionary. When the Spelling and Grammar Checker highlights the word "sining", click the appropriate word in the Suggestions box, and then click Change.

Explore   3. If necessary, read Steps 9 and 10 in the Review Assignments to learn about adding Web addresses and e-mail addresses to a document. Below the company's mailing address, add the company Web address in all uppercase: WWW.G&B.NET.

       4. Change the top and left margins to 1.5 inches.

       5. Center the first five lines of the document (containing the form title and the company address).

       6. Format the first line of the document (the form title) in 16-point Arial, with italics.

       7. Format lines 2 through 5 (the address, including the Web address) in 12-point Arial.

Explore 8. Replace all instances of G&B, except the first one (in the Web address), with the complete company name, Gygs and Bytes. Use the Find Next button to skip an instance of the search text.

9. Format the blank ruled lines as a numbered list. Customers will use these blank lines to write in the names of authorized employees.

Explore 10. Format the entire document using 1.5 spacing. Then triple-space the numbered list (with the blank lines) and the Signature and Title lines as follows:
   a. Select the numbered list with the blank lines.
   b. Triple-space the selected text using the line spacing button on the Formatting toolbar.
   c. Select the "Signed:" and the "Title:" lines, and then press F4.

11. Save the document.

12. Drag "Customer Number:" up to position it above "Customer Name".

Explore 13. Select "Customer Name:", "Customer Number:", and "Address:". Press Ctrl+B to format the selected text in bold. Note that it is sometimes easier to use this keyboard shortcut instead of the Bold button on the Formatting toolbar.

14. Delete the phrase "all employees" and replace it with "all authorized personnel".

Explore 15. Select the phrase "all authorized personnel will be required to show a photo I.D." Press Ctrl+I to format the selected text in italics. It is sometimes easier to use this keyboard shortcut instead of the Italic button on the Formatting toolbar.

16. Insert your name in the form, in the "Customer Name:" line. Format your name without boldface, if necessary.

17. Insert your address, left aligned, without bold, below the heading "Address:".

18. Click the Print Preview button on the Standard toolbar to check your work.

Explore 19. Click the Shrink to Fit button on the Print Preview toolbar to reduce the entire document to one page. Word reduces the font sizes slightly in order to fit the entire form on one page. Close the Print Preview window and save your work.

Explore 20. Use the Print command on the File menu to open the Print dialog box. Print two copies of the document by changing the Number of copies setting in the Print dialog box.

Explore 21. You can find out the number of words in your documents by using the Word Count command on the Tools menu. Use this command to determine the number of words in the document, and then write that number in the upper-right corner of the printout.

22. Save and close the document, and then exit Word.

Case 2. Advertising Brochure for the CCW Web Site The *Carson College Weekly* is a student-run newspaper published through the Carson College Student Services Association. The newspaper is distributed around campus each Friday. The online version of the newspaper is posted on the CCW Web site on Thursdays. Local businesses have a long-established tradition of advertising in the print version of the newspaper, and the paper's advertising manager, Noah McCormick, would like to ensure that this same tradition carries over to the online newspaper. When he sends out the monthly statements to his print advertisers, he would like to include a one-page brochure encouraging them to purchase an online ad. He has copied the text of the brochure from the CCW Web site and saved it as unformatted text in a Word document.

1. Open the file **CCW** from the Cases folder for Tutorial 2 on your Data Disk, and save the file as **CCW Brochure** in the same folder.

2. Correct any spelling or grammar errors. Take time to make sure the right correction is selected in the Suggestions list box before you click Change. Proofread for any words that are spelled correctly but used incorrectly.

Explore
3. If necessary, read Steps 9 and 10 in the Review Assignments to learn about adding Web addresses and e-mail addresses to a document. Below *Carson College Weekly*, add the newspaper's Web address in all uppercase: WWW.CARSON.CCW.EDU, and then press Enter. At the end of the document, insert a space, type "advertising@carson.ccw.edu", (without the quotation marks), type a period, and then press Enter.

4. In the second to last sentence, replace "the CCW Advertising Office" with your name.

5. Change the right margin to 1.5 inches and the left margin to 2 inches.

6. Format the entire document in 12-point Times New Roman.

7. Format the four paragraphs below "Did you know?" as a bulleted list.

8. Drag the third bullet (which begins "You can include . . . ") up to the top of the bulleted list.

9. Format the first two lines of the document using a font, font size, and alignment of your choice. Use bold or italics for emphasis.

10. Format the entire document using 1.5 line spacing.

11. Add a comment to the first line (*Carson College Weekly*) asking Noah if he would like you to leave a printed copy of the brochure in his mailbox. Close the Reviewing Pane and the Reviewing toolbar when you are finished.

12. Save your work, preview the document, and then switch back to Normal view to make any changes you think necessary.

13. Print the document.

14. Save and close the document, and then exit Word.

Case 3. *Productivity Training Summary for UpTime* Matt Patterson is UpTime's marketing director for the Northeast region. The company provides productivity training for large companies across the country. Matt wants to provide interested clients with a one-page summary of UpTime's productivity training sessions.

1. If necessary, start Word, make sure your Data Disk is in the appropriate disk drive, and check your screen to make sure your settings match those in the tutorials.

2. Open the file **UpTime** from the Tutorial 2 Cases folder on your Data Disk, and save it as **UpTime Training Summary** in the same folder.

3. Change the title at the beginning of the document to a 16-point sans serif font. Be sure to pick a font that looks professional and is easy to read. (Remember to use the Undo and Redo buttons as you work to correct any editing mistakes.)

4. Center and bold the title and Web address.

5. Delete the word "general" from the second sentence of the first paragraph after the document title.

6. Convert the list of training components following the first paragraph to an indented, numbered list.

7. Under the heading "Personal Productivity Training Seminar," delete the last sentence from the first paragraph, the one beginning with "This seminar improves".

8. Under the heading "Personal Productivity Training Seminar," delete the phrase "at the seminar" from the first sentence in the second paragraph.

9. In the first paragraph under the heading "Management Productivity Training," move the first sentence (beginning with "UpTime provides management training") to the end of the paragraph.

10. Switch the order of the first and second paragraphs under the "Field Services Technology and Training" heading.

11. Search for the text "your name", and replace it with your first and last name. Use the Bold button and the Underline button on the Formatting toolbar to format your name in boldface, with an underline.

12. Change the top margin to 1.5 inches.

13. Change the left margin to 1.75 inches.

14. Bold and italicize the heading "Personal Productivity Training Seminar" and then use the Format Painter to copy this heading's format to the headings "Management Productivity Training" and "Field Services Technology and Training". Turn off the Format Painter when you're finished.

Explore

15. Select both occurrences of the word "free" in the second paragraph under the "Field Services Technology and Training" heading. Press Ctrl+I to format the selected text in italics.

16. Save and preview the document.

17. Print the document, and then close the file, and exit Word.

Case 4. Product Description for Ridge Top   Thomas McGee is vice president of sales and marketing at Ridge Top, an outdoor and sporting-gear store in Conshohocken, Pennsylvania. Each year Thomas and his staff mail a description of new products to Ridge Top's regular customers. Thomas has asked you to edit and format the first few pages of this year's new products' description.

1. If necessary, start Word, make sure your Data Disk is in the appropriate disk drive, and check your screen to make sure your settings match those in the tutorials.

2. Open the file **Ridge** from the Tutorial 2 Cases folder on your Data Disk, and save it as **RidgeTop Guide** in the same folder.

3. Use the Spelling and Grammar checker to correct any errors in the document. Because of the nature of this document, it contains some words that the Word dictionary on your computer may not recognize. It also contains headings that the Spelling and Grammar checker may consider sentence fragments. As you use the Spelling and Grammar checker, use the Ignore All button, if necessary, to skip over brand names.

4. Delete the phrase "a great deal" from the first sentence of the paragraph below the heading "Snuggle Up to These Prices." (Remember to use the Undo and Redo buttons to correct any editing mistakes as you work.)

5. Reverse the order of the first two paragraphs under the heading, "You'll Eat Up the Prices of This Camp Cooking Gear!"

6. Cut the last sentence of the first full paragraph ("Prices are good through . . . ") from the document. Then move the insertion point to the end of the document, press the Enter key twice, and insert the cut sentence as a new paragraph. Format it in 12-point Arial, and italicize it.

7. Format the Ridge Top tip items as a numbered list.

Explore 8. Reorder the items under the "Ridge Top Tips" heading by moving the fourth product idea and the following blank paragraph to the top of the list.

9. Search for the text "your name", and replace with your first and last name.

Explore 10. Experiment with two special paragraph alignment options: first line and hanging. First, select everything from the heading "Ridge Top Guarantees Warmth at Cool Prices" through the paragraph just before the heading "Ridge Top Tips". Next, click Format on the menu bar, click Paragraph, click the Indents and Spacing tab if necessary, click the Help button in the upper-right corner of the dialog box, click the Special list arrow, and review the information on the special alignment options. Experiment with both the First line and the Hanging options. When you are finished, return the document to its original format by choosing the none option.

11. Justify all the paragraphs in the document. (*Hint*: To select all paragraphs in the document at one time, click Edit on the menu bar, and then click Select All.)

12. Replace all occurrences of "RidgeTop" with "Ridge Top". (You may have already made this correction when you checked spelling in the document.)

13. Apply a 12-point, bold, sans serif font to each of the headings. Be sure to pick a font that looks professional and is easy to read. Use the Format Painter to copy the formatting after you apply it once using the Font list box.

14. Change the title's and subtitle's font to the same font you used for the headings, except set the size to 16 point.

15. Bold the title and subtitle.

16. Underline the names and prices for all of the brand name products.

17. Save and preview the document.

18. Print the document, and then close the file, and exit Word.

INTERNET ASSIGNMENTS

Student Union

The purpose of the Internet Assignments is to challenge you to find information on the Internet that you can use to create effective documents. The actual assignments are updated and maintained on the Course Technology Web site. Log on to the Internet and use your Web browser to go to the Student Union on the New Perspectives Series site at **www.course.com/NewPerspectives/studentunion**. Click the Online Companions link, and then click the link for this text.

QUICK CHECK ANSWERS

Session 2.1

1. Click at the beginning of the document, and then click the Spelling and Grammar button on the Standard toolbar. In the Spelling and Grammar dialog box, review any errors highlighted in color. Grammatical errors appear in green; spelling errors appear in red. Review the possible corrections in the Suggestions list box. To accept a suggested correction, click it in the Suggestions list box. Then click Change to make the correction and continue searching the document for errors.

2. (a) ↓; (b) Ctrl+End; (c) Page Down

3. (a) Double-click the word; (b) click at the beginning of the block, and then drag until the entire block is selected; (c) double-click in the selection bar next to the paragraph, or triple-click in the paragraph.

4. (a) the blank space in the left margin area of the Document window that allows you to easily select entire lines or large blocks of text; (b) the button on the Standard toolbar that redoes an action you previously reversed using the Undo button; (c) the process of moving text by first selecting the text, and then pressing and holding the mouse button while moving the text to its new location in the document, and finally releasing the mouse button

5. You might use the Undo button to remove the bold formatting you had just applied to a word. You could then use the Redo button to restore the bold formatting to the word.

6. False

7. Cut and paste removes the selected material from its original location and inserts it in a new location. Copy and paste makes a copy of the selected material and inserts the copy in a new location; the original material remains in its original location.

8. Click Edit on the menu bar, click Replace, type the search text in the Find what text box, type the replacement text in the Replace with text box, click Find Next or click Replace all.

Session 2.2

1. The default top and bottom margins are 1 inch. The default left and right margins are 1.25 inches.

2. Align-left: each line flush left, ragged right; Align-right: each line flush right, ragged left; Center: each line centered, ragged right and left.; Justify: each line flush left and flush right

4. You might use the Format Painter to copy the formatting of a heading to the other headings in the document.

5. Click the Underline button on the Formatting toolbar, type the word, and then click the Underline button again to turn off underlining.

6. Select the paragraphs, and then click the Numbering button on the Formatting toolbar.

7. Select the title, click the Font list arrow, and click Arial in the list of fonts. Then click the Font Size list arrow, and click 14.

8. Select the text you want to change, click the Line Spacing list arrow on the Formatting toolbar, and then click the line spacing option you want. Or select the text, and then press Ctrl+1 for single spacing, Ctrl+5 for 1.5 line spacing, or Ctrl+2 for double spacing.

In this tutorial you will:

- Set tab stops

- Divide a document into sections

- Change the vertical alignment of a section

- Center a page between the top and bottom margins

- Create a header with page numbers

- Create a table

- Sort the rows in a table

- Modify a table's structure

- Format a table

CREATING
A MULTIPLE-PAGE REPORT

Writing a Recommendation for Tyger Networks

CASE

Tyger Networks

Tyger Networks is a consulting company in Madison, Wisconsin that specializes in setting up computer networks for small businesses and organizations. Susan Launspach, the program director at New Hope Social Services, recently contacted Tyger Networks about linking the computer networks at New Hope's three main offices. The offices are scattered throughout southern Wisconsin in Madison, Janesville, and Milwaukee. Each office has its own self-contained computer network. To make it easier for a social worker in one office to access data stored on a computer in another office, Susan would like to establish some kind of connection between the three networks.

Caitilyn Waller, an account manager at Tyger Networks, is responsible for the New Hope account. In a phone call, she explained to Susan that connecting the three offices will create a new type of a network known as a wide area network (WAN). Because Susan is unfamiliar with networking terminology, Caitilyn offered to write a report that summarizes the options for creating this type of a network. Working with a task force of sales and technical personnel, Caitilyn compiled the necessary information in a multipage document. Now Caitilyn would like you to help her finish formatting the report. She also needs some help adding a table to the end of the report. Once the report is completed, Susan will present it to the board of directors at New Hope Social Services.

In this tutorial, you will format the report's title page so that it has a different layout from the rest of the report. The title page will contain only the title and subtitle and will not have page numbers like the rest of the report. You also will add a table to the report that summarizes the costs involved in creating a WAN.

In this session you will review the task force's recommendation report. Then you will learn how to set tab stops, divide a document into sections, center a page between the top and bottom margins, create a header, and create a table.

Planning **the Document**

As head of the task force, Caitilyn divided the responsibility for the report among the members of the group. Each person gathered information about one topic and wrote the appropriate section of the report. Then Caitilyn compiled all the information into a coherent and unified report. In addition, she took care to follow the company's guidelines for content, organization, style, and format.

Because Caitilyn knows that some members of the New Hope board of directors will not have time to read the entire report, she began the report with an executive summary. The body of the report provides an in-depth explanation of the options for establishing a WAN. At the end of the report, she summarizes the costs of these options. The report's style follows established standards of business writing, and emphasizes clarity, simplicity, and directness.

In accordance with the company style guide, Caitilyn's report will begin with a title page, with the text centered between the top and bottom margins. Every page except the title page will include a line of text at the top, giving a descriptive name for the report, as well as the page number. The text and headings will be formatted to match all reports created at Tyger Networks, and will follow company guidelines for layout and text style.

Opening **the Report**

Caitilyn already has combined the individual sections into one document. She also has begun formatting the report by changing the font size of headings, adding elements such as bold and italics, and by indenting paragraphs. You'll open the document and perform the remaining formatting tasks on page 1, as indicated in Figure 3-1.

Figure 3-1 INITIAL DRAFT OF REPORT (PAGE 1)

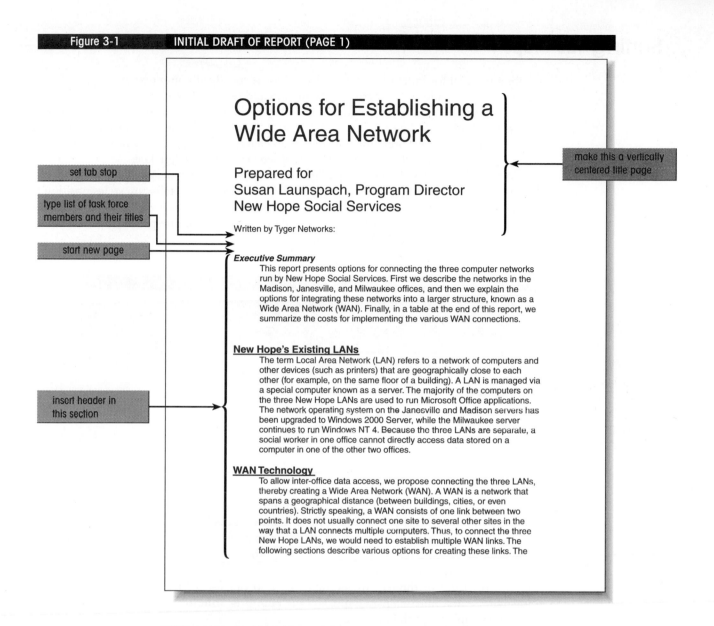

To open the document:

1. Start Word, and place your Data Disk in the appropriate drive.

2. Open the file **WAN** from the Tutorial folder in the Tutorial.03 folder on your Data Disk.

3. To avoid altering the original file, save the document as **New Hope WAN Report** in the Tutorial folder in the Tutorial.03 folder on your Data Disk.

4. Make sure your screen matches the figures in this tutorial. In particular, be sure to display the nonprinting characters and switch to Normal view if necessary.

Setting Tab Stops

Tabs are useful for indenting paragraphs and for vertically aligning text or numerical data in columns. A **tab** adds space between the margin and text in a column or between text in one column and text in another column. A **tab stop** is the location where text moves when you press the Tab key. When the Show/Hide button ¶ is pressed, the nonprinting tab character appears wherever you press the Tab key. A tab character is just like any other character you type; you can delete it by pressing the Backspace key or the Delete key.

Word provides several **tab-stop alignment styles**. The five major styles are left, center, right, decimal, and bar, as shown in Figure 3-2. The first three tab-stop styles position text in a similar way to the Align Left, Center, and Align Right buttons on the Formatting toolbar. The difference is that with a tab, you determine line by line precisely where the left, center, or right alignment should occur.

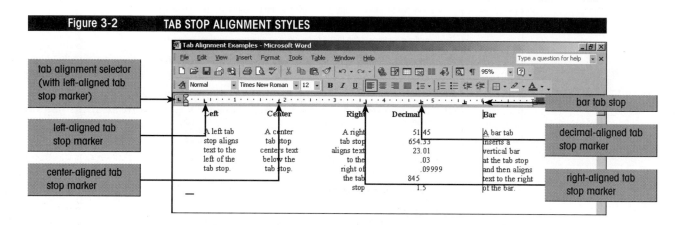

Figure 3-2   TAB STOP ALIGNMENT STYLES

The default tab stops on the ruler are **Left tabs**, which position the left edge of text at the tab stop and extend the text to the right. **Center tabs** position text so that it's centered evenly on both sides of the tab stop. **Right tabs** position the right edge of text at the tab stop and extend the text to the left. **Decimal tabs** position numbers so that their decimal points are aligned at the tab stop. **Bar tabs** insert a vertical bar at the tab stop and then align text to the right of the bar. In addition, you also can use a **First Line Indent tab**, which indents the first line of a paragraph, and the **Hanging Indent tab**, which indents every line of a paragraph *except* the first line.

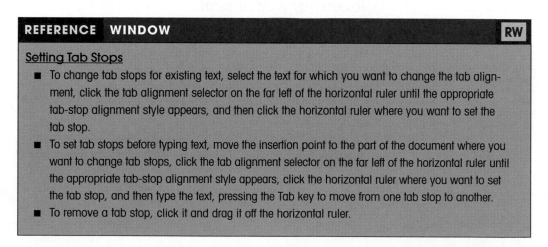

REFERENCE WINDOW   **RW**

Setting Tab Stops
- To change tab stops for existing text, select the text for which you want to change the tab alignment, click the tab alignment selector on the far left of the horizontal ruler until the appropriate tab-stop alignment style appears, and then click the horizontal ruler where you want to set the tab stop.
- To set tab stops before typing text, move the insertion point to the part of the document where you want to change tab stops, click the tab alignment selector on the far left of the horizontal ruler until the appropriate tab-stop alignment style appears, click the horizontal ruler where you want to set the tab stop, and then type the text, pressing the Tab key to move from one tab stop to another.
- To remove a tab stop, click it and drag it off the horizontal ruler.

The Word default tab-stop settings are every one-half inch, as indicated by the small gray tick marks at the bottom of the ruler shown in Figure 3-3. You set a new tab stop by selecting a tab-stop alignment style (from the tab alignment selector at the left end of the horizontal ruler) and then clicking the horizontal ruler to insert the tab stop. You can remove a tab stop from the ruler by clicking it and dragging the tab stop off the ruler.

Figure 3-3	RULER WITH TAB STOPS

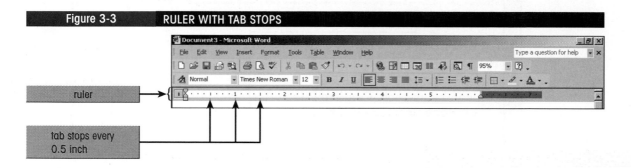

ruler

tab stops every 0.5 inch

You should never try to align columns of text by adding extra spaces with the spacebar. Although the text might seem precisely aligned in the document window, it might not be aligned when you print the document. Furthermore, if you edit the text, the extra spaces might disturb the alignment. However, if you edit text aligned with tabs, the alignment remains intact. If you want to align a lot of text in many columns, it is better to use a table, as described later in this tutorial.

To align columns using tabs, you can type some text, and press the Tab key. The insertion point then moves to the next tab stop to the right, where you can type more text. You can continue in this way until you type the first row of each column. Then you can press the Enter key, and begin typing the next row of each column. However, sometimes you'll find that text in a column stretches beyond the next default tab stop, and as a result the columns fail to line up evenly.

In the Tyger Networks report, you need to type the list of task force members and their titles. As you type, you'll discover whether Word's default tab stops are appropriate for this document, or whether you need to add a new tab stop.

To enter the task force list using tabs:

1. Verify that nonprinting characters are displayed, and then move the insertion point to the line below the text "Written by Tyger Networks:."

2. Type **Caitilyn Waller** and then press the **Tab** key. A tab character appears, and the insertion point moves to the first tab stop after the *r* in "Waller." This tab stop is located at the 1.5-inch mark on the horizontal ruler. See Figure 3-4.

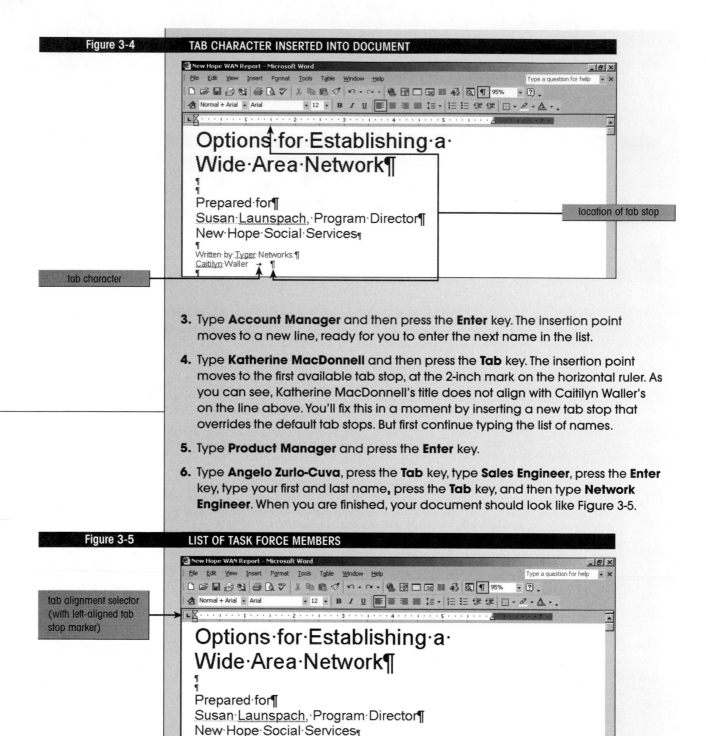

Figure 3-4 TAB CHARACTER INSERTED INTO DOCUMENT

location of tab stop

tab character

3. Type **Account Manager** and then press the **Enter** key. The insertion point moves to a new line, ready for you to enter the next name in the list.

4. Type **Katherine MacDonnell** and then press the **Tab** key. The insertion point moves to the first available tab stop, at the 2-inch mark on the horizontal ruler. As you can see, Katherine MacDonnell's title does not align with Caitilyn Waller's on the line above. You'll fix this in a moment by inserting a new tab stop that overrides the default tab stops. But first continue typing the list of names.

5. Type **Product Manager** and press the **Enter** key.

6. Type **Angelo Zurlo-Cuva**, press the **Tab** key, type **Sales Engineer**, press the **Enter** key, type your first and last name, press the **Tab** key, and then type **Network Engineer**. When you are finished, your document should look like Figure 3-5.

Figure 3-5 LIST OF TASK FORCE MEMBERS

tab alignment selector (with left-aligned tab stop marker)

your first and last name should appear here

titles do not align neatly

The list of names and titles is not aligned properly. You'll fix this by inserting a new tab stop.

To add a new tab stop to the horizontal ruler:

1. Click and drag the mouse pointer to select the list of task force members and titles.

2. Make sure the current tab-stop alignment style is left tab **L**, as shown in Figure 3-5. If **L** is not selected, click the **tab alignment selector** one or more times until **L** appears.

3. Click the **tick mark** on the ruler that occurs at 2.5 inches. Word automatically inserts a left tab stop at that location and removes the tick marks to its left. The column of titles shifts to the new tab stop.

4. Deselect the highlighted text and then move the insertion point anywhere in the list of names and titles. See Figure 3-6.

| Figure 3-6 | LEFT TAB STOP ON RULER |

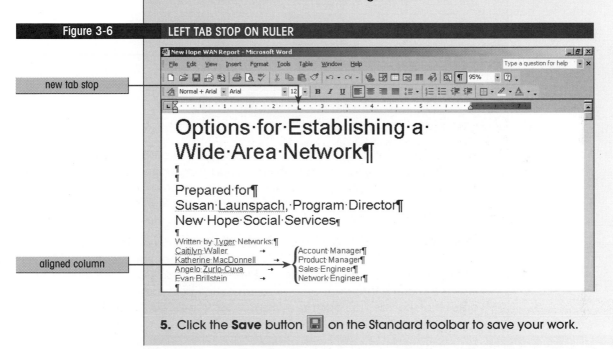

5. Click the **Save** button on the Standard toolbar to save your work.

The two columns of information are now aligned, as Caitilyn requested. Notice that Word changed the tab stops only for the selected paragraphs, not for all the paragraphs in the document. Next, you need to change the layout of the title page.

Formatting **the Document in Sections**

According to the company guidelines, the title page of the report should be centered between the top and bottom margins of the page. To format the title page differently from the rest of the report, you need to divide the document into sections. A **section** is a unit or part of a document that can have its own page orientation, margins, headers, footers, and vertical alignment. Each section, in other words, is like a mini-document within a document.

To divide a document into sections, you insert a **section break** (a dotted line with the words "Section Break") that marks the point at which one section ends and another begins. Sections can start on a new page or continue on the same page. You can insert a section break with the Break command on the Insert menu.

To insert a section break after the title:

1. Position the insertion point immediately to the left of the "E" in the heading "Executive Summary." You want the text above this heading to be on a separate title page and the executive summary to begin on the second page of the report.

2. Click **Insert** on the menu bar, and then click **Break** to open the Break dialog box. See Figure 3-7.

Figure 3-7	BREAK DIALOG BOX

You can use this dialog box to insert several types of breaks into your document, including a **page break**, which moves the text after it onto a new page. Instead of inserting a page break, however, you will insert a section break that indicates both a new section and a new page. Later in this session, you will use another method to insert a page break into the document.

3. Under "Section break types" click the **Next page** option button, and then click the **OK** button. A double-dotted line and the words "Section Break (Next Page)" appear before the heading "Executive Summary," indicating that you have inserted a break that starts a new section on the next page. The status bar indicates that the insertion point is on page 2, section 2. See Figure 3-8.

Figure 3-8	SECTION BREAK

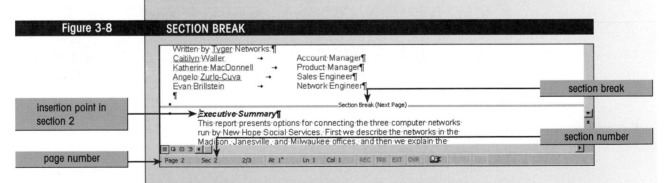

TROUBLE? If you see a single dotted line and the words "Page Break", you inserted a page break rather than a section break. Click the Undo button on the Standard toolbar, and then repeat Steps 1 through 3.

Now that the title page is a separate section and page from the rest of the report, you can make changes affecting only that section, leaving the rest of the document unchanged.

Changing the Vertical Alignment of a Section

You're ready to center the text of page 1 vertically on the page. But first you will switch to the Print Preview window, so you can more easily observe your changes to page 1.

To see the document in Print Preview:

1. Click the **Print Preview** button on the Standard toolbar to open the Print Preview window.

2. Click the **Multiple Pages** button on the Print Preview toolbar, and then click and drag across the top three pages in the list box to select "1 × 3 Pages." The three pages of the report are reduced in size and appear side by side. See Figure 3-9. Although you cannot read the text on the pages, you can see the general layout.

Figure 3-9 | REPORT IN PRINT PREVIEW WINDOW

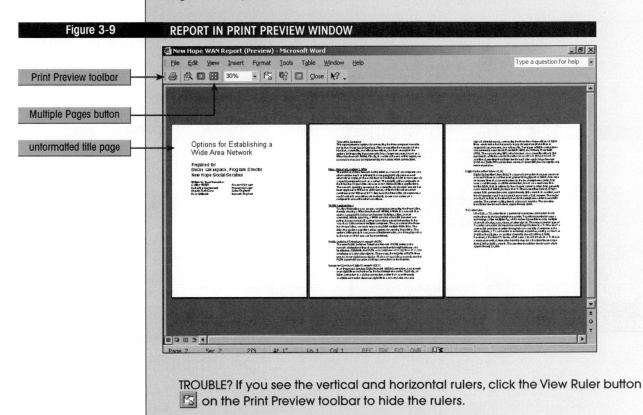

Print Preview toolbar

Multiple Pages button

unformatted title page

TROUBLE? If you see the vertical and horizontal rulers, click the View Ruler button on the Print Preview toolbar to hide the rulers.

Now you can change the vertical alignment to center the lines of text between the top and bottom margins. The **vertical alignment** specifies how a page of text is positioned on the page between the top and bottom margins—flush at the top, flush at the bottom, or centered between the top and bottom margins.

You'll center the title page text from within the Print Preview window.

To change the vertical alignment of the title page:

1. Click the **Magnifier** button 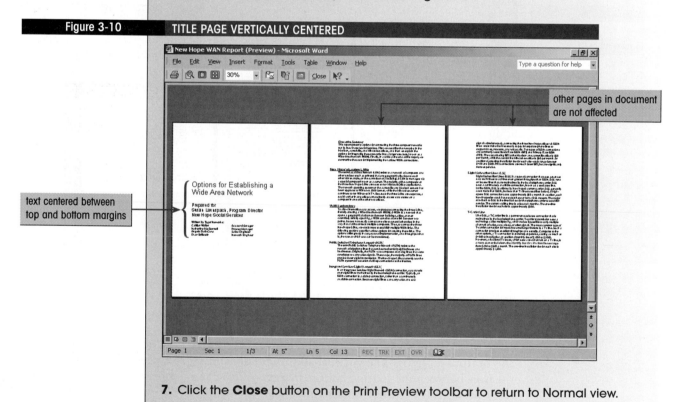 on the Print Preview toolbar once to deselect it.

2. Click the **leftmost page** in the Print Preview window to move the insertion point to page 1 (the title page). The status bar indicates that page 1 is the current page.

   TROUBLE? If the size of page 1 increases when you click it, you selected the Magnifier button in Step 1 instead of deselecting it. Click the Multiple Pages button on the Print Preview toolbar, drag to select "1 × 3 Pages," and then repeat Step 1.

3. Click **File** on the menu bar, and then click **Page Setup**. The Page Setup dialog box opens.

4. Click the **Layout** tab. In the Apply to list box, select **This section** (if it is not already selected) so that the layout change affects only the first section, not both sections, of your document.

5. Click the **Vertical alignment** list arrow, and then click **Center** to center the pages of the current section—in this case, just page 1—vertically between the top and bottom margins.

6. Click the **OK** button to return to the Print Preview window. The text of the title page is centered vertically, as shown in Figure 3-10.

Figure 3-10 **TITLE PAGE VERTICALLY CENTERED**

other pages in document are not affected

text centered between top and bottom margins

Options for Establishing a Wide Area Network

7. Click the **Close** button on the Print Preview toolbar to return to Normal view.

You have successfully centered the title page text. Next, you turn your attention to inserting a descriptive name for the report and the page number at the top of every page.

Adding **Headers**

The report guidelines at Tyger Networks require a short report title and the page number to be printed at the top of every page except the title page. Text that is printed at the top of every page is called a **header**. For example, the page number, tutorial number, and tutorial name printed at the top of the page you are reading is a header. Similarly, a **footer** is text that is printed at the bottom of every page. (You'll have a chance to work with footers in the Review Assignments at the end of this tutorial.)

When you insert a header or footer into a document, you switch to Header and Footer view. The Header and Footer toolbar is displayed, and the insertion point moves to the top of the document, where the header will appear. The main text is dimmed, indicating that it cannot be edited until you return to Normal or Print Layout view.

You'll create a header for the main body of the report (section 2) that prints "Options for Establishing a Wide Area Network" at the left margin and the page number at the right margin.

To insert a header for section 2:

1. Click anywhere after the section break, so that the insertion point is located in section 2 and not in section 1.

2. Click **View** on the menu bar, and then click **Header and Footer**. The Word window changes to Header and Footer view, and the Header and Footer toolbar appears in the document window. The header area appears in the top margin of your document surrounded by a dashed line and displays the words "Header -Section 2-". See Figure 3-11. (If the Header and Footer toolbar covers the header area, drag the toolbar below the header area, similar to its position in Figure 3-11.)

Figure 3-11	CREATING A HEADER

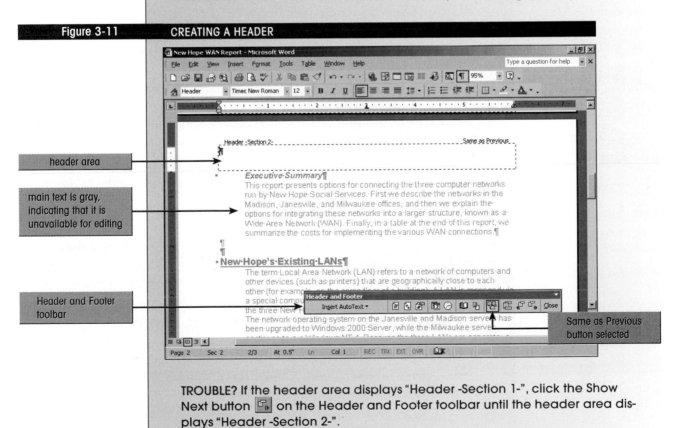

header area

main text is gray, indicating that it is unavailable for editing

Header and Footer toolbar

Same as Previous button selected

TROUBLE? If the header area displays "Header -Section 1-", click the Show Next button on the Header and Footer toolbar until the header area displays "Header -Section 2-".

TROUBLE? If the main text of the document doesn't appear on the screen, click the Show/Hide Document Text button 🔲 on the Header and Footer toolbar, and continue with Step 3.

3. Click the **Same as Previous** button 🔳 on the Header and Footer toolbar so that the button is *not* selected. When Same as Previous is selected, Word automatically inserts the same header text as for the previous section. You deselected it to ensure that the text of the current header applies only to the current section (section 2), and not to the previous section (section 1).

4. Type **Options for Establishing a Wide Area Network**. The title is automatically aligned on the left. See Figure 3-12.

Figure 3-12   **HEADER TEXT**

report title

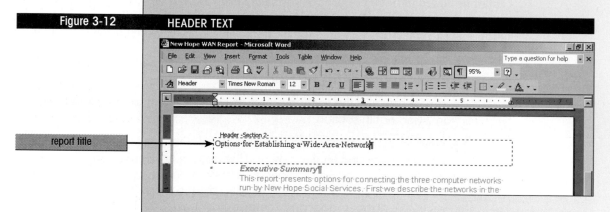

5. Press the **Tab** key to move the insertion point to the right margin of the header area. (Notice that by default the header contains center and right-align tab stops.)

6. Type the word **Page** and press the **spacebar** once.

7. Click the **Insert Page Number** button 🔲 on the Header and Footer toolbar. The page number "2" appears at the right-aligned tab. The page number in the header looks like you simply typed the number 2, but you actually inserted a special instruction telling Word to insert the correct page number on each page. Now consecutive page numbers will print on each page of the header within this section.

8. Click the **Close** button on the Header and Footer toolbar to return to Normal view, and then save your changes.

Notice that you can't see the header in Normal view. To see exactly how the header will appear on the printed page, you will switch to the Print Preview window. *Note:* you can also use Print Layout view.

To view the header and margins in Print Preview:

1. Click the **Print Preview button** 🔲 on the Standard toolbar. The three pages of the document are displayed as they were earlier in the Print Preview window, although this time you can see a line of text at the top of pages 2 and 3. To read the header text, you need to increase the magnification.

2. If necessary, click the **Magnifier** button 🔲 on the Print Preview toolbar to select it.

3. Move the pointer 🔍 over the second page of the document and then click the header text at the top of the page. The Print Preview window zooms in on the header text for page 2, as shown in Figure 3-13.

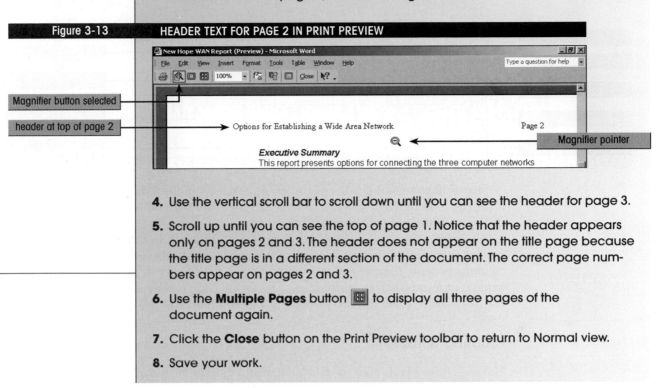

| Figure 3-13 | HEADER TEXT FOR PAGE 2 IN PRINT PREVIEW |

Magnifier button selected

header at top of page 2

Options for Establishing a Wide Area Network   Page 2

Magnifier pointer

Executive Summary
This report presents options for connecting the three computer networks

4. Use the vertical scroll bar to scroll down until you can see the header for page 3.

5. Scroll up until you can see the top of page 1. Notice that the header appears only on pages 2 and 3. The header does not appear on the title page because the title page is in a different section of the document. The correct page numbers appear on pages 2 and 3.

6. Use the **Multiple Pages** button 🔳 to display all three pages of the document again.

7. Click the **Close** button on the Print Preview toolbar to return to Normal view.

8. Save your work.

The report now has the required header. You have formatted Caitlyn's report so that the results are professional-looking, clearly presented, and easy to read. Next, you will add a table that summarizes the costs of the various WAN options.

Inserting Tables

Using Word, you can quickly organize data and arrange text in an easy-to-read table format. A **table** is information arranged in horizontal rows and vertical columns. As shown in Figure 3-14, table rows are commonly referred to by number (row 1, row 2, and so forth), while columns are commonly referred to by letter (column A on the far left, then column B and so forth). However, you do not see row and column numbers on the screen. The area where a row and column intersect is called a **cell**. Each cell is identified by a column and row label. For example, the cell in the upper-left corner of a table is cell A1 (column A, row 1), the cell to the right of that is cell B1, the cell below cell A1 is A2, and so forth. The table's structure is shown by **gridlines**, which are light gray lines that define the rows and columns. By default, gridlines do not appear on the printed page. You can emphasize specific parts of a table on the printed page by adding a **border** (a line the prints along the side of a table cell).

Figure 3-14 ELEMENTS OF A WORD TABLE

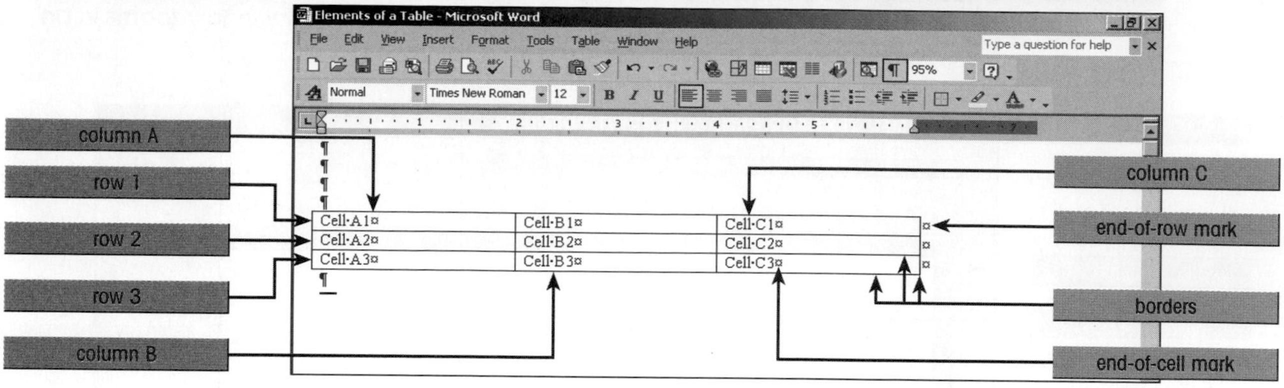

Depending on your needs, you can create a blank table and then insert information into it (as you'll do next), or you can convert existing text into a table (as you'll do in the Case Problems at the end of this tutorial).

You may be wondering why you can't use tabs to align text in columns. Tabs work well for smaller amounts of information, such as two columns with three or four rows, but tabs and columns become tedious and difficult to work with when you need to organize a larger amount of more complex information. The Word Table feature allows you to quickly organize data and to place text and graphics in a more legible format.

Creating a Table

You can create a table with equal column widths quickly by using the Insert Table button on the Standard toolbar. (You will use this technique to create the table Caitilyn requested.) You also can create a table by dragging the Draw Table pointer to draw the table structure you want. (You'll practice this method in the Case Problems.) However you create a table, you can modify it by using commands on the Table menu or the buttons on the Tables and Borders toolbar.

Caitilyn wants you to create a table that summarizes information in the Tyger Networks report. Figure 3-15 shows a sketch of what Caitilyn wants the table to look like. The table will allow the members of the New Hope board of directors to see at a glance the cost of each option. The top row of the table, called the **heading row**, identifies the type of information in each column.

Figure 3-15 TABLE SKETCH

Type of Connection	Monthly Charge
ISDN	$50 to $60
DSL	$80
T1	$1000 to $2000

Inserting a Page Break

Before you begin creating the table, you need to insert a page break so that the table will appear on a separate page.

To insert a page break:

1. Verify that the document is displayed in Normal view.

2. Press **Ctrl+End** to position the insertion point at the end of the report.

3. Press **Ctrl+Enter**. A dotted line with the words "Page Break" appears in the document window. *Note*: You also can add a page break using the Break dialog box you used earlier to insert a section break.

   TROUBLE? If you do not see the words "Page Break," check to make sure the document is displayed in Normal view.

4. Scroll down until the page break is positioned near the top of the document window.

The insertion point is now at the beginning of a new page, where you want to insert the table.

Inserting a Blank Table

You'll use the Insert Table button to insert a blank table structure into the new page. Then you can type the necessary information directly into the table.

To create a blank table using the Insert Table button:

1. Click the **Insert Table** button 📄 on the Standard toolbar. A drop-down grid resembling a miniature table appears below the Insert Table button. The grid starts with four rows and five columns for the table. You can drag the pointer to select as many rows and columns as you need. In this case, you need four rows and two columns.

2. Position the pointer in the upper-left cell of the grid, and then click and drag the pointer down and across the grid until you highlight four rows and two columns. As you drag the pointer across the grid, Word indicates the size of the table (rows by columns) at the bottom of the grid.

3. When the table size is 4 × 2, release the mouse button. An empty table, four rows by two columns, appears in your document with the insertion point blinking in the upper-left corner (cell A1). The two columns are of equal width. Each cell contains an end-of-cell mark, and each row contains an end-of-row mark. See Figure 3-16.

| Figure 3-16 | EMPTY TABLE IN NORMAL VIEW |

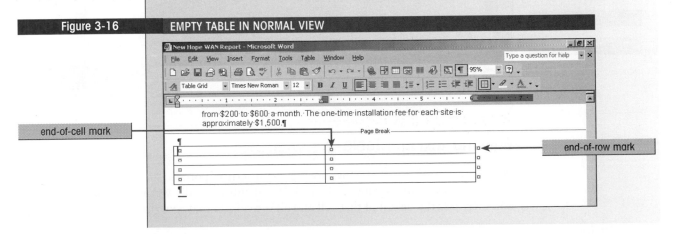

> TROUBLE? If your table is displayed in Print Layout view, switch to Normal view and then compare your table to Figure 3-16.
>
> TROUBLE? If you don't see the end-of-cell and end-of-row marks, you need to show nonprinting characters. Click the Show/Hide button ¶ on the Standard toolbar to show nonprinting characters.
>
> TROUBLE? If you see the Tables and Borders toolbar displayed along with the new blank table, close it. You will learn how to use the Tables and Borders toolbar later in this tutorial.

When working with tables and graphics, it's helpful to switch to Print Layout view, which allows you to get a better sense of the overall layout of the page, including the headers. Also, some special table features are only available in Print Layout view. You'll switch to Print Layout view in the following steps.

To display the table structure in Print Layout view:

1. Click the **Print Layout View** button 🔳. If necessary, change the **Zoom** setting (in the Standard toolbar) to **100%**. The table is displayed in Print Layout view, where you can see the column widths indicated on the horizontal ruler. Also, notice that the document header is visible in Print Layout view.

2. Move the mouse pointer over the empty table. The Table Move handle appears in the table's upper-left corner, and the Table Resize handle appears in the lower-right corner. You don't need to use either of these handles now, but you should understand their function. To quickly select the entire table, you can click the Table Move handle. Then you can move the entire table by dragging the Table Move handle. To change the size of the entire table, you could drag the Table Resize handle. See Figure 3-17.

Figure 3-17   **EMPTY TABLE IN PRINT LAYOUT VIEW**

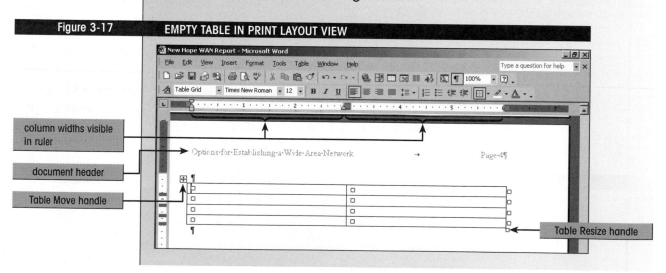

Entering Text in a Table

You can enter text in a table by moving the insertion point to a cell and typing. If the text takes up more than one line in the cell, Word automatically wraps the text to the next line and increases the height of that cell and all the cells in that row. To move the insertion point to another cell in the table, you can either click in that cell or use the Tab key. Figure 3-18 summarizes the keystrokes for moving the insertion point within a table.

Figure 3-18 | **KEYSTROKES FOR MOVING AROUND A TABLE**

PRESS	TO MOVE THE INSERTION POINT
Tab or →	One cell to the right, or to the first cell in the next row
Shift+Tab or ←	One cell to the left, or to the last cell in the previous row
Alt+Home	To the first cell of the current row
Alt+End	To the last cell of the current row
Alt+PageUp	To the top cell of the current column
Alt+PageDown	To the bottom cell of the current column
↑	One cell up in the current column
↓	One cell down in the current column

Now you are ready to insert information into the table.

To insert data into the table:

1. Verify that the insertion point is located in cell **A1** (in the upper-left corner).

2. Type **Type of Connection**.

3. Press the **Tab** key to move to cell B1. See Figure 3-19.

Figure 3-19 | **ENTERING TEXT IN THE TABLE**

pressing Tab moved insertion point to cell B1

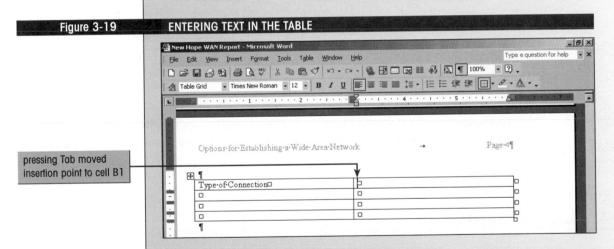

TROUBLE? If Word created a new paragraph in cell A1 rather than moving the insertion point to cell B1, you accidentally pressed the Enter key instead of the Tab key. Press the Backspace key to remove the paragraph mark, and then press the Tab key to move to cell B1.

4. Type **Monthly Charge** and then press the **Tab** key to move to cell A2. Notice that when you press the Tab key in the last column of the table, the insertion point moves to the first column in the next row.

You have finished entering the heading row, the row that identifies the information in each column. Now you can enter the information about the various WAN options.

To continue entering information in the table:

1. Type **ISDN** and then press the **Tab** key to move to cell B2.

2. Type **$50 to $60** and then press the **Tab** key to move the insertion point to cell A3.

3. Type the remaining information for the table, as shown in Figure 3-20, pressing the **Tab** key to move from cell to cell. Don't worry if the text in your table doesn't wrap the same way as shown here. You'll change the column widths in the next session.

Figure 3-20   **TABLE WITH COMPLETED INFORMATION**

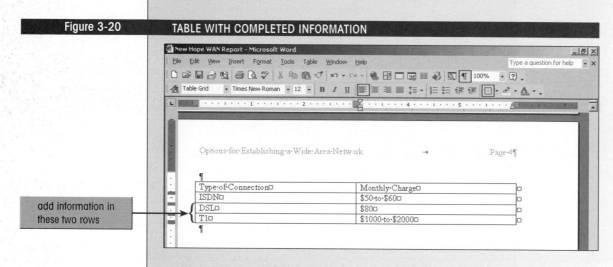

add information in these two rows

TROUBLE? If a new row (row 5) appeared at the bottom of your table, you pressed the Tab key when the insertion point was in cell B4, the last cell in the table. Click the Undo button on the Standard toolbar to remove row 5 from the table.

4. Save your work.

Keep in mind that many document-editing features, such as the Backspace key, the copy-and-paste feature, the Undo button, and the AutoCorrect feature, work the same way in a table as they do in the rest of the document. As you do in a paragraph, you must select text in a table to edit it. You will edit and format this table in the next session.

Session 3.1 QUICK CHECK

1. Define the following in your own words:
   a. tab stop
   b. cell
   c. table
   d. decimal-aligned tab stop
   e. section (of a document)

2. Explain how to center the title page vertically between the top and bottom margins.

3. What is the difference between a header and a footer?

4. Describe how to insert a blank table consisting of four columns and six rows.

5. How do you move the insertion point from one row to the next in a table?

6. How do you insert the page number in a header?

7. Explain how to insert a new tab stop.

8. Describe a situation in which you would want to divide a document into sections.

9. Describe a situation in which it would be better to use a table rather than tab stops.

10. Explain how to select an entire table.

SESSION 3.2	In this session you will learn how to change the table you just created. First, you will display the Tables and Borders toolbar and rearrange the existing rows, and then you will learn how to add and delete rows and columns. Next, you will format the table to improve its appearance.

Displaying the Tables and Borders Toolbar

The **Tables and Borders toolbar** contains a number of useful buttons that simplify the process of working with tables. You'll display the Tables and Borders toolbar in the following steps.

To open the Tables and Borders toolbar:

1. If you took a break after the previous session, make sure Word is running and that the New Hope WAN Report document is open. Check that the nonprinting characters are displayed, that the document is displayed in Print Layout view, and that the document is scrolled so that the table is visible.

2. Click the **Tables and Borders** button 🖼 on the Standard toolbar. The Tables and Borders toolbar appears.

3. Move the mouse pointer over the table. The Draw Table pointer ✐ appears. You can use this pointer to add new rows or columns in a table, and to add borders between cells. You'll have a chance to practice using this pointer in the Case Problems at the end of this tutorial. For now you'll turn it off.

4. Click the **Draw Table** button 🖉 on the Tables and Borders toolbar. The pointer changes to an I-beam pointer I.

5. If necessary, drag the Tables and Borders toolbar down and to the right, so that it doesn't block your view of the table, as shown in Figure 3-21.

Figure 3-21 POSITIONING THE TABLES AND BORDERS TOOLBAR

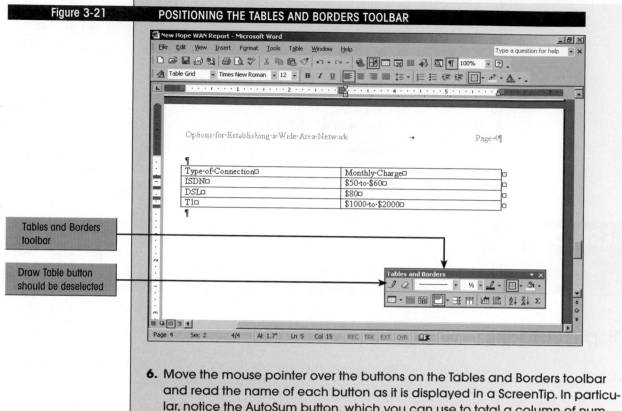

6. Move the mouse pointer over the buttons on the Tables and Borders toolbar and read the name of each button as it is displayed in a ScreenTip. In particular, notice the AutoSum button, which you can use to total a column of numbers; the Merge Cells button, which you can use to combine multiple cells into one cell; and the Split Cells button, which you can use to divide one cell into multiple cells. You'll have a chance to practice using these buttons in the Review Assignments and Case Problems at the end of this tutorial. Notice also the two Sort buttons, which you can use to rearrange the rows in a table. You will use the Sort Ascending button in the next section.

Sorting Rows in a Table

The term **sort** refers to the process of rearranging information in alphabetical, numerical, or chronological order. When you sort a table, you arrange the rows based on the contents of one of the columns. For example, you could sort the table you just created based on the contents of the Type of Connection column—either in ascending alphabetical order (from *A* to *Z*) or in descending alphabetical order (from *Z* to *A*). Alternately, you could sort the table based on the contents of the Monthly Charge column—either in descending numerical order (highest to lowest) or in ascending numerical order (lowest to highest). When you sort table data, Word usually does not sort the heading row along with the other information, but instead leaves the heading row at the top of the table.

Caitilyn would like you to sort the table in ascending alphabetical order, based on the contents of the Type of Connection column. You start by positioning the insertion point in that column.

To sort the information in the table:

1. Click cell **A2** (which contains the text "ISDN"). The insertion point is now located in the Type of Connection column.

2. Click the **Sort Ascending** button 🔠 on the Tables and Borders toolbar. Rows 2 through 4 are now arranged alphabetically according to the text in the Type of Connection column. Note that Word did not sort the header row along with the other rows. The header row remains in its original position at the top of the table. See Figure 3-22.

Figure 3-22	TABLE AFTER BEING SORTED

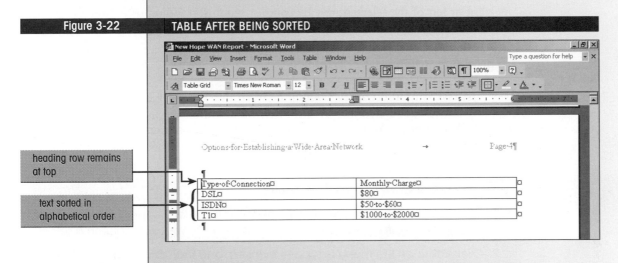

heading row remains at top

text sorted in alphabetical order

TROUBLE? If the sort was unsuccessful, immediately click the Undo button on the Standard toolbar, and then repeat Steps 1 and 2.

Caitilyn stops by and asks you to add an "Installation Fee" column. She also would like you to insert a new row with information about a Fractional T1 connection.

Modifying an Existing Table Structure

You will often need to modify a table structure by adding or deleting rows and columns. Figure 3-23 summarizes ways to insert or delete rows and columns in a table.

Figure 3-23	WAYS TO INSERT OR DELETE TABLE ROWS AND COLUMNS

TO	DO THIS
Insert a row within a table	Select the row below where you want the row added, click Table on the menu bar, point to Insert, and then click Rows Above.
	Select the row below where you want the row added, and then click the Insert Rows button on the Standard toolbar.
Insert a row at the end of a table	Position the insertion point in the cell at the far right of the bottom row, then press the Tab key.
Insert a column within a table	Select the column to the right of where you want the column added, click Table on the menu bar, point to Insert, then click Columns to the Right.
	Select the column to the right of where you want the column added, then click the Insert Columns button on the Standard toolbar.
Insert a column at the end of a table	Select the end-of-row markers to the right of the table, click Table on the menu bar, point to Insert, then click Columns to the Left.
	Select the end-of-row markers to the right of the table, and then click the Insert Columns button on the Standard toolbar.
Delete a row	Select the row or rows to be deleted, click Table on the menu bar, point to Delete, and then click Rows.
Delete a column	Select the column or columns to be deleted, click Table on the menu bar, point to Delete, and then click Columns.

When you select part of a table, new buttons sometimes appear on the Standard toolbar to help you modify the table structure. For instance, when you select a column, the Insert Columns button appears to help you insert a new column in the table. In most cases, however, you'll find it easiest to use menu commands to add and delete rows and columns, because the menu commands allow you to specify exactly where you want to modify the table. For instance, by using a menu command, you can indicate whether you want to insert a column to the right or left of the selected row. By contrast, the Insert Columns button always inserts a new column to the left of the selected column.

Inserting Columns in a Table

Your first task is to insert a new column between the Type of Connection column and the Monthly Charge column. This column will contain information on the Installation Charge for each WAN option. You need to begin by selecting the column to the left of the location where you want to insert a column.

To insert a column in the table:

1. Click in cell **A1** (which contains the heading "Type of Connection") and drag the mouse pointer down until the entire Type of Connection column is selected.

2. Click **Table** on the menu bar, point to **Insert**, and then click **Columns to the Right**. A new column is inserted in the table to the right of the Type of Connection column.

   Note: If you had selected two columns in Step 1, Word would have inserted two new columns in the table. If you had selected three columns, Word would have inserted three columns, and so on.

3. Click in the new cell **B1** and enter the Installation Charge heading and data shown in Figure 3-24.

| Figure 3-24 | NEW INSTALLATION CHARGE COLUMN |

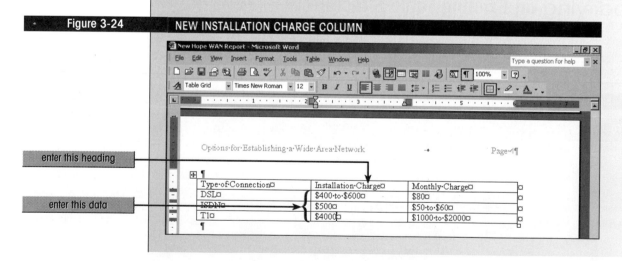

Inserting Rows in a Table

Next you need to insert a row with information on a more economical type of T1 connection, called a fractional T1 connection. You could insert this row in its alphabetical position in the table (below the DSL row). But it's quicker to add the row to the end of the table, and then resort the table.

To insert a row at the bottom of the table:

1. Click the bottom cell in the Monthly Charge column (which contains "$1000 to $2000"). The insertion point is now located in the last cell in the table.

2. Press the **Tab** key. A blank row is added to the bottom of the table.

   TROUBLE? If a blank row is not added to the bottom of the table, click the Undo button on the Standard toolbar. Check to make sure the insertion point is in the rightmost cell of the bottom row, and then press the Tab key.

3. Enter the following information in the new row:

   Type of Connection: **Fractional T1**

   Installation Charge: **$1500**

   Monthly Charge: **$200 to $600**

4. Click anywhere in the Type of Connection column, and then click the **Sort Ascending** button on the Tables and Borders toolbar. The table rows are rearranged in alphabetical order, with the Fractional T1 row positioned below the DSL row, as shown in Figure 3-25.

Figure 3-25	SORTED TABLE WITH NEW ROW

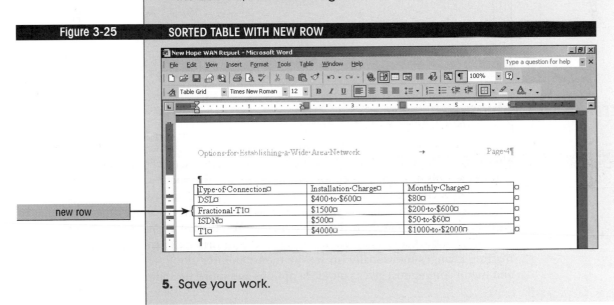

5. Save your work.

After reviewing the table, Caitilyn decides not to include the information on the full T1 connection, because it is far too expensive for New Hope's current budget. She asks you to delete the T1 row.

Deleting Rows and Columns in a Table

With Word, you can delete either the contents of the cells or the structure of the cells. To delete the contents of a table, you select one or more cells, and then press the Delete key. However, to delete both the contents and structure of a selected row or column from the table entirely, you must use one of the methods described earlier in Figure 3-23. Right now you'll use a menu command to delete the T1 row.

To delete a row using the Table menu:

1. Click the selection bar next to row 5 to select the T1 row. (Select the T1 row, at the bottom of the table, *not* the Fractional T1 row.)

2. Click **Table** on the menu bar, point to **Delete**, and then click **Rows**. The selected row is deleted from the table. See Figure 3-26.

Figure 3-26   **TABLE AFTER DELETING ROW**

row removed from table

3. Save your work.

Formatting Tables

Word provides a variety of ways to enhance the appearance of the tables you create. You can alter the width of the columns and the height of the rows, or change the alignment of text within the cells or the alignment of the table between the document's left and right margins. You can also change the appearance of the table borders, and add a shaded background. If you happen to be in a hurry, you can format an entire table at one time using the **Table AutoFormat command** on the Table menu. (You'll have a chance to practice using this command in the Case Problems at the end of this tutorial.) In general, however, making formatting changes individually (using the mouse pointer along with various toolbar buttons and menu commands) gives you more options and more flexibility.

Changing Column Width and Row Height

Sometimes you'll want to adjust the column widths in a table to make the text easier to read. If you want to specify an exact width for a column, you should use the Table Properties command on the Table menu. However, it's usually easiest to drag the column's right border to a new position. Alternately, you can double-click a column border to have the column width adjust automatically to accommodate the widest entry in the column.

The Type of Connection column and the Monthly Charge column are too wide for the information they contain. You'll change these widths by dragging the column borders, using the ruler as a guide. Keep in mind that to change the width of a column, you need to drag the column's right-hand border.

To change the width of columns by dragging the borders:

1. Verify that the table is displayed in Print Layout view. Also, make sure that the insertion point is located anywhere within the table, without any part of the table selected.

2. Move the pointer over the border between columns A and B (in other words, over the right border of column A, the "Type of Connection" column). The pointer changes to ◄||►.

3. Press and hold down the **Alt** key and the mouse button. The column widths are displayed in the ruler, as shown in Figure 3-27. (The widths on your computer might differ slightly.)

Figure 3-27   COLUMN WIDTHS DISPLAYED IN RULER

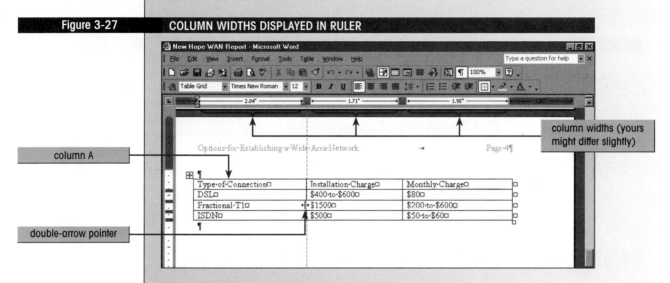

4. While holding down the **Alt** key, drag the pointer to the left until column A is about **1.4** inches wide, and then release the mouse button and the Alt key. As the width of column A decreases, the width of column B (the Installation Charge column) increases. However, the overall width of the table does not change.

   TROUBLE? If you can't get the column width to exactly 1.4 inches, make it as close to that width as possible.

Now you need to adjust the width of both columns B and C. You could do this by dragging the column border, as you did for column A. But it's much faster to double-click the right-hand border of each column.

To change the width of columns B and C:

1. Double-click the right-hand border of column B (the Installation Charge column). The column shrinks, leaving just enough room for the widest entry in the column (the column heading "Installation Charge").

2. Repeat this procedure to adjust the width of column C (the Monthly Charge column). All three columns in the table are now just wide enough to accommodate the column headings.

You also can change the height of rows by dragging a border. You'll make row 1 (the header row) taller so it is more prominent.

To change the height of row 1:

1. Position the pointer over the bottom border of the header row. The pointer changes to .

2. Press and hold down the **Alt** key and the mouse button. The row heights are displayed in the vertical ruler.

3. While holding down the **Alt** key, drag the pointer down until row 1 is about **0.45** inches high, then release the mouse button and the Alt key. Notice that the height of the other rows in the table is not affected by this change. See Figure 3-28.

Figure 3-28   **TABLE WITH NARROWER COLUMNS AND A WIDER HEADING ROW**

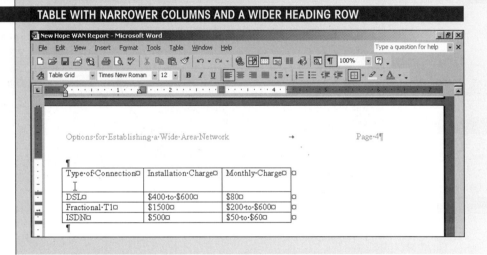

Aligning Text Within Cells

Aligning the text within the cells of a table makes the information easier to read. For example, aligning a column of numbers or percentages along the right margin helps the reader to compare the values quickly. At the same time, centering a row of headings makes a table more visually appealing. You can align text within the active cell the same way you do other text—with the alignment buttons on the Formatting toolbar. However, the Alignment buttons on the Tables and Borders toolbar provide more options.

Caitilyn would like you to align the data in the Installation Charge and Monthly Charge columns along the right side of the columns. The table also would look better with the headings centered. You'll begin by selecting and formatting all of columns B and C.

To right-align the numerical data and center the headings:

1. Move the pointer to the top of column B until the pointer changes to ↓. Press and hold the left mouse button, and then drag right to select columns B and C.

2. Click the **Align Right** button ☰ on the Formatting toolbar. The numbers line up along the right edges of the cells.

TROUBLE? If more than just the numbers and column headings are right-aligned within the table, you may have selected the wrong block of cells. Click the Undo button on the Standard toolbar, and then repeat Steps 1 through 3.

Notice that in the process of formatting columns B and C, you right-aligned two of the headings ("Installation Charge" and "Monthly Charge"). You will reformat those headings in the next step, when you center the text in row 1 both horizontally and vertically in each cell.

3. Click the selection bar next to row 1. All of row 1 is selected.

4. Click the **Align** list arrow on the Tables and Borders toolbar to display a palette of nine alignment options.

5. Click the **Align Center** button in the middle of the palette. The text is centered both horizontally and vertically in the row.

6. Click anywhere in the table to deselect the row, and then save your work. See Figure 3-29.

Figure 3-29	TABLE WITH NEWLY ALIGNED TEXT

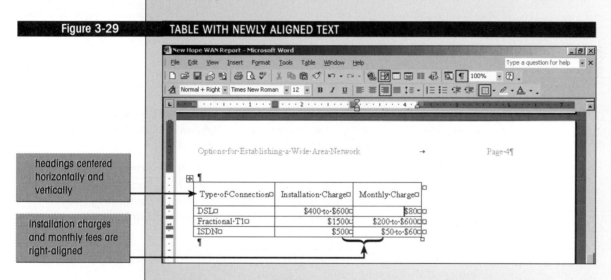

headings centered horizontally and vertically

installation charges and monthly fees are right-aligned

TROUBLE? If more than just the heading row is centered, click the Undo button on the Standard toolbar, and then repeat Steps 3 through 6.

Changing Borders

Gridlines and borders are different parts of a table. **Gridlines** are light gray lines that indicate the structure of the table on the screen but do not show up on the printed page. **Borders** are darker lines overlaying the gridlines, which do appear on the printed page. When you create a table using the Insert Table button, Word automatically applies a thin black border, so you can't actually see the underlying gridlines.

After you have created a table, you can add new borders or erase existing borders by using the buttons on the Tables and Borders toolbar. You can modify an existing border by changing its **line weight** (its thickness). You can also choose a different **line style**—for instance, you can change a single straight-line border to a triple dotted line.

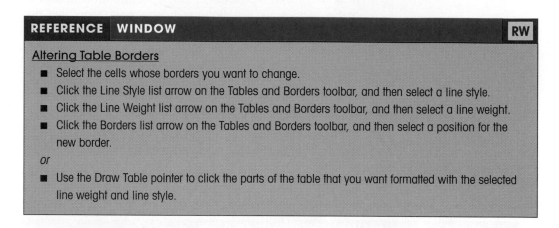

REFERENCE WINDOW   **RW**

Altering Table Borders

- Select the cells whose borders you want to change.
- Click the Line Style list arrow on the Tables and Borders toolbar, and then select a line style.
- Click the Line Weight list arrow on the Tables and Borders toolbar, and then select a line weight.
- Click the Borders list arrow on the Tables and Borders toolbar, and then select a position for the new border.

or

- Use the Draw Table pointer to click the parts of the table that you want formatted with the selected line weight and line style.

To modify the table's borders:

1. Select row 1 (the heading row).

2. Click the **Line Weight** list arrow ⬚ on the Tables and Borders toolbar, and then click **2 ¼ pt**. Next you will examine the options available in the List Style list. Currently, a single straight-line border is selected.

3. Click the **Line Style** list arrow ⬚ on the Tables and Borders toolbar, and then scroll down to view the various options. Note that you can remove borders (without removing the underlying gridlines) by selecting the No Border option. Caitilyn prefers a simple border, so you decide not to change the current selection.

4. Press the **Esc** key. The Line Style list closes. You have selected a single straight-line border, with a thickness of 2 points.

5. Click the **Borders** list arrow ⬚ on the Tables and Borders toolbar. A palette of options appears. You want to insert a thick border at the bottom of Row 1, so you need to use the Bottom Border option.

6. Click the **Bottom Border** ⬚ option (in the bottom row of the Borders palette, third from the left). The new border style is applied to the bottom border of row 1.

7. Click anywhere in the table to deselect the row. See Figure 3-30.

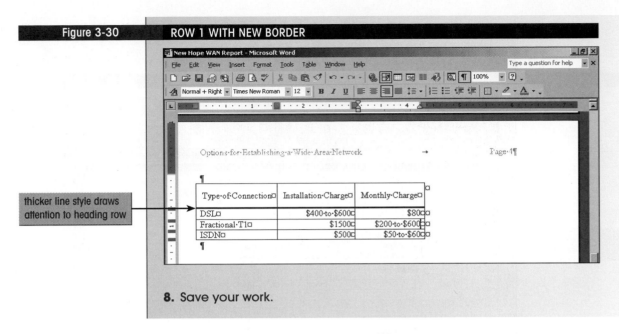

Figure 3-30   ROW 1 WITH NEW BORDER

thicker line style draws attention to heading row

8. Save your work.

Changing the borders has made the table more attractive. You'll finish formatting the table by adding shading to the cells containing the headings.

Adding Shading

Adding **shading** (a gray or colored background) is useful in tables when you want to emphasize headings, totals, or other important items. Generally, when you add shading to a table, you also need to bold the shaded text to make it easier to read.

You will now add a light gray shading to the heading row and then format the headings in bold.

To add shading to the heading row and change the headings to bold:

1. Click the selection bar to the left of row 1 to select the heading row of the table.

2. Click the **Shading Color** list arrow 🎨 ▾ on the Tables and Borders toolbar. A palette of shading options opens.

3. Point to the fifth gray square from the left, in the top row. The ScreenTip "Gray-15%" appears.

4. Click the **Gray-15%** square. A light gray background appears in the heading row. Now you need to format the text in bold to make the headings stand out from the shading.

5. Click the **Bold** button 🅱 on the Formatting toolbar to make the headings bold. The wider letters take up more space, so Word breaks one or more of the headings into two lines within row 1.

TROUBLE? If any of the headings break incorrectly (for example, if the "n" in "Installation" moves to the next line), you might need to widen columns to accommodate the bold letters. Drag the column borders as necessary to adjust the column widths so that all the column headings are displayed correctly.

6. Click in the table to deselect row 1. Your table should look like Figure 3-31, although the line breaks in your table may differ.

Figure 3-31 | BOLDED HEADINGS WITH SHADING

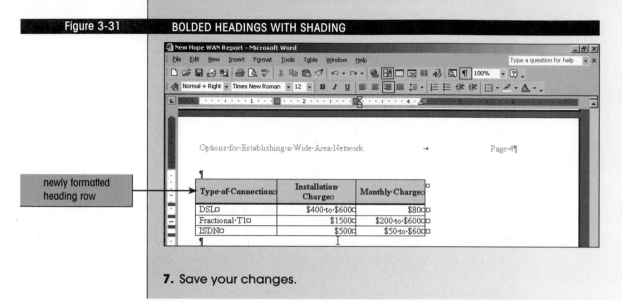

newly formatted
heading row

7. Save your changes.

Centering a Table

If a table doesn't fill the entire page width, you can center it between the left and right margins. The Center button on the Formatting toolbar centers only text within each selected cell. It does not center the entire table across the page. To center a table across the page (between the left and right margins), you need to use the Table Properties command.

Caitilyn thinks the table would look better if it was centered between the left and right margins.

To center the table across the page:

1. Click anywhere in the table, click **Table** on the menu bar, and then click **Table Properties**. The Table Properties dialog box opens.

2. Click the **Table** tab if necessary.

3. In the Alignment section click the **Center** option. See Figure 3-32.

Figure 3-32   **TABLE TAB OF THE TABLE PROPERTIES DIALOG BOX**

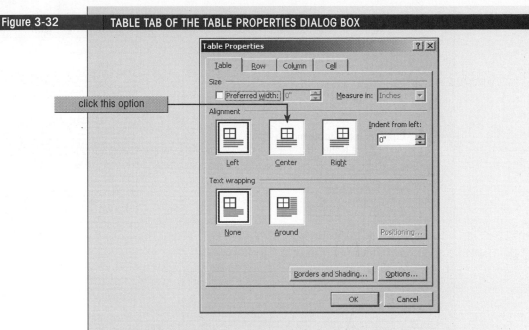

click this option

4. Click the **OK** button. The table centers between the left and right margins.

5. Save your work and then close the Tables and Borders toolbar.

Now that you're finished with the table, you want to print a copy of the full report for Caitilyn. You'll preview the report first.

To preview the report:

1. Click the **Print Preview** button 🔍 on the Standard toolbar to open the Print Preview window.

2. Use the **Multiple Pages** button 🖽 on the Print Preview toolbar to display all four pages of the report. Verify that the table is properly formatted.

3. Click the **Print** button 🖨 on the Print Preview toolbar to print the report, and then close the document and exit Word.

You now have a hard copy of the New Hope report including the table, which summarizes the costs for creating a WAN. Your four-page report should look like Figure 3-33. You give the report to Caitilyn, so that she can add a brief introduction to the table.

Figure 3-33 NEW HOPE WAN REPORT

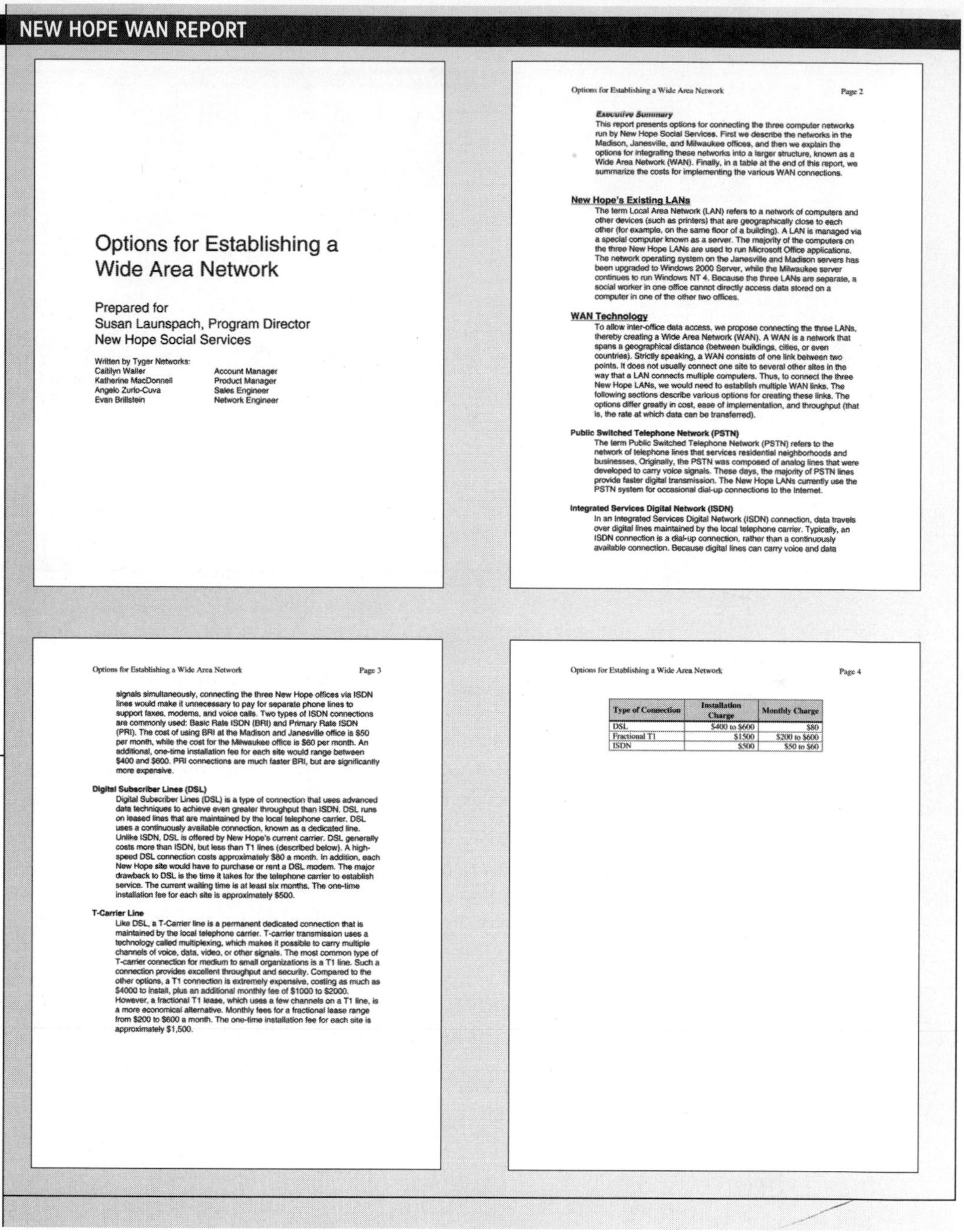

Options for Establishing a Wide Area Network

Prepared for
Susan Launspach, Program Director
New Hope Social Services

Written by Tyger Networks:

Caitilyn Waller	Account Manager
Katherine MacDonnell	Product Manager
Angelo Zurlo-Cuva	Sales Engineer
Evan Brillstein	Network Engineer

Options for Establishing a Wide Area Network — Page 2

Executive Summary
This report presents options for connecting the three computer networks run by New Hope Social Services. First we describe the networks in the Madison, Janesville, and Milwaukee offices, and then we explain the options for integrating these networks into a larger structure, known as a Wide Area Network (WAN). Finally, in a table at the end of this report, we summarize the costs for implementing the various WAN connections.

New Hope's Existing LANs
The term Local Area Network (LAN) refers to a network of computers and other devices (such as printers) that are geographically close to each other (for example, on the same floor of a building). A LAN is managed via a special computer known as a server. The majority of the computers on the three New Hope LANs are used to run Microsoft Office applications. The network operating system on the Janesville and Madison servers has been upgraded to Windows 2000 Server, while the Milwaukee server continues to run Windows NT 4. Because the three LANs are separate, a social worker in one office cannot directly access data stored on a computer in one of the other two offices.

WAN Technology
To allow inter-office data access, we propose connecting the three LANs, thereby creating a Wide Area Network (WAN). A WAN is a network that spans a geographical distance (between buildings, cities, or even countries). Strictly speaking, a WAN consists of one link between two points. It does not usually connect one site to several other sites in the way that a LAN connects multiple computers. Thus, to connect the three New Hope LANs, we would need to establish multiple WAN links. The following sections describe various options for creating these links. The options differ greatly in cost, ease of implementation, and throughput (that is, the rate at which data can be transferred).

Public Switched Telephone Network (PSTN)
The term Public Switched Telephone Network (PSTN) refers to the network of telephone lines that services residential neighborhoods and businesses. Originally, the PSTN was composed of analog lines that were developed to carry voice signals. These days, the majority of PSTN lines provide faster digital transmission. The New Hope LANs currently use the PSTN system for occasional dial-up connections to the Internet.

Integrated Services Digital Network (ISDN)
In an Integrated Services Digital Network (ISDN) connection, data travels over digital lines maintained by the local telephone carrier. Typically, an ISDN connection is a dial-up connection, rather than a continuously available connection. Because digital lines can carry voice and data

Options for Establishing a Wide Area Network — Page 3

signals simultaneously, connecting the three New Hope offices via ISDN lines would make it unnecessary to pay for separate phone lines to support faxes, modems, and voice calls. Two types of ISDN connections are commonly used: Basic Rate ISDN (BRI) and Primary Rate ISDN (PRI). The cost of using BRI at the Madison and Janesville office is $50 per month, while the cost for the Milwaukee office is $60 per month. An additional, one-time installation fee for each site would range between $400 and $600. PRI connections are much faster BRI, but are significantly more expensive.

Digital Subscriber Lines (DSL)
Digital Subscriber Lines (DSL) is a type of connection that uses advanced data techniques to achieve even greater throughput than ISDN. DSL runs on leased lines that are maintained by the local telephone carrier. DSL uses a continuously available connection, known as a dedicated line. Unlike ISDN, DSL is offered by New Hope's current carrier. DSL generally costs more than ISDN, but less than T1 lines (described below). A high-speed DSL connection costs approximately $80 a month. In addition, each New Hope site would have to purchase or rent a DSL modem. The major drawback to DSL is the time it takes for the telephone carrier to establish service. The current waiting time is at least six months. The one-time installation fee for each site is approximately $500.

T-Carrier Line
Like DSL, a T-Carrier line is a permanent dedicated connection that is maintained by the local telephone carrier. T-carrier transmission uses a technology called multiplexing, which makes it possible to carry multiple channels of voice, data, video, or other signals. The most common type of T-carrier connection for medium to small organizations is a T1 line. Such a connection provides excellent throughput and security. Compared to the other options, a T1 connection is extremely expensive, costing as much as $4000 to install, plus an additional monthly fee of $1000 to $2000. However, a fractional T1 lease, which uses a few channels on a T1 line, is a more economical alternative. Monthly fees for a fractional lease range from $200 to $600 a month. The one-time installation fee for each site is approximately $1,500.

Options for Establishing a Wide Area Network — Page 4

Type of Connection	Installation Charge	Monthly Charge
DSL	$400 to $600	$80
Fractional T1	$1500	$200 to $600
ISDN	$500	$50 to $60

Session 3.2 QUICK CHECK

1. How do you adjust the width of the columns in a table?
2. Explain how to alter the border on the bottom of a heading row.
3. Define the following terms in your own words:
   a. line weight
   b. line style
   c. border
   d. shading

4. Explain how to add a row to the bottom of a table.

5. What's the fastest way to modify a column to accommodate the widest entry in the column?

6. In what order would the following numbers appear in a table if you sorted them in ascending numerical order: 25, 10, 75, 45?

7. How do you center a table between the left and right margins?

REVIEW ASSIGNMENTS

Susan Launspach, the program director at New Hope Social Services, has contacted Caitilyn Waller about another issue related to the agency's local area networks (LANs). Since last January, employees at the Madison office have experienced a number of problems, including malfunctioning printers and difficulty retrieving e-mail. Susan would like to hire Tyger Networks to resolve the network problems, a process known as troubleshooting. To secure the necessary funding, she needs a report outlining the basic issues, which she can then distribute to New Hope's board of directors. Working with a task force at Tyger Networks, Caitilyn has completed a draft of this report. It's your job to format the report and add a table at the end. When you're finished, she would like you to create a separate document that lists only the new equipment recommended by Tyger Networks. Complete the following:

1. If necessary, start Word, make sure your Data Disk is in the appropriate disk drive, and check your screen to make sure your settings match those in the tutorial. Display non-printing characters as necessary and switch to Print Layout view.

2. Open the file **Trouble** from the Review folder for Tutorial 3 on your Data Disk, and then save it as **Troubleshooting Report** in the same folder.

3. Select the list of task force members and their titles, and then insert a left tab stop 2.5 inches from the left margin.

4. Replace "Evan Brillstein" with your name.

5. Divide the document into two sections. Insert a section break so that the executive summary begins on a new page.

Explore   6. Vertically align the first section of the document using the Justified alignment option in the Page Setup dialog box, and view the results in Print Preview.

Explore   7. Add a footer to section 2. Click View on the menu bar, and then click Header and Footer. Use the Word online Help system to learn the functions of the buttons on the Header and Footer toolbar. Then, on the Header and Footer toolbar, click the Switch Between Header and Footer button to move to the footer area, then use the Show Next button (if necessary) to move from the section 1 footer to the section 2 footer. Click the Same as Previous button to deselect it. Using the same techniques you used to create a header in the tutorial, create a footer for section 2 that reads "Troubleshooting Network Problems Report" at the left margin. Insert the current date at the right margin. (*Hint*: Use the Insert Date button on the Header and Footer toolbar to insert the date.) Use the Formatting toolbar to format the footer and date in 9-point bold Arial.

8. Create a header for section 2 that aligns your name at the left margin and centers the page number preceded by the word "Page". Don't forget to deselect the Same as Previous button. (*Hint*: To center the page number, use the second tab stop.) Click Close on the Header and Footer toolbar, and then save your work so far.

9. Insert a page break at the end of the document, and then create the table shown in Figure 3-34.

Figure 3-34

Troubleshooting Options	Explanation	Cost
Onsite Troubleshooting	40 hours of onsite troubleshooting, at $120 an hour	$4800
Cable Checker	3 devices for each office, at $225 a piece	$675
Cable Tester	1 device to be shared among the three offices	$1300

10. Display the Tables and Borders toolbar, and then sort the Troubleshooting Options column in ascending order..

11. Insert a new row just below the Cable Tester row, and then enter the following information into the new row:

    Troubleshooting option: Onsite Training

    Explanation: Informational seminar for all Madison employees

    Cost: $300

12. Modify the widths of columns A and C to accommodate only the widest entry in each, and then right-align the data in the Cost column.

13. Increase the height of the heading row and format it appropriately using shading and boldface. Center the headings vertically and horizontally in their cells.

Explore 14. Add a 2¼-point straight-line border around the outside of the table. (*Hint*: Select the entire table, select the line weight, and then use the Outside Border option in the Borders list box.) Add a double ½-point border at the bottom of the heading row.

15. Center the table on the page and then save your work.

16. Use the Table Move handle to select the entire table. Copy the table, open a new, blank document, and paste a copy of the table into the new document. Use the Delete command on the Table menu to delete the Onsite Training and Onsite Troubleshooting rows. Save the document as **Equipment List** in the Review folder for Tutorial 3. Close the document.

17. In the Troubleshooting Report document, insert a new row at the end of the table.

Explore 18. Select cells A6 and B6 (the two leftmost cells in the new row) and then click the Merge Cells button on the Tables and Borders toolbar. Type the text "TOTAL" into the new, merged cell, and then format the text so that it aligns on the right side of the cell. Apply boldface and shading to the new, merged cell to match the heading row.

Explore 19. Click the cell to the right of the TOTAL cell (cell C6) and then click the AutoSum button on the Tables and Borders toolbar. Word automatically sums the various costs, and displays the total ($7075.00) in cell C6.

Explore 20. Change the cost of the Onsite Training to $250, click cell C6, and then click the AutoSum button again. Word automatically updates the total.

21. Save your work, preview the report, print it, and close the document. Close the Tables and Borders toolbar, and then exit Word.

CASE PROBLEMS

Case 1. Sun Porch Bookstore Annual Report As manager of Sun Porch Bookstore in San Diego, California, you must submit an annual report to the Board of Directors. Complete the following:

1. If necessary, start Word, make sure your Data Disk is in the appropriate drive, and check your screen to make sure your settings match those in the tutorials. Switch to Print Layout view.

2. Open the file **SunRep** from the Cases folder for Tutorial 3 on your Data Disk, and save it as **Sun Porch Report** in the same folder.

3. Divide the document into two sections. Begin section 2 with the introduction on a new page.

Explore ▶ 4. Format the title ("Annual Report") and the subtitle ("Sun Porch Bookstore") using the font and font size of your choice. Center the first section vertically, and then select the title and subtitle and center them horizontally using the Center button on the Formatting toolbar. Note that you can combine horizontal and vertical alignment styles.

Explore ▶ 5. Click in section 1, and then create a header for the entire document that aligns your name on the left margin, and the current date on the right margin. Click the Show Next button on the Header and Footer toolbar to view the header text for section 2. Click the Same as Previous button to deselect it.

Explore ▶ 6. While in Header and Footer view, click the Switch between Header and Footer button to switch to the footer area for section 2. Press the Tab key to move the insertion point to the center tab stop, and then type the word "Page" followed by a space and the page number (using the Insert Page Number button on the Header and Footer toolbar). Insert a space, type the word "of", insert another space, and then click the Insert Number of Pages button on the Header and Footer toolbar to insert the total number of pages in the document. Close Header and Footer view when you are finished.

7. Select the list of members under the heading "Board of Directors." Insert a left tab stop 4.0 inches from the left margin, and then save your work.

8. Insert a page break at the end of the document, and then insert a table consisting of four rows and three columns.

9. Insert the headings "Name", "Title", and "Duties". Fill in the rows with the relevant information about the store personnel, which you will find listed in the report in the "Store Management and Personnel" section. Add new rows as needed.

10. Adjust the table column widths so the information is presented attractively.

11. Increase the height of the heading row, use the Tables and Borders toolbar to center the column headings horizontally and vertically, and then bold them.

12. Insert a row in the middle of the table, and add your name to the list of store managers. Adjust the column widths as needed.

13. Format the heading row with a light gray shading of your choice, and then change the outside border of the table to a single 2¼-point line weight.

14. Center the table on the page.

15. Save, preview, print, and close the document. Close the Tables and Borders toolbar, and then exit Word.

Case 2. Top Flight Travel's "Masterpiece Tour" Report Each year Top Flight Travel sponsors a "Masterpiece" tour, which shepherds travelers through a two-week, whirlwind tour of the artistic masterpieces of Europe. The tour director has just completed a report summarizing the most recent tour. It's your job to format the report, which includes one table. Complete the following:

1. If necessary, start Word, make sure your Data Disk is in the appropriate drive, and check your screen to make sure your settings match those in the tutorials. Switch to Print Layout view.

2. Open the file named **Tour** from the Cases folder for Tutorial 3 on your Data Disk, and then save it as **Masterpiece Tour Report** in the same folder.

3. Replace "Your Name" in the first page with your first and last name.

4. Divide the document into two sections. Begin the second section on a new page, with the summary that starts "This report summarizes and evaluates."

5. Vertically align the first section using the Center alignment option.

6. Create a header for section 2 only that contains the centered text "Top Flight Travel". (*Hint*: To center text in the header, use the second tab stop. Deselect the Same as Previous button before you begin.) Format the header text using italics and the font size of your choice.

Explore ▶ 7. On the Header and Footer toolbar, click the Switch Between Header and Footer button to move to the footer area of the document. Using the same techniques you used to create a header in the tutorial, create a footer for section 2 only that aligns "Evaluation Report" on the left margin and the date on the right margin. (*Hint*: Deselect the Same as Previous button first, and then use the Insert Date button on the Header and Footer toolbar to insert the date.) Close Header and Footer view.

Explore ▶ 8. Display the Tables and Borders toolbar. In the table, select the text in column A (the left column), bold the text, and then click the Change Text Direction button (on the Tables and Borders toolbar) twice so that text is formatted vertically, from bottom to top. Adjust the width of column A to accommodate the newly rotated text.

9. Adjust the other row and column widths as necessary.

10. Delete the blank row 2.

11. Format column A with a light colored shading of your choice.

12. Change the border around column A to 2¼-point line weight. Adjust the row heights, if necessary, to display each row heading in one line.

13. Save, preview, print, and close the document. Close the Tables and Borders toolbar, and then exit Word.

Case 3. Contact List for Flower Box Bakery Ken Yamamoto recently opened Flower Box Bakery, a wholesale bakery catering to upscale cafes and tea shops in suburban St. Louis. He has just acquired a list of potential sales contacts from the local chamber of commerce via e-mail. The information consists of names, phone numbers, and managers for a number of new cafes and restaurants in the St. Louis area. The information is formatted as simple text, with the pieces of information separated by commas. Ken asks you to convert this text into a table and then format the table to make it easy to read. Complete the following:

1. Open the file **Contacts** from the Cases folder for Tutorial 3 on your Data Disk, and then save it as **Sales Contacts** in the same folder.

Explore 2. Select the entire document, click Table on the menu bar, point to Convert, and then click Text to Table. In the Convert Text to Table dialog box, make sure the settings indicate that the table should have three columns and that the text is separated by commas. Also, select the "AutoFit to contents" option button, to ensure that columns are sized appropriately, and then click the OK button. Word converts the list into a table.

3. Replace the name "Christian Brook" with your first and last name.

4. Insert a new row at the top of the table and insert some appropriate headings.

Explore 5. When you need to format a table quickly, you can allow Word's AutoFormat command to do the work for you. Click anywhere in the table, click Table on the menu bar, and then click Table AutoFormat to open the Table AutoFormat dialog box. Scroll down the Table styles list box to see the available options. Click options that interest you, and observe the sample tables in the Preview box. Note that you can deselect the checkboxes in the "Apply special formats to" section to remove boldface or shading from columns or rows that don't require it. Select a table style that you think is appropriate for the Contacts table, deselect check boxes as you see fit, and then click the Apply button.

6. Sort the table alphabetically by column A.

Explore 7. Place the pointer over the Table Resize handle, just outside the lower-right corner of the table. Drag the double-arrow pointer to increase the height and width of each cell to a size of your choice. Notice that all the parts of the table increase proportionally.

8. Save your work. Preview the table and then print it.

9. Close the document, and then exit Word.

Case 4. Brochure for Camp Winnemac Angela Freedman is the publicity director for Camp Winnemac, a sleep-away camp for girls located in Northern Michigan. She asks you to create an informational flier announcing the dates for Camp Winnemac's two summer sessions. She gives you a sketch, similar to the one shown in Figure 3-35. You decide to take advantage of the Word table features to structure the information in the sketch.

Figure 3-35

Camp Winnemac	Summer Sessions for Girls Ages 8 to 12	
	Ultimate Sports Rock climbing, kayaking and white water rafting June 6 through July 2	**Equestrian Skills** Western and English style, for new and experienced riders July 6 through August 15
	Camp Winnemac is located in Michigan's Northern Peninsula, and boasts over 140 acres of forests, streams, and trails. The campgrounds include a heated pool, a modern stable, eight log cabin dormitories, and a full-sized dining hall and kitchen. For information, contact Angela Freedman at 456-818-0000.	

1. Open a new, blank document and save it as **Camp Winnemac** in the Cases folder for Tutorial 3.

2. If necessary, switch to Print Layout view and display rulers and the Tables and Borders toolbar.

3. Click the Draw Table button on the Tables and Borders toolbar, if necessary, to select the button and change the pointer to a pencil shape (the Draw Table pointer).

4. Select a single-line line style, with a line weight of 1½ points.

Explore 5. Click in the upper-left corner of the document (near the paragraph mark), and then drag down and to the right to draw a rectangle about 6 inches wide and 3.5 inches high.

Explore 6. Continue to use the Draw Table pointer to draw the columns and rows shown in Figure 3-35. For example, to draw the column border for the "Camp Winnemac" column, click at the top of the rectangle, where you want the column to begin, and drag down to the bottom of the rectangle. Use the same technique to draw rows. If you make a mistake, use the Undo button. To delete a border, click the Eraser button on the Tables and Borders toolbar, click the border you want to erase, and then click the Eraser button again to turn it off. Don't expect to draw the table perfectly the first time. You may have to practice awhile until you become comfortable with the Draw Table pointer, but once you can use it well, you will find it a helpful tool for creating complex tables. Click the Draw Table button on the toolbar again to turn it off.

Explore 7. In the left column, type the text "Camp Winnemac". With the pointer still in that cell, click the Change Text Direction button (on the Tables and Borders toolbar) twice to position the text vertically. Format the text in 26-point Times New Roman, and then center it in the cell using the Align Center option on the Tables and Borders toolbar. (*Hint*: You will probably have to adjust and readjust the row and column borders throughout this project, until all the elements of the table are positioned properly.)

8. Type the remaining text, as shown in Figure 3-35. Replace the name "Angela Freedman" with your own name. Use bold and italic as shown in Figure 3-35 to draw attention to key elements. Use the font styles, font sizes, and alignment options you think appropriate.

Explore 9. Click the Drawing button on the Standard toolbar to display the Drawing toolbar. Now you can insert the Camp Winnemac logo in the upper-right cell, using one of the tools on the Drawing toolbar. Click the upper-right cell, which at this point should be blank. Click the AutoShapes button on the Drawing toolbar, point to Basic Shapes, click the Sun shape. A box appears in the cell with the text "Create your drawing here." Click anywhere within the upper-right cell. The sun shape is inserted in the cell or somewhere nearby. The sun is selected, as indicated by the small circles, called selection handles, that surround it. If necessary, drag the sun to position it neatly within the cell. If the sun is not the right shape, click the lower-right selection handle, and drag up or down to adjust the size of the sun so that it fits within the cell borders more precisely. With the sun still selected, click the Fill Color list arrow on the Drawing toolbar, and then click a light pink square in the color palette.

10. Adjust column widths and row heights so that the table is attractive and easy to read.

Explore 11. Now that you have organized the information using the Word table tools, you can remove the borders so that the printed flier doesn't look like a table. Click the Table Move handle to select the entire table, click Table on the menu bar, click Table Properties, click the Table tab, click the Borders and Shading button, and then click the Borders tab, click the None option, click the OK button, and then click the OK button again. The borders are removed from the flier, leaving only the underlying gridlines, which will not appear on the printed page.

12. Save your work, preview the flier, make any necessary adjustments, print it, and then close the document and exit Word.

INTERNET ASSIGNMENTS

Student Union

The purpose of the Internet Assignments is to challenge you to find information on the Internet that you can use to create effective documents. The actual assignments are updated and maintained on the Course Technology Web site. Log on to the Internet and use your Web browser to go to the Student Union on the New Perspectives Series site at **www.course.com/NewPerspectives/studentunion**. Click the Online Companions link, and then click the link for this text.

QUICK CHECK ANSWERS

Session 3.1

1. a. the location where text moves when you press the Tab key
   b. the intersection of a row and a column in a table
   c. information arranged in horizontal rows and vertical columns
   d. a tab stop that aligns numerical data on the decimal point
   e. a unit or part of a document that can have its own page orientation, margins, headers, footers, and vertical alignment

2. Insert a section break, move the insertion point within the section you want to align, click File, click Page Setup, click the Layout tab, select Center in the Vertical alignment list box, make sure "This section" is selected in the Apply to list box, and then click OK.

3. A header appears at the top of a page, whereas a footer appears at the bottom of a page.

4. Move the insertion point to the location where you want the table to appear. Click the Insert Table button on the Standard toolbar. In the grid, click and drag to select four columns and six rows, and then release the mouse button.

5. If the insertion point is in the cell at the far right in a row, press the Tab key. Otherwise, press the ↓ key.

6. Click View on the menu bar, click Header and Footer, verify that the insertion point is located in the Header area, press Tab to move the insertion point to where you want the page number to appear, and then click the Insert Page Number button on the Header and Footer toolbar.

7. Select the text whose tab alignment you want to change, click the tab alignment selector on the far left of the horizontal ruler until the appropriate tab stop alignment style appears, and then click in the horizontal ruler where you want to set the new tab stop.

8. You may want to divide a document into sections if you wanted to center only part of the document between the top and bottom margins.

9. It's better to use a table rather than tab stops when you need to organize more than a few columns of information.

10. Click the Table Move handle.

Session 3.2

1. Drag the right border of each column to a new position.

2. Select the row. Click the Line Style list arrow on the Tables and Borders toolbar and select a line style. Click the Line Weight list arrow on the Tables and Borders toolbar and select a line weight. Click the Borders list arrow on the Tables and Borders toolbar and then click the Bottom Border option.

3. **a.** the thickness of the line used to create a border

   b. the style of the line used to create a border

   c. the outline of a row, cell, column, or table

   d. a gray or colored background used to highlight parts of a table

4. Click the cell at the far right in the bottom row of the table, and then press the Tab key.

5. Double-click the column's right-hand border.

6. 10, 25, 45, 75

7. Click anywhere in the table, click Table on the menu bar, click Table Properties, click the Table tab, click Center, and then click OK.

OBJECTIVES

In this tutorial you will:

- Identify desktop-publishing features
- Create a title with WordArt
- Work with hyperlinks
- Create newspaper-style columns
- Insert and edit graphics
- Wrap text around a graphic
- Incorporate drop caps
- Use symbols and special typographic characters
- Add a page border

DESKTOP PUBLISHING A NEWSLETTER

Creating a Newsletter for Wide World Travel

CASE

Wide World Travel, Inc.

Wide World Travel, Inc. hosts international tours for travelers of all ages. Recently, the company has expanded its business by selling clothes and shoes specifically designed for the frequent traveler. Max Stephenson, one of the Wide World tour guides, has taken on the job of managing this new retail venture. In order to generate business, he wants to include an informational newsletter with each set of airline tickets mailed from the main office. He has asked you to help him create the newsletter.

Max has already written the text of the newsletter, which describes some of the most popular items sold by Wide World Travel. Now Max wants you to transform this text into an eye-catching publication that is neat, organized, and professional looking. He would like the newsletter to contain headings (so the customers can scan it quickly for interesting items) as well as a headline that will give the newsletter a memorable look. He wants you to include a picture that will reinforce the newsletter content.

In this tutorial, you'll plan the layout of the newsletter and then add some information about the Wide World Travel Web site. Then you'll get acquainted with the desktop-publishing features and elements you'll need to use to create the newsletter. Also, you'll learn how desktop publishing differs from other word-processing tasks and from Web page design. You'll format the title using an eye-catching design and divide the document into newspaper-style columns to make it easier to read. To add interest and focus to the text, you'll include a piece of art. You'll then fine-tune the newsletter layout, give it a more professional appearance with typographic characters, and put a border around the page to give the newsletter a finished look.

SESSION 4.1

In this session you will see how Max planned his newsletter and learn about desktop-publishing features and elements. Then you will add and remove a hyperlink, create the newsletter title using WordArt, modify the title's appearance, and format the text of the newsletter into newspaper-style columns.

Planning the Document

The newsletter will provide a brief overview of some popular items sold by Wide World Travel. Like most newsletters, it will be written in an informal style that conveys information quickly. The newsletter title will be eye-catching and will help readers quickly identify the document. Newsletter text will be split into two columns to make it easier to read, and headings will help readers scan the information quickly. A picture will add interest and illustrate the newsletter's content. Drop caps and other desktop-publishing elements will help draw readers' attention to certain information and make the newsletter design attractive and professional.

Elements of Desktop Publishing

Desktop publishing is the production of commercial-quality printed material using a desktop computer system from which you can enter and edit text, create graphics, compose or lay out pages, and print documents. In addition to newsletters, you can desktop publish brochures, posters, and other documents that include text and graphics. In the Case Problems, you'll have to create a brochure. The following elements are commonly associated with desktop publishing:

- High-quality printing. A laser printer or high-resolution inkjet printer produces final output.
- Multiple fonts. Two or three font types and sizes provide visual interest, guide the reader through the text, and convey the tone of the document.
- Graphics. Graphics, such as horizontal or vertical lines (called rules), boxes, electronic art, and digitized photographs help illustrate a concept or product, draw a reader's attention to the document, and make the text visually appealing.
- Typographic characters. Typographic characters such as typographic long dashes, called em dashes (—), in place of double hyphens (--), separate dependent clauses; typographic medium-width dashes, called en dashes (–), are used in place of hyphens (-) as minus signs and in ranges of numbers; and typographic bullets (•) signal items in a list.
- Columns and other formatting features. Columns of text, pull quotes (small portions of text pulled out of the main text and enlarged), page borders, and other special formatting features that you don't frequently see in letters and other documents distinguish desktop-published documents.

You'll incorporate many of these desktop-publishing elements into the Wide World Travel newsletter for Max.

Word's Desktop-Publishing Features

Successful desktop publishing requires that you first know what elements professionals use to desktop publish a document. Figure 4-1 defines some of the desktop-publishing features included in Word. Max wants you to use these features to produce the final newsletter shown in Figure 4-2. The newsletter includes some of the typical desktop-publishing elements that you can add to a document using Word.

Figure 4-1	WORD DESKTOP PUBLISHING FEATURES
ELEMENT	**DESCRIPTION**
Columns	Two or more vertical blocks of text that fit on one page
WordArt	Text modified with special effects, such as rotated, curved, bent, shadowed, or shaded letters
Clip art	Prepared graphic images that are ready to be inserted into a document
Drop cap	Oversized first letter of word beginning a paragraph that extends vertically into two or more lines of the paragraph
Typographic symbols	Special characters that are not part of the standard keyboard, such as em dashes (—), copy-right symbols (©), or curly quotation marks (")

Figure 4-2   WIDE WORLD TRAVEL NEWSLETTER

Travel in Style!

Wide World Tours

After countless trips abroad, our tour leaders have mastered the art of traveling light. The secret, they explain, is to pack a few well-made, light-weight items that you can wash in a sink and dry overnight on a line. Unless you lived in a large city with numerous specialty stores, finding good traveling clothes used to be nearly impossible. But now you can purchase everything you need for a fast-paced Wide World tour at the Wide World Web site. This newsletter describes a few of our most popular items. To learn more about other Wide World products, call us at 283-333-9010 or visit our Web site at www.wideworldtravel.com.

Easy Moving Knitware

Unbelievably versatile, these knit garments are so adaptable that you can wear them from the train station to the outdoor market to the theater with just a change of accessories. They combine the softness of cotton with the suppleness of Flexistyle®, a wrinkle-resistant synthetic fabric.

The cardigan has side vents for a graceful drape and looks great layered over the knit shell. The pants have comfortable elasticized waistbands and side-seam pockets. Available in Midnight Black, Azure, and Coffee. Sizes: XS, S, M, L, and XL.

Resilient Straw Hat

If you're planning a trip to sunny climes, bring along this eminently packable broad-brimmed hat. Crunch it in a ball and stuff it into your suitcase. When you unpack, the hat will spring back to its original, elegant shape—guaranteed! Available in Cream and Taupe. Sizes: S, M, L, and XL.

Comfort Trekkers

These amazingly supportive walking shoes combine the comfort of hiking boots with the style of light-weight athletic shoes, giving your feet both stability and support. Wear them to explore a mysterious medieval city in the morning, and then hike a mountain trail after lunch. Available in Antique Black and Desert Brown, in whole and half sizes.

Desktop Publishing Versus Web Page Design

In many ways, desktop-published documents are similar to another kind of document known as a Web page. As you probably know, a **Web page** is a document that can contain specially formatted text, graphics, video, and audio. A Web page is stored on a computer as a collection of electronic files and is designed to be viewed in a special program called a **browser**. You probably have experience using a browser such as Microsoft Internet Explorer to explore Web pages on the Internet.

Like desktop-published documents, Web pages often include drop caps, multiple fonts, and graphics. However, you must use these elements differently when designing a Web page than when desktop publishing a document. Figure 4-3 summarizes some basic distinctions between desktop publishing and Web page design.

Figure 4-3	DESKTOP-PUBLISHED DOCUMENTS COMPARED TO WEB PAGES
DESKTOP PUBLISHING	**WEB PAGE DESIGN**
Reader sees the entire page at one time. Large areas of white space or uneven columns are therefore very noticeable in a desktop-published document.	Reader sees only the portion of the Web page that is displayed in the browser window.
Use of color increases printing costs. For this reason, many desktop-published documents are designed to be printed on a black and white printer.	The use of color does not affect the cost of producing the Web page.
The quality of the printer greatly affects the appearance of graphics in the printed page. Thus, desktop publishers usually prefer simple graphics that print well on laser printers.	The quality of graphics is most affected by the type of electronic file in which the graphic is stored.
The page is static. The only devices that can be used to catch the reader's attention are desktop-publishing elements, such as headlines, columns, and graphics.	Parts of the page can be animated, or include video. Also, Web pages often convey information or attract the reader's attention by using sound.
The reader cannot interact with a desktop-published document.	The reader can interact with a Web page by clicking links that display other Web pages or by entering information into a form on the Web page.

Now that you are familiar with some basic concepts related to desktop publishing, you can begin work on Max's newsletter. Your first task is to insert some information about the Wide World Travel Web site in the first section. To do this, you need to understand how to work with specially formatted text called hyperlinks.

Working with Hyperlinks

As mentioned in Figure 4-3, Web pages often include special text called **hyperlinks** (or simply **links**) that you can click to display other Web pages. You can also use hyperlinks in Word documents that will be read **online** (that is, on a computer).

For example, if you type an e-mail address and then press Enter, Word will automatically format the e-mail address as a hyperlink. (Hyperlink text is usually formatted in blue with an underline.) When you press Ctrl and click an e-mail hyperlink, an e-mail program opens automatically, ready for you to type a message. (If you completed the Review Assignments for Tutorial 2, you already have experience using e-mail hyperlinks.)

In the same way, Word will automatically format a Web page address, or **URL**, as a hyperlink. (One example of a Web address is www.microsoft.com.) When you press Ctrl and click a Web page address that has been formatted as a hyperlink, your computer's browser opens automatically and attempts to display that Web page. (The browser may not actually be able to display the Web page if your computer is not currently connected to the Internet, or if the Web page is unavailable for some other reason.)

Including hyperlinks in a Word document is very useful when you plan to distribute it via e-mail and have others read it online. For instance, if you include your e-mail address in a memo to a potential customer, the customer can click the e-mail address to begin typing an e-mail message to you in reply. However, when you know that your document will only be distributed on paper, it's a good idea to remove any hyperlinks so that the e-mail address or Web address is formatted the same as the rest of the document. This helps ensure that a desktop-published document has a uniform look. To remove a hyperlink, right-click the hyperlink and then click Remove Hyperlink in the shortcut menu. Once you remove the hyperlink, the Web address or e-mail address remains in the document, but is no longer formatted in blue with an underline.

Max would like you to complete the newsletter text by adding a reference to the Wide World Travel Web site. He does not want the company's Web address formatted as a hyperlink, so you will have to remove the hyperlink after typing the Web address. He has saved the newsletter text in a document named Clothes. You'll begin by opening the document that contains the unformatted text of the newsletter, often called **copy**.

To open the newsletter document and add the Web address:

1. Start Word, and place your Data Disk in the appropriate drive. Make sure your screen matches the figures in this tutorial. In particular, be sure to display non-printing characters and switch to Normal view.

2. Open the file **Clothes** from the Tutorial folder in the Tutorial.04 folder on your Data Disk.

3. To avoid altering the original file, save the document as **Travel Clothes** in the Tutorial folder in the Tutorial.04 folder on your Data Disk.

4. If necessary, change the Zoom setting (in the Standard toolbar) to 100% and switch to Normal view.

5. Click at the end of the second paragraph (after the phone number) press the **spacebar**, and then type the following: **or visit our Web site at www.wideworldtravel.com**

6. Type a period at the end of the Web address, and then press the **Enter** key. The Web address is formatted as a hyperlink, in a blue font with an underline.

7. Move the mouse pointer over the hyperlink. A ScreenTip appears, with the complete URL (including some extra characters that a browser needs to display the Web page). The ScreenTip also displays instructions for displaying the Wide World Travel Web site. See Figure 4-4.

Figure 4-4	HYPERLINK WITH SCREENTIP

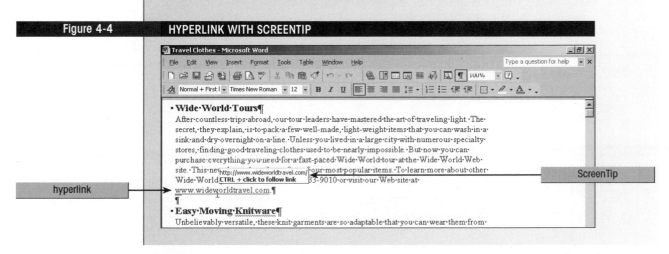

Max tells you that the Wide World Travel Web site is being updated, so it is not yet available online. So instead of clicking the link to test it, you will remove the hyperlink. This will ensure that the Web address is formatted to match the rest of the paragraph.

To remove the hyperlink:

1. Right-click the text **www.wideworldtravel.com**. A shortcut menu opens, as shown in Figure 4-5.

Figure 4-5   HYPERLINK MENU

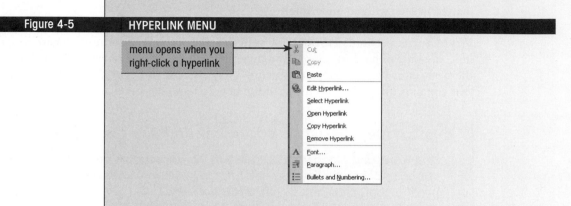

2. Click **Remove Hyperlink**. The shortcut menu closes and the text is now formatted in black to match the rest of the paragraph.

You have finished adding the information about the company's Web site to the newsletter. Now that the newsletter contains all the necessary details, you can turn your attention to adding a headline.

Using WordArt to Create a Headline

Max wants the title of the newsletter, "Travel in Style," to be eye-catching and dramatic, as shown earlier in Figure 4-2. WordArt, available in Word and other Microsoft Office programs, provides great flexibility in designing text with special effects that expresses the image or mood you want to convey in your printed documents. With WordArt, you can apply color and shading, as well as alter the shape and size of the text. You can easily "wrap" the document text around WordArt shapes.

Note that you begin creating WordArt by clicking a button on the Drawing toolbar. When you first display the Drawing toolbar, Word switches to Print Layout view. As a rule, Print Layout view is the most appropriate view to use when you are desktop publishing with Word because it shows you exactly how the text and graphics fit on the page. The vertical ruler that appears in Print Layout view helps you position graphical elements more precisely.

REFERENCE WINDOW **RW**

<u>Creating Special Text Effects Using WordArt</u>
- Click the Drawing button on the Standard toolbar to display the Drawing toolbar.
- Click the Insert WordArt button on the Drawing toolbar.
- Click the style of text you want to insert, and then click the OK button.
- Type the text you want in the Edit WordArt Text dialog box.
- Click the Font and Size list arrows to select the font and font size you want.
- If you want, click the Bold or Italic button, or both.
- Click the OK button.
- With the WordArt selected, drag any handle to reshape and resize it. To keep the text in the same proportions as the original, press and hold down the Shift key while you drag a handle.

You're ready to use WordArt to create the newsletter title. First you will display the Drawing toolbar. Then you will choose a WordArt style and type the headline text.

To create the title of the newsletter using WordArt:

1. Press **Ctrl+Home** to move the insertion point to the beginning of the document.

2. If the Drawing toolbar is not displayed on your screen, click the **Drawing** button on the Standard toolbar. The Drawing toolbar appears at the bottom of the screen. Word switches to Print Layout view.

   TROUBLE? If the Drawing toolbar is not positioned at the bottom of the Document window, drag it there by its title bar. If you do not see the Drawing toolbar anywhere, right-click the Standard toolbar, and then click Drawing on the shortcut menu.

3. If necessary, click **View** on the menu bar and then click **Ruler** to display the vertical and horizontal rulers, and then verify that the Zoom setting is 100%.

4. Click the **Insert WordArt** button on the Drawing toolbar. The WordArt Gallery dialog box opens, displaying 30 different WordArt styles.

5. Click the WordArt style in the second row from the top, second column from the right, as shown in Figure 4-6.

Figure 4-6   WORDART STYLES

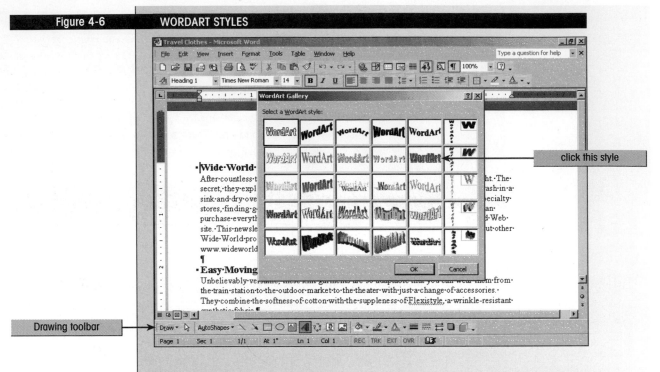

Drawing toolbar

6. Click the **OK** button. The Edit WordArt Text dialog box opens, displaying the default text "Your Text Here," which you will replace with the newsletter title.

7. Type **Travel in Style** to replace the default text with the newsletter title. Notice the toolbar at the top of the Edit WordArt Text dialog box, which you could use to apply boldface and italics, or to change the font or font style. You don't need to use these options now, but you might choose to when creating headlines for other documents.

8. Click the **OK** button. The Edit WordArt Text dialog box closes and the WordArt image is inserted at the beginning of the newsletter. The "Wide World Tours" heading moves to the right to accommodate the new headline. See Figure 4-7.

   TROUBLE? If you see a border around the headline, the WordArt is currently selected. Click anywhere outside of the border to deselect the WordArt.

Figure 4-7   WORDART HEADLINE INSERTED INTO DOCUMENT

headline

first line moves over to make room for WordArt

Eventually, you will position the headline so that it appears at the very top of the document, stretching from margin to margin. But for now, you can leave it in its current position.

Selecting a WordArt Object

The WordArt image you have created is not regular text. You cannot edit it as you would other text, by moving the insertion point to it and typing new letters, or by selecting part of it and using the buttons on the Formatting toolbar. Unlike regular text, a WordArt headline is considered an **object**—that is, something that lies on top of the document. To edit a WordArt object in Word, you must first click it to select it. Then you can make changes using special toolbar buttons and dialog boxes, or by dragging it with the mouse.

Max would like you to make several changes to the newsletter headline. Before you can do this, you need to select it.

To select the WordArt headline:

1. Click the WordArt headline. The headline is surrounded by a black border with eight small black squares (called resize handles). The WordArt toolbar also appears. See Figure 4-8.

Figure 4-8	SELECTED HEADLINE

resize handles

WordArt toolbar

Editing a WordArt Object

Now that the WordArt object is selected, you can modify its appearance (color, shape, size, and so forth) using the buttons on the Drawing toolbar or the WordArt toolbar. First of all, Max would like you to edit the WordArt by adding an exclamation mark at the end of the headline. While you're making that change, he would like you to format the headline in italics.

To change the font and formatting of the WordArt object:

1. Verify that the WordArt object is selected, as indicated by the resize handles.

2. Click the **Edit Text** button on the WordArt toolbar. The Edit WordArt Text dialog box opens. As you recall, you used this dialog box earlier when you first created the WordArt headline.

3. Click at the end of the headline (after the "e" in Style") and type ! (an exclamation mark).

4. Click the **Italic** button in the Edit WordArt Text dialog box. The headline in the Text box is now formatted in italics, with an exclamation mark at the end.

5. Click the **OK** button. The Edit WordArt Text dialog box closes, allowing you to see the edited headline in the document.

Changing the Shape of a WordArt Object

You can quickly change the shape of a WordArt object using the **WordArt Shape** button on the WordArt toolbar. Right now, the WordArt headline has a straight shape, without any curve to it. Max wants to use an arched shape.

To change the shape of the WordArt object:

1. Verify that the WordArt headline is selected, and then click the **WordArt Shape** button [Abc] on the WordArt toolbar.

2. Move the mouse pointer over the options in the palette to display a ScreenTip with the name of each shape. As you can see, the Plain Text shape (a straight line) is currently selected.

3. Click the **Inflate Top** shape (fourth row down, fifth column from the left), as shown in Figure 4-9.

Figure 4-9	WORDART SHAPES

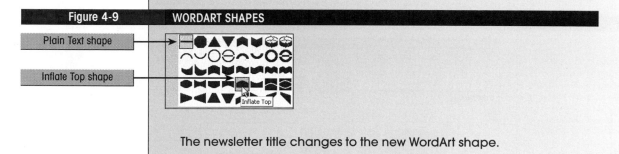

The newsletter title changes to the new WordArt shape.

The headline has the shape you want. Now you can take care of positioning the WordArt object above the newsletter text.

Wrapping Text Below the WordArt Object

At this point, the WordArt object is on the same line as the heading "Wide World Tours." Max would like you to set the WordArt on its own line at the top of the document. To do this, you need to change the way the text flows, or **wraps**, around the WordArt object.

You can wrap text around objects many different ways in Word. For example, you can have the text wrap above and below the object, through it, or wrap the text to follow the shape of the object, even if it has an irregular shape. Text wrapping is often used in newsletters to prevent text and graphics from overlapping, to add interest, and to prevent excessive open areas, called white space, from appearing on the page. The Text Wrapping button on the WordArt or Picture toolbar provides some basic choices, whereas the Layout tab of the Format Picture dialog box provides more advanced options. Because you want to use a relatively simple option—wrapping text so that it flows below the WordArt headline—you'll use the Text Wrapping button on the WordArt toolbar. You'll have a chance to use the Format Picture dialog box in the Case Problems at the end of this tutorial.

To wrap the newsletter text below the WordArt headline:

1. With the WordArt object selected, click the **Text Wrapping** button [🖾] on the WordArt toolbar. A menu of text wrapping options opens.

2. Click **Top and Bottom**. The text drops below the newsletter title. The WordArt is still selected, but instead of handles in the shape of square boxes, you see small circles. A number of other items appear around the WordArt object, as shown in Figure 4-10. You can use the handles shown in Figure 4-10 to change the size and position of the WordArt object. You'll learn the meaning of the anchor symbol shortly. Don't be concerned if yours is not in the same position as the one in Figure 4-10.

Figure 4-10	WORDART AFTER WRAPPING TEXT

Positioning and Sizing the WordArt Object

After you choose a text wrap style for a WordArt object, you can adjust its size and position in the document. To position a WordArt object, click it and drag it with the mouse pointer. To widen any WordArt object, drag one of its resize handles. To keep the object the same proportion as the original, hold down the Shift key as you drag the resize handle. This prevents "stretching" the object more in one direction than the other.

Max asks you to widen the headline so it fits neatly within the newsletter margins. As you enlarge the headline, you can practice dragging the WordArt object to a new position.

To position and enlarge the WordArt object:

1. Move the mouse pointer over the headline.

2. Use the ✛ pointer to drag the WordArt object to the right, until it is centered over the top of the newsletter.

3. Click the **Undo** button on the Standard toolbar to undo the move. The headline returns to its original position, aligned along the left-hand margin. Note that you can use this same technique to drag a WordArt object to any location in a document. (You'll learn more about dragging objects later in this tutorial, when you insert a picture into the newsletter.)

4. With the WordArt object still selected, position the pointer over its lower-right resize handle. The pointer changes to ⬊.

5. Press and hold the **Shift** key while you drag the resize handle to the right margin, using the horizontal ruler as a guide. See Figure 4-11. As you drag the handle, the pointer changes to ┼. If necessary, repeat the procedure to make the exclamation mark line up with the right margin.

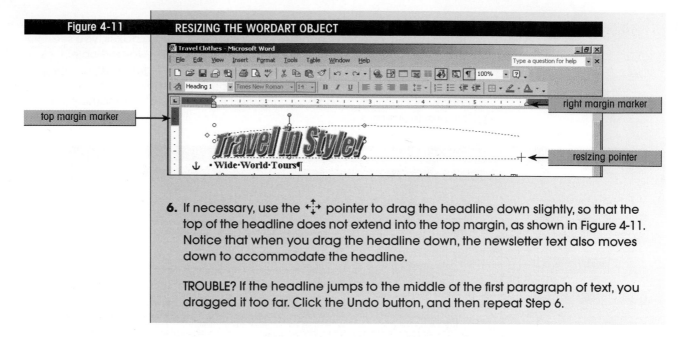

Figure 4-11 RESIZING THE WORDART OBJECT

6. If necessary, use the pointer to drag the headline down slightly, so that the top of the headline does not extend into the top margin, as shown in Figure 4-11. Notice that when you drag the headline down, the newsletter text also moves down to accommodate the headline.

   TROUBLE? If the headline jumps to the middle of the first paragraph of text, you dragged it too far. Click the Undo button, and then repeat Step 6.

In addition to moving and resizing the WordArt headline, you can drag the rotation handle to rotate the headline. You can also use the adjustment handle to increase or decrease the arch at the top of the headline. You'll have a chance to practice these techniques in the Review Assignments at the end of this tutorial. Right now you need to turn your attention to the anchor symbol on the left side of the WordArt object.

Anchoring the WordArt Object

At some point after you wrap text around a document, you need to make sure the WordArt object is properly positioned within the document as a whole—a process known as **anchoring**. The process draws its name from the anchor symbol in the left margin, which indicates the position of the WordArt relative to the text. (The anchor symbol is only visible after you wrap text around the document.) To ensure that changes to the text (such as section breaks) do not affect the WordArt, you need to anchor the WordArt to a blank paragraph before the text. At this point, the WordArt anchor symbol is probably located to the left of the first paragraph (the heading "Wide World Tours"). However, yours may be in a different position (for instance, it might be positioned above and to the left of the WordArt). In the next set of steps, you will move the anchor to a new, blank paragraph at the beginning of the document.

To anchor the WordArt object to a blank paragraph:

1. Press **Ctrl+Home**. The insertion point moves to the beginning of the newsletter text (that is, to the left of the first "W" in the heading "Wide World Tours"). The WordArt object is no longer selected; you cannot see the anchor at this point.

2. Press the **Enter** key. A new paragraph symbol is inserted at the beginning of the document.

3. Click the WordArt object. The selection handles and the anchor symbol appear.

4. Click the anchor and drag it to the left of the new, blank paragraph, as shown in Figure 4-12.

| Figure 4-12 | PROPERLY ANCHORED WORDART |

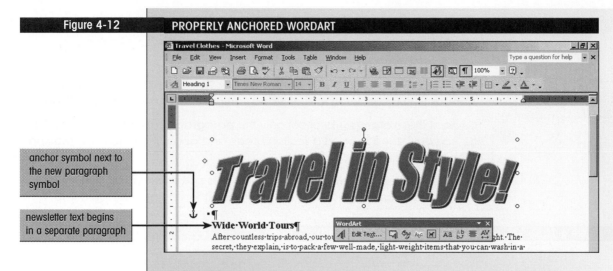

anchor symbol next to the new paragraph symbol

newsletter text begins in a separate paragraph

TROUBLE? If your WordArt headline is positioned below the new paragraph symbol, drag it up slightly to position it above the new paragraph symbol. If you notice any other differences between your headline and the one shown in Figure 4-12, edit the headline to make it match the figure. For example, you may need to drag the WordArt left or right slightly, or you may need to adjust its size by dragging one of its resize handles.

5. Click anywhere in the newsletter to deselect the WordArt, and then save your work.

Your WordArt is now finished. Max congratulates you on your excellent work. The headline will definitely draw attention to the newsletter, encouraging potential customers to read the entire document.

Formatting Text in Newspaper-Style Columns

Because newsletters are meant for quick reading, they are usually laid out in newspaper-style columns. In newspaper-style columns, a page is divided into two or more vertical blocks, or columns. Text flows down one column, continues at the top of the next column, flows down that column, and so forth. The narrow columns and small type size allow the eye to take in a lot of text, thus allowing a reader to scan a newspaper quickly for interesting information.

When formatting a document in columns, you can click where you want the columns to begin and then click the Columns button on the Formatting toolbar. However, the Columns command on the Formatting menu offers more options. Using the Columns command, you can insert a vertical line between columns. The Columns command also gives you more control over exactly what part of the document will be formatted in columns.

Max wants you to divide the text below the title into two columns and add a vertical line between them.

To apply newspaper-style columns to the body of the newsletter:

1. Position the insertion point at the beginning of the second paragraph (to the left of the first "W" in "Wide World Tours").

2. Click **Format** on the menu bar, and then click **Columns**. The Columns dialog box opens.

3. In the Presets section, click the **Two** icon.

4. Click the **Line between** check box to select it. The text in the Preview box changes to a two-column format with a vertical rule between the columns.

   You want these changes to affect only the paragraphs after the WordArt headline, so you'll need to insert a section break and apply the column formatting to the text after the insertion point.

5. Click the **Apply to** list arrow, and then click **This point forward** to have Word automatically insert a section break at the insertion point. See Figure 4-13.

Figure 4-13   **COMPLETED COLUMNS DIALOG BOX**

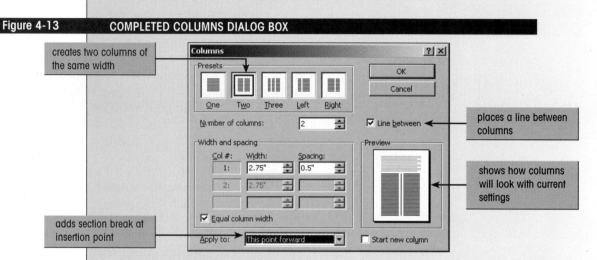

creates two columns of the same width

places a line between columns

shows how columns will look with current settings

adds section break at insertion point

6. Click the **OK** button to return to the Document window. A continuous section break appears below the WordArt title. The word "continuous" indicates that the new section continues on the same page as the preceding page—in other words, the newsletter text and the WordArt title will print on the same page, even though they lie in different sections. The text in Section 2 is formatted in two columns.

To get a good look at the columns, you need to change the zoom setting so you can see the entire page at one time.

To zoom out to display the whole page:

1. Click the **Zoom** list arrow on the Standard toolbar, and then click **Whole Page**. Word displays the entire page of the newsletter so that you can see how the two-column format looks on the page. See Figure 4-14. Note that the Whole Page Zoom setting is only available in Print Layout view. You should use it whenever you want to have the entire page displayed as you edit it.

Figure 4-14   **WHOLE PAGE VIEW SHOWING TWO COLUMNS**

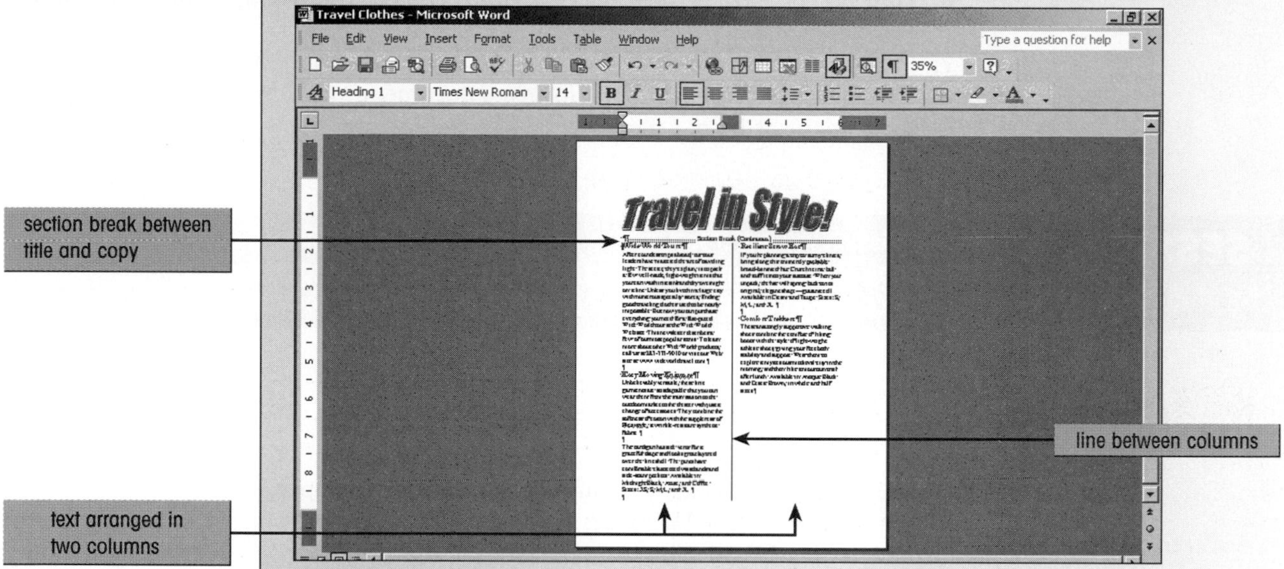

section break between
title and copy

line between columns

text arranged in
two columns

TROUBLE? Your columns may break at a slightly different line from those shown in the figure. This is not a problem; just continue with the tutorial.

The newsletter headline is centered on the page, and the copy is in a two-column format. The text fills the left column but not the right column. You'll fix this later, after you add a graphic and format some of the text.

2. Click the **Zoom** list arrow again, and then click **Page Width**. The Page Width option reduces the zoom setting enough to make the page span the width of the document window. Now you can read the text again.

3. Save your work.

Keep in mind that you can modify the structure of columns in a document by reformatting the document with three or more columns, or return the document to its original format by formatting it as one column. You can also insert column breaks to force text to move from one column to the next. You'll have a chance to practice modifying the columns in the Case Problems at the end of this tutorial.

Session 4.1 QUICK CHECK

1. Describe four elements commonly associated with desktop publishing.
2. Describe at least two differences between a desktop-published document and a Web page.
3. In your own words, define the following terms:
   a. desktop publishing
   b. Web page
   c. copy
   d. anchor
4. True or False: When using Word's desktop-publishing features, you should display your document in Normal view.

5. True or False: You can edit WordArt just as you would edit any other text in Word.

6. How do you change the text of a WordArt object after you have inserted it into a Word document?

7. What is the purpose of the WordArt Shape button on the WordArt toolbar?

8. True or False: When you first format a document into newspaper-style columns, the columns will not necessarily be of equal length.

SESSION 4.2

In this session you will insert, resize, and crop clip art, and change the way the text wraps around the clip art. Then you'll create drop caps, insert typographic symbols, balance columns, place a border around the newsletter, and print the newsletter.

Inserting Graphics

Graphics, which can include drawings, paintings, photographs, charts, tables, designs, or even designed text such as WordArt, add variety to documents and are especially appropriate for newsletters. Word allows you to draw pictures in your document, using the buttons on the Drawing toolbar. To produce professional-looking graphics, it's easier to create a picture in a special graphics program and then save the picture as an electronic file. (You may already be familiar with one graphics program, **Paint**, which is included as part of the Windows operating system.)

Instead of creating your own art in a graphics program, you can take a piece of art on a piece of paper (such as a photograph) and scan it—that is, run it through a special machine called a scanner. A **scanner** is similar to a copy machine except that it saves a copy of the image as an electronic file, instead of reproducing it on a piece of paper. (As you may know, many modern copy machines also function as scanners.) You can also use a digital camera to take a photograph that is then stored as an electronic file.

Electronic files come in several types, many of which were developed for use in Web pages. In desktop publishing, you will most commonly work with **bitmaps**—a type of file that stores an image as a collection of tiny dots, which, when displayed on a computer monitor or printed on a page, make up a picture. There are several types of bitmap files, the most common of which are:

- BMP: Used by Microsoft Paint to store graphics you create. These files, which have the .bmp file extension, tend to be very large.

- GIF: Suitable for most types of simple art. A GIF file is compressed, so it doesn't take up much room on your computer. A GIF file has the file extension .gif.

- JPEG: Suitable for photographs and drawings. Even more compressed than GIF files. A JPEG file has the file extension .jpg.

- TIFF: Commonly used for photographs or scanned images. TIFF files have the file extension .tif and are usually much larger than GIF or JPEG files.

Once you have stored a piece of art as an electronic file, you can insert it into a document using the Picture commands on the Insert menu. You'll have a chance to explore some of these commands in the Review Assignments and Case Problems at the end of this tutorial.

If you don't have time to prepare your own art work, you can take advantage of **clip art**—a collection of pre-made, copyright-free images included along with Word. A number of clip art selections are stored on your computer when you install Microsoft Word. You can also download additional clip art from the Web. (You'll have a chance to look for clip art on the Web in the Case Problems at the end of this tutorial.) You begin inserting clip art by opening the Clip Art Task Pane. From there you can open the Clip Organizer, which gives you access to a series of folders containing various categories of clip art. Then you copy an image to the Office Clipboard, close the Clip Organizer, and paste the image into the document.

To add visual appeal to the Wide World Travel newsletter, you will insert a piece of clip art now. Max wants you to use a graphic that reflects the newsletter content.

To insert the clip art image of an airplane into the newsletter:

1. If you took a break after the previous session, make sure Word is still running, the Travel Clothes newsletter is open, the document is in Print Layout view, and the nonprinting characters are displayed. Also verify that the Drawing toolbar is displayed.

2. Click the **Insert Clip Art** button 🖼 on the Drawing toolbar. The Insert Clip Art Task Pane opens, as shown in Figure 4-15. You can use the top part of this Task Pane to search for graphics related to a specific topic. You can also click the Clip Organizer option (near the bottom) to open a dialog box where you can browse among the various images stored on your computer. You'll use the Clip Organizer in the next step.

Figure 4-15	INSERT CLIP ART TASK PANE

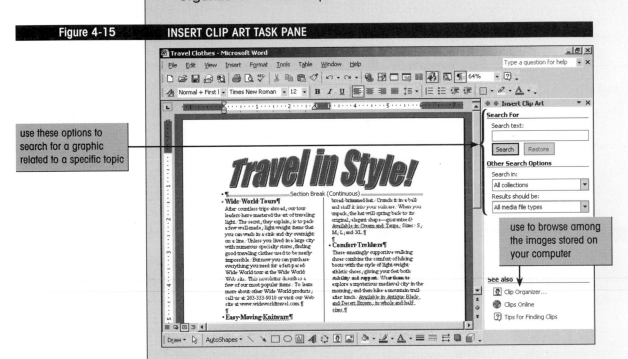

use these options to search for a graphic related to a specific topic

use to browse among the images stored on your computer

TROUBLE? If you see the Add Clips to Organizer dialog box, click Now. This will organize the clip art installed on your computer into folders, so that you can then use the Clip Organizer dialog box to select a piece of clip art. This dialog box will appear the first time you attempt to use clip art on your computer.

3. Click **Clip Organizer** near the bottom of the Task Pane. The Microsoft Clip Organizer opens, with the Favorites folder selected in the Collection List. This dialog box works similar to Windows Explorer. You click the plus signs next to folders to display subfolders. The images stored in subfolders are displayed in the right-hand pane. Clip art in Word is stored in subfolders within the Office Collections folder. See Figure 4-16. (You might see different folders from those shown in Figure 4-16, but you should see the Office Collections folder.)

Figure 4-16 | MICROSOFT CLIP ORGANIZER

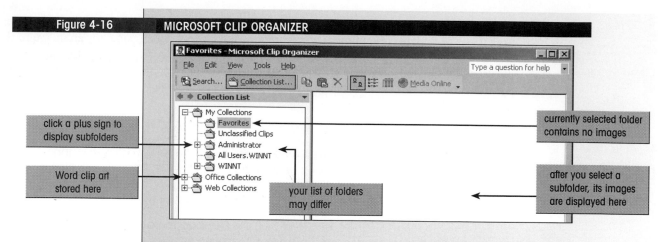

click a plus sign to display subfolders

Word clip art stored here

your list of folders may differ

currently selected folder contains no images

after you select a subfolder, its images are displayed here

4. Click the plus sign next to the **Office Collections** folder. A list of subfolders within the Office Collections folder appears. This list of folders, which is created when you install Word, organizes clip art images into related categories. The folders with plus signs next to them contain subfolders or clip art images.

5. Scroll down and examine the list of folders. Click any plus signs to open subfolders, and then click folders to display clip art images in the right-hand pane.

6. Click the plus sign next to the **Transportation** folder to display its subfolders, and then click the **Transportation** folder to select it. Three images stored in the Transportation folder are displayed in the right-hand pane.

TROUBLE? If you don't see any images in the Transportation folder, click the Travel folder to select it and display an image of an airplane in a blue circle.

7. Move the pointer over the image of the airplane in the blue circle. An arrow button appears.

8. Click the arrow button. A menu of options opens, as shown in Figure 4-17.

Figure 4-17 | IMAGE IN THE TRANSPORTATION FOLDER SELECTED

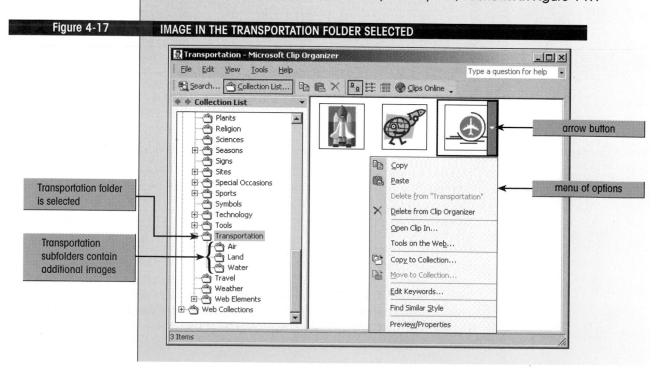

Transportation folder is selected

Transportation subfolders contain additional images

arrow button

menu of options

9. Click **Copy** in the menu. The image is copied to the Office Clipboard.

10. Click the **Close** button ☒ to close the Microsoft Clip Organizer, and then click **Yes** when you see a dialog box asking if you want to save the item on the Clipboard. You return to the Document window.

Now that you have copied the image to the Clipboard, you can paste it into the document at the insertion point. Max asks you to insert the graphic in the paragraph below the heading "Tours." Before you insert the image, you will close the Task Pane.

To paste the clip art into the document:

1. Close the Insert Clip Art Task Pane.

2. Position the insertion point to the left of the word "After" in the beginning of the first paragraph below the heading "Wide World Tours."

3. Click the **Paste** button 🖺 on the Standard toolbar. The image is inserted into the document at the insertion point. The image nearly fills the left column.

4. Save the document.

5. Click the airplane image to select it. Like the WordArt object you worked with earlier, the clip art image is an object with resize handles that you can use to change its size. The Picture toolbar appears whenever the clip art object is selected. See Figure 4-18.

Figure 4-18	NEWSLETTER WITH THE CLIP ART OBJECT INSERTED

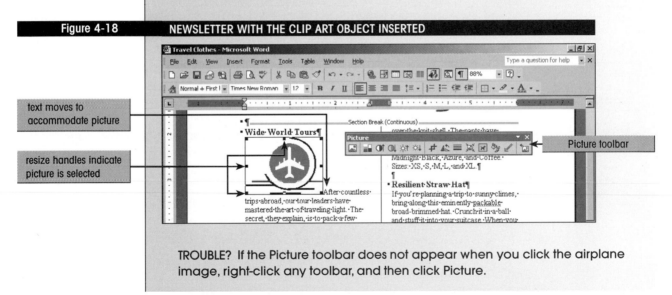

text moves to accommodate picture

resize handles indicate picture is selected

Picture toolbar

TROUBLE? If the Picture toolbar does not appear when you click the airplane image, right-click any toolbar, and then click Picture.

Max would like the image to be smaller so it doesn't distract attention from the text. You'll make that change in the next section.

Resizing a Graphic

You often need to change the size of a graphic so that it fits better into your document. This is called **scaling** the image. You can resize a graphic by either dragging its resize handles or, for more precise control, by using the Format Picture button on the Picture toolbar.

For Max's newsletter, the dragging technique will work fine.

To resize the clip art graphic:

1. Make sure the clip art graphic is selected.

2. Drag the lower-right resize handle up and to the left until the dotted outline forms a rectangle about 1.5 inches wide. Remember to use the horizontal ruler as a guide. See Figure 4-19. *Note:* You don't have to hold down the Shift key, as you do with WordArt, to resize the picture proportionally.

Figure 4-19	RESIZING THE GRAPHIC

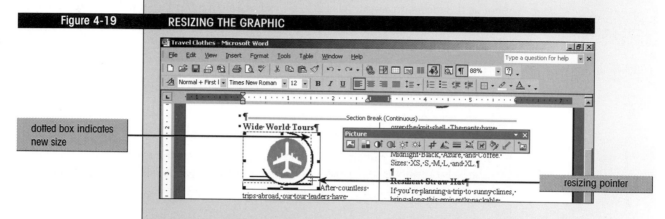

dotted box indicates new size

resizing pointer

3. Release the mouse button. The airplane image is now about half as wide as the left-hand column.

Max wonders if the graphic would look better if you deleted part of the horizontal line on the left side of the image. You'll make that change in the next section.

Cropping a Graphic

You can **crop** the graphic—that is, cut off one or more of its edges—using either the Crop button on the Picture toolbar or the Format Picture dialog box. Once you crop a graphic, the part you cropped is hidden from view. It remains a part of the graphic image, so you can change your mind and restore a cropped graphic to its original form.

To crop the airplane graphic:

1. If necessary, click the clip art to select it. The resize handles appear.

2. Click the **Crop** button on the Picture toolbar. The pointer changes to . To crop the graphic, you must position this pointer over a middle handle on any side of the graphic.

3. Position the pointer directly over the middle resize handle on the left side of the picture.

4. Press and hold down the mouse button. The pointer changes to .

5. Drag the handle to the right. As you drag, a dotted outline appears to indicate the new shape of the graphic. Position the left border of the dotted outline along the left border of the blue circle. See Figure 4-20.

Figure 4-20   **CROPPING THE GRAPHIC**

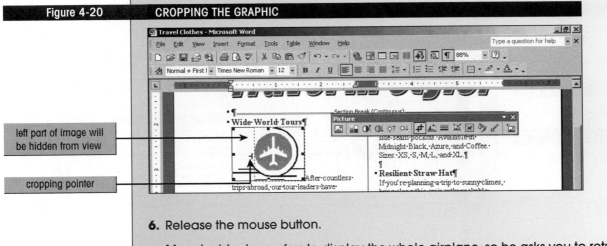

left part of image will be hidden from view

cropping pointer

6. Release the mouse button.

Max decides he prefers to display the whole airplane, so he asks you to return to the original image.

7. Click the **Undo** button on the Standard toolbar. The cropping action is reversed, and the full image reappears.

Rotating a Graphic

Max still isn't happy with the appearance of the graphic, because of the amount of white space on the left side. He suggests rotating the image, so that the airplane is positioned horizontally on the page. Use the Rotate Left button on the Picture toolbar to rotate the image.

To rotate the airplane graphic:

1. If necessary, click the clip art to select it. The resize handles appear.

2. Click the **Rotate Left** button on the Picture toolbar. The graphic rotates 90 degrees to the left. The resize handles change to circles, just as they did when you adjusted the position of the WordArt headline earlier. You can drag the green rotation handle to rotate the graphic, but it's easier to continue using the Rotate Left button.

3. Click again. The graphic rotates another 90 degrees, leaving the airplane upside down.

4. Click again. The graphic rotates another 90 degrees. Now the airplane appears to be flying across the page from left to right. See Figure 4-21.

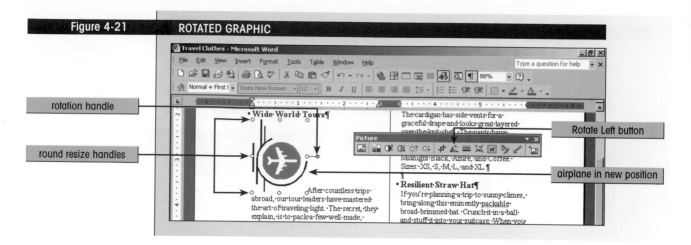

Figure 4-21   ROTATED GRAPHIC

Now Max wants you to make the text wrap to the right of the graphic, making the airplane look as if it's flying into the text.

Wrapping Text Around a Graphic

For the airplane to look as though it flies into the newsletter text, you need to make the text wrap around the image. Earlier, you used the Top and Bottom text wrapping to position the WordArt title above the columns of text. Now you'll try the Tight text wrapping option to make the text follow the shape of the plane.

To wrap text around the airplane graphic:

1. Verify that the airplane graphic is selected.

2. Click the **Text Wrapping** button ▣ on the Picture toolbar. A menu of text wrapping options appears.

3. Click **Tight**. The text wraps to the right of the airplane, following its shape.

4. Click anywhere in the text to deselect the graphic, and then save the newsletter. Your screen should look similar to Figure 4-22.

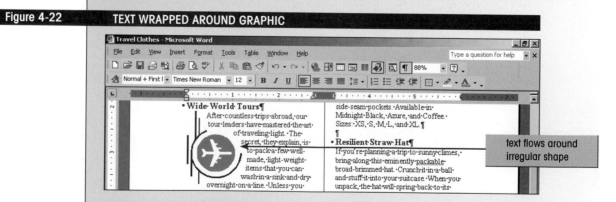

Figure 4-22   TEXT WRAPPED AROUND GRAPHIC

The Text Wrapping button should provide all the options you need for most situations. In some cases, however, you might want to use the more advanced options available in the Format Picture or Format WordArt dialog box. You'll have a chance to explore these options in one of the Case Problems.

Moving a Graphic

Finally, Max asks you to move the graphic down to the middle of the paragraph, so that it is not so close to the heading. You can do this by dragging the graphic to a new position. Like WordArt, a clip art graphic is anchored to a specific paragraph in a document. When you drag a graphic (including WordArt) to a new paragraph, the anchor symbol moves to the top of that paragraph. When you drag a graphic to a new position within the same paragraph, the anchor symbol remains in its original position and only the graphic moves. You'll see how this works when you move the airplane graphic.

To move the graphic:

1. Verify that the graphic is selected. You should see an anchor symbol to the left of the graphic, indicating that the graphic is anchored to the first paragraph below the heading "Wide World Tours." (It may look like the graphic is actually anchored to the heading.)

2. Move the mouse pointer over the graphic.

3. Click and drag the pointer down. As you move the pointer, a dotted outline appears indicating the new position of the graphic.

4. Position the dotted outline in the middle of the paragraph, aligned along the left margin, and then release the mouse button. The graphic moves to its new position, but the anchor remains at the top of the paragraph. See Figure 4-23.

Figure 4-23	GRAPHIC IN NEW POSITION

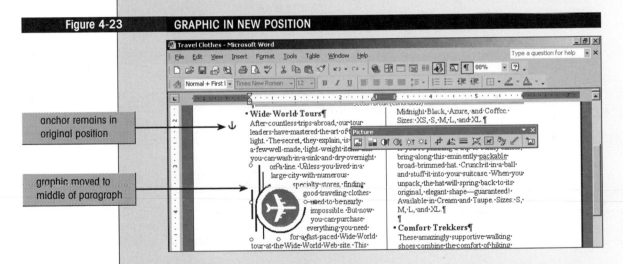

anchor remains in original position

graphic moved to middle of paragraph

5. Click anywhere outside the graphic to deselect it.

TROUBLE? If paragraph text wraps to the left of the graphic, you need to drag the graphic further to the left, so that it aligns along the left-hand margin.

The image of the airplane draws the reader's attention to the beginning of the newsletter, but the rest of the text looks plain. Max suggests adding a drop cap at the beginning of each section.

Inserting Drop Caps

A **drop cap** is a large, capital letter that highlights the beginning of the text of a newsletter, chapter, or some other document section. The drop cap usually extends from the top of the first line of the paragraph down two or three succeeding lines of the paragraph. The text of the paragraph wraps around the drop cap. Word allows you to create a drop cap for the first letter of the first word of a paragraph.

You will create a drop cap for the first paragraph following each heading in the newsletter. The drop cap will extend two lines into the paragraph.

To insert drop caps in the newsletter:

1. Click in the paragraph below the heading "Wide World Tours" (the paragraph where you inserted the graphic).

2. Click **Format** on the menu bar, and then click **Drop Cap**. The Drop Cap dialog box opens.

3. In the Position section, click the **Dropped** icon.

4. Click the **Lines to drop** down arrow once to change the setting from 3 to 2. You don't need to change the default distance from the text. See Figure 4-24.

Figure 4-24	DROP CAP DIALOG BOX

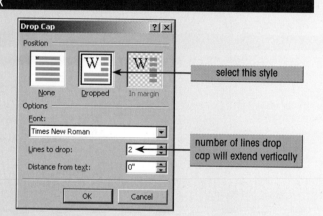

5. Click the **OK** button to close the dialog box, and then click anywhere in the newsletter to deselect the new drop cap. Word formats the first character of the paragraph as a drop cap.

6. Click anywhere in the newsletter text to deselect the drop cap.

   Note: Word re-wraps the text around the graphic to accommodate the drop cap above. If the paragraph text wraps to the left of the graphic, drag it closer to the left margin. See Figure 4-25.

   TROUBLE? Don't be concerned if Word now marks the "fter" of "After" as a grammatical error. Word considers drop caps to be objects, not regular text. By formatting the *A* in "After" as a drop cap, you essentially deleted the regular character *A*. Because the remaining regular characters "fter" do not appear in the dictionary, Word marks it as a potential error.

| Figure 4-25 | DROP CAP BEGINS THE PARAGRAPH |

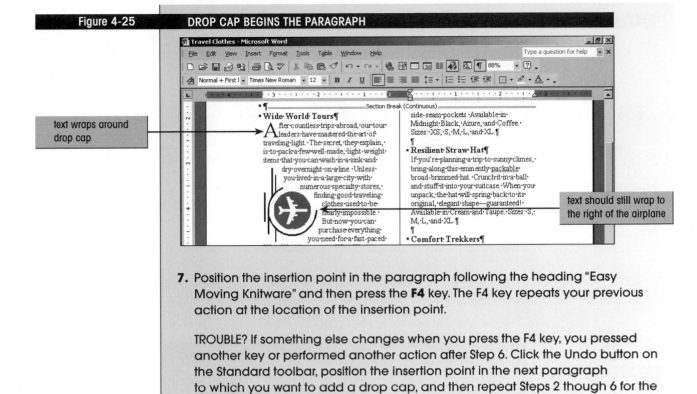

text wraps around drop cap

text should still wrap to the right of the airplane

7. Position the insertion point in the paragraph following the heading "Easy Moving Knitware" and then press the **F4** key. The F4 key repeats your previous action at the location of the insertion point.

TROUBLE? If something else changes when you press the F4 key, you pressed another key or performed another action after Step 6. Click the Undo button on the Standard toolbar, position the insertion point in the next paragraph to which you want to add a drop cap, and then repeat Steps 2 though 6 for the paragraph specified in Step 7.

8. Continue using the **F4** key to add drop caps to the paragraphs following the remaining two headings.

The newsletter looks more lively with the drop caps. Next, you turn your attention to inserting a registered trademark symbol beside a trademark name.

Inserting Symbols and Special Characters

In printed publications, it is customary to change some of the characters available on the standard keyboard into more polished looking characters called **typographic symbols**. For instance, while you might type two hyphens to indicate a dash, in a professionally produced version of that document the two hyphens would be changed to one long dash (called an em dash because it is approximately as wide as the letter "m"). In the past, desktop publishers had to rely on special software to insert and print a document containing typographic symbols, but now you can let Microsoft Word do the work for you.

Word's AutoCorrect feature automatically converts some standard characters into more polished looking typographic symbols as you type. For instance, as Max typed the information on the Resilient Straw Hat, he typed two hyphens after the words "elegant shape." As he began to type the next word "guaranteed," Word automatically converted the two hyphens into an em dash. Figure 4-26 lists some of the other characters that AutoCorrect automatically converts to typographic symbols. In most cases you need to press the spacebar and type more characters before Word will insert the appropriate symbol. You'll have a chance to practice using AutoCorrect to insert typographic symbols in the Review Assignments at the end of this tutorial.

Figure 4-26   COMMON TYPOGRAPHIC SYMBOLS

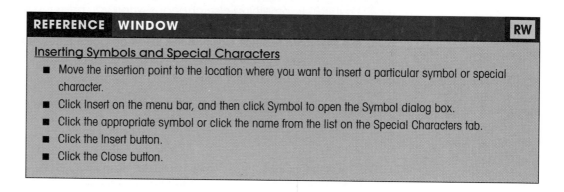

TO INSERT THIS SYMBOL OR CHARACTER	TYPE	WORD CONVERTS IT TO
em dash	word--word	word—word
smiley	:)	☺
copyright symbol	(c)	©
registered trademark symbol	(r)	®
trademark symbol	(tm)	™
ordinal numbers	1st, 2nd, 3rd, etc.	1st, 2nd, 3rd, etc.
fractions	1/2, 1/4	½, ¼
arrows	--> or <--	→ or ←

To insert typographic characters into a document after you've finished typing it, you can use the Symbol command on the Insert menu.

REFERENCE WINDOW   **RW**

Inserting Symbols and Special Characters

- Move the insertion point to the location where you want to insert a particular symbol or special character.
- Click Insert on the menu bar, and then click Symbol to open the Symbol dialog box.
- Click the appropriate symbol or click the name from the list on the Special Characters tab.
- Click the Insert button.
- Click the Close button.

Max noticed that he forgot to insert a registered trademark symbol (®) after the trademarked name "Flexistyle." He asks you to insert this symbol now, using the Symbol command on the Insert menu.

To insert the registered trademark symbol:

1. Scroll down to display the paragraph below the heading "Easy Moving Knitware," and then click to the right of the word "Flexistyle." (Take care to click between the final "e" and the comma.)

2. Click **Insert** on the menu bar, and then click **Symbol** to open the Symbol dialog box.

3. If necessary, click the **Special Characters** tab. See Figure 4-27.

Figure 4-27   **INSERTING A TYPOGRAPHIC SYMBOL**

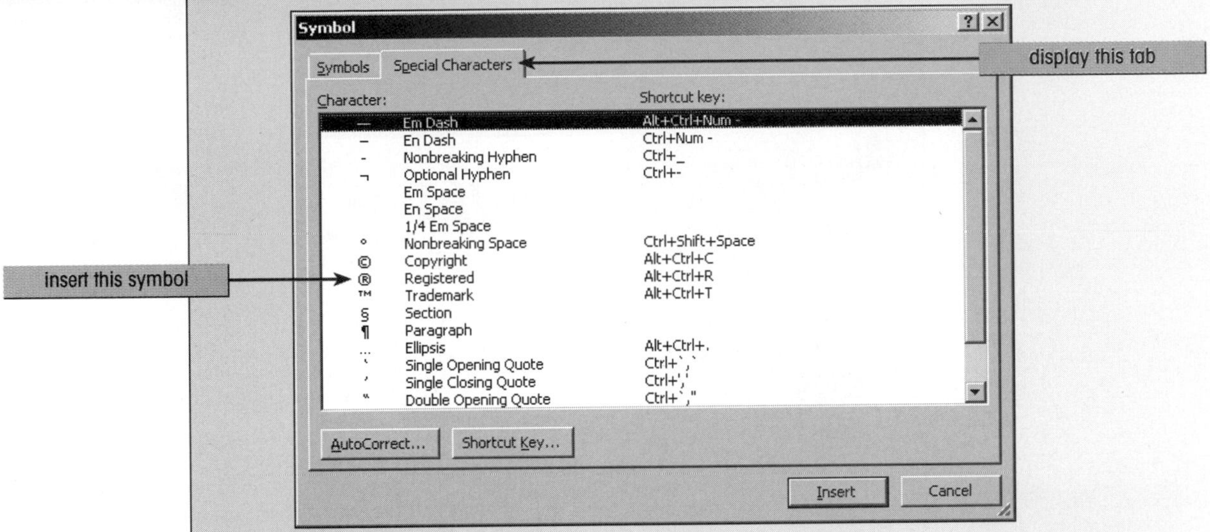

4. Click **Registered** to select it, and then click the **Insert** button.

5. Click the **Close** button to close the Symbol dialog box. Word inserts an ® immediately after the word "Flexistyle."

Next, you decide to adjust the columns of text so they are approximately the same length.

Balancing the Columns

You can shift text from one column to another by adding blank paragraphs to move the text into the next column or by deleting blank paragraphs to shorten the text so it will fit into one column. The problem with this approach is that any edits you make could throw off the balance. Instead, Word can automatically **balance** the columns, or make them of equal length.

To balance the columns:

1. Position the insertion point at the end of the text in the right column, just after the period following the word "sizes."

Next, you need to change the zoom to Whole Page so you can see the full affect of the change.

2. Click the **Zoom** list arrow on the Standard toolbar, and then click **Whole Page**.

3. Click **Insert** on the menu bar, and then click **Break**. The Break dialog box opens.

4. Below "section break types," click the **Continuous** option button.

5. Click the **OK** button. Word inserts a continuous section break at the end of the text. As shown in Figure 4-28, Word balances the text between the two section breaks.

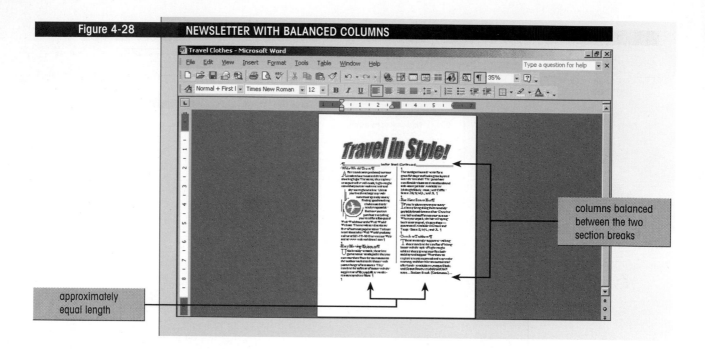

Figure 4-28   NEWSLETTER WITH BALANCED COLUMNS

columns balanced between the two section breaks

approximately equal length

Drawing a Border Around the Page

You can add definition to a paragraph or an entire page by adding a border. Right now, Max wants to add a border around the newsletter. (In the Case Problems at the end of this tutorial, you'll learn how to add a border around individual paragraphs.)

To draw a border around the newsletter:

1. Make sure the document is in Print Layout view and that the zoom setting is set to Whole Page so that you can see the entire newsletter.

2. Click **Format** on the menu bar, and then click **Borders and Shading**. The Borders and Shading dialog box opens.

3. Click the **Page Border** tab. You can use the Setting options on the left side to specify the type of border you want. In this case, you want a simple box.

4. In the Setting section, click the **Box** option. Now that you have selected the type of border you want, you can choose the style of line that will be used to create the border.

5. In the Style list box, scroll down and select the ninth style down from the top (the thick line with the thin line underneath), and then verify that the Apply to list option is set to **Whole document**. See Figure 4-29. (While the Borders and Shading dialog box is open, notice the Shading tab, which you can use to add a colored background to a page. You'll have a chance to use this tab in the Case Problems at the end of this tutorial.)

Figure 4-29   ADDING A BORDER TO THE NEWSLETTER

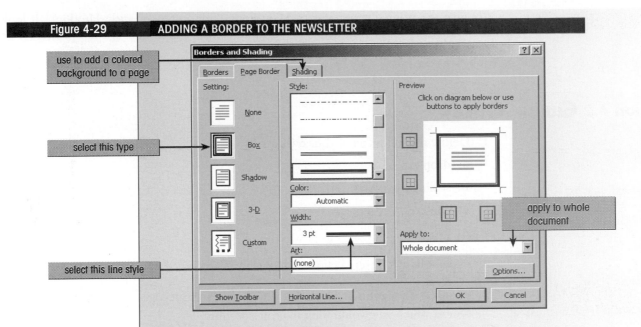

use to add a colored background to a page

select this type

select this line style

apply to whole document

6. Click the **OK** button, and then save your work. The newsletter is now surrounded by an attractive border, as shown in Figure 4-30.

Figure 4-30   NEWSLETTER WITH BORDER

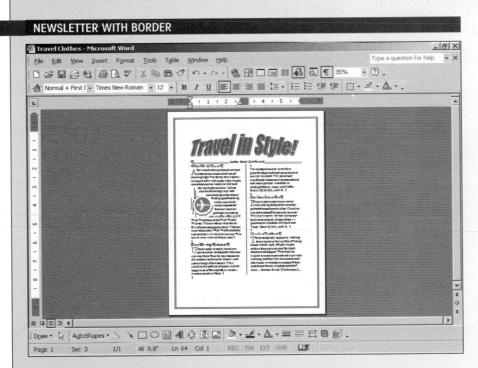

7. Create a footer that centers **Prepared by your name** and the current date at the bottom of the document. Be sure to replace **your name** with your first and last name. Format the footer in a small font to make it as unobtrusive as possible.

8. Preview the newsletter and then print it. Unless you have a color printer, the WordArt headline and the airplane will print in black and white.

9. If necessary, click the **Close** button on the Print Preview toolbar to return to Print Layout view, then close the newsletter and exit Word.

You give the printed newsletter to Max, along with a copy on disk. He thinks it looks great and thanks you for your help. He'll print it later on a high-quality color printer (to get the best resolution for printing multiple copies).

Session 4.2 QUICK CHECK

1. Define the following in your own words:

   a. **drop cap**

   b. **scaling**

   c. **clip art**

   d. **balance**

2. Explain how to insert a clip art graphic in Word.

3. Describe a situation in which you would want to scale a graphic. Describe a situation in which you would want to crop a graphic.

4. True or False: When inserting a drop cap, you can specify the number of lines you want the drop cap to extend into the document vertically.

5. Describe two different methods for inserting the registered trademark symbol in a document.

6. Besides the Symbol command on the Insert menu, what is another way of entering typographic symbols?

7. Describe the process for drawing a border around the page.

REVIEW ASSIGNMENTS

Max's Wide World Travel newsletter was a success; the sales for the advertised items were brisk. Now he has been asked to create a newsletter describing the highlights of some recent Wide World Travel tours. Max has already written the text of the newsletter and asks you to transform it into a professional-looking newsletter. Complete the following:

1. If necessary, start Word and make sure your Data Disk is in the appropriate disk drive. Check your screen to make sure your settings match those in the tutorial and that the nonprinting characters and Drawing toolbar are displayed.

2. Open the file **Travel** from the Review folder for Tutorial 4 on your Data Disk, and then save it as **Travel Highlights** in the same folder.

3. In the first paragraph after the heading "Wide World Tours," replace "YOUR NAME" with your first and last name.

4. In the first paragraph after the heading "Wide World Tours" (after the phone number), insert the following: "or visit our Web site at www.wideworldtravel.com." Then press Enter to insert a blank line. Remove the hyperlink from the Web address.

5. At the top of the document, create the headline "Wide World Highlights" using WordArt. In the WordArt Gallery, choose the third style from the right in the third row down from the top (the rainbow style with the shadow).

6. Change the shape of the WordArt object to Triangle Up, and then edit the WordArt text to add italics.

7. Apply the Top and Bottom wrapping style to the WordArt object.

8. Insert a blank paragraph at the beginning of the document, anchor the WordArt headline to the new paragraph, and then save your work. If the WordArt moves below the new paragraph symbol, drag it up above the new paragraph. When you are finished, the anchor symbol should be positioned to the left of the new paragraph symbol, with the WordArt object positioned above the new paragraph symbol.

9. If necessary, enlarge the WordArt object to span the entire width of the page. Be sure to hold down the Shift key while you drag. When you are finished, the WordArt object should be approximately .5 inches high on the left end, and about 1 inch tall at the center.

Explore ▶ 10. Practice dragging the adjustment handle (the yellow diamond on the left) up and down to change the slope of the WordArt image. Click the Undo button to undo each change. When you are finished, the adjustment handle should be located to the left of the middle resize handle on the left edge of the WordArt object.

Explore ▶ 11. Practice dragging the rotation handle to rotate the WordArt object. When you are finished, return the headline to its original, horizontal position.

12. Position the insertion point to the left of the first word in the first heading, and then format the newsletter text in two columns using the Columns dialog box. Insert a section break so that the columns formatting is applied to the part of the newsletter after the insertion point. Do not insert a line between columns. View the new columns in Print Layout view, using the Whole Page zoom setting.

13. Return to Page Width zoom, and then click to the left of the paragraph that begins "We prefaced our adventure . . . "

14. Insert the clip art graphic of the Eiffel Tower from the Buildings folder.

15. Select and resize the graphic so it is approximately 1.5 inches square.

16. Crop the image vertically on the left and right. When you are finished, the image

should be approximately 1 inch wide.

17. Use the Undo button to undo the cropping.

18. Wrap text around the graphic using the Tight wrapping option.

19. Add a drop cap for the first paragraph following each heading, using the default settings for the Dropped position.

Explore 20. Scroll to display the paragraph below the heading "Wide World Tours." Click after the last "s" in "Wide World Adventures," press the spacebar, and then type "(tm)" (without the quotation marks). Word's AutoCorrect feature converts the letters in parentheses to the trademark symbol. Save your work and then open a new, blank document, and practice using AutoCorrect to insert the typographic symbols shown earlier in Figure 4-26. When you are finished, close the document without saving your changes.

Explore 21. You can change the alignment of text in newspaper-style columns using the alignment buttons on the Formatting toolbar. Select both columns of text by clicking before the first word of the heading "Wide World Tours," pressing and holding down the Shift key, and then clicking after the last word of text in the second column ("square"). Use the Justify button on the Formatting toolbar to justify the text.

22. Balance the columns. If the words in the last line of the newsletter text are spaced too far apart after you insert the section break, click at the end of the line and then press Enter to move the section break to the next line.

23. Add a border around the page using a border style of your choice.

24. Preview, save, and print the newsletter. When you are finished, close the document and exit word.

CASE PROBLEMS

Case 1. City of Santa Fe, New Mexico Caroline Hestwood is the manager of information systems for the city of Santa Fe. She and her staff, along with the city manager, have just decided to convert all city computers from the Windows 98 operating system to Windows 2000 and to standardize applications software on the latest version of Microsoft Office. Caroline writes a monthly newsletter on computer operations and training, so this month she decides to devote the newsletter to the conversion. Complete the following:

1. If necessary, start Word, make sure your Data Disk is in the appropriate drive, and check your screen to make sure your settings match those in the tutorial.

2. Open the file **Convert** from the Cases folder for Tutorial 4 on your Data Disk, and then save the file as **Software Conversion** in the same folder.

Explore

3. If the text you want to format as WordArt has already been typed, you can begin creating your WordArt by selecting the text in the document. Select the text of the newsletter title, "Software Update." (Do not select the paragraph symbol at the end of the title.) Click the Insert WordArt button on the Drawing toolbar, and then choose the WordArt style in the third row down, first column on the left. Verify that "Software Update" appears in the Edit WordArt Text dialog box, and then click OK.

4. Set the wrapping style to Top and Bottom, insert a new paragraph, and then anchor the WordArt to the new paragraph.

5. Edit the WordArt object to set the font to 32-point Arial bold, and then apply the Arch Up (Curve) shape to the object. Resize the WordArt object so that it spans the width of the page from left margin to right margin and so that its maximum height is about 1 inch. (*Hint*: Use the resize handles while watching the horizontal and vertical rulers in Print Layout view to adjust the object to the appropriate size.)

6. Center and italicize the subtitle of the newsletter, "Newsletter from the Santa Fe Information Management Office."

7. Replace "INSERT YOUR NAME HERE" with your name, then center and italicize the line containing your name.

8. Insert a continuous section break before the subtitle.

Explore

9. You can emphasize paragraphs within a document by putting a border around one or more paragraphs and by adding shading. To learn how, select the subtitle and the line after it (containing your name). Click Format on the menu bar, and then click Borders and Shading. In the Borders and Shading dialog box, select the Box style on the Borders tab, click the Shading tab, select a light, see-through color from the Fill grid, such as Gray-15%, and then click OK.

10. Select everything in the newsletter from the heading "The Big Switch" through the last word in the document. Then use the Columns button in the Standard toolbar to format the body of the newsletter into two newspaper-style columns. Examine the newsletter to find the new section break.

Explore

11. Position the insertion point at the beginning of the first paragraph under the heading "Training on MS Office," and then open the Insert Clip Art Task Pane. In the Search text box, type Computer and then click Search. A group of clip art images appears in the Insert Clip Art Task Pane. Click an image that illustrates the newsletter content. The image is inserted into the newsletter. Close the Insert Clip Art Task Pane.

Explore

12. Resize the picture so that it is 35% of its original size. Instead of dragging the resize handles as you did in the tutorial, select the picture, and then click the Format Picture button on the Picture toolbar to open the Format Picture dialog box. Click the Size tab. Adjust the Height and Width settings to 35% in the Scale section, and make sure the Lock aspect ratio check box is selected. Click OK.

13. Use the appropriate Picture toolbar button to select the Tight wrapping option.

Explore   14. You can use the Replace command to replace standard word processing characters with typographic characters. To replace every occurrence of two dashes (– –) with an em dash (—), position the insertion point at the beginning of the first paragraph of text. Click Edit on the menu bar, and then click Replace. In the Find what text box, type two hyphens (--), and then press the Tab key to move the insertion point to the Replace with text box. Click the More button to display additional options, and then click the Special button at the bottom of the dialog box. Click Em Dash in the list. Word displays the special code for em dashes in the Replace with text box. Click the Replace All button. When the operation is complete, click the OK button, and then click the Close button.

Explore   15. Preview the newsletter. If it does not fit on one page, click the Shrink to Fit button on the Print Preview toolbar.

16. Insert a border around the newsletter. Use a border style of your choice.

17. If necessary, balance the columns.

18. Save and print the newsletter, and then close it and exit Word.

Case 2. Morning Star Movers Martin Lott is the executive secretary to Whitney Kremer, director of personnel for Morning Star Movers (MSM), a national moving company with headquarters in Minneapolis, Minnesota. Whitney assigned you the task of preparing the monthly newsletter News and Views, which provides news about MSM employees. You decide to update the layout and to use the desktop-publishing capabilities of Word to design the newsletter. You will use text assembled by other MSM employees for the body of the newsletter. Complete the following:

1. If necessary, start Word, make sure your Data Disk is in the appropriate drive, and check your screen to make sure your settings match those in the tutorial.

2. Open the file **Movers** from the Cases folder for Tutorial 4 on your Data Disk, and then save it as **Movers Newsletter** in the same folder.

3. Use the Find and Replace command to replace all instances of the name "Katrina" with your first name. Then replace all instances of "Pollei" with your last name.

4. Click at the end of the first section (to the right of the space after "contact her at") and then type "thurlow@msm.net" (without the quotes) followed by a period. Press Enter to insert a blank line, and then remove the hyperlink.

5. Create a "News and Views" WordArt title for the newsletter. Use the WordArt style in the third row down, fourth column from the left, and set the font to 24-point Arial bold. Set the wrapping style to Top and Bottom, and then anchor the WordArt to a new, blank paragraph.

6. Resize the WordArt object proportionally so that the title spans the width of the page from left margin to right margin and so that the height of the title is about 1 inch. (*Hint*: Use the resize handles while watching the horizontal and vertical rulers in Print Layout view to adjust the object to the appropriate size.)

7. Make sure the WordArt object is positioned above the new paragraph, and then format the body of the newsletter into two newspaper-style columns. Place a vertical rule between the columns.

Explore 8. You can change the structure of a newsletter by reformatting it with additional columns. Change the number of columns from two to three using the same technique you used in the previous step (that is, the Columns command on the Format menu). Make sure that the Equal column width check box is selected.

Explore 9. You can insert your own graphics, stored as an electronic file, just as quickly as you can insert clip art. Position the insertion point at the beginning of the paragraph below the heading "MSM Chess Team Takes Third." Click Insert on the menu bar, point to Picture, and then click From File. Look in the Cases folder for Tutorial 4 on your Data Disk, select the file named Knight, and then click the Insert button.

Explore 10. You can delete a graphic by selecting it, and then pressing the Delete key. To practice this technique, click the Knight graphic to select it, and then press the Delete key. To reinsert the graphic, click the Undo button.

11. Scale the height and the width of the picture to 60% of its original size. (*Hint*: To scale the size, click the Format Picture button on the Picture toolbar, and then set the Scale values on the Size tab, making sure the Lock aspect ratio check box is selected.) Close the Format Picture dialog box when you are finished.

Explore 12. In addition to cropping a picture with the Crop button, you can use the Format Picture dialog box. Using this dialog box allows you to be more precise because you can specify exact cropping measurements. To try it now, click the Format Picture button on the Picture toolbar, click the Picture tab, and change the values in the Crop from text boxes. Crop 0.3, 0.4, 0.2, and 0.4 inches from the left, right, top, and bottom of the picture, respectively.

Explore 13. You already know how to wrap text around a graphic or WordArt object using the Text Wrapping button. In some situations, however, you might need additional options to gain even more control over how text wraps in a document. To view these options now, click the Format Picture button on the Picture toolbar, click the Layout tab, and then click Advanced. Click the Tight icon, and notice the additional settings at the bottom of the Advanced Layout dialog box. Among other things, you can specify to what side the text should wrap and the distance to preserve between the text and the graphic. Click the Right only option button, click OK, and then click OK again. Keep in mind that you can also access the Advanced Layout dialog box from the Format WordArt dialog box.

Explore ▷ 14. Format drop caps in the first paragraph after each heading except the "MSM Chess Team Takes Third" heading. Use the default settings for number of lines, but change the font of the drop cap to Arial.

15. View the entire page. If necessary, decrease the height of the WordArt title or change the page margins until the entire newsletter fits onto one page and until each column starts with a heading.

16. Add a border around the entire page of the newsletter using the Page Border command.

17. Save the newsletter, and then preview and print it. Close the document and exit Word.

Case 3. *Wild Grains Grocery Cooperative* Mary Ann Hansen is the publicity director for Wild Grains Grocery Cooperative in Athens, Georgia. Local residents pay a membership fee to join the co-op, and then receive a 10% discount on all purchases. Many members don't realize that they can take advantage of other benefits—such as free cooking classes and monthly mailings with recipe cards and coupons. To spread the word, Mary Ann would like to create a brochure describing the benefits of joining the co-op. She has already written the text of the brochure. She would like the brochure to consist of one piece of paper folded in three parts, like a standard business letter, with text on both sides of the paper. Complete the following:

1. If necessary, start Word, make sure your Data Disk is in the appropriate drive, and check your screen to make sure your settings match those in the tutorial.

2. Open the file **Grains** from the Cases folder for Tutorial 4 on your Data Disk, and then save it as **Wild Grains Brochure**.

3. Below the cornucopia graphic, click after the Web address, insert a blank line and then type your first and last name. Remove the hyperlink from the Web address.

4. Format the entire document in three columns of equal width. Do not include a vertical line between columns. Don't be concerned that part of the text overflows onto a second page.

5. Click at the end of the list of member benefits (after the word "country") and press Ctrl+Enter to insert a page break. Click the Bullets button to remove the bullet from the new paragraph.

Explore ▷ 6. You are already familiar with adding section breaks and page breaks to a document. You can also add a column break, which forces the text after the insertion point to move to the next column. Click at the beginning of the heading "Join Now!" (just to the left of the "J"), click Insert on the menu bar and then click Break. Under Break Types, click Column break, and then click OK. Insert another column break before the heading "Member Benefits." On the second page, click at the top of the left-hand column, press Enter a few times to insert some blank paragraphs, and then insert another column break. (Don't be concerned if the new paragraph marks don't align.) Press Ctrl+End to move the insertion point to the end of the document and insert another column break.

7. Change the zoom setting to Whole Page and review your work. The document should consist of two pages, with three columns each. The graphic and the co-op address should appear in the middle column on the second page.

Explore 8. Click the cornucopia graphic in the second page, click the Copy button on the Standard toolbar, click to the left of the heading "Join Now!" and then add two blank paragraphs. Click in the first new paragraph (at the top of the column) and then click the Paste button on the Standard toolbar. The middle column of the first page now contains the graphic, with the heading "Join Now!" below, followed by two paragraphs of text.

9. Click in the left-hand column of page 2, and then delete all but one of the paragraph marks. With the insertion point located at the only remaining paragraph mark in the left-hand column, insert the WordArt text "WHY JOIN?" In the WordArt Gallery select the style in the fourth column from the left, third row down (the rainbow style with a shadow). Be sure to type "WHY JOIN?" in all uppercase letters in the Edit WordArt Text dialog box, and format the text in boldface. Save your work.

Explore 10. Select the WordArt object, and then click the WordArt Vertical Text button on the WordArt toolbar. The heading is positioned vertically in the left-hand column of page 2.

11. Increase the size of the WordArt object (by dragging a resize handle) so that the WordArt spans the height of the column—do *not* press Shift as you drag the handle—and the letters spread out to fill the height of the column. When you are finished, the WordArt object should be approximately 6 inches high. If you increase the size too much, the WordArt will jump to the next column. If that happens, click the Undo button and try again.

Explore 12. Click the Format WordArt button on the WordArt toolbar. In the Format WordArt dialog box, click the Colors and Lines tab, click the Color list arrow, click the black square in the upper-left hand corner of the palette, and then click OK. The WordArt changes from a rainbow style to all black. Save your work.

Explore 13. Use the Copy button on the Formatting toolbar to copy the "WHY JOIN?" WordArt object to the Office Clipboard. Paste a copy of the WordArt object in the right-hand column of page 2, and then change the text to "WILD GRAINS". When you are finished, page 2 should consist of the "WHY JOIN?" WordArt in the left-hand column, the graphic and address information in the middle column, and the "WILD GRAINS" WordArt in the right-hand column. Zoom to Whole Page view and examine your work.

14. If necessary, add paragraph breaks to the center column to center the graphic and the text vertically in relation to the WordArt titles. Adjust the size of the WordArt as necessary.

15. Use the Page Setup command on the File menu to center both pages vertically. (*Hint*: Use the Vertical alignment setting in the Layout tab.)

Explore ▸ 16. To print the brochure, you need to print the first page and print the second page on the reverse side. Click File on the menu bar, click Print, click the Pages option button, type 1, and then click OK. Retrieve the printed page, and then insert it into your printer's paper tray so that "WHY JOIN?" prints on the reverse side of the list of member benefits; likewise, "WILD GRAINS" should print on the reverse side of the "Welcome to Wild Grains" text. Whether you should place the printed page upside down or right-side up depends on your printer. You may have to print a few test pages until you get it right. When you finish, you should be able to turn page 1 (the page with the heading "Welcome to Wild Grains") face up, and then fold it inward like a business letter, along the two column borders. Fold the brochure so that the "WILD GRAINS" column lies on top.

17. Save and close the document, and then exit Word.

Case 4. New Job Newsletter You've just moved to a new part of the country and decide to send out a newsletter to friends and family describing your new job. In the one-page newsletter, you'll include articles about you and your colleagues, your new job, your new responsibilities, and future plans. You'll desktop publish the copy into a professional-looking newsletter. Complete the following:

1. If necessary, start Word, make sure your Data Disk is in the appropriate drive, and check your screen to make sure your settings match those in the tutorial.

2. Write two articles to include in the newsletter; save each article in a separate file.

3. Plan the general layout of your newsletter.

4. Create a title for your newsletter with WordArt.

5. Save the document as **New Job** in the Cases folder for Tutorial 4.

Explore ▸ 6. Insert the current date and your name as author below the title.

7. Insert the articles you wrote into your newsletter. Position the insertion point where you want the first article to appear, click Insert on the menu bar, click File, select the article you want to insert, and then click the Insert button. Repeat to insert the second article.

Explore ▸ 8. Format your newsletter with multiple columns.

9. Insert at least one clip art picture into your newsletter. If your computer is connected to the Internet, use the Clips Online option in the Insert Clip Art Task Pane to access Microsoft's online collection of clip art. Follow the directions on the screen to search for an image that illustrates the content of your newsletter. Download the image to your computer, and then insert it into the newsletter.

Explore ▸ 10. Wrap text around the graphic, and then add at least two drop caps in the newsletter.

11. Create a border around the page and then add shading to the entire document using the Shading tab in the Borders and Shading dialog box. (*Hint*: Press Ctrl+A to select the entire document, open the Borders and Shading dialog box, select a page border, click the Shading tab, select a light, transparent color from the Fill grid, such as Gray-15%, and then click OK.)

12. Save and print the newsletter, and then close the document and exit Word.

INTERNET ASSIGNMENTS

Student Union

The purpose of the Internet Assignments is to challenge you to find information on the Internet that you can use to create effective documents. The actual assignments are updated and maintained on the Course Technology Web site. Log on to the Internet and use your Web browser to go to the Student Union on the New Perspectives Series site at **www.course.com/NewPerspectives/studentunion**. Click the Online Companions link, and then click the link for this text.

QUICK CHECK ANSWERS

Session 4.1

1. List any four of the following: The printing is of high-quality; the document uses multiple fonts; the document incorporates graphics; the document uses typographic characters; the document uses columns and other special formatting features.

2. List any two of the following: In desktop publishing the reader sees the entire page at one time while in a Web page the reader sees only part of the page at a time; in desktop publishing the use of color increases printing costs, while in Web design, color itself does not affect the cost of producing a Web page; in desktop publishing the quality of the printer greatly affects the appearance of graphics in the printed page, while in Web design the quality of graphics is most affected by the type of electronic file in which the graphic is stored; in desktop publishing the page is static, while in Web design parts of the page can be animated, or include video and audio; the reader cannot interact with a desktop-published document, while it is possible to interact with a Web page by clicking hyperlinks.

3. (a) Using a desktop computer system to produce commercial-quality printed material. With desktop publishing, you can enter and edit text, create graphics, lay out pages, and print documents. (b) A document that can contain specially formatted text, graphics, video, and audio. A Web page is stored on a computer as a collection of electronic files and is designed to be viewed in a special program called a browser. (c) Unformatted text (d) A symbol that appears in the left margin, which shows a WordArt object's position in relation to the text.

4. False

5. False

6. To resize a WordArt object, select the object and drag its resize handles. To resize the WordArt object proportionally, press and hold the Shift key as you drag a resize handle.

   To change the text of a WordArt object, click the object to select it, click the Edit Text button on the WordArt toolbar, edit the text in the Edit WordArt Text dialog box, and then click OK.

7. The WordArt Shape button allows you to change the basic shape of a Word-Art object.

8. True

Session 4.2

1. (a) a large, uppercase letter that highlights the beginning of the text of a newsletter, chapter, or some other document section; (b) resizing an image to better fit a document; (c) existing, copyright-free artwork that you can insert into your document; (d) to make columns of equal length

2. Position the insertion point at the location where you want to insert the image, click the Insert Clip Art button on the Drawing toolbar, click Clip Organizer in the Task Pane, open the folder containing the image you want, click the arrow button on the image, click Copy, and then close the Clip Organizer. Finally, paste the graphic into the document.

3. You might scale a graphic to better fit the width of a column of text. You might crop a graphic to emphasize or draw attention to a particular part of the image or to eliminate unnecessary borders.

4. True

5. Click where you want to insert the symbol in the document, click Insert on the menu bar, click Symbol, click the Special Characters tab in the Symbol dialog box, click Registered Trademark in the list, click the Insert button, and then click the Close button. Type "(tm)".

6. using the AutoCorrect feature, which lets you type certain characters and then changes those characters into the corresponding symbol

7. Click Format on the menu bar, click Borders and Shading, click the Page Border tab in the Borders and Shading dialog box, select the border type you want in the Setting section, choose a line style from the Style list box, make sure Whole document appears in the Apply to list box, and then click OK.

New Perspectives on

MICROSOFT WORD 2002

Read This Before You Begin

To the Student

Data Disks

To complete the Level II tutorials, Review Assignments, and Case Problems, you need three Data Disks. Your instructor will either provide you with the Data Disks or ask you to make your own. You will also need storage space on your computer's hard drive.

If you are making your own Data Disks, you will need **three** blank, formatted high-density disks. You will need to copy a set of files and/or folders from a file server, standalone computer, or the Web onto your disk. Your instructor will tell you which computer, drive letter, and folders contain the files you need. You could also download the files by going to **www.course.com** and following the instructions on the screen.

The information below shows you which folders go on your disks, so that you will have enough disk space to complete all the tutorials, Review Assignments, and Case Problems:

Data Disk 1
Write this on the disk label:
Data Disk 1: Word 2002 Tutorial 5
Put this folder on the disk:
Tutorial.05

Data Disk 2
Write this on the disk label:
Data Disk 2: Word 2002 Tutorial 6 (Tutorial and Review)
Put these folders on the disk:
Tutorial.06\Tutorial and Tutorial.06\Review

Data Disk 3
Write this on the disk label:
Data Disk 3: Word 2002 Tutorial 6 (Cases)
Put this folder on the disk:
Tutorial.06\Cases

Before you begin Tutorial 7, copy the Tutorial.07 folder to your hard drive.

When you begin each tutorial, be sure you are using the correct Data Disk (or that you have copied the necessary files to your hard drive). Refer to the "File Finder" chart at the back of this text for more detailed information on which files are

used in which tutorials. See the inside front or inside back cover of this book for more information on Data Disk files, or ask your instructor or technical support person for assistance.

Course Labs

The Word Level II tutorials feature an interactive Course Lab to help you understand Internet: World Wide Web concepts. The Lab Assignments at the end of Tutorial 7 refer to this Lab.

To start a Lab, click the **Start** button on the Windows taskbar, point to **Programs**, point to **Course Labs**, point to **New Perspectives Course Labs**, and click the name of the Lab you want to use.

Using Your Own Computer

If you are going to work through this book using your own computer, you need:

- **Computer System** Microsoft Windows 98, NT, 2000 Professional, or higher must be installed on your computer. This book assumes you have installed Microsoft Word 2002 on your computer. To complete Tutorial 7, you also need to have Microsoft Excel 2002 installed on your computer. Depending on the options chosen when you installed Word, you may need access to the Microsoft Office XP installation CD in order to install additional features. (The tutorial steps provide information on installing these features as you need them.)

- **Data Disks** You will not be able to complete the tutorials or exercises in this book using your own computer until you have your Data Disks.

- **Course Labs** See your instructor or technical support person to obtain the Course Lab software for use on your own computer.

Visit Our World Wide Web Site

Additional materials designed especially for you are available on the World Wide Web. Go to www.course.com/NewPerspectives.

To the Instructor

The Data Disk Files and Course Labs are available on the Instructor's Resource Kit for this title. Follow the instructions in the Help file on the CD-ROM to install the programs to your network or standalone computer. For information on creating Data Disks or the Course Labs, see the "To the Student" section above. Please note:

students need to install the data files for Tutorial 7 onto their hard drives due to the complexity of the tutorial.

You are granted a license to copy the Data Files and Course Labs to any computer or computer network used by students who have purchased this book.

CREATING
STYLES, OUTLINES, TABLES, AND TABLES OF CONTENTS

Writing a Business Plan for Safe Site Inc.

CASE

SafeSite Inc.

Pamela Morris and Maya Siu have been friends since college, where they both majored in computer science. Since graduation a few years ago, they have been working for e-commerce companies—companies that sell their products over the Web. Typically, customers make e-commerce purchases by typing information into a form on a Web page and then clicking a button. The information is then sent to the company via the Internet. One problem with this arrangement is that many customers hesitate to send private information, such as credit card numbers, over the Internet because they fear that a third party might intercept this information and use it for fraudulent purposes. To help protect their customers' privacy, e-commerce companies employ a variety of security measures. Still, many consumers continue to avoid e-commerce sites because they don't understand how effective these security measures are.

With this in mind, Pamela and Maya are developing a new Web site, called SafeSite, that will allow consumers to look up security ratings for e-commerce companies. Pamela and Maya have already established a new business, SafeSite Inc., which will market the Web site. Like many Web businesses, SafeSite Inc. will ultimately generate revenue by selling advertising space. The more popular their site becomes with e-commerce customers, the more Maya and Pamela will be able to charge for advertising on SafeSite.

Maya and Pamela are ready to quit their jobs to work full-time on SafeSite. Before they can do that, they must secure a start-up loan from First Bank of the Pacific. To obtain the loan, they must write a business plan—a report that details all aspects of starting a new business, including the market for the business, operations, financial, and personnel information. They have written part of the plan and have asked you to help them work on it.

In this session, you will see how Maya and Pamela planned their report. Then you'll open the report and use the Microsoft Word Thesaurus to edit the report. You'll learn about using fonts and templates, and then modify, create, and apply template styles to format the report. Finally, you will create a new template for use in future SafeSite documents.

Planning the Document

Before they began working on their business plan, Maya and Pamela consulted a number of resources, including the U.S. government Small Business Administration (SBA). They know that a thorough business plan informs prospective investors about the purpose, organization, goals, and projected profits of the proposed business. It also analyzes the target industry, including available market research. Most importantly, a business plan should convince potential investors that the venture is viable, well-conceived, and worthy of funding.

Maya and Pamela want to organize their business plan in a standard manner. According to information on the SBA's Web site, the body of a business plan can be divided into four parts: the description of the business; the marketing plan; the financial management plan; and the management plan. In addition, a business plan should include an executive summary, supporting documents, and financial projections. Maya and Pamela have completed some of these sections, and have saved them in a Word document named SafeSite.

Maya and Pamela have begun to format the document, but want you to check the fonts, headers, and styles and make sure the formatting is consistent. They also need you to create a table of contents and create a new folder in which to store your version of the document.

Creating a New Folder

You'll begin by opening the current draft of the business plan. Pamela wants you to create a new folder in which to store the business plan and any related files. That way she can easily copy the entire folder to a floppy disk and transfer the files to her home computer. You'll create the folder, and then save the document in the new folder, using a different filename.

To open the document and save it in a new folder:

1. Start Word, if necessary, make sure your Data Disk is in the appropriate drive, and check the screen. Make sure that nonprinting characters are displayed.

2. Open the file **SafeSite** from the Tutorial subfolder in the Tutorial.05 folder on your Data Disk.

3. Switch to Normal view, if necessary.

4. Click **File** on the menu bar, and then click **Save As** to display the Save As dialog box. You'll now create a new folder called Business Plan within the Tutorial folder.

5. Click the **Create New Folder** button 📁 located near the top of the Save As dialog box. The New Folder dialog box opens, as shown in Figure 5-1.

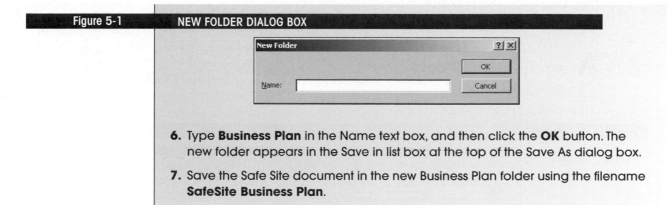

Figure 5-1   NEW FOLDER DIALOG BOX

6. Type **Business Plan** in the Name text box, and then click the **OK** button. The new folder appears in the Save in list box at the top of the Save As dialog box.

7. Save the Safe Site document in the new Business Plan folder using the filename **SafeSite Business Plan**.

Before you begin formatting the SafeSite business plan, read through it carefully to check for word usage. You can find synonyms for overused words by using Word's built-in Thesaurus.

Using the Thesaurus

In the paragraph above the last heading in the SafeSite business plan document, the word "market" occurs twice in one sentence. Pamela asks you to replace the second occurrence with another word that has the same meaning. You can do this using the Thesaurus. The **Thesaurus** is a Word feature that contains a list of words and their synonyms. Similar to a thesaurus reference book, the Word Thesaurus lets you look up a specific word to find its synonyms and related words. Then you can immediately insert an appropriate synonym into a document. The Thesaurus is a useful editing tool that helps make your word choices varied and exact.

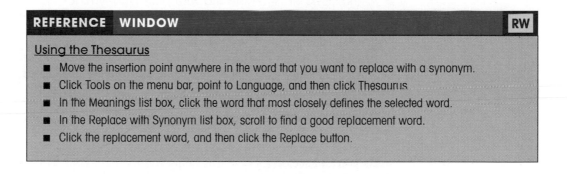

REFERENCE WINDOW   **RW**

Using the Thesaurus
- Move the insertion point anywhere in the word that you want to replace with a synonym.
- Click Tools on the menu bar, point to Language, and then click Thesaurus.
- In the Meanings list box, click the word that most closely defines the selected word.
- In the Replace with Synonym list box, scroll to find a good replacement word.
- Click the replacement word, and then click the Replace button.

You'll now use the Thesaurus to find a synonym for the word "market."

To find synonyms using the Thesaurus:

1. Click **Edit** on the menu bar, click **Find**, and then use the Search and Replace dialog box to find the sentence that begins "We are prepared to refine our site."

2. In the sentence that begins "We are prepared to refine our site," click the second occurrence of the word **market**.

3. Click **Tools** on the menu bar, point to **Language**, and then click **Thesaurus**. The Thesaurus: English (U.S.) dialog box opens. The word "market" appears in the Looked Up list box. A list of possible meanings for "market" appears in the Meanings list. "Marketplace" is selected in the Meanings list. A list of synonyms for "marketplace" appears to the right. Your Thesaurus dialog box should look similar to Figure 5-2, although your list of synonyms may differ.

Figure 5-2	FINDING SYNONYMS FOR MARKET

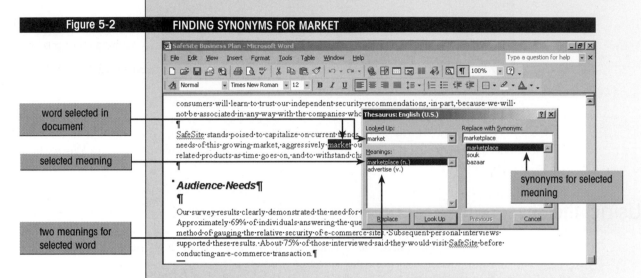

word selected in document

selected meaning

two meanings for selected word

synonyms for selected meaning

Whenever you use the Thesaurus, be sure to select the correct meaning for the word you're looking up. For example, in the business plan, the selected occurrence of "market" means advertise, not marketplace. You need to select this meaning before you can view the correct synonyms.

4. Click **advertise (v.)** in the Meanings list box. (Note that the "v." in parentheses indicates that the word is a verb.) The synonyms for "advertise" appear in the Replace with Synonym list box on the right. Pamela thinks that "promote" is the best synonym.

5. Click **promote** in the Replace with Synonym list box to highlight it, and then click the **Replace** button. The Thesaurus dialog box closes, and the word "promote" replaces the word "market" in the document.

6. Save your work.

As you can see, the Thesaurus helps you increase your word power as you write. Now that the text of the chapter is finished, you can work on its appearance. To create a professional-looking document, you need to understand how to use fonts effectively.

Choosing Fonts

The Word default font, Times New Roman, is useful for many situations. But in some cases, you may want to choose a different font. Times New Roman was specifically designed for narrow-column newspaper text. For reports (such as business plans), Web pages, and other documents that have wider columns, a wider font is sometimes easier to read. Here are some general principles that might help you decide which fonts to use in your documents:

- It's common practice to use a serif font for the main text. A **serif** is a small embellishment at the tips of the lines of a character, as shown in Figure 5-3. "Sans" is French for "without," thus, a **sans serif font** is a font without embellishments.

Figure 5-3 — SERIF AND SANS SERIF FONTS

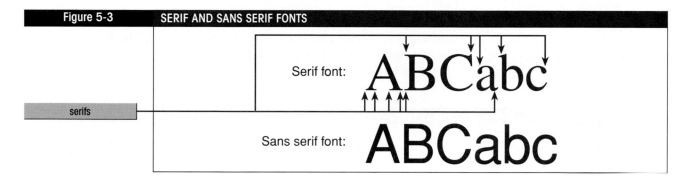

serifs

- Common serif fonts include Book Antiqua, Courier, Garamond, and Times New Roman, some of which are shown in Figure 5-4. Because serif fonts are easy to read, they are appropriate not only for main text, but also for titles and headings.

Figure 5-4 — SAMPLE SERIF FONTS

- Examples of common sans serif fonts include Arial, Arial Narrow, Century Gothic, and Lucida Console, some of which are shown in Figure 5-5. Large blocks of text in sans serif font can be harder to read than serif fonts, so you should use sans serif fonts for titles, headings, headers and footers, captions, and other special parts of a document.

Figure 5-5	SAMPLE SANS SERIF FONTS

Arial
Arial Narrow
Century Gothic

- Avoid all-uppercase sans serif text, which is difficult to read. All-uppercase serif font is easier to read, but mixed uppercase and lowercase text in any font is better still.
- Avoid unusual or fancy fonts except in certificates, invitations, advertisements, and other specialty documents. Examples of specialty fonts include Brush Script, Impact, Monotype Corsiva, and Stencil. Some specialty fonts are shown in Figure 5-6.

Figure 5-6	SAMPLE SPECIALTY FONTS

Brush Script

Monotype Corsiva

STENCIL

- Avoid excessive changes in fonts and font attributes. Typically, the text of a document should include only one or two fonts—one for the main paragraphs and another one for the titles and headings. Excessive use of boldface and italics makes a document appear cluttered and sloppy and detracts attention from the document's content.
- You can add special effects to most fonts by adjusting the formatting settings in the Font dialog box. (To open this dialog box, click Format on the menu bar, and then click Font.) For example, you can format a font as small caps (a reduced version of regular capital letters), superscript (slightly above the main line), subscript (slightly below the main line), outline (only the outline of the letters), or with shadows. Figure 5-7 shows some common font effects. Take care not to overuse special effects, or your document will look messy.

Figure 5-7	COMMON FONT EFFECTS

SMALL CAPS

Super^{script}

Sub_{script}

Outline

Shadow

Pamela wants you to choose some appropriate fonts and apply them to the business plan.

Applying Styles

Now that you understand how to use fonts effectively, you're ready to learn how to apply them quickly to text. It's often helpful to use the Format Painter to copy formatting (including fonts) from one paragraph to another. However, when you're working on a long document, it is easier to use the sets of predefined formats known as **styles**. Every Word document opens with a set of styles that includes Normal (the default style for paragraphs in a Word document), Heading 1, Heading 2, and Heading 3. Word's default Normal style is 12-point Times New Roman, left alignment, with single-line spacing.

All styles used in a document are listed in the Style list on the Formatting toolbar. Figure 5-8 shows the default styles available with a new, blank document. Note that the Style list will rarely be so short, because every time you change the formatting in a document (for example, by adding a bulleted list or underlining a heading), Word adds your formatting choices to the Style list as new styles.

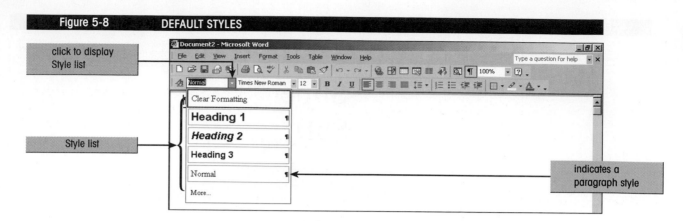

Figure 5-8   DEFAULT STYLES

click to display
Style list

Style list

indicates a
paragraph style

The easiest way to apply a style is to select the text you want to format, and then select a style in the Style list. However, if you plan to work extensively with styles in a document, you may prefer to use the options in the Styles and Formatting Task Pane. You can also use the Reveal Formatting Task Pane, which summarizes all the formatting applied to selected text. (You'll have a chance to use the Styles and Formatting Task Pane later in this tutorial. You'll use the Reveal Formatting Task Pane in the Case Problems at the end of this tutorial.)

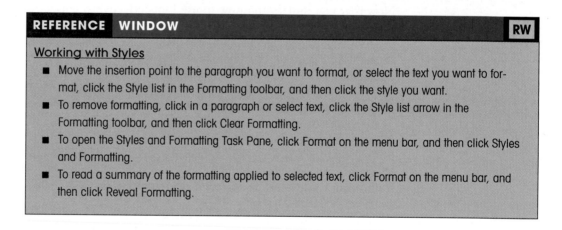

REFERENCE WINDOW   **RW**

Working with Styles

- Move the insertion point to the paragraph you want to format, or select the text you want to format, click the Style list in the Formatting toolbar, and then click the style you want.
- To remove formatting, click in a paragraph or select text, click the Style list arrow in the Formatting toolbar, and then click Clear Formatting.
- To open the Styles and Formatting Task Pane, click Format on the menu bar, and then click Styles and Formatting.
- To read a summary of the formatting applied to selected text, click Format on the menu bar, and then click Reveal Formatting.

Pamela and Maya used Word's default styles to format the headings in their business plan. However, after looking over the document, Pamela notices some inconsistencies. For example, she forgot to apply the Heading 1 style to the "Executive Summary" heading at the beginning of the document. You'll use the Style list to apply the Heading 1 style.

To apply a style:

1. Scroll up to the beginning of the document, and then click anywhere in the **Executive Summary** heading.

2. Click the **Style** list arrow in the Formatting toolbar. The Style list opens, as shown in Figure 5-9. The Style list contains the default styles included with all new Word documents (shown earlier in Figure 5-8), and styles for additional formatting (such as the bulleted list format) applied by Maya and Pamela. You want to apply the Heading 1 style.

| Figure 5-9 | STYLE LIST FOR SAFESITE BUSINESS PLAN DOCUMENT |

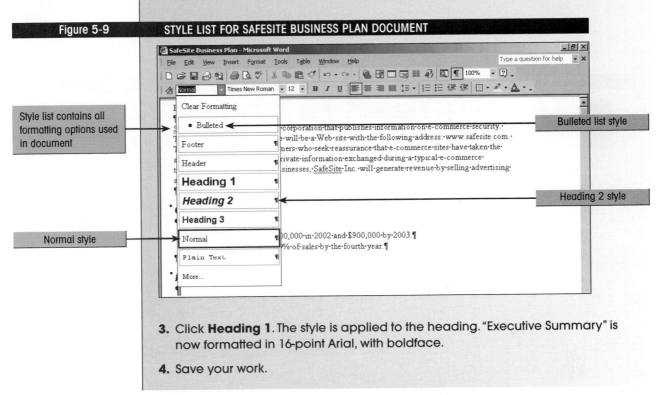

Style list contains all formatting options used in document

Bulleted list style

Heading 2 style

Normal style

3. Click **Heading 1**. The style is applied to the heading. "Executive Summary" is now formatted in 16-point Arial, with boldface.

4. Save your work.

Now that you are familiar with the Word Style list, you are ready to learn how to add other predefined styles to a document. You do this by using a Word template.

Using a Template

A **template** is a set of predefined styles designed for a specific type of document. For example, Word provides templates for formatting reports, brochures, memos, letters, and resumes. The Word default template, the Normal template, contains the Normal paragraph style described earlier. You can change the available styles by attaching a different template to a document. You can also use a Word template as the basis for a completely new document.

Another Word feature related to templates is known as a theme. A **theme** is a unified design for a document and can include background colors, horizontal and vertical lines, and graphics. Themes include colorful backgrounds and borders, and are designed for Web pages and other documents that you plan to present online. Typically, they are not suitable for business-related reports (such as a business plan).

Pamela wants to use the Word Professional Report template to format the business plan. She explains that you can see the styles available in this template by opening it from the New Documents Task Pane.

To review the styles in the Professional Report template:

1. Click **File** on the menu bar, and then click **New**. The New Document Task Pane opens.

2. Under the "New From Template" heading, click **General Templates**. The Templates dialog box opens. The tabs in this dialog box list a variety of templates which you can use as the basis for letters, reports, memos, and many other kinds of documents.

3. Click the **Reports** tab, if necessary. As shown in Figure 5-10, the Reports tab displays the templates that you can use to create reports. (Your Templates dialog box might contain more or fewer templates than the ones shown in Figure 5-10.) You're interested in the Professional Report template.

Figure 5-10 | TEMPLATES DIALOG BOX

tabs contain templates for several types of documents

Reports template tab

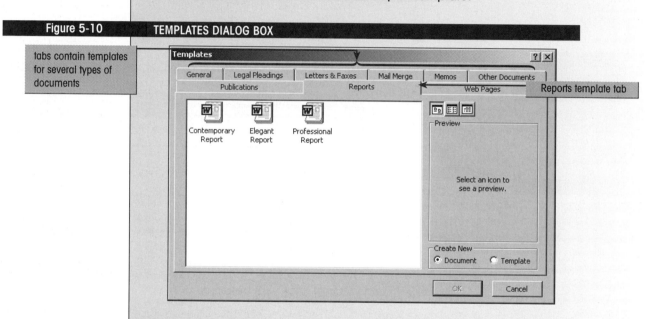

4. Click **Professional Report** and then click **OK**. The template opens in the Document window. It contains placeholder text formatted with the template styles.

   TROUBLE? If you see a message indicating that the Professional Report template is not installed, insert the Microsoft Office XP CD into your CD-ROM drive, and then click the OK button. If the Office XP CD is not available to you, choose another template.

5. Click the **Style** list arrow on the Formatting toolbar, examine the styles included in the template, press **Esc** to close the Style list, scroll through the document to view the formatted text, and then close the template.

You could use this template to create a new document by selecting the placeholder text and typing new text. However, the SafeSite Business Plan document already contains formatted headings. In this case, it makes more sense to attach the template to the existing document (that is, to the SafeSite Business Plan document), and then have Word apply the template styles automatically. (You'll use a template as the basis for a new document in the Review Assignments at the end of this chapter.)

Attaching a Template

You attach a template to a document using the Templates and Add-ins command on the Tools menu. Typically, Word's template files are stored in a subfolder of the Microsoft Office folder, in the Program Files folder. However, they may be stored in a different folder on your computer. Once you select the template file you want to attach, you need to select the "Automatically update document styles" check box in the Templates and Add-ins dialog box. This checkbox ensures that the templates styles are added to the document's Style list.

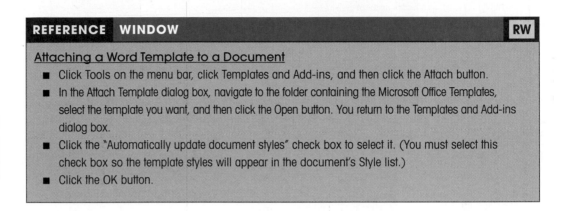

REFERENCE WINDOW   **RW**

Attaching a Word Template to a Document

- Click Tools on the menu bar, click Templates and Add-ins, and then click the Attach button.
- In the Attach Template dialog box, navigate to the folder containing the Microsoft Office Templates, select the template you want, and then click the Open button. You return to the Templates and Add-ins dialog box.
- Click the "Automatically update document styles" check box to select it. (You must select this check box so the template styles will appear in the document's Style list.)
- Click the OK button.

Pamela asks you to attach the Professional Report template to the SafeSite Business Plan document. The Professional Report template file is included on your Data Disk.

To preview and attach the Professional Report template to the business plan:

1. Click **Tools** on the menu bar, and then click **Templates and Add-ins**. The Templates and Add-ins dialog box opens.

2. Click the **Attach** button. The Attach Template dialog box opens. Use the Look in list arrow to open the Tutorial subfolder within the Tutorial.05 folder on your Data Disk.

3. If necessary, click **Professional Report** in the file list, as shown in Figure 5-11.

Figure 5-11	TEMPLATE SELECTED IN ATTACH TEMPLATE DIALOG BOX

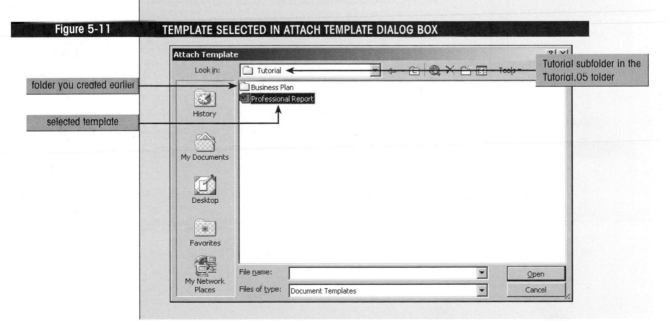

4. Click the **Open** button. The Attach Template dialog box closes, and you return to the Templates and Add-ins dialog box.

5. Click the **Automatically update document styles** check box to select it. Your Templates and Add-ins dialog box should look similar to the one in Figure 5-12.

Figure 5-12	TEMPLATES AND ADD-INS DIALOG BOX

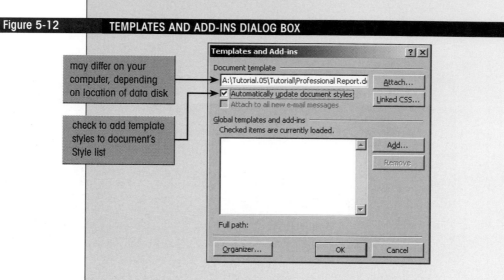

may differ on your computer, depending on location of data disk

check to add template styles to document's Style list

6. Click the **OK** button. The Templates and Add-ins dialog box closes, and you return to the Document window. The document is now formatted using the styles of the Professional Report template, as shown in Figure 5-13.

Figure 5-13	DOCUMENT FORMATTED WITH TEMPLATE STYLES

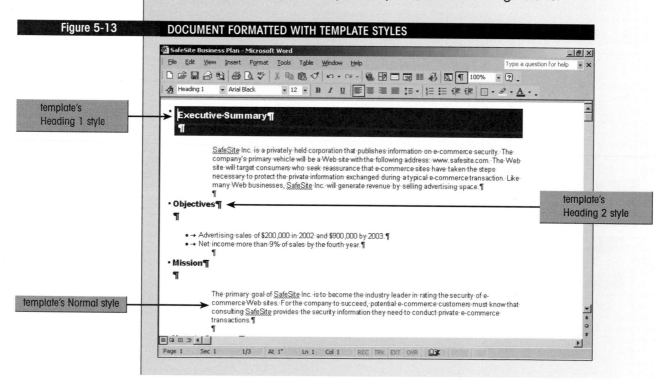

template's Heading 1 style

template's Heading 2 style

template's Normal style

7. Click the **Executive Summary** heading and read the style name in the Style list box. The template's Heading 1 style includes a black background and white text.

8. Click in the paragraph below the "Executive Summary" heading, and read the style name in the Style list box. The template's Normal style includes a paragraph indentation, and a 10-point Arial font.

9. Click the **Style** list arrow on the Formatting toolbar, and scroll through the list of template styles. Note that the styles with paragraph marks next to them are considered paragraph styles. When you click a paragraph style, the paragraph containing the insertion point is formatted (whether or not the entire paragraph is selected). The styles with lowercase a's are character styles. When you select a character style, only the text you have selected is formatted. You'll learn more about character and paragraph formatting later in this tutorial. Figure 5-14 shows examples of character and paragraph styles.

| Figure 5-14 | TEMPLATE CHARACTER AND PARAGRAPH STYLES |

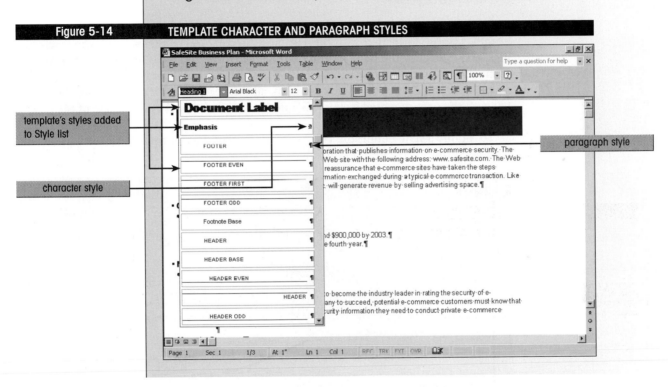

Applying Template Styles

After you attach a template to a document, you often need to correct formatting problems. For instance, the Normal style paragraphs in the report document are indented slightly. However, the bulleted lists in the document are not. Pamela asks you to fix this problem by applying the template's List Bullet 2 style, a bulleted list style that includes paragraph indentation.

To apply template styles to the document:

1. Press the **Esc** key to close the style list.

2. Select the bulleted list of objectives near the beginning of the document. Take care to select both items in the list, as well as the paragraph mark at the end of each item. Do not, however, select the paragraph mark below the bulleted list.

3. Click the **Style** list arrow on the Formatting toolbar, scroll down, and then click **List Bullet 2**. The list of objectives is indented further to the right and formatted with square bullets.

   TROUBLE? If the list is formatted without bullets, you may have clicked "List 2" rather than "List Bullet 2." Click the Undo button on the Standard toolbar and try again.

4. Use the List Bullet 2 style to format the bulleted lists below the headings "Keys to Success" and "Market Analysis Summary."

5. Save your work.

Modifying a Style

After looking over the document, Pamela decides that she wants to italicize the second-level headings (those formatted with the Heading 2 style). You could select all the level-2 headings, and then click the Italic button on the Formatting toolbar. However, it's more efficient to change the style definition, which specifies the particular font, size, and format for that style. Once you change the style definition, all the headings with that style will be reformatted with the new, modified style. This automatic updating makes styles one of the most flexible and helpful Word tools.

To modify a style definition, you move the insertion point to the text formatted with the style you want to change, and then open the Styles and Formatting Task Pane.

REFERENCE WINDOW   **RW**

Modifying a Style

- Click Format on the menu bar, and then click Styles and Formatting to open the Styles and Formatting Task Pane.
- In the Styles and Formatting Task Pane, right-click the style you want to modify, and then click Modify.
- In the Modify Style dialog box, use the toolbar buttons to select formatting. For other formatting changes, use the Format list button.
- If you want to save your style changes to the original template file, select the Add to template check box. If you don't select this check box, your style changes will be saved only to the template attached to the active document.
- To update all text in the document with the modified style, select the Automatically update check box.

You're ready to add italics to the Heading 2 style. You'll start by moving the insertion point to a heading formatted with the Heading 2 style.

To change the Heading 2 style to italics:

1. Click the **Objectives** heading near the beginning of the document.

2. Click **Format** on the menu bar, and then click **Styles and Formatting**. The Styles and Formatting Task Pane opens. As shown in Figure 5-15, it contains a list that you can use to apply styles. The box at the top of the Task Pane contains the name of the style applied to the paragraph that contains the insertion point—in this case, the Heading 2 style. Note that you could click the Select All button to select all the text in the document that is formatted with the Heading 2 style.

Figure 5-15   **STYLES AND FORMATTING TASK PANE**

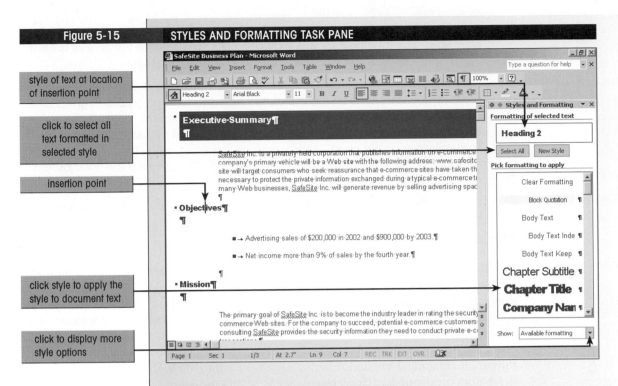

style of text at location of insertion point

click to select all text formatted in selected style

insertion point

click style to apply the style to document text

click to display more style options

3. Scroll the Pick formatting to apply list until you can see "Heading 2" in the list.

4. In the Pick formatting to apply list, right-click **Heading 2**. A shortcut menu opens.

5. Click **Modify** in the shortcut menu. The Modify Style dialog box opens, as shown in Figure 5-16. This dialog box contains a toolbar that you can use to apply common formatting options. For other formatting changes, you can use the Format list button. The dialog box also includes a preview of the selected style and a description of all its formatting attributes.

Figure 5-16   **MODIFY STYLE DIALOG BOX**

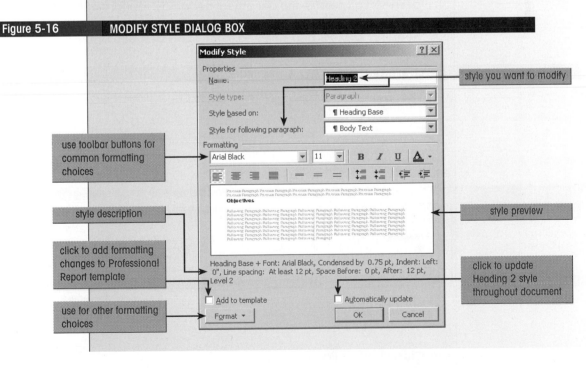

style you want to modify

use toolbar buttons for common formatting choices

style description

style preview

click to add formatting changes to Professional Report template

use for other formatting choices

click to update Heading 2 style throughout document

6. In the Modify Style dialog box, point to the toolbar buttons and read their names. Notice that the Font box indicates that the Heading 2 style font is Arial Black. The Font Size box indicates that the font size is 11 points.

7. Click the **Format** list button in the lower-left corner of the dialog box, and review the commands on the menu that appears. When you are finished, press the **Esc** key to close the menu. (You'll use this Format menu in the Case Problems at the end of this tutorial. Keep in mind that it includes many of the same options as the main Format menu in the Word menu bar.) Now, you want to add italics to the Heading 2 style. You can do this by using the Italic button on the toolbar.

8. Click the **Italic** button ⬚ on the Modify Style dialog box toolbar. The word "Italic" is added to the style description.

Now you need to indicate how you want to apply the modified style. If you want to save your style changes to the original template file (that is, to the original Professional Report template file), you select the Add to template check box. If you don't select this check box, your style changes are saved only to the template attached to the active document. Pamela does not want you to change the original Professional Report template file, so you will not select the Add to template check box. However, you need to indicate that you want Word to format all Heading 2 text in the active document with italics. You can do this by selecting the Automatically update check box.

To update the Heading 2 style and return to the document:

1. Click the **Automatically update** check box to insert a check mark, and then click the **OK** button. The Modify Style dialog box closes. You return to the Document window, where the Styles and Formatting Task Pane remains open.

2. Save your work and then scroll through the document to view the new style definition applied to the document headings. Text formatted with the Heading 2 style is now italicized, making the headings more noticeable. Note that the Heading 2 style is also italicized in the Task Pane. See Figure 5-17.

Figure 5-17   NEW FONT DEFINITION APPLIED DOCUMENT

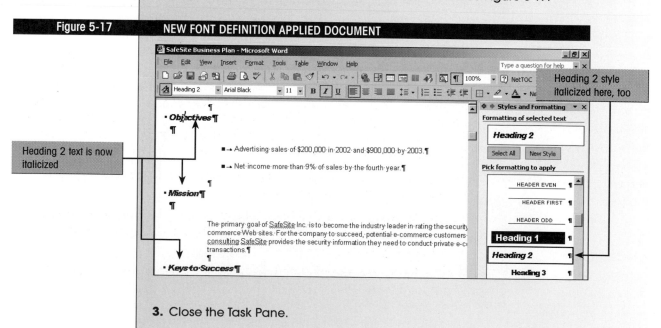

3. Close the Task Pane.

Defining New Styles

To add interest to the business plan, Maya asks you to create, or define, a new style that includes all the characteristics of the Normal style, plus a light gray background. She plans to use this new style to emphasize the paragraph under the "Executive Summary" heading, and for other parts of the business plan that she hasn't written yet.

Defining, or creating, a new style is similar to modifying an existing style. To define a new style, you assign it a name and give it a new style definition. You can define a style two different ways: by example and by using the New Style dialog box.

REFERENCE WINDOW   **RW**

Defining New Styles

- Select text formatted with a style that you want to use as the basis of the new style.
- Apply the formatting you want to include in the style.
- With the newly formatted text selected, type a name for the new style in the Style list box, and then press the Enter key.

or

- Select text formatted with a style that you can use as the basis of the new style.
- Open the Styles and Formatting Task Pane, and then click the New Style button.
- In the New Style dialog box, use the toolbar buttons or the Format button to specify the formatting you want to include in the style.
- Type a name for the style in the Style text box.
- Click the Style Type list arrow, and click Paragraph or Character.
- To add the new style to the template file attached to the document, select the Add to template check box.
- To update the document with the new style, select the Automatically update check box.

Maya wants you to define a new style called Summary that contains all the formatting elements of the Normal style, plus a light gray background. She also wants the style to align the paragraph along the left margin. You'll start by selecting a paragraph that is formatted with the Normal style, and then apply the formatting you want.

To apply the formatting you want to include in the style:

1. Select the paragraph of text under the heading "Executive Summary" (the paragraph that begins "SafeSite Inc. is a privately held corporation"). This paragraph is formatted with the Normal style. You want the new style to include all the characteristics of this paragraph, plus a light gray shading. You can add this shading by using the Borders and Shading command on the Format menu.

2. Click **Format** on the menu bar, and then click **Borders and Shading**. The Borders and Shading dialog box opens.

3. Click the **Shading** tab, and in the palette of shading options, click the fourth square from the left on the top row (gray 12.5%), and then click the **OK** button. The Borders and Shading dialog box closes.

4. Click the **Decrease Indent** button 🔲 twice. The paragraph moves left, so that it is aligned on the left margin.

5. Deselect the paragraph and review the formatting change. A light gray background has been added to the paragraph, as shown in Figure 5-18. It is also aligned on the left margin.

Figure 5-18 | **NEWLY FORMATTED PARAGRAPH**

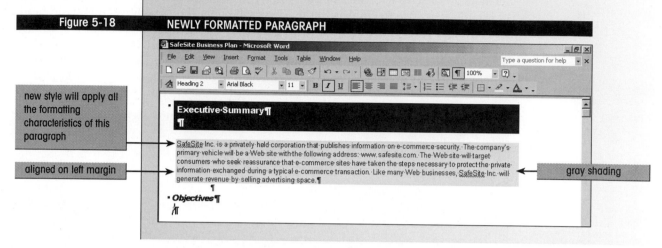

Now that the paragraph is formatted the way you want, you can use its formatting to define a new style. As you will see in the next set of steps, Word added the new formatting (with the 12.5% gray screen) to the Style list.

To define a new style:

1. Click the **Style** list arrow in the Formatting toolbar, and scroll down until you see Left .08". Word created this new style when you applied the gray shading to the selected paragraph. You could use this new style whenever you want to format a paragraph in Arial 10-point text, with a gray background, and aligned on the left margin. However, the style's name (Left .08") is not very descriptive. Instead of using the styles created automatically by Word, it is usually better to create a new style yourself, with a descriptive name of your choice. Pamela wants to name the new style "Summary," so that she and Maya remember that it is designed for summary paragraphs at the beginning a document.

2. Press the **Esc** key. The Style list closes.

3. Click anywhere within the paragraph with the gray background.

4. Click the **Style** list box, type **Summary**, and then press **Enter**.

5. Open the **Style** list. As shown in Figure 5-19, the style named Left .08" has been replaced with a style named "Summary." (The styles in the list are arranged alphabetically, so you'll find "Summary" near the end of the list.)

Figure 5-19   **NEWLY DEFINED STYLE**

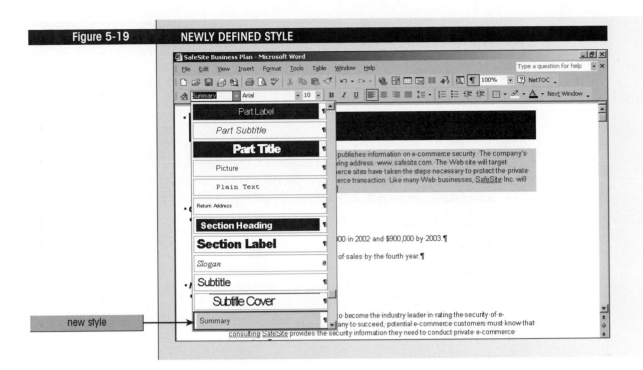

new style

Creating a New Template

The document now contains all the styles that Pamela and Maya will use when creating other important documents for SafeSite Inc. They ask you to save these styles as a new template, which they can use to create SafeSite documents.

By default, Word offers to save your new template in the Template folder. You can access any templates saved to this folder later using the New command on the File menu. For this tutorial, however, you'll save your template in the same folder as the rest of your data files.

REFERENCE WINDOW   **RW**

<u>Creating and Using a New Template</u>
- Create a new document containing all the styles you want to include in your template, save it as a Word document, and then delete all text from the document.
- Click File on the menu bar, click Save As, click the Save as type list arrow, and then click Document Template.
- Verify that the Templates folder is displayed in the Save in list box. If you save your template to this folder, it will appear as one of the options in the Templates dialog box. If you prefer, you can save the template in a different location, such as a folder on your Data Disk.
- Type a descriptive name for the template in the File name text box, click the Save button, and then close the template.
- To begin creating a document based on a template stored in the Template folder, click File on the menu bar, click New, click General Templates in the New Document Task Pane, click the icon for your template in the General tab, and then click the OK button. Create the document, applying styles as necessary. Save the new document as a Word document.
- To begin creating a document based on a template saved in any location, open a blank document, and then attach the template (as described earlier in this tutorial) using the Templates and Add-ins command on the Tools menu. If you prefer, you can open the template and then save it as a Word document.

You're ready to save the styles in the document as a new template. You'll save the template to the Business Plan folder that you created earlier, so that you can easily give it to Pamela and Maya. Your first step is to save the SafeSite Business Plan document, preserving your work so far. Then you will delete the text in the document and save it with a new name as a template.

To save the styles of the current document as a new template:

1. Click the **Save** button 🖫 on the Standard toolbar to preserve your work. Be certain you have saved the document before proceeding to the next step.

2. Press **Ctrl+A** and then press **Delete**. The text of the document is selected and then deleted, but the styles are still available from the Style list box.

3. Click **File** on the menu bar, click **Save As**, click the **Save as type** list arrow, and then click **Document Template**. The Templates folder is displayed in the Save in list box. Because you want your new template handy, you'll save it to a different location.

4. Use the **Save in** list arrow to switch to the Business Plan folder on your Data Disk, where you originally saved the Safe Site Business Plan document. Now you need to enter a descriptive name for the template, which will be used as the basis for all future SafeSite company documents.

5. Change the filename to **SafeSite Company Documents**, and then click the **Save** button.

The new template is now saved and ready for whenever Pamela wants to create a SafeSite document. To begin creating a document based on this template, she must open a blank document, and then attach the template (as described earlier in this tutorial) using the Templates and Add-ins command on the Tools menu. Alternately, she can open the template and then save it as a Word document. Either way, the template styles will be available to her via the Style list.

> **To verify that the new template contains all the necessary styles:**
>
> 1. Click the **Style** list arrow and review the Style list. Note that it contains the new Summary style you created earlier.
>
> 2. Press the **Esc** key to close the Style list, and then close the template as you would close any Word document.

The template you have just created will make it easy for Pamela and Maya to create new documents. You'll give them a copy on a disk after you have completed your work on the business plan.

Session 5.1 QUICK CHECK

1. Explain how to create a new folder.

2. What is the Thesaurus?

3. Use the Thesaurus to find at least two synonyms for the word "business" when it is used to refer to an individual company.

4. Define scrif and sans serif fonts. When would you use each of these types of fonts? Give two examples of each type of font.

5. Explain how to attach a Word template to a document.

6. Explain how to create a new template and attach it to a document.

7. How do you modify a predefined style?

8. Explain how to define a new style by example.

SESSION 5.2

In this session, you will learn how to rearrange parts of a document using Outline view. You'll also learn how to improve the appearance of the right margin by hyphenating the document. Finally, you'll add a footnote to the document that will help readers locate additional information.

Using Outline View

An **outline** is a list of the basic points of a document and the order in which they are presented. Once you have formatted a document with heading styles, you can use Word's Outline view to display an outline that shows as much of the document as you specify. For instance, you can display only text formatted with Heading 1, text formatted with Heading 1 and Heading 2, or all the text in the document, including text formatted with the Normal style. In Outline view, you can see and edit as many as nine levels of headings in a document. As with any outline, the broadest or most general topic is the level-1 heading (that is, text formatted in the Heading 1 style), and the remaining topics become increasingly narrow or more specific with second-level headings (text formatted in the Heading 2 style) and subsequent headings (Heading 3 style, and so on).

Outline view simplifies the process of reorganizing a document. To select an entire section, you click the white plus sign next to that section's heading. To move a section after you select it, you click the Move Up or Move Down button on the Outlining toolbar. You can also use the Outlining toolbar to change the precedence of headings. For instance, you might want to demote a level-1 heading to a level-2 heading, or to promote a level-3 heading to a level-1 heading. Note that some kinds of formatting (such as the Heading 1 formatting with the black background) are not visible in Outline view. To ensure that you can see all the text, including text with special formatting, you need to deselect the Show Formatting button in the Outlining toolbar.

REFERENCE WINDOW **RW**

Creating and Editing Outlines

- Format a document with heading styles.
- Click the Outline View button.
- To ensure that you can see all the text, including text with special formatting, click the Show Formatting button to deselect it.
- Use the Show Level list arrow to display the desired number of headings.
- To move a section, click the white plus sign next to the section's heading, and then click the Move Up button or the Move Down button until the section has moved to the desired location.
- Use the Promote button or the Demote button to increase or decrease the levels of headings.
- Click the Show Level list arrow, and then click to display the entire document again.
- Click the Normal View button.

After reviewing the organization of the business plan, Maya decides that the topic "Current Competition" should appear before the topic "Market Definition." You start by switching to Outline view.

To use Outline view:

1. Open the **SafeSite Business Plan** document. Display nonprinting characters in Normal view.

2. Make sure the insertion point is at the beginning of the document, and then click the **Outline View button** 🔲 in the lower-left corner of the Document window. The Outlining toolbar appears. This toolbar contains two list boxes. You can use the Outline Level list box to apply a heading level to text. You can use the Show Level list box to display the desired number of levels in an outline. In this case, you need to use the Show Level list box to display the first- and second-level headings in the document.

3. Locate the Show Level list arrow by using the mouse pointer to display its name in a ScreenTip. (The Show Level box currently displays the text "Show All Levels".)

4. Click the **Show Level** list arrow, and then click **Show Level 2**. You see only the level-1 and level-2 headings in the document.

5. If you see the level-2 headings (beginning with "Objectives") but not the level-1 headings (beginning with "Executive Summary"), you need to click the **Show Formatting** button in the Outlining toolbar to deselect it. At this point, your outline should look similar to Figure 5-20. Notice that the headings are displayed in the outline without the rest of the document text. The plus sign next to each line of text indicates that the text is a heading, rather than part of the main text of the document. The underlines indicate text that is not visible.

Figure 5-20   DOCUMENT IN OUTLINE VIEW

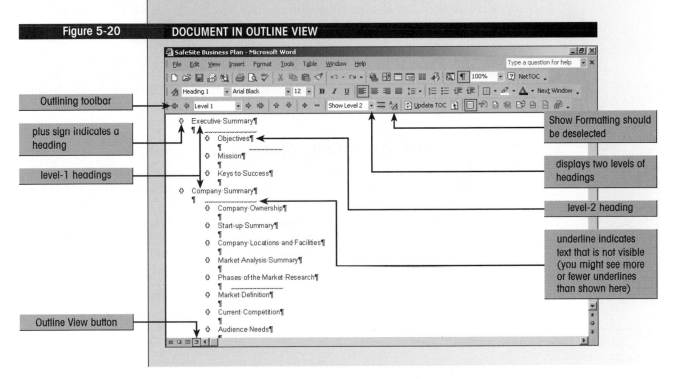

Now that you see only the headings of the business plan, you can change the organization by reordering some headings and changing the level of others.

Moving Headings in an Outline

You can rearrange the order of topics in an outline by moving the headings up and down. When you move a heading in Outline view, any text below that heading (indicated by the underline) moves with it. First, you'll move the section "Current Competition" so that it appears before the topic "Market Definition." As you work in Outline view, keep in mind that the Undo button reverses any mistakes, just as in Normal view.

To move headings in Outline view:

1. Click the **white plus sign** next to the heading "Current Competition." The heading and the paragraph mark following it are selected.

2. Click the **Move Up** button on the Outlining toolbar. The heading and the text below it move above the heading "Market Definition." Note that each time you click the Move Up button, the selected section moves above the preceding section. To move a section down, you would use the Move Down button. You can also use the mouse to drag sections up and down.

Now that the topics of the outline are in logical order, you realize that one level-2 heading (formatted in the Heading 2 style) should actually be a level-3 heading (formatted in the Heading 3 style).

Promoting and Demoting Headings in an Outline

You can easily change the levels of headings in Outline view. To **promote** a heading means to increase the level of a heading—for example, to change a level-3 heading to a level-2 heading. To **demote** a heading means to decrease the level—for example, to change a level-1 heading to a level-2 heading.

While reviewing the business plan, Maya notices that the heading "Audience Needs" should be a level-3 heading, below the level-2 heading "Market Definition." She also wants to add other level-3 headings below the "Market Definition" heading. You'll demote the "Audience Needs" heading, and then add two new level-3 headings.

To demote a heading and then add new headings:

1. Click anywhere in the heading "Audience Needs," and then click the **Demote** button on the Outlining toolbar. (Take care not to click the Demote to Body Text button by mistake, which would make the heading part of the main text of the document, rather than a heading.) The heading moves right and becomes a level-3 heading, formatted with the Heading 3 style. Note that promoting a heading in Outline view is similar to demoting a heading. You place the insertion point in the desired heading and click the Promote button.

   TROUBLE? If the heading now has a square next to it rather than a plus sign, you clicked the Demote to Body Text button by mistake. Click the Undo button on the Formatting toolbar, and then repeat Step 1.

2. Click at the beginning of the heading "Audience Needs," and then press the **Enter** key. A new heading is inserted in the outline.

3. Click in the new heading and type **Audience Demographics**. The new level-3 heading is now formatted in the Heading 3 style. You can't see the formatting, however, because the Show Formatting button in the Outlining toolbar is deselected.

4. Press the **Enter** key, verify that Level 3 is still selected in the Outline Level list box, and then type **Potential for Audience Growth**. Your outline, with the new level-3 headings, should now look like the one in Figure 5-21. You will probably see rectangles next to the first two level-3 headings and a plus sign next to the last level-3 heading. All that matters is that the last three headings are level-3 headings.

Figure 5-21	REVISED OUTLINE

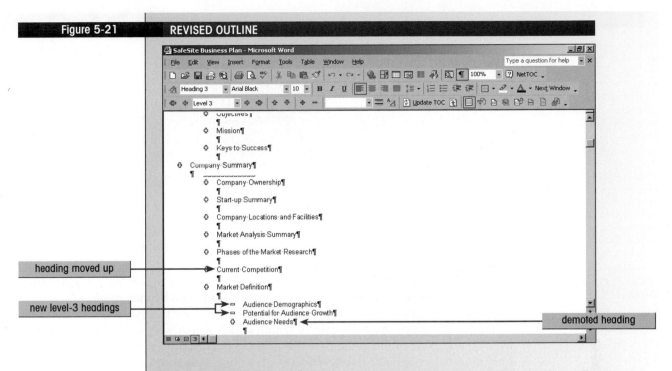

5. Save your work, switch to Normal view, and then scroll through the entire document. The heading you demoted ("Audience Needs") is now formatted in Heading 3 style, as are the two new headings you added. Note that when you moved the Current Competition heading, the entire section moved with it.

Pamela explains that she will print the outline later. To do so, she will display the document in Outline view, display the number of headings she wants to include in the outline, and then click the Print button on the Standard toolbar.

Now you're ready to address some other concerns. First, Pamela has noticed that the right edges of most of the paragraphs in the document are uneven. You'll correct this problem in the next section.

Hyphenating a Document

One potential problem with left-aligned text is excessive raggedness along the right margin. You can reduce raggedness by justifying the text, but that introduces another problem: Word inserts extra white space between words to stretch the lines of text to align along the right margin. Sometimes, this causes unsightly **rivers**, that is, blank areas running through the text of a page, as shown in Figure 5-22.

Figure 5-22	RIVERS WITHIN JUSTIFIED TEXT

This illustrates rivers that appear in text. **Rivers** are wide, empty spaces that occur between words in columns of text that are justified. Rivers are more likely to occur when the column is very narrow or the font size is large. Sometimes hyphenation can help reduce the number of rivers in text. Other times, reducing the font size or increasing the column width will help.

Hyphenating the text can sometimes reduce the raggedness in left-aligned text or reduce the rivers in justified text. Use the Word Hyphenation feature to hyphenate a document one or two ways: automatically, in which case Word decides where to divide a word; or manually, in which case you can accept, reject, or change the suggested hyphenation.

To hyphenate a document, you need to specify a width for the **hyphenation zone**, which is the distance from the right margin within which words will be hyphenated. A smaller hyphenation zone results in more words being hyphenated, but creates a less-ragged right margin. A larger hyphenation zone results in fewer hyphenated words but a more-ragged right margin. In justified text, increasing the number of hyphenated words reduces the amount of white space inserted between words. You also can specify the number of successive lines that can end with hyphenated words. Too many lines in a row ending in a hyphen can be distracting and difficult to read.

Pamela asks you to hyphenate the business plan to eliminate as much raggedness as possible. This means you need to decrease the hyphenation zone.

To set the hyphenation zone and hyphenate the newsletter:

1. Verify that the document is displayed in Normal view.

2. With the insertion point anywhere in the document, click **Tools** on the menu bar, point to **Language**, and then click **Hyphenation**. The Hyphenation dialog box opens.

3. Decrease the Hyphenation zone to **0.1"**.

4. Change the Limit consecutive hyphens setting to **3**. This prevents Word from hyphenating words at the end of more than three lines in a row.

5. Click the **Automatically hyphenate document** check box to insert a check. See Figure 5-23.

Figure 5-23	HYPHENATING A DOCUMENT

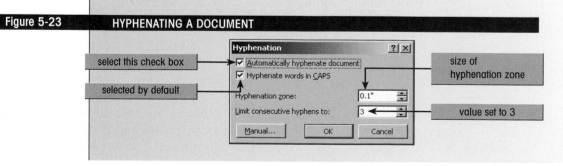

6. Click the **OK** button. Word hyphenates the document as needed. Scroll the document so that the paragraph under the heading "Phases of Market Research" is at the top of the Document window. You can now see several hyphenated words, as shown in Figure 5-24.

TROUBLE? If your document is not hyphenated as shown in Figure 5-24, repeat Steps 1-6, making sure to click the Automatically hyphenate check box to insert a check.

Figure 5-24   **DOCUMENT WITH AUTOMATIC HYPHENATION**

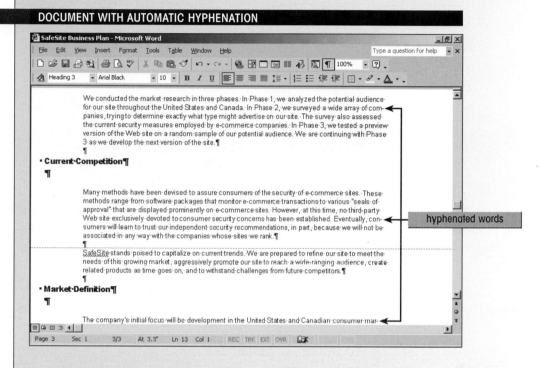

TROUBLE? If you see a dialog box indicating that the Hyphenation feature is not currently installed, click Yes, and, if necessary, insert the Office XP CD into the CD-ROM drive. If you don't have access to the Office XP CD, click No, and then simply read the rest of this section. Your document will not be hyphenated as described here.

7. Save your work.

Look through your document to make sure you like how Word has hyphenated it. If you don't like the hyphenation, you can click the Undo button, repeat the preceding steps, and then click the Manual button instead. Word now will stop at each word before it is hyphenated to let you accept or reject the suggested hyphenation. In this case, Pamela is satisfied with the automatic hyphenation.

Adding Footnotes and Endnotes

The sentence under the heading "Audience Needs" refers to the results of a survey. Pamela wants to include the survey results in an appendix at the end of the business plan and reference these results in a footnote.

A **footnote** is a line of text that appears at the bottom of the printed page and often includes an explanation, the name of a source, or a cross-reference to another place in the document. When all notes for a document are gathered together and printed at the end of the document, instead of at the bottom of each page, they are called **endnotes**. Usually, a document will contain footnotes or endnotes, but not both. You can insert footnotes and endnotes into a Word document with the Footnote command on the Insert menu. When you insert footnotes and endnotes in Normal view, Word opens a special window where you can type the footnote (or endnote text) and see the footnote (or endnote) number at the same time.

REFERENCE WINDOW   RW

Inserting Footnotes or Endnotes

- Switch to Normal view, and position the insertion point where you want the footnote or endnote number to appear.
- Click Insert on the menu bar, point to Reference, and then click Footnote to open the Footnote and Endnote dialog box.
- Click the Footnote button if you want the note to appear at the bottom of the page, or click the Endnote button if you want the note to appear at the end of the document, and then click Insert.
- Type the text of the footnote or endnote in the Footnotes window.
- Close the Footnotes window.
- To delete a footnote or endnote, highlight the footnote or endnote number in the document and press the Delete key.

Now you'll insert a footnote in the business plan that refers the reader to the survey information in the appendix.

To insert a footnote:

1. Make sure the document is in Normal view, click **Edit** on the menu bar, click **Find**, and then use the Find and Replace dialog box to find the phrase **for the service SafeSite will provide**. Close the Find and Replace dialog box.

2. Click at the end of the sentence (to the right of the period after "provide"). This is where you will add the footnote number.

3. Click **Insert** on the menu bar, point to **Reference**, and then click **Footnote**. The Footnote and Endnote dialog box opens.

4. Make sure the **Footnotes** option button is selected, the Number format is set to "1, 2, 3...," and the Start at setting is set to 1.

5. Click the **Insert** button. A footnote number is inserted into the text, and the insertion point moves to the Footnotes window. See Figure 5-25.

Figure 5-25   **CREATING A FOOTNOTE**

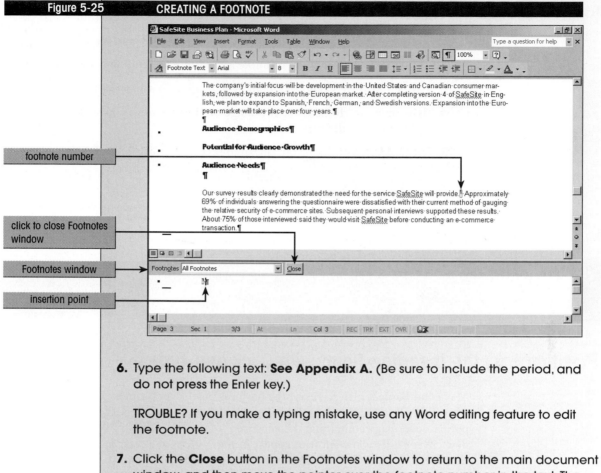

6. Type the following text: **See Appendix A.** (Be sure to include the period, and do not press the Enter key.)

   TROUBLE? If you make a typing mistake, use any Word editing feature to edit the footnote.

7. Click the **Close** button in the Footnotes window to return to the main document window, and then move the pointer over the footnote number in the text. The footnote is displayed in a box over the number. Next, to see the footnote as it will print at the bottom of the page, you need to switch to Print Layout view.

8. Switch to Print Layout view, and scroll to the bottom of page 3 to view the footnote.

9. Save your work.

To delete a footnote or endnote, highlight the footnote or endnote number in the document and press the Delete key. When you delete the number, Word automatically deletes the text of the footnote or endnote and renumbers the remaining notes consecutively.

You can move a footnote or endnote using the cut-and-paste method. Select and cut the note number from the document, and then paste it anywhere in your document. Again, Word renumbers the notes consecutively and places the footnote on the same page as its reference number. You can edit the text of an endnote or footnote by clicking in the footnote or endnote while in Print Layout view, or by double-clicking the footnote number in the main text.

Session 5.2 QUICK CHECK

1. Why would you want to move headings up and down in an outline?

2. What happens when you promote a heading? When you demote a heading?

3. Explain how to promote or demote a heading in a Word outline.

4. True or False: To take full advantage of Outline view, you should apply the Word predefined heading styles first.

5. What does the term "river" mean in relation to justified text?

6. What is the hyphenation zone? If you increase its size, how does that affect the number of hyphenated words?

7. What is the difference between a footnote and an endnote?

SESSION 5.3

In this session, you will learn how to position the insertion point with Click and Type and how to insert the current date. You'll also learn how to highlight text with colors and adjust character and paragraph spacing. Finally, you'll create a table of contents.

Positioning the Insertion Point with Click and Type

Maya and Pamela plan to revise the business plan several times. To help them keep track of who worked on each draft and the date each draft was created, they ask you to create a temporary cover page containing the necessary information. To draw attention to the text of the new cover page, you want it to appear in the middle of a separate page. You could position the insertion point at the beginning of a blank page and press the Enter key until you have inserted the appropriate number of paragraph marks. But it is much easier to use the Word **Click and Type** feature, which allows you to double-click a blank area of a page and immediately begin typing. Word inserts the necessary paragraph marks and applies the proper formatting to position the text in that particular area of the page. Keep in mind that Click and Type only works in Print Layout view.

To create the new cover page for the document, you'll first verify that the Click and Type feature is turned on. Then you'll insert a new page, double-click the center of the blank page, and begin typing the centered text.

To create a title page using Click and Type:

1. Verify that the **SafeSite Business Plan** document is open, that nonprinting characters are displayed, and that the document is displayed in Print Layout view.

2. Display the horizontal and vertical rulers.

3. Click **Tools** on the menu bar, and then click **Options**. The Options dialog box opens.

4. Click the **Edit** tab, verify that the **Enable click and type** check box (in the lower-left corner of the Edit tab) contains a check mark, and then click the **OK** button.

5. Press **Ctrl+Home** to move the insertion point to the beginning of the document. Before inserting the new page, you need to insert a blank paragraph, and then clear formatting from it. Otherwise, the Heading 1 style would apply to the cover page.

6. Press **Enter** to insert a new paragraph, press ↑ to move the insertion point up to the new paragraph, click the **Style** list arrow on the Formatting toolbar, scroll to the top of the Style list, and then click **Clear Formatting**.

7. Press **Ctrl+Enter** to insert a page break, and then press ↑ to move the insertion point up to the new page. As you will see, when you move the pointer over a blank area of a page, the pointer changes shape to reflect the alignment that will be applied to text in that area.

You've inserted a new page that is formatted in the Normal style. Now you're ready to use Click and Type. As you will see, when you move the pointer over a blank area of a page, the pointer changes shape to reflect the alignment that will be applied to text in that area.

To use Click and Type to insert new text in a blank page:

1. Move the pointer over a blank area of the page, near the left margin. The pointer changes to $\text{I}^{\equiv}$, indicating that if you click in that spot, the text will be left-aligned.

2. Move the pointer over a blank area of the page, near the right margin. The pointer changes to $^{\equiv}\text{I}$, indicating that if you click in that spot, the text will be right-aligned.

3. Move the pointer over the center of the page, about 4 inches down from the top margin. (Use the vertical ruler on the left side of the screen as a guide.) The pointer changes to $\text{I}_{\equiv}$, indicating that if you click in that spot the text will be center-aligned.

4. Double-click. Word inserts the appropriate number of paragraph marks and positions the insertion point where you double-clicked. See Figure 5-26.

TROUBLE? If the paragraph marks appear and then disappear, you may have triple-clicked. Repeat Steps 3 and 4.

Figure 5-26	INSERTION POINT POSITIONED WITH CLICK AND TYPE

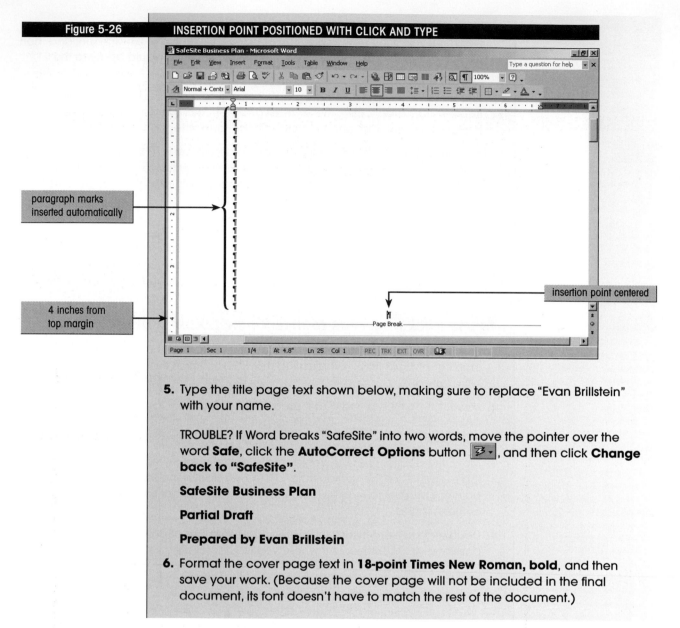

paragraph marks inserted automatically

4 inches from top margin

insertion point centered

5. Type the title page text shown below, making sure to replace "Evan Brillstein" with your name.

   TROUBLE? If Word breaks "SafeSite" into two words, move the pointer over the word **Safe**, click the **AutoCorrect Options** button 🛛▾, and then click **Change back to "SafeSite"**.

   SafeSite Business Plan

   Partial Draft

   Prepared by Evan Brillstein

6. Format the cover page text in **18-point Times New Roman, bold**, and then save your work. (Because the cover page will not be included in the final document, its font doesn't have to match the rest of the document.)

Inserting the Current Date

Next, Pamela asks you to add the current date to the cover page. You could begin typing the date and have Word finish it for you using AutoComplete. But by using the Insert Date and Time command on the Insert menu, you can take advantage of its formatting options. You can use this command to insert both the current date and the time into a document.

To insert the date into the title page:

1. Click at the end of your name, and then press the **Enter** key to move the insertion point to a new line.

2. Click **Insert** on the menu bar, and then click **Date and Time**. The Date and

Time dialog box opens, as shown in Figure 5-27. The Available formats list box contains the current date and time in a variety of formats. Notice the Update automatically check box, which you could click if you wanted Word to update the date and time each time you open the document. In this case, you want to insert today's date, without Word updating it when you reopen the document.

Figure 5-27	DATE AND TIME DIALOG BOX

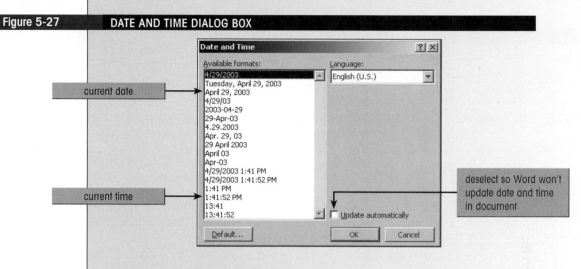

current date

current time

deselect so Word won't update date and time in document

3. In the Available formats list box, click the format that provides the day of the week and the date—for example, Monday, April 29, 2003.

4. Click the **OK** button. Word inserts the date into the title page.

5. Verify that the date is formatted in 18-point Times New Roman, bold, to match the rest of the title page text.

Next, Pamela explains that she plans to ask several colleagues to review the business plan, and she wants to makes sure they know that the document is not yet completed. She asks you to draw attention to the words "Partial Draft" in the cover page.

Highlighting Text with Color

The **Highlight** button on the Formatting toolbar works like an electronic highlighting pen; you use it to shade parts of a document with color. It is useful when you need to draw attention to specific text. If you want, you can click the Highlight list arrow to select a highlighting color from the palette of options. But most people prefer yellow (which is selected by default) because its light shade makes it easy to read the text.

Pamela asks you to use the yellow highlighting to draw attention to the words "Partial Draft" on the cover page.

To highlight the title page text:

1. Select the words **Partial Draft**.

2. Click the **Highlight** list arrow in the Formatting toolbar. A color palette appears. Yellow background is applied to the selected text. The highlighting will alert anyone who reviews the plan that it is not yet final. See Figure 5-28.

3. Click the yellow square (in the upper-left corner).

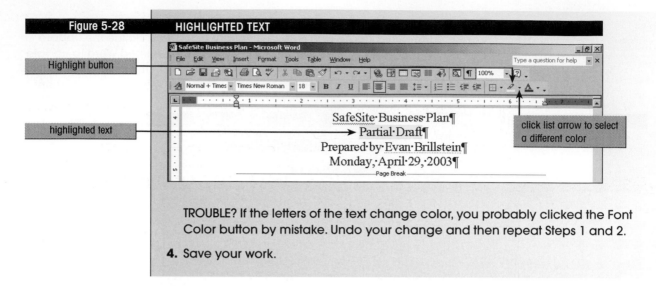

Figure 5-28   **HIGHLIGHTED TEXT**

Highlight button

highlighted text

SafeSite·Business·Plan¶
Partial·Draft¶
Prepared·by·Evan·Brillstein¶
Monday,·April·29,·2003¶
————Page Break————

click list arrow to select a different color

TROUBLE? If the letters of the text change color, you probably clicked the Font Color button by mistake. Undo your change and then repeat Steps 1 and 2.

4. Save your work.

Finally, you decide the cover page text would be easier to read if you added space between the characters. While you're at it, you'll also adjust some paragraph spacing within the business plan.

Changing Character and Paragraph Spacing

As you know, you can quickly change the spacing between lines of a document to make it single-spaced, 1.5-spaced, or double-spaced. (If you prefer, you can choose even more precise line-spacing options by using the Paragraph command on the Format menu.)

To add polish to a document, you can also adjust the spacing between characters or between individual paragraphs. Adjusting **character spacing** is useful when you want to emphasize titles, whereas adjusting **paragraph spacing** allows you to fine-tune the appearance of specially formatted elements, such as a bulleted list.

Adjusting Spacing Between Characters

Word offers a number of ways to adjust the spacing between characters. In some situations, you might want to use kerning, the process of adjusting the spacing between combinations of characters to improve their appearance. In most documents, however, it's easiest to select a group of characters and then uniformly expand or condense the spacing between them. Notice that space between characters is measured in points, with one point equal to $\frac{1}{72}$ of an inch.

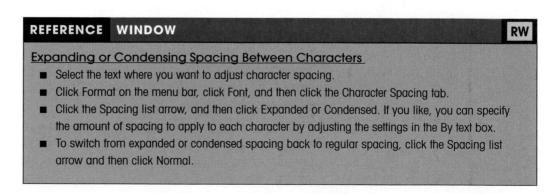

REFERENCE WINDOW   **RW**

Expanding or Condensing Spacing Between Characters

- Select the text where you want to adjust character spacing.
- Click Format on the menu bar, click Font, and then click the Character Spacing tab.
- Click the Spacing list arrow, and then click Expanded or Condensed. If you like, you can specify the amount of spacing to apply to each character by adjusting the settings in the By text box.
- To switch from expanded or condensed spacing back to regular spacing, click the Spacing list arrow and then click Normal.

You want to expand the spacing between the characters in the cover page. You'll do that now.

To adjust character spacing in the cover page:

1. Select the cover page text.

2. Click **Format** on the menu bar, and then click **Font**. The Font dialog box opens.

3. Click the **Character Spacing** tab, if necessary. This tab, shown in Figure 5-29, offers a number of ways to adjust the spacing between characters.

Figure 5-29	ADJUSTING CHARACTER SPACING

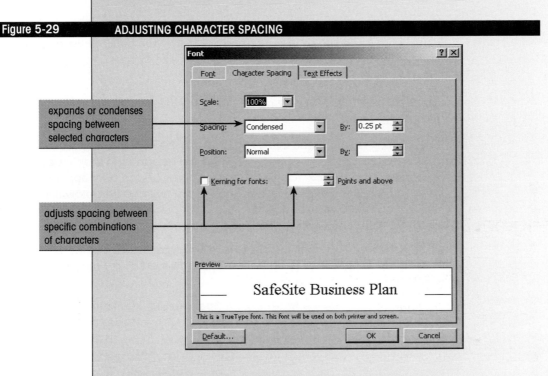

expands or condenses spacing between selected characters

adjusts spacing between specific combinations of characters

4. Click the **Spacing** list arrow, and then click **Expanded**.

5. Change the number of points between characters (in the top By text box) to **1.5**.

6. Observe the expanded spacing (applied to the first line of the selected text) in the Preview box.

7. Click the **OK** button, and then click anywhere in the cover page to deselect the text. Notice the increased space between characters in the title page text.

Now that the cover page is finished, you turn your attention to adjusting the spacing before and after the bulleted list on page 3.

Adjusting Spacing Between Paragraphs

In a single-spaced document, such as the SafeSite business plan, you might need to insert extra space before specially formatted items, such as bulleted lists. As with character spacing, paragraph spacing is measured in points.

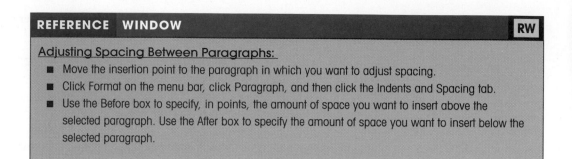

REFERENCE WINDOW   **RW**

Adjusting Spacing Between Paragraphs:
- Move the insertion point to the paragraph in which you want to adjust spacing.
- Click Format on the menu bar, click Paragraph, and then click the Indents and Spacing tab.
- Use the Before box to specify, in points, the amount of space you want to insert above the selected paragraph. Use the After box to specify the amount of space you want to insert below the selected paragraph.

Pamela has asked you to insert extra space before the bulleted list on page 3, under the heading "Market Analysis Summary."

To change the paragraph spacing before and after the bulleted list:

1. Click **Edit** on the menu bar, click **Find**, use the Find and Replace dialog box to find the paragraph that begins **Before we began**, and then close the Find and Replace dialog box. You need to insert some space between this paragraph (which begins "Before we began") and the bulleted list below it. To accomplish this, you could insert space after the paragraph, or insert space before the first bullet. You'll insert space after the paragraph.

2. With the insertion point located in the paragraph that begins "Before we began," click **Format** on the menu bar, and then click **Paragraph**. The Paragraph dialog box opens.

3. If necessary, click the **Indents and Spacing** tab. See Figure 5-30. As mentioned earlier, you can use the Line spacing settings to choose precise line-spacing options. You'll use the After box now to specify, in points, the amount of space you want to insert below the selected paragraph.

Figure 5-30   **CHANGING PARAGRAPH SPACING**

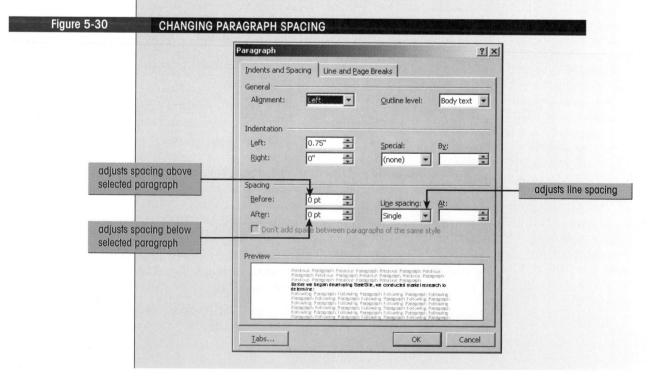

4. Click the up arrow in the After text box twice to change the setting to **12 pt**.

5. Observe the effects of this new setting in the Preview box.

6. Click the **OK** button. Space is added between the paragraph that begins "Before we began" and the first bullet. The first bullet is now positioned 12 points (about ⅛ of an inch) below the preceding paragraph.

Your work on this draft of the business plan is almost completed. Before you finish, Pamela asks you to create a table of contents, which usually is one of the last tasks you perform when creating a document.

Creating a Table of Contents

Word can create a table of contents with page numbers for any document to which you have applied heading styles in the form of Heading 1, Heading 2, and so forth. Note that if you add or delete text later and one or more headings moves to a new page, the table of contents will not be updated automatically to reflect the change. However, you can easily update the table of contents by right-clicking anywhere in the table of contents, and then clicking Update Field. The page numbers in a Word table of contents are actually hyperlinks that you can use to jump to a particular part of the document.

REFERENCE WINDOW   **RW**

Creating a Table of Contents
- Make sure you have applied heading styles such as Heading 1, Heading 2, and Heading 3. (Note that it is possible to create a table of contents from other heading styles, but Word uses the Heading 1, Heading 2, etc., styles by default.)
- Click Insert on the menu bar, point to Reference, and then click Index and Tables.
- Click the Table of Contents tab in the Index and Tables dialog box.
- Click the Formats list arrow and select a style, set Show levels to the number of heading levels you want to show, verify that the Show page numbers check box is selected, and then click the OK button.
- To delete a table of contents, select it and press the Delete key.
- To update a table of contents, right-click it, click Update Field, and then click Update entire table.

The current draft of the SafeSite business plan is fairly short, but the final document will be much longer. Pamela asks you to create a table of contents for the business plan now, and insert it on a new page, just after the title page. Then, as Pamela adds sections to the business plan, she can update your original table of contents.

To insert the table of contents:

1. Move the insertion point to the end of the date on the cover page, and press **Ctrl+Enter** to insert a new page. Before inserting the table of contents, you need to clear formatting from this new page.

2. Click the **Style** list arrow, and then click **Clear Formatting**. The new paragraph is formatted in the Normal style. Next, you need to add a heading for the table of contents.

3. Click the **Bold** button 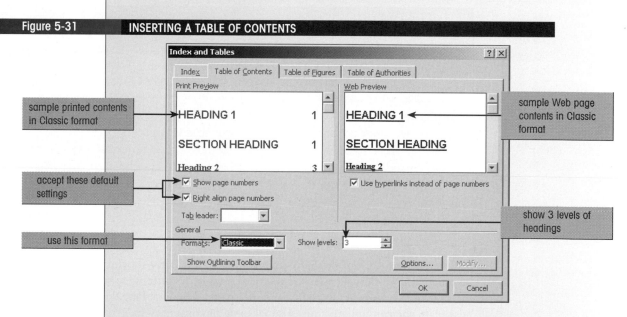 B on the Formatting toolbar, type **Contents**, click B again to turn off bold formatting, and then press **Enter** three times. The insertion point is now located where you want to insert the table of contents.

4. Click **Insert** on the menu bar, point to **Reference**, and click **Index and Tables**. The Index and Tables dialog box opens.

5. Click the **Table of Contents** tab, if necessary. Word provides a variety of formats for a table of contents. In this case, you'll use the Classic format.

6. Click the **Formats** list arrow and then click **Classic**. The Print Preview box shows a sample of a table of contents formatted with the Classic format. (The Web Preview box shows you what the table of contents would look like if you saved your Word document as a Web page and viewed it in a Web browser such as Microsoft Explorer.)

   Note that the Show page numbers check box is selected by default, so the table of contents will include a page number for each heading. By default, the Use hyperlinks instead of page numbers check box is selected. This setting means that Word will make each entry in the table of contents (each heading and page number) a hyperlink that links to the relevant section in the document. You can accept this default setting. Even if you deselected this check box, Word would still format the page numbers as hyperlinks. Finally, because the document contains three levels of headings, you can leave the Show levels setting at 3. See Figure 5-31.

Figure 5-31   INSERTING A TABLE OF CONTENTS

sample printed contents in Classic format

accept these default settings

use this format

sample Web page contents in Classic format

show 3 levels of headings

7. Click the **OK** button. Word searches for any text formatted with styles Heading 1, Heading 2, and Heading 3, and then assembles that text and its corresponding page number in a table of contents. The table of contents appears below the "Contents" heading.

8. The text is gray to indicate that Word considers the table of contents a single object. Note that this gray highlighting does not indicate that the table of contents is selected. To select the entire table of contents, you would have to click and drag to its left, in the selection bar.

9. Press **Ctrl** and click a heading in the Table of Contents. That section of the document is displayed in the Document window. Continue experimenting using the hyperlinks in the table of contents.

You'll have a chance to experiment with Word's table of contents feature more extensively in the Review Assignments and Case Problems at the end of this tutorial. Among other things, you will update a table of contents and delete one. You'll also learn another way to move quickly among the headings in a document—browsing by heading with the Select Browse object button in the vertical scroll bar.

With the table of contents inserted in the business plan, you're ready to print the document.

To print the document:

1. Save your work.

2. Preview, and then print the business plan. If you see a dialog box asking about updating the table of contents, go ahead and update the entire table. Your completed document should look like Figure 5-32. Notice that the yellow highlighting on the cover page appears as a gray background on a black and white printout.

Figure 5-32   **COMPLETED DOCUMENT (PAGES 1 AND 2)**

SafeSite Business Plan
Partial Draft
Prepared by Evan Brillstein
Tuesday, April 29, 2003

Contents

EXECUTIVE SUMMARY	3
Objectives	3
Mission	3
Keys to Success	3
COMPANY SUMMARY	3
Company Ownership	4
Start-up Summary	4
Company Locations and Facilities	4
Market Analysis Summary	4
Phases of the Market Research	4
Current Competition	5
Market Definition	5
Audience Demographics	5
Potential for Audience Growth	5
Audience Needs	5

Figure 5-32 | **COMPLETED DOCUMENT (PAGE 3)**

Executive Summary

SafeSite Inc. is a privately held corporation that publishes information on e-commerce security. The company's primary vehicle will be a Web site with the following address: www.safesite.com. The Web site will target consumers who seek reassurance that e-commerce sites have taken the steps necessary to protect the private information exchanged during a typical e-commerce transaction. Like many Web businesses, SafeSite Inc. will generate revenue by selling advertising space.

Objectives

- Advertising sales of $200,000 in 2002 and $900,000 by 2003.
- Net income more than 9% of sales by the fourth year.

Mission

The primary goal of SafeSite Inc. is to become the industry leader in rating the security of e-commerce Web sites. For the company to succeed, potential e-commerce customers must know that consulting SafeSite provides the security information they need to conduct private e-commerce transactions.

Keys to Success

- The ability to supply unfailingly accurate information on industry-wide e-commerce security.
- Reputation for respectability and reliability in the e-commerce community, as evidenced by favorable reviews in trade magazines.
- Up-to-date assessments of consumer needs.

Company Summary

SafeSite Inc. is a new company that seeks to publish the most accurate information on e-commerce security in the industry. The company's Web site will serve consumers who seek reassurance before making online purchases.

Figure 5-32	COMPLETED DOCUMENT (PAGE 4)

Company Ownership

SafeSite Inc. has been established as a Limited Liability corporation based in Santa Clara County. As of this writing, the corporation is entirely owned by its principal operators.

Start-up Summary

Total start-up expenses (including legal costs, initial Web site design and testing, and computer equipment) are $26,175. We require start-up assets of $75,000 in initial cash to cover additional site development and office expenses.

Company Locations and Facilities

The company will soon move to new office space in the Silicon Valley area of California, the heart of the U.S. high-tech industry. Initially, SafeSite Inc. requires a four-room suite of offices, with fiber-optic network cabling and a full T1 connection.

Market Analysis Summary

Before we began developing SafeSite, we conducted market research to determine:

- Profile of target audience

- Size of target audience

- Profile of potential advertisers

- Number of potential advertisers

The answers to these questions are crucial to the continued development and the future marketing of SafeSite. We must understand the nature of our audience (the people who will access SafeSite to look up security information). In addition, we must accurately identify our potential advertisers.

Phases of the Market Research

We conducted the market research in three phases. In Phase 1, we analyzed the potential audience for our site throughout the United States and Canada. In Phase 2, we surveyed a wide array of companies, trying to determine exactly what type might advertise on our site. The survey also assessed the current security measures employed by e-commerce companies. In Phase 3, we tested a preview version of the Web site on a random sample of our potential audience. We are continuing with Phase 3 as we develop the next version of the site.

Figure 5-32	COMPLETED DOCUMENT (PAGE 5)

Current Competition

Many methods have been devised to assure consumers of the security of e-commerce sites. These methods range from software packages that monitor e-commerce transactions to various "seals of approval" that are displayed prominently on e-commerce sites. However, at this time, no third-party Web site exclusively devoted to consumer security concerns has been established. Eventually, consumers will learn to trust our independent security recommendations, in part, because we will not be associated in any way with the companies whose sites we rank.

SafeSite stands poised to capitalize on current trends. We are prepared to refine our site to meet the needs of this growing market, aggressively promote our site to reach a wide-ranging audience, create related products as time goes on, and to withstand challenges from future competitors.

Market Definition

The company's initial focus will be development in the United States and Canadian consumer markets, followed by expansion into the European market. After completing version 4 of SafeSite in English, we plan to expand to Spanish, French, German, and Swedish versions. Expansion into the European market will take place over four years.

Audience Demographics

Potential for Audience Growth

Audience Needs

Our survey results clearly demonstrated the need for the service SafeSite will provide.[1] Approximately 69% of individuals answering the questionnaire were dissatisfied with their current method of gauging the relative security of e-commerce sites. Subsequent personal interviews supported these results. About 75% of those interviewed said they would visit SafeSite before conducting an e-commerce transaction.

---
[1] See appendix A.

SafeSite Business Plan   Page **5**

Page breaks in your document occur at different locations, depending on the fonts you used. Don't be concerned about this. Scroll through your document and add return characters as necessary so that the lines of text are well-grouped.

3. Close the document, and then exit Word.

You now have a printed copy of the business plan, which you take to Pamela and Maya.

Session 5.3 QUICK CHECK

1. Explain how to position the insertion point in the middle of a blank page without pressing Enter to insert paragraph marks.

2. True or False: If you use the Date and Time dialog box to insert the current date in your document, Word will automatically revise the date each time you open the document.

3. Describe a situation in which you would highlight text in a document, and then explain how to do so.

4. What is the difference between character spacing and paragraph spacing?

5. True or False: It is only possible to adjust the spacing before a paragraph.

6. Explain the steps required to create a table of contents in Word.

REVIEW ASSIGNMENTS

Maya and Pamela received the start-up funding they wanted and successfully launched SafeSite, which has proven popular with e-commerce consumers. Now that they have the Web site up and running, they would like to expand SafeSite Inc. by selling a software package called SafeDesign. Web designers can use SafeDesign to build security into their e-commerce sites from the bottom up. Before Pamela and Maya can begin marketing SafeDesign, they need to develop a technical support strategy. They have written a summary of their customer training and support policies, and have asked you to help edit and format the document.

1. Start Word, if necessary, and open the file SafeDesign from the Review folder for Tutorial 5 on your Data Disk.

2. Make sure that nonprinting characters and the ruler are displayed. If necessary, switch to Normal view.

3. Create a new folder called **SafeDesign Technical Support** (within the Review folder for Tutorial 5).

4. Save the file in the new folder as **SafeDesign Policies**.

5. Use the Thesaurus to replace "personnel" (in the second paragraph after the heading "Introducing SafeDesign") with a different word.

6. Attach the Professional Report template to the document. (This template is in the Review folder for Tutorial 5.) Remember to select the Automatically update document styles check box.

7. Apply the Heading 1 style to the first line of the document, "SafeDesign Support Policies." Apply the Heading 2 style to all of the headings in the body of the document: "Introducing SafeDesign," "Classes," "Technical Support," "Using Technical Support," "Average Wait Times," and "Frequently Asked Questions." Do not apply a style to the company address and phone number at the top of the document.

8. Create a new style by example for the company address, phone numbers, and Web address at the top of the document. The style should format text in 12-point Arial bold, centered on the page, with character spacing expanded (insert 1.5 points between each character). Name the style "Company Address." Click anywhere in the document outside the first six lines, and verify that the new style is available in the Style list box on the Formatting toolbar.

Explore   9. Create a new character style (a style that formats only selected characters) for the word "SafeDesign." To create the style: open the Styles and Formatting Task Pane, click the New Style button, type Software Name in the Name text box, click the Style type list arrow, click Character, click the Bold button, click the Italic button, click the Format list arrow, click Font, click the Character Spacing tab, change the spacing to expanded with 1.5 points between characters, and then click the OK button twice. Select the second instance of "SafeDesign" in the document (in the sentence that begins "Our new software, SafeDesign"). Click Software Name in the Task Pane. Apply the Software Name style to the third instance of "SafeDesign" (in the next paragraph, in the sentence that begins "That's why we are committed").

Explore 10. Modify the Heading 1 style so that it formats text with center alignment, using the small caps font effect, in 16-point Arial Black. (*Hint:* To make the font changes, click the Font list button in the Modify Style dialog box, click Font, and then use the tabs of the Font dialog box to make your selections.) Close the Styles and Formatting Task Pane when you are finished.

11. Under the heading "Using Technical Support," select the list of three technical support options (beginning with "Call our telephone support" and ending with "and your technical support plan"), and then apply the List Bullet style. Under the heading "Average Wait Times," apply the List Bullet style to the list of waiting times for the four technical support plans (Levels I through IV). Add 12 points of space before the first bullet in each list.

12. Using Outline view, reorganize the document so the "Classes" section comes after the "Average Wait Times" section.

13. Demote the headings "Using Technical Support" and "Average Wait Times" to make them level-3 headings, and then switch to Normal view to review your changes.

14. Below the heading "Technical Support," after the period at the end of the second sentence, insert the following footnote: "As the needs and resources of your company change, you can modify your technical support plan. Changes can be made only at the expiration of the current contract period."

15. Hyphenate the document with a hyphenation zone of 0.1", using automatic hyphenation. Limit consecutive hyphens to 2.

16. Create a cover page for the document. To prevent the formatting of the document title from affecting the new page, insert a new paragraph at the beginning of the document, clear formatting from it, and then insert a new page. Switch to Print Layout view. Use Click and Type to insert your name on one line, and the word "Draft" on another line in the center of the page. Highlight the word "Draft" to call attention to it.

Explore 17. Start a new line and insert the current date and time, using a format that includes seconds. Click the Update automatically check box. (If the date is highlighted in yellow, select the date, click the Highlight list arrow, and then click None.) Note the time inserted into the document, save your work, and close the document. Reopen the document and notice that the time has been updated. Wait a few seconds, click the date and time, and then press F9. Note that the time is updated again.

18. Insert a table of contents on a new page immediately after the cover page as follows: insert a new page after the cover page, clear formatting, and insert the boldface heading "Contents". Insert a table of contents formatted with the Fancy format for your table of contents. (If the Fancy format is not available, choose another.) Be sure to include the necessary number of heading levels. Test one of the headings to make sure it links to that section in the document.

Explore 19. In addition to using the table of contents to move around in a document, you can use the Select Browse Object button on the vertical scroll bar. Press Ctrl+Home to move the insertion point to the beginning of the document, click the Select Browse Object button (the circle near the bottom of the vertical scroll bar). A palette of options opens. Move the pointer over the buttons in the palette and review the name of each option. Click the Go To button in the palette, and then use the Go To tab of the Find and Replace dialog box to move the insertion point to the top of page 3. Close the Find and Replace dialog box. Click the Select Browse Object button again, click the Browse by Heading button, and then click the double blue down arrow button (at the bottom of the vertical scroll bar) to move from one heading to the next. Use the double blue up arrow button to browse up through the document by heading.

20. Save the document and then print it. If you are asked if you want to update the table of contents, go ahead and update the entire table.

21. Use the SafeDesign Policies document to create a new blank template called **SafeDesign Template**. Save the new template in the SafeDesign Technical Support folder on your Data Disk.

Explore 22. To keep a Style list from getting overcrowded, you can delete unnecessary styles. (Note that you can't delete default styles, such as Heading 1 and Heading 2.) Delete the block quotation style from the template as follows: open the Styles and Formatting Task Pane, right-click the block quotation style in the Task Pane Style list, click Delete, and then click Yes. Save your changes to the template and then close it.

23. Open a blank document and attach the SafeDesign Template to it. Be sure to select the Automatically update document styles check box. Verify that the template headings are available in the Styles and Formatting Task Pane, save the new document as **Additional Policies** in the SafeDesign Technical Support folder on your Data Disk, and then close the document.

Explore 24. To experiment with using a Word template as the basis for a new document, click File on the menu bar, and then click New. Click General Templates in the New Document Task Pane. Click the tabs in the New dialog box to review the various templates provided with Word. Some tabs include icons for Wizards, which guide you through the steps involved in creating complicated documents such as Web pages. Click the General tab. Note that if you create a new template and save it in the Templates folder, it will appear as an option on this tab. Click the Letters and Faxes tab, click the Elegant Fax icon, and then click the OK button. A document opens with placeholder text for all the elements of a fax cover sheet. Following instructions in the template, create a fax sheet that you could use to fax the SafeDesign document from SafeSite Inc. to Peter Bennigan at First Bank of the Pacific. Use information that you make up, and type a brief message in the Notes/Comments area. To select a check box, double-click it. Save the document as **Fax Cover Sheet** in the SafeDesign Technical Support folder on your Data Disk, preview it, print it, and then close it.

25. Close any open documents and exit Word.

CASE PROBLEMS

Case 1. Rosewood Interiors Geoffrey Browne is the sales manager for Rosewood Interiors, a furniture store in Boulder, Colorado, that until recently specialized in contemporary furnishings. In response to customer requests, the store has begun stocking more traditional style furniture. Now Geoffrey needs to provide his sales associates with some tips on selling this new stock. He has created a draft of a document and has asked for your help.

1. Start Word, if necessary, open the file **Furniture** from the Cases folder for Tutorial 5 on your Data Disk, and save it as **Rosewood Traditional Furniture**.

2. Switch to Outline view, display two levels of headings, and then promote the section "Guidelines for Helping Customers" to a level-1 heading. Reorder the document so the introduction section is the first section of the document.

Explore 3. Print the outline without showing the formatting of the headings.

4. Switch to Normal view, and change the font of the Title style and the Heading 1 style to a sans serif font. (*Hint*: Use the Font list box in the Modify Style dialog box.)

5. Change the font of the Normal style to a serif font other than Times New Roman.

6. Click at the end of the telephone number at the top of the document, press the Enter key twice, type "Draft Prepared by", and then type your name. Highlight the new line, using the color of your choice.

7. Format the four lines containing the store's name, address, and phone number using one of the font effects (such as small caps) available in the Font dialog box. Adjust the character spacing as necessary to make the text easy to read.

8. In the last paragraph of the document, change "consult" to one of its synonyms in the Thesaurus.

9. At the end of the first bullet (following the word "brochure"), insert the following foot-note: "The Traditional Interiors brochure is available at the Customer Service desk."

10. Hyphenate the document using automatic hyphenation with a hyphenation zone of .25. Limit consecutive hyphens to 3.

11. Click in the paragraph above the table (which begins "Here is a list"), and change the paragraph spacing after the paragraph to 12 points.

12. Insert a table of contents for the document above the introduction, using the Formal style. Because the document is so short, you do not need page numbers, so you can des-elect the Show page numbers check box. Keep the Use hyperlinks instead of page num-bers check box selected. Check the headings in the table of contents to make sure they work as hyperlinks.

Explore 13. In the body of the document, change the heading "Guidelines for Helping Customers" to "Guidelines for Assisting Customers". Now that you've changed the heading, you need to update the table of contents as follows: right-click the table of contents, and then click Update Field in the shortcut menu.

14. Save your changes. Preview the document for problems, fix any formatting problems, and then print the document.

Explore 15. Word's AutoCorrect feature allows you to preserve formatted text and then insert it into documents later simply by typing a few characters. To see how this works, select the store's name, address, and phone number at the top of the document, as well as the blank paragraph below the phone number. Click Tools on the menu bar, click AutoCorrect Options, click the AutoCorrect tab, type "Rosewood Address" (without the quotation marks) in the Replace text box, verify that the Formatted text option button is selected, click the Add button, and then click the OK button. To try out the new AutoCorrect entry, close the Rosewood Traditional Furniture document, open a blank document, type Rosewood Address, and then press the spacebar. Verify that the formatted text is inserted into the document, and save the document as **Store Address** in the Cases folder for Tutorial 5. Now you can delete your AutoCorrect entry as follows: click Tools, click AutoCorrect Options, scroll down and select the Rosewood Address entry in the list box, click the Delete button, and then click the OK button. Close the Store Address document and exit Word.

Case 2. Brochure for Meals & Menus Clarissa Ruffolo and Tom Jenkins own Meals & Menus, an upscale catering service that specializes in home entertaining for people who like to socialize but don't have time to cook. Tom has prepared a brochure with the company's lat-est menu choices, which he formatted using the Word default heading styles. However, he is not happy with the brochure's appearance and has asked for your help.

1. Start Word, if necessary, and check your screen, making sure that nonprinting charac-ters are displayed.

2. Open the file **Meals** from the Cases folder for Tutorial 5 on your Data Disk, and save it as **Meals & Menus**. Notice that the headings in the document are formatted using the Word default Heading1 and Heading 2 styles.

3. Attach the template named **Menu Template**, which is stored in the Cases folder for Tutorial 5, to the current document. Remember to select the Automatically update document styles check box. Verify that the document's styles are updated to reflect the template's styles.

4. Apply the Bulleted List style (with the diamond-shaped bullet) to all the bulleted lists in the document. (If you find that Word automatically transformed the bullets in the document to diamonds, go ahead and apply the style anyway so that all the bullets have the same line spacing.)

Explore

5. You can use the Reveal Formatting Task Pane to check the formatting in a document. To try it now, click Format on the menu bar, click Reveal Formatting, select the heading "Our Famous Desserts," and then, in the Reveal Formatting Task Pane, review the description of formatting applied to this text. Note that the Task Pane even lists the outline level for the selected text, which in this case is Level 2. Select the heading "A Final Word" and review the heading applied to it. Note that this is a Level 1 heading.

Explore

6. Click the list arrow in the Task Pane title bar, and then click Styles and Formatting to open the Styles and Formatting Task Pane. Select the heading "Our Famous Desserts" (which is formatted in the Heading 2 style), and then click Select All in the Styles and Formatting Task Pane. All the text in the document formatted with the Heading 2 style is selected. Scroll through the document to review these headings. Close the Task Pane.

7. In Outline view, display two levels of headings, and then promote the headings "Lunch," "Dinner," and "Our Famous Desserts," to level-1 headings.

Explore

8. Move the "Our Famous Desserts" heading up, to make it the first heading in the document, above "Bagel Brunch." This time, instead of clicking the Move Up button, select the heading, and then drag it up to the beginning of the document.

9. Print the outline with only the headings displayed, and then switch back to Normal view.

10. In the first sentence under the heading "Our Famous Desserts," use the Thesaurus to find a synonym for "delectable."

Explore

11. Switch to Print Layout view, press Ctrl+Home, press Ctrl+Enter, and then clear formatting from the new page. Scroll down to display the heading "Our Famous Desserts," and notice that you inadvertently cleared formatting from this heading. Click the Undo button until "Our Famous Desserts" is again formatted in the Heading 1 style, and the new page is removed. Now insert a new paragraph at the beginning of the page. Clear formatting from the new paragraph, insert a new first page, move the insertion point up to the new page, select the Company Name style, and then use Click and Type to insert "Meals & Menus" (without the quotation marks) about 3 inches down, in the center of the page. Notice how the Click and Type Feature automatically applies the selected style.

12. Press Enter, select the Company Address style, and then type the following:

2567 Rowley

Madison, Wisconsin 53708

Prepared by Your Name

Be sure to replace "Your Name" with your first and last name.

Explore   13. Insert the current date below your name, in the format of your choice. Click the Update automatically check box so that Word shows the current date each time you open the document. Right-click the date to open a shortcut menu. Notice the command "Update Field," which you can use to update the date the next time you open the document.

14. Modify the Company Address style so that it applies a sans serif font with expanded character spacing. (*Hint:* To select expanded character spacing, click the Format button in the Modify Style dialog box, and then click Font.)

Explore   15. You can use the Styles and Formatting Task Pane to display a list of all the styles currently in use in a document. To display this list now, open the Styles and Formatting Task pane, click the Show list arrow (at the bottom of the Task Pane), and then click Formatting in Use. A list of the styles used in the document appears. Review the list and then close the Task Pane.

16. Save, preview, and print the document, and then exit Word.

Case 3. The Business of Basketball As part of the requirements for your advanced writing class, your writing group has written a term paper on "The Business of Basketball." Your assignment is to edit the preliminary outline.

1. Start Word, if necessary, and check your screen, making sure that nonprinting characters are displayed. Open the file **Business** from the Cases folder for Tutorial 5 on your Data Disk.

2. In the Cases folder for Tutorial 5, create a new folder called **Writing Project**, and then save the document in the new folder as **Business of Basketball**.

3. Using Outline view, reorder the headings so that "Team Philosophy" follows "Management Style."

4. Demote the section "Marketing" to make it a second-level heading.

5. Print the completed outline of the document, with the Show Formatting feature turned off.

6. Use the Thesaurus to find a synonym to replace "lucrative" in the first sentence under the heading "Introduction."

Explore   7. Scroll to the table in the document, and add the following endnote to the table heading: "Data taken from www.basketballnews.com, May 25, 2002." Take care to select the Endnotes option button rather than the Footnotes option button in the Footnote and Endnote dialog box. In the Endnotes list box, make sure that End of document is selected, so that the note will be placed at the end of the report. When you are finished typing the note, scroll up to the end note number in the document, and place the pointer over the number to display the end note text.

8. Change the Heading 1 style to a sans serif font.

Explore   9. Create a new character style (a style that formats only selected characters) for the author names. To create the style: open the Styles and Formatting Task Pane, click New Style, type Author Name in the Name text box, click the Style type list arrow, click Character, click the Bold button, if necessary, click the Italic button, select 12-point Arial, and then click OK. Apply the new style to the author names (on the first page).

10. Add your name to the list of authors on the first page, format it with the Author Name style, and then add highlighting to your name.

11. Create a table of contents on a separate page, following the heading "Table of Contents." Use the Formal style.

Explore 12. Drag in the Selection bar to select the table of contents, and then press Delete. Insert a new table of contents using the Classic style.

13. Save your work, preview the document, print it, and then close it. When you are finished, exit Word.

Case 4. Washington State Budget Mona Parks is an economic analyst for the governor's office in the state of Washington. She is responsible for compiling a preliminary draft of the governor's annual budget proposal, a document that will ultimately incorporate information from over 100 state agencies. Each year she begins her work on the budget draft by creating an outline using Word's outline numbered list feature. She has asked you to help.

1. Start Word, if necessary, making sure that nonprinting characters are displayed.

2. Open a new Word document, and save it as **Preliminary Budget Draft** in the Cases folder for Tutorial 5 on your Data Disk.

Explore 3. In addition to creating an outline using document headings, you can create a numbered list in outline format using the Numbering button on the Formatting toolbar. To begin creating the budget outline: display the document in Normal or Print Layout view, insert a new line, click the Numbering button on the Formatting toolbar, and type "Governor's Message". Press Enter and type "Budget Highlights". Press Enter and type "Summaries by Agencies".

Explore 4. To demote a level-1 heading to a level-2 heading, you can click the Increase Indent button on the Formatting toolbar. To demote a level-2 heading to a level-3 heading, you click the Increase Indent button again. You'll use these options now as you type the list of agencies under the heading "Summaries by Agencies." To type this list: press Enter, click the Increase Indent button, type "Department of Agriculture", press the Enter key, click the Increase Indent button, type "Research", press Enter, type "County Outreach", press Enter, click the Decrease Indent button once, and then type "Department of Commerce".

5. Continue using the techniques described in Step 4 to add the following text to the outline:
   c. Department of Justice
      i. Juvenile Justice Program
      ii. Appeals Court
      iii. Public Defenders
   d. Department of Parks and Recreation
   e. Department of Education

Explore 6. Now that you have created your outline, you can format it using the Word default heading styles. Select your outline numbered list, click Format on the menu bar, click Bullets and Numbering, and then click Outline Numbered tab. Click the second style from the right, in the bottom row (which uses the form I. Heading 1, A. Heading 2), and then click OK.

7. Switch to Outline view, and reorganize the list of departments in alphabetical order. Print the outline and then switch to Normal view.

8. Click at the beginning of the document, click the Numbering button to deselect it, and then add the following title and subtitle to the beginning of the document: Preliminary Budget for the State of Washington, Draft Prepared by Your Name. (Replace "Your Name" with your first and last name.) On a line after your name, insert the current date in a format that includes the day of the week.

9. Format the title, subtitle, and date appropriately, and then save this formatting as a new style named "Budget Title".

10. Save your work, preview the document, and print it.

11. Create a new template named **Budget Template**, based on the Preliminary Budget Draft document. Save the template in the Cases folder for Tutorial 5, close it, and then exit Word.

QUICK CHECK ANSWERS

Session 5.1

1. In the Save As dialog box, click the New Folder button, type the name of the folder, and then click the OK button.

2. The Thesaurus is a feature you can use to find synonyms for words in a document.

3. The following are synonyms for "business" when it is used to refer to an individual company: company, corporation, conglomerate, establishment, partnership, firm, multinational, transnational, small business, enterprise, venture, concern, and organization.

4. A serif font is a font in which each character has a small embellishment (called a serif) at its tips. A sans serif font is a font in which the characters do not have serifs. Serif fonts are useful for the main text of a document because they are easy to read. Sans serif fonts are best for headings and titles. Two examples of serif fonts are Times New Roman and Garamond. Two examples of sans serif fonts include Arial and Century Gothic.

5. Click Tools on the menu bar, and then click Templates and Add-ins. Click the Attach button. In the Attach Template dialog box, navigate to the folder containing the template, select the template you want, and then click the Open button. Click the Automatically update document styles check box to select it. Click the OK button to attach the template to your document.

6. First, create a new document containing all the styles you want to include in the new template, save it as a Word document, and delete all text from the document. Then save the file as a Document Template. Verify that the Templates folder is displayed in the Save in list box. If you save your template to this folder, it will appear as one of the options in the New dialog box. If you prefer, you can save the template in a different location.

7. Move the insertion point to text formatted with the style you want to modify. Click Format on the menu bar, and then click Styles and Formatting. In the Styles and Formatting Task Pane, click the Show list arrow and then click Custom. In the Format Settings dialog box, click the Styles button (in the lower-left corner). In the Style dialog box, verify that the style you want to modify is selected in the Styles text box and then click Modify. In the Modify Style dialog box, use the toolbar buttons for common formatting options. For other formatting changes, use the Format button. If you want your style changes saved in the original template file, select the Add to template check box. If you don't select this check box, your style changes will only be saved to the template attached to the active document. To update all text in the document with the modified style, select the Automatically update check box. Click the OK button. In the Style dialog box, click the Close button.

8. Format a paragraph with the font, margins, alignment, spacing, and other elements that you want for the style, and then select the paragraph. Click the Style text box on the Formatting toolbar. Type the name of the new style (replacing the current style name), and then press the Enter key.

Session 5.2

1. By moving the headings in an outline, you can reorganize the document text.

2. When you promote a heading, it becomes a higher-level heading in the outline. For example, you could promote a level-2 heading to a level-1 heading. When you demote a heading, it becomes a lower-level heading. For example, you could demote a level-1 heading to a level-2 or level-3 heading.

3. To promote a heading, click that heading in Outline view, and then click the Promote button on the Outlining toolbar. To demote a heading, click that heading, and then click the Demote button.

4. True

5. A river is a blank area running through the text of a page.

6. The hyphenation zone is the distance from the right margin within which words will be hyphenated. Increasing its size reduces the number of hyphenated words.

7. A footnote appears at the bottom of a page, whereas an endnote appears at the end of a document.

Session 5.3

1. Double-click a blank area of a page using the Click and Type pointer.

2. False

3. It is sometimes helpful to highlight text that you want to delete from a document later, or to draw a colleague's attention to an important section. To highlight text, first select it, and then click the Highlight button on the Formatting toolbar.

4. Character spacing affects the positioning of individual characters, whereas paragraph spacing affects the spacing between paragraphs.

5. False

6. Make sure you have applied heading styles such as Heading 1, Heading 2, and Heading 3. Click Insert on the menu bar, point to Reference, and then click Index and Tables. Click the Table of Contents tab in the Index and Tables dialog box. Select a predefined style in the Formats list box, set the show-levels number to the number of heading levels you want to show, verify that the Show page numbers check box is selected, and then click the OK button.

OBJECTIVES

In this tutorial you will:

- Learn about the Mail Merge process

- Use the Mail Merge Wizard

- Select a main document

- Create a data source

- Insert merge field codes into a main document

- Preview a merged document

- Complete a mail merge

- Edit an existing data source

- Sort and filter records

CREATING
FORM LETTERS AND MAILING LABELS

Writing a Form Letter for Palm Tree Athletic Club

CASE

Palm Tree Athletic Club

Maria Fuentes is the facilities manager for Palm Tree Athletic Club, a chain of health and fitness clubs with branches located throughout the state of Florida. The chain has just completed major renovations at several branches, which forced club members to endure a lot of dust, noise, and inconvenience. Maria wants to show the club's gratitude by inviting each member to sign up for three free hours with a certified personal trainer. She plans to send a letter to each member announcing the free offer.

Maria doesn't have time to type personal letters to each of the club's many members. Instead, she plans to create a **form letter** that contains the information she wants to send all members. The form letter will also contain specific details for individual members, such as name, address, and favorite type of exercise equipment. Maria will create the form letter using Word's Mail Merge features. She has already written the letter, but she needs to add the personal information for each member. She asks you to create the form letter, as well as the mailing labels for the envelopes.

In this tutorial, you'll use Word's Mail Merge Wizard to help Maria create a form letter, mailing labels, and a telephone directory. First you'll open the letter that will serve as the main document. Next you'll create a data source that contains the name and address of each member who will receive the customized letter. Then you'll have Word merge the main document with the data source. Finally, you'll use the data source document to create mailing labels for the envelopes. You'll also create a telephone list containing the number of each branch of the Palm Tree Athletic Club.

**SESSION
6.1**

In this session, you will see how Maria planned her letter. You'll open the form letter, start the Mail Merge Wizard, create a data source with specific member information that will be inserted into the form letter, and then merge the form letter with the data source.

Planning the Form Letter

Maria hopes to generate good will for the Palm Tree Athletic Club by offering each member three free hours with a personal trainer. Maria's letter is designed to inform members about the offer and mention improvements to the club that might appeal to each member. Her letter is organized to capture the reader's attention. First she thanks club members for their patience during the renovations, and then she briefly describes the free offer. Finally, she encourages members to review the new schedules for their favorite type of exercise class.

Maria writes in a friendly, informal style. She uses a standard business-letter format and plans to print the letters on stationery preprinted with the company letterhead.

Understanding the Merge Process

Maria asks you to use Word's Mail Merge features to create the form letters. The term **merge** refers to the process of combining information from two separate documents to create many final documents, each containing customized information. In Word, the two separate documents are called a main document and a data source.

A **main document** is a document (such as a letter) that contains standard text and placeholders (called **merge fields**) that mark where variable information (such as a name or an address) will be inserted. Maria's main document is a letter that looks like Figure 6-1, except that merge fields will replace the red text.

Figure 6-1   **MARIA'S MAIN DOCUMENT**

[Date]

[First Name] [Last Name]
[Address Line 1]
[City], **FL** [ZIP Code]

Dear [First Name]:

As you've probably noticed, your branch of the Palm Tree Athletic Club has been
undergoing major renovations. You'll be happy to know that we have finally cleared
away the rubble. We've installed the new equipment, including a new suite of [Favorite
Equipment] machines, and are laying the new carpet next week. We want to thank you
for your patience while we knocked down walls and expanded our facilities. We realize
you put up with a lot of inconvenience (not to mention noise and dust).

As a sign of our gratitude, we invite you to sign up for three free hours with one of our
certified personal trainers. Just bring this letter to your branch of the Palm Tree Athletic
Club and sign up for six half-hour sessions at times that are convenient for you. Our
trainers are available Monday through Saturday.

While you're at the club, take a look at our new schedule for [Favorite Class] classes. We
hope you'll like the additional weekend options. (We've had many requests for these over
the past few months.)

We look forward to seeing you at Palm City Athletic Club.

Sincerely yours,

Maria Fuentes
Facilities Manager

A **data source** is a document that contains information, such as members' names and
addresses, that will be inserted into the main document. Maria's data source will include the
name and address of each club member, as well as information about each member's preferred exercise machine and favorite class.

Inserting information from a data source into a main document produces a final document called a **merged document**. Figure 6-2 illustrates how the data source and main
document combine to form a merged document.

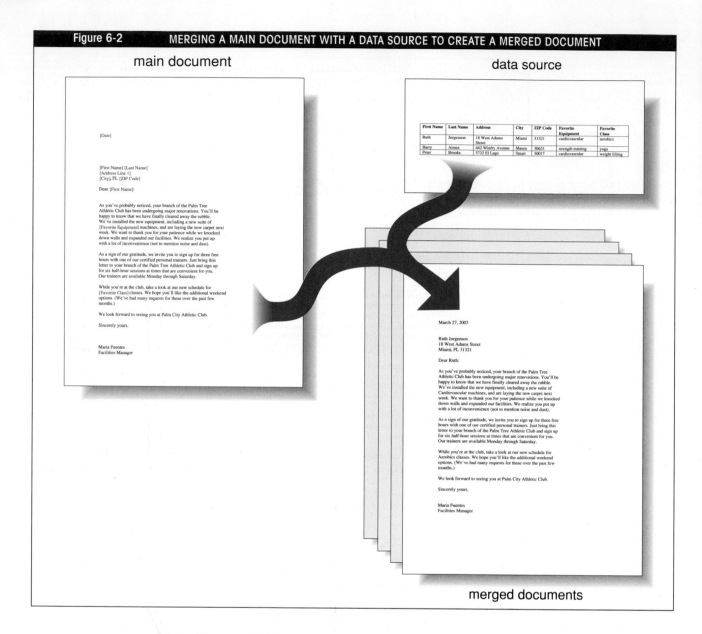

Figure 6-2   MERGING A MAIN DOCUMENT WITH A DATA SOURCE TO CREATE A MERGED DOCUMENT

Mail Merge Fields

During a merge, the merge fields (the placeholders for text that changes in the main document) instruct Word to retrieve information from the data source. For example, one merge field in the main document might retrieve a name from the data source; another merge field might retrieve an address. For each club member listed in the data source, Word will create a new, separate letter in the final merged document. Thus, if the data source contains five sets of member names and addresses, the merged document will contain five separate letters, each one containing a different member name and address in the appropriate places.

You insert merge fields in a main document using the Insert Merge Fields dialog box. You can distinguish merge fields from the other text of the main document because each merge field name is enclosed by pairs of angled brackets—like this: << >>.

Data Fields and Records

A data source is a table of information similar to the one shown in Figure 6-3. The **header row**, the first row of the table, contains the name of each merge field. The cells below the header row contain the specific information that replaces the merge field in the main document. This information is called **data**. Each row of data in the table makes up a complete **record**, or all the information about one individual or object. For a mail merge to work smoothly, every record in the data source must have the same set of merge fields.

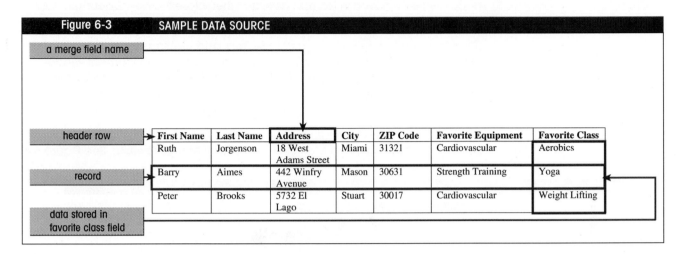

Figure 6-3   SAMPLE DATA SOURCE

First Name	Last Name	Address	City	ZIP Code	Favorite Equipment	Favorite Class
Ruth	Jorgenson	18 West Adams Street	Miami	31321	Cardiovascular	Aerobics
Barry	Aimes	442 Winfry Avenue	Mason	30631	Strength Training	Yoga
Peter	Brooks	5732 El Lago	Stuart	30017	Cardiovascular	Weight Lifting

Data sources are commonly used to store names and addresses. However, you can also create data sources with inventory records, records of suppliers, or records of equipment. After you understand how to manage and manipulate the records in a data source, you'll be able to use them for many different types of information.

Using the Mail Merge Wizard

Word's **Mail Merge Wizard** is a special feature that walks you through the six steps involved in merging documents. These steps are:

- Select the type of document you want to use as the main document. Possible types of main documents include letters, envelopes, and e-mails.
- Select the document you want to use as the main document. You can type a new document or edit an existing one.
- Select the list of recipients (that is, the data source) you want to use for the merge. You can use an existing data source or create a new one.
- Complete the main document by adding merge fields.
- Preview the merged document.
- Complete the mail merge.

You can access the Mail Merge Wizard via the Mail Merge Task Pane. Once you are familiar with merging documents, you can also use the buttons on the Mail Merge toolbar to perform the same tasks described by the Mail Merge Wizard. Maria asks you to start the Mail Merge Wizard now.

To start Word and open the Mail Merge Wizard:

1. Start Word, insert your Data Disk in the appropriate drive, verify that a new, blank document is displayed in Normal view, and then close the New Document Task Pane, if necessary.

2. Click **Tools** on the menu bar, point to **Letters and Mailings**, and then click **Mail Merge Wizard**. The Mail Merge Task Pane opens and the Document window switches to Print Layout view. The Mail Merge Task Pane displays information and options related to the first step in merging documents. Depending on how your computer is set up, you might also see the Mail Merge toolbar.

3. If you do not see the Mail Merge toolbar, click **Tools** on the menu bar, point to **Letters and Mailings**, and then click **Show Mail Merge Toolbar**. See Figure 6-4.

Figure 6-4	WORD'S MAIL MERGE FEATURES

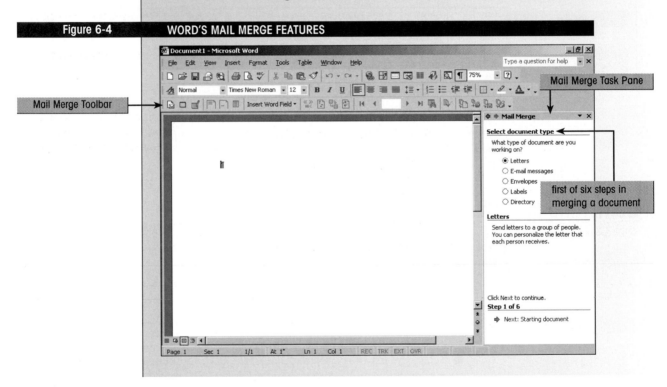

With the Mail Merge Task Pane open, you are ready to perform the first two steps in merging a document.

Selecting a Main Document

According to the Mail Merge Wizard, your first task is to specify the type of main document you want to use for the merge. The Mail Merge Wizard provides a number of options, including e-mail messages and labels. In this case, you want to create a letter.

To specify the type of merged document to create:

1. Verify that the **Letters** option button is selected in the Mail Merge Task Pane.

2. At the bottom of the Task Pane, click **Next: Starting document**. The Mail Merge Task Pane displays information and options that you can use to select a starting document—that is, to select a main document.

When selecting a main document, you have three choices: use the document currently displayed in the Document window; start a new document from a template; or open an existing document. Maria has already written the letter she wants to send to all Palm Tree Athletic Club members, so you don't need to create a new document. Instead, you'll use an existing document.

To select a starting, or main, document:

1. In the Mail Merge Task Pane, click the **Start from existing document** option button (just below the "Select starting document" heading). A list box appears, with an Open button below it.

2. Click **Open**. The Open dialog box appears. You'll use this dialog box to open Maria's document.

3. Use the Look in list arrow to select the **Tutorial** folder in the Tutorial.06 folder on your Data Disk.

4. Click **Club** and then click **Open**. The document named Club opens.

5. Switch to **Normal** view, zoomed to **100%**. Note that the "Use the current document" option button is now selected in the Task Pane, indicating that you will use the current document. Also, note that the title bar indicates that the newly opened document (which was originally named "Club") is now named "Document1." At the bottom of the Task Pane, you can see the next step in the mail merge process. See Figure 6-5.

Figure 6-5	**MAIN DOCUMENT OPEN IN DOCUMENT WINDOW**

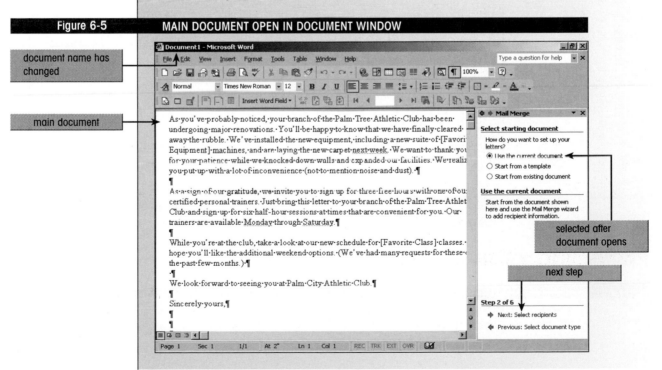

Next you need to tell Word where to find the list of recipients for Maria's letter.

Selecting a Data Source

As you learned earlier, a data source is a table of information. In a typical mail merge, the data source contains a list of names and addresses, but it can also contain additional, customized fields. You can use many kinds of files as data sources for a mail merge including simple Word tables, Excel worksheets, Access databases, or a special file designed to store addresses for Microsoft Office applications.

When performing a mail merge, you can select a data source file that already contains names and addresses, or you can create a new data source, enter names and addresses into it, and then merge it with the main document. In this section, you will create a data source using the tools provided by the Mail Merge Wizard. This involves two steps: deciding which fields to include in the data source, and entering address information.

Selecting Fields to Include in the Data Source

You need to create a data source that contains club member information, including address, favorite exercise equipment, and preferred type of class. Maria compiled all the necessary information by asking each member to fill out a form when they first joined the club. Figure 6-6 shows one of these forms.

Figure 6-6	MEMBER INFORMATION FORM

Palm Tree Athletic Club

First Name ___Barry___ Last Name ___Aimes___

Address ___442 Winfrey Ave___ City ___Mason___ , Florida

ZIP Code ___30631___

Favorite Equipment ___strength training___

Favorite Class ___spinning___

Your job is to create a data source to store all the data found in the member information forms. When you create your data source, therefore, you must include the field names shown in Figure 6-7.

Figure 6-7   **FIELD NAMES TO INCLUDE IN DATA SOURCE**

Field Names	Description
First Name	Member's first name
Last Name	Member's last name
Address	Member's street address
City	Member's city (in Florida)
ZIP Code	Member's ZIP code
Favorite Equipment	Member's favorite type of exercise equipment
Favorite Class	Member's favorite type of exercise class

When you create a new data source from within the Mail Merge Wizard, Word provides a number of default fields such as First Name, Last Name, and Company. You can customize the data source by adding new fields and removing the default fields that you don't plan to use. As you create a data source, keep in mind that each field name must be unique; you can't have two fields with the same name. Although the order of field names in the data source doesn't affect their placement in the main document, arrange them logically so you can enter information quickly and efficiently. For example, you'll probably want the First Name field next to the Last Name field. Finally, note that if you include spaces in your field names, Word will replace the spaces with underscores. For example, Word transforms the field name First Name into First_Name.

REFERENCE WINDOW   **RW**

Creating a Data Source

- In Step 3 of the Mail Merge Wizard, select the Type a new list option button, and then click Create.
- In the New Address List dialog box, click the Customize button.
- In the Customize Address List dialog box, click a field you want to delete, click the Delete button, and then click the Yes button. Continue to delete any unnecessary fields.
- To add a new field, click the Add button, type the name of the field in the Add Field dialog box, and then click the OK button.
- To rearrange the order of the field names, click a field name, and then click the Move Up or Move Down button.
- Click the OK button to close the Customize Address List dialog box.
- In the New Address List dialog box, enter information for the first record, click the New Entry button, and type another record. Continue until you are finished entering information into the data source, and then click the Close button.

You're ready to begin creating the data source for Maria's form letter.

To begin creating the data source:

1. In the bottom of the Task Pane, click **Next: Select recipients**, and then click the **Type a new list** option button in the Task Pane.

2. Below the heading "Type a new list" click **Create**. The New Address List dialog box opens, as shown in Figure 6-8. You will use this dialog box to enter a complete set of information for one person—that is, enter one record into the data source. Before you begin entering information, you need to customize the list of fields to match the list shown earlier in Figure 6-7.

Figure 6-8   CREATING A DATA SOURCE

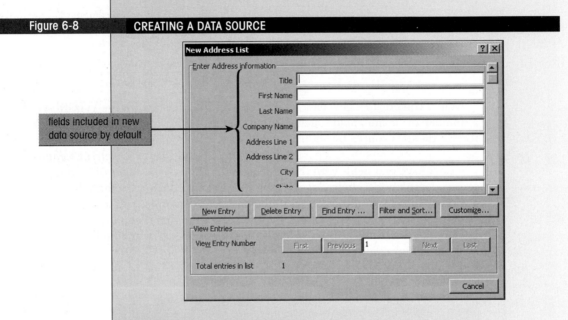

fields included in new
data source by default

3. Click the **Customize** button. The Customize Address List dialog box opens. Here you can delete the fields you don't need, and add new ones. You'll start by deleting fields.

4. In the Field Names list box, click **Title** (if necessary), and then click the **Delete** button. A message appears asking you to confirm the deletion.

5. Click the **Yes** button. The Title field is deleted from the list of field names.

6. Continue using the Delete button to delete the following fields: Company Name, Address Line 2, State, Country, Home Phone, Work Phone, and E-mail Address. Next you need to add some new fields. When you add a new field, it is inserted below the selected field, so you will start by selecting the last field in the list.

7. Verify that **ZIP Code** is selected, and then click the **Add** button. The Add Field dialog box opens, instructing you to type a name for your field.

8. Type **Favorite Equipment**, click the **OK** button, and then use the Add button to add a **Favorite Class** field. When you are finished, your Customize Address List dialog box should look like the one shown in Figure 6-9. You could use the Move Up and Move Down buttons to rearrange the field names (for instance, to move the Favorite Class field above the Favorite Equipment field), but in this case the order is fine. You are finished customizing the list of field names.

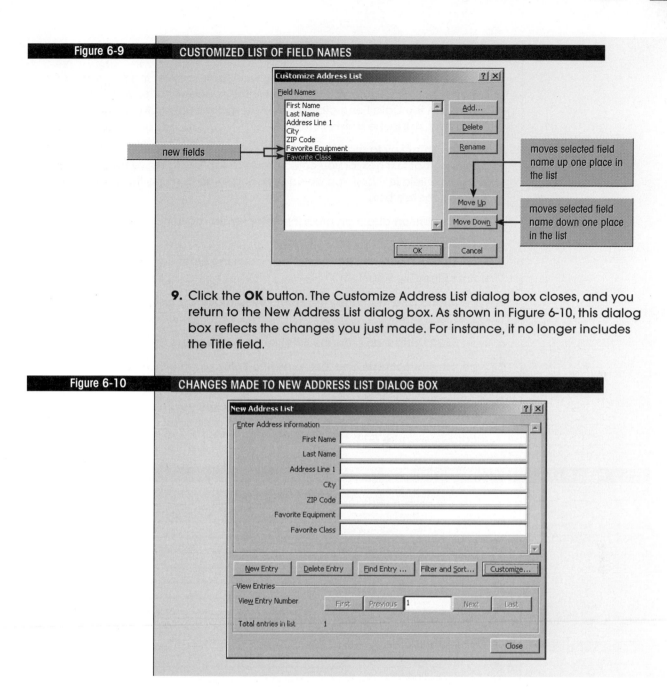

Figure 6-9   **CUSTOMIZED LIST OF FIELD NAMES**

new fields

moves selected field name up one place in the list

moves selected field name down one place in the list

9. Click the **OK** button. The Customize Address List dialog box closes, and you return to the New Address List dialog box. As shown in Figure 6-10, this dialog box reflects the changes you just made. For instance, it no longer includes the Title field.

Figure 6-10   **CHANGES MADE TO NEW ADDRESS LIST DIALOG BOX**

Now that you have specified the fields you want to use, you are ready to enter the member information into the data source.

Entering Data into a Data Source

You are now ready to begin entering information about each club member into the data source. Maria gives you three completed Member Information Forms (shown earlier in Figure 6-6). She asks you to transfer the information from the paper forms into the data source. Each paper form will equal one new record in the data source. You'll use the New Address List dialog box to begin entering information.

To enter data into a record using the data form:

1. Click the **First Name** text box, and then type **Ruth** to enter the first name of the first member. Make sure you do not press the spacebar after you finish typing an entry in the Data Form dialog box. Add spaces only in the text of the main document, not in the data source.

2. Press the **Enter** key to move the insertion point to the Last Name field. You could also click that text box, or you could press the Tab key to move the insertion point to the next field text box. You would press Shift + Tab to move the insertion point to the previous text box.

3. Type **Jorgenson** and then press the **Enter** key to move the insertion point to the Address Line 1 field.

4. Type **18 West Adams Street**, and then press the **Enter** key to move the insertion point to the City field.

5. Type **Miami** and then press the **Enter** key to move the insertion point to the ZIP Code field.

6. Type **31321** and then press the **Enter** key to move to the Favorite Equipment field.

7. Type **cardiovascular**, and then press the **Enter** key. The insertion point is now in the Favorite Class field.

8. Type **step aerobics** but do *not* press the Enter key yet. The number at the bottom of the dialog box tells you that so far, the data source contains only one record. See Figure 6-11.

Figure 6-11   COMPLETED RECORD 1

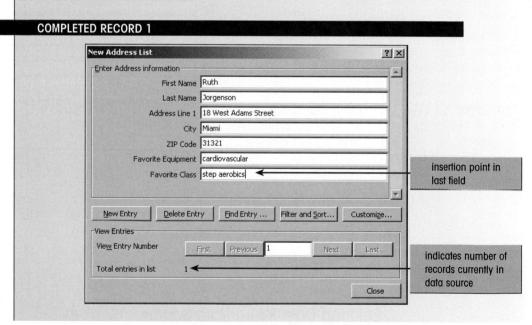

You have completed the information for the first record of the data source document. Now you're ready to enter the information for the next two records. You can create a new record by clicking the New Entry button, or by pressing the Enter key twice. In the steps below, you use the New Entry button.

To add additional records to the data source:

1. Click the **New Entry** button. This creates a new, blank record. The Total entries in list number, at the bottom of the dialog box, tells you that you're editing the second record.

2. Enter the information shown in Figure 6-12 into the new record.

Figure 6-12	COMPLETED RECORD 2

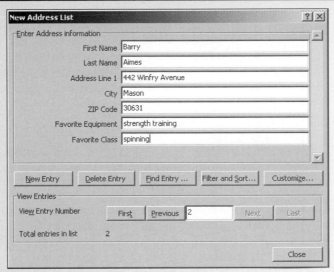

3. After entering data into the last field, press **Enter** twice. Note that you can use the Enter key or the New Entry button to create a blank record.

4. Enter the information for the third record, as shown in Figure 6-13.

Figure 6-13	COMPLETED RECORD 3

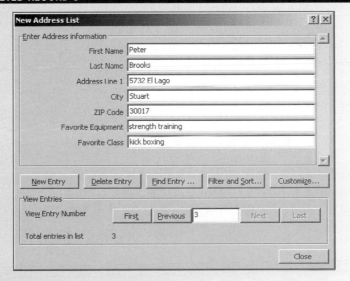

TROUBLE? If a new, blank record opens, you pressed the Enter key twice at the end of the third record or you clicked the New Entry button in the New Address List dialog box. Click the Delete Entry button to remove the unneeded fourth record.

You have entered the records for three members. Next you need to proofread each record to make sure you typed the information correctly. Any misspelled names or other typos in the final letters will reflect poorly on Palm Tree Athletic Club.

Displaying Records in a Data Source

You can display specific records in the data source by using the First, Previous, Next, and Last buttons. You'll use these buttons now to proofread each record in the data source.

To display the first record:

1. Click the **First** button at the bottom of the New Address List dialog box. The current record number (to the right of the Previous button) changes to 1, and the first record appears, with information about Ruth Jorgenson.

2. Proofread the data by comparing your information with Figure 6-11. Make any necessary corrections by selecting the text and retyping it.

3. Click the **Next** button. The "View Entry Number" changes to 2, and the information for the second record (for Barry Aimes) appears. Compare your record with Figure 6-12.

4. Click the **Last** button to review the last record (for Peter Brooks) in the data source. Compare your record with Figure 6-13. Make any necessary corrections.

Maria's data source eventually will contain hundreds of records for Palm Tree Athletic Club members. The current data source, however, contains only the records Maria wants to work with now.

You are finished entering records into the data source. Next you need to save the data source.

Saving a Data Source

When you create a data source in the Mail Merge Wizard, Word saves it as a Microsoft Office Address List, which is a special file designed to store address information for any Microsoft Office program.

Maria asks you to close the New Address List dialog box. In the process, you will save the data source as a Microsoft Office Address List.

To save the data source:

1. In the New Address List dialog box, click **Close**. The Save Address List dialog box opens, as shown in Figure 6-14. By default, Word offers to save the file to the My Data Sources folder, which is a subfolder of the My Documents folder. In this case, however, you will save the data source to your Data Disk. Notice that the Save as type box indicates that the data source will be saved as a Microsoft Office Address Lists file.

Figure 6-14 SAVING THE DATA SOURCE

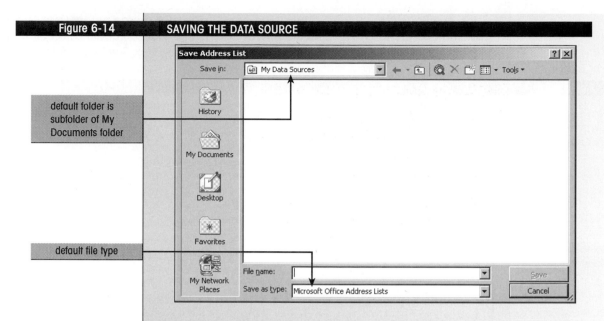

default folder is subfolder of My Documents folder

default file type

2. Use the Save in list arrow to select the **Tutorial** folder within the Tutorial.06 folder on your Data Disk.

3. Click the **File name** text box, type **Club Data**, and then click the **Save** button. The Mail Merge Recipients dialog box opens, as shown in Figure 6-15. Here you can see the data source displayed as a table. The header row, at the top, contains the names of each field in the table. Each row below the header row consists of one complete record. (You need to scroll right to see all the fields.) You can use this dialog box to rearrange the records in the list and to choose which members you want to include in the mail merge. You'll use this dialog box later in this tutorial. For now, you'll close it.

Figure 6-15 DATA DISPLAYED AS A TABLE

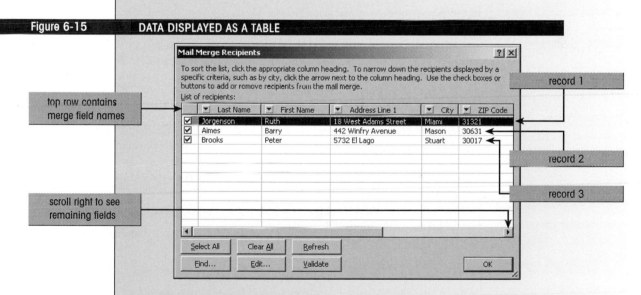

top row contains merge field names

scroll right to see remaining fields

record 1

record 2

record 3

4. Click the **OK** button. The Mail Merge Recipients dialog box closes. You return to the Document window. The Mail Merge Task Pane indicates that you have selected an Office Address List file named Club Data.mdb as your data source.

The Task Pane also indicates that the next step in the mail merge process is writing (in this case, editing) the main document. Finally, note that you could click Edit recipient list to reopen the Mail Merge Recipients dialog box. See Figure 6-16.

Figure 6-16   SELECTED DATA SOURCE

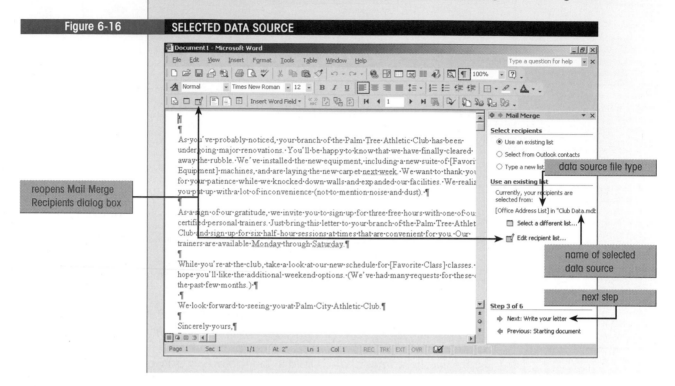

Editing a Main Document

In the first two steps of the Mail Merge Wizard, you selected Maria's letter as your main document. This letter is open on your screen, next to the Mail Merge Task Pane. In the third step, you selected, created, and saved the data source. Now you will turn your attention back to the main document. You'll edit Maria's letter to add the current date and the merge fields.

Adding a Date Field

You already know how to use the Insert Date and Time dialog box to add the current date to a document. If you select the Update automatically check box, Word inserts a **date field**, which tells Word to provide the current date each time the document is opened. A date field is similar to a merge field—the information it displays varies. However, you do not have to include a date field in the data source.

Maria wants the date to appear at the top of the document, just below the company logo on the printed stationery.

To insert the date field:

1. In the Mail Merge Task Pane, click **Next: Write your letter**. The Mail Merge Task Pane displays information and options related to working with the main document. If you had originally selected a new, blank document as your main document, you would need to write the text of the form letter now. In this case, you will edit the existing letter.

2. Make sure the insertion point is at the beginning of the form letter, on the first blank line. Maria already adjusted the page's top margin to leave room for the letterhead on the company stationery. You will insert the date on the first line of the document.

3. Click **Insert** on the menu bar, and then click **Date and Time**. The Date and Time dialog box opens. You will use the Update automatically check box to have Word revise the date every time you open the document.

4. Click the third month-day-year format in the Available formats list, and then click the **Update automatically** check box to select it. See Figure 6-17.

| Figure 6-17 | INSERTING A DATE FIELD |

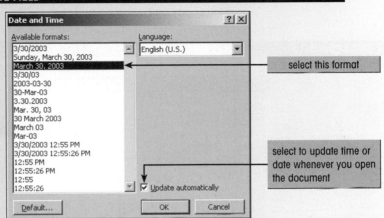

TROUBLE? The date in your Date and Time dialog box will differ from the one shown in Figure 6-17. Just click the format that includes the month, the day, and the year, as in March 3, 2003.

5. Click the **OK** button. The current date appears in the document. Now, whenever you or Maria print the merged document letter for Palm Tree Athletic Club's members, the current date will appear.

TROUBLE? If you see {TIME \@ "MMMM d, yyyy"} instead of the date, your system is set to display field codes. To view the date, click Tools on the menu bar, click Options, click the View tab, click the Field codes check box to remove the check mark and then click the OK button.

You're now ready to insert the merge fields for the letter's inside address.

Inserting Merge Fields

Maria's letter is a standard business letter, so you'll place the member's name and address below the date. You'll use merge fields for the member's first name, last name, address, city, and zip code. You must enter proper spacing and punctuation around the fields so that the information in the merged document will be formatted correctly. The Mail Merge Task Pane includes links, such as the Address block link, that you can use to insert a standard set of fields. The More items link offers more flexibility because it allows you to insert fields one at a time, rather than in predefined groups.

To insert a merge field:

1. Press the **Enter** key six times to leave space between the date and the first line of the inside address.

2. Click **More items** in the Mail Merge Task Pane. The Insert Merge Fields dialog box opens. (You could also use the Insert Merge Field button on the Mail Merge toolbar to open this dialog box.) As shown in Figure 6-18, the Database Fields option button is selected, indicating that the dialog box displays all the fields in the data source.

   TROUBLE? If you see a different list, the Address Fields option button may be selected rather than the Database Fields option button. Click the Database Fields option button to select it.

Figure 6-18	INSERTING MERGE FIELDS INTO THE MAIN DOCUMENT

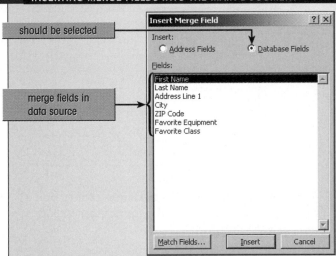

3. In the Fields list, click **First Name** if necessary, click the **Insert** button, and then click the **Close** button. The Insert Merge Fields dialog box closes, and a special instruction called a merge code is inserted into the document. The merge field consists of the field name surrounded by angled brackets << >> (also called chevrons).

   TROUBLE? If you make a mistake and insert the wrong merge field, select the entire merge field, including the chevrons, press the Delete key, and then insert the correct merge field.

4. Depending on how your computer is set up, you might see a gray background behind the merge field. If you do *not* see the gray background, click **Tools** on the menu bar, click **Options**, and then click the **View** tab in the Options dialog box. If necessary, change the **Field Shading** setting to **Always**, and then click the **OK** button.

Later, when you merge the main document with the data source, Word will replace the field code with information from the First Name field in the data source. Now, you're ready to insert the merge fields for the rest of the inside address. You'll add the necessary spacing and punctuation to the main document as well.

To insert the remaining merge fields for the inside address:

1. Press the **spacebar** to insert a space after the First Name field, click the **Insert Merge Fields** button 🔲 on the Mail Merge toolbar, click **Last Name** in the Insert Merge Field dialog box, click the **Insert** button, and then click the **Close** button. Word inserts the Last Name merge field into the form letter.

2. Press the **Enter** key to move the insertion point to the next line, click 🔲, click **Address Line 1** in the Insert Merge Field dialog box, click the **Insert** button, and then click the **Close** button. Word inserts the Address Line 1 merge field into the form letter.

3. Press the **Enter** key to move the insertion point to the next line, click 🔲, click **City** in the Insert Merge Field dialog box, click the **Insert** button, and then click the **Close** button. Word inserts the City merge field into the form letter.

4. Type **,** (a comma), press the **spacebar** to insert a space after the comma, and then type **FL** to insert the abbreviation for the state of Florida. If Palm Tree Athletic Club had members outside Florida, you would need to use the State field name in the data source and also in the main document form letter. Because all of the members live in Florida, you can make the state name part of the main document, where it will be the same for every letter.

5. Press the **spacebar** to insert a space after FL, and then insert the ZIP Code merge field. Word inserts the ZIP Code merge field into the form letter. See Figure 6-19.

Figure 6-19	FORM LETTER WITH MERGE FIELDS

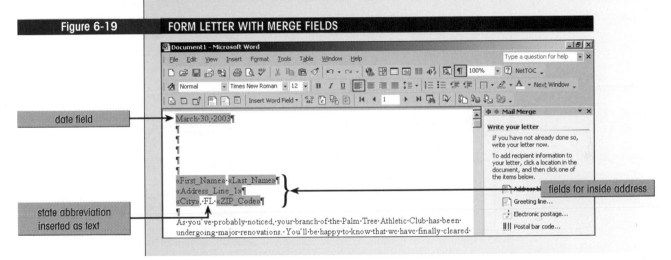

The inside address is set up to match the form for a standard business letter. You can now add the salutation of the letter, which will contain each member's first name.

To insert the merge field for the salutation:

1. Press the **Enter** key twice to leave a line between the inside address and the salutation, type **Dear**, and then press the **spacebar**.

2. Insert the **First Name** field into the document.

3. Type **:** (a colon). This completes the salutation.

   TROUBLE? If the Office Assistant asks if you want help writing the letter, click "Just type the letter without help."

You'll personalize the letter even more by including references to each member's favorite class and exercise equipment.

To finish personalizing the letter:

1. Select the placeholder **(Favorite Equipment)** (including the brackets) in the first paragraph of the form letter. You'll replace this phrase with a merge field.

2. Use the Insert Merge Field dialog box to insert the **Favorite Equipment** merge field. Word replaces your placeholder with the Favorite Equipment merge field.

3. If necessary, press the **spacebar** to insert a space between the field and the next word, "machines."

4. Replace **(Favorite Class)** in the first sentence of the third main paragraph of the form letter with the **Favorite Class** field, and make sure there is a space between the merge field and the next word, "classes." Your document should look like Figure 6-20.

Figure 6-20   FORM LETTER AFTER INSERTING MERGE FIELDS

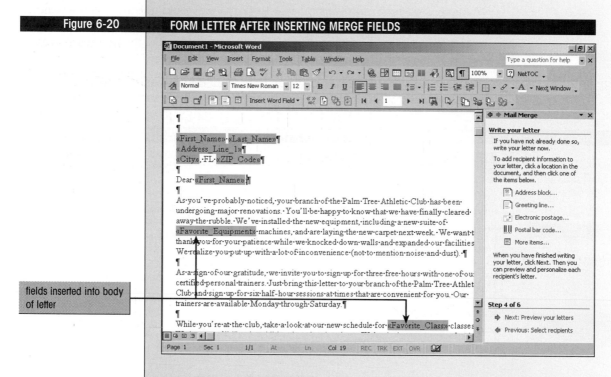

fields inserted into body of letter

5. Carefully check your document to make sure all the field names and spacing are correct. Now that you have inserted all the merge fields, you need to save the main document with a new name.

   TROUBLE? If you see an error, edit the document as you would any other Word document. If you inserted an incorrect merge field, delete the entire merge field, and then insert the correct one.

6. Save the letter as **Club Letter with Field Codes** in the Tutorial subfolder within the Tutorial.06 folder on your Data Disk.

The main document now contains all the necessary merge fields, but not the data. To include data, you merge the main document and the data source. First, however, you should preview the merged document.

Previewing the Merged Document

According to the Mail Merge Wizard, your next step is to preview the merged document to see how the letter will look after Word inserts the information for each member. When you preview the merged document, you can check one last time for any missing spaces between the merge codes and the surrounding text. You can also look for any other formatting problems, and, if necessary, make final changes to the data source.

To preview the merged document:

1. In the Mail Merge Task Pane, click **Next: Preview your letters**. The Task Pane displays information and options related to previewing the merged document. The data for the first record replaces the merge fields in the form letter. See Figure 6-21. Scroll to the top of the document so you can see the inside address and salutation. Carefully check the letter to make sure the text and formatting are correct. In particular, check to make sure that the spaces before and after the merged data are correct because it is easy to omit spaces or add extra spaces around merge fields. Finally, notice that both the Task Pane and the Go to Record box in the Mail Merge toolbar indicate which record is currently displayed in the document.

| Figure 6-21 | FIRST LETTER WITH MERGED DATA |

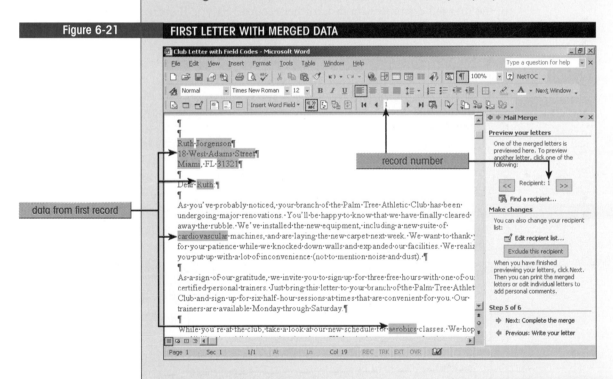

2. If you need to make any changes to the form letter, click **Previous: Write your letter** in the Task Pane, edit the document, save your changes, and then click **Next: Preview your letters** in the Task Pane. When you are finished, your screen should look like Figure 6-21. Before you finish previewing your merged document, you should review the data for the other two records.

3. Click the **Next Record** button ▶ in the Mail Merge toolbar to display the data for Barry Aimes in the letter. (*Note:* You can also use the right-facing double-arrow button in the Task Pane to display the next record.)

4. Click ▶ in the Mail Merge toolbar to display the data for Peter Brooks in the letter.

5. Click the **First Record** button ◀ in the Mail Merge toolbar to redisplay the first record in the letter (with data for Ruth Jorgenson).

The form letter (main document) of the mail merge is completed. At this stage you could also use the Mail Merge Task Pane to make changes to the data source, but Maria says the data source is fine for now. You are ready for the final step, completing the merge.

Merging the Main Document and Data Source

Now that you've created the form letter (main document) and the list of member information (data source), you're ready to merge the two files and create personalized letters to send to Palm Tree Athletic Club members. Because the data source consists of three records, you'll create a merged document with three pages, one letter per page.

You could merge the data source and main document directly to the printer using the Merge to Printer button on the Mail Merge toolbar. Then Word immediately prints the merged document without saving it as a separate file. However, Maria wants to keep a copy of the merged document on disk for her records. So you'll merge the data source and main document to a new document.

To complete the mail merge:

1. In the Mail Merge Task Pane, click **Next: Complete the merge**. As shown in Figure 6-22, the Task Pane displays options related to merging the main document and the data source. You can use the Print option (or the Merge to Printer button 📇 on the Mail Merge toolbar) to merge directly to the printer. Or, you can use the Edit individual letters option (or the Merge to New Document button 🗐 on the Mail Merge toolbar) to merge to a new document.

| Figure 6-22 | LAST STEP OF MAIL MERGE WIZARD |

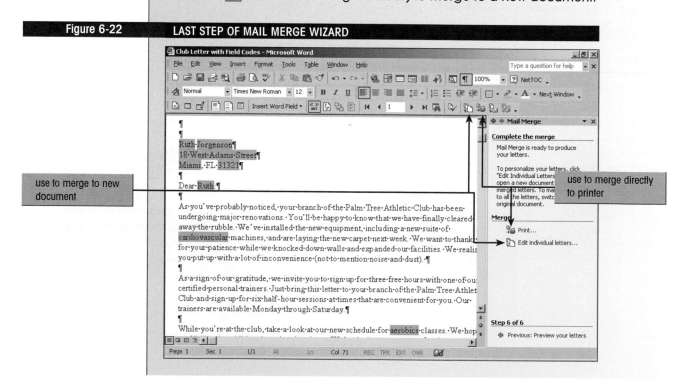

2. Click **Edit individual letters** in the Mail Merge Task Pane. The Merge to New Document dialog box opens. Here, you need to specify which records you want to include in the merge. You want to include all the records in the data source.

3. Verify that the All option button is selected, and then click the **OK** button. Word creates a new document called Letters1, which contains three pages, one for each record in the data source. The form letter with the merge field codes (Club Letter with Field Codes) remains open, as indicated by its button in the taskbar. See Figure 6-23.

Figure 6-23	MERGED DOCUMENT

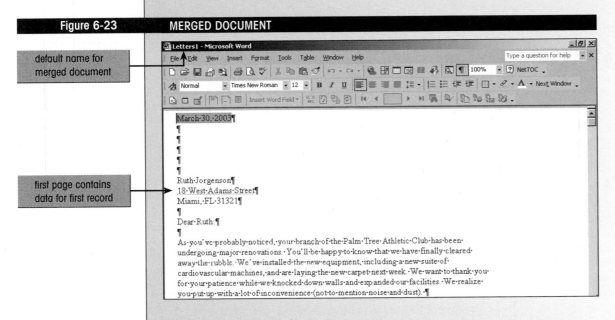

default name for merged document

first page contains data for first record

4. Save the merged document in the Tutorial subfolder in the Tutorial.06 folder, using the filename **Club Merged Letters1**.

5. Click the **Print Preview** button 🔍 on the Standard toolbar to switch to Print Preview.

6. Click the **Zoom Control** list arrow on the Print Preview toolbar, and then click **Page Width** so the text is large enough to read. Next you will use the Select Browse Object button (at the bottom of the vertical scroll bar) to move from one page to the next.

7. Click the **Select Browse Object** button 🔘, click the **Browse by Page** button 🗎 in the palette, and then click the **Previous Page** button 🔼 or **Next Page** button 🔽 below the vertical scroll bar to move to the beginning of each letter. Note that each letter is addressed to a different member and that the favorite equipment and class vary from one letter to the next.

8. Click the **Close** button on the Print Preview toolbar to return to Normal view, and then save and close the Club Merged Letters1 document. The document named Club Letter with Field Codes reappears, along with the last step of the Mail Merge Wizard.

> **9.** Close the Mail Merge Task Pane but leave the Mail Merge toolbar displayed. If you are not taking a break before the next session, you can leave the Club letter with Field Codes document open. If you are taking a break, close all open documents (saving any changes) and exit Word.

You have completed the six steps of the Mail Merge Wizard and generated a merged document. In the next session you will learn how to use additional features of the Mail Merge Wizard.

Session 6.1 QUICK CHECK

1. Define the following in your own words:
   a. form letter
   b. main document
   c. data source
   d. merge field
   e. record

2. All the information about one individual or object in a data source is called a
   _____ .

3. True or False: For a mail merge to work properly, every record in the data source must have the same set of fields.

4. Suppose you want to insert information for a field named "Gender" into the data source. How would you do it?

5. What type of file do you create when you create a data source from within the Mail Merge Wizard?

6. Explain how to insert a field code into a main document.

7. Explain how to merge to a new document.

SESSION 6.2

In this session you will edit a data source, sort records in a data source, filter a data source to display only certain records, create mailing labels, and create a telephone directory.

Editing a Data Source

After you complete a mail merge, you may find that you need to make some changes to the data source and redo the merge. For instance, now Maria wants to add some records to the data source.

You can edit a data source in two ways—from within the program used to create the data source in the first place, or from within the Mail Merge Wizard. If you are familiar with the program used to create the data source, it's often simplest to edit the file from within that program. For example, if you were using an Excel worksheet as your data source, you could open the file in Excel, edit it (perhaps by adding new records), save it, and then reselect the file as your data source. You can use Microsoft Access to edit a data source created in Word, but it's easier to edit it from within Word, using the buttons on the Mail Merge toolbar.

REFERENCE   WINDOW   RW

Editing a Data Source

- If you did not use the Mail Merge Wizard to create your data source, open the program you used to create the data source, edit the file, save it and close it.
- Click the Open Data Source button on the Mail Merge toolbar, navigate to the folder containing the data source, select the data source, and then click the Open button.

or

- Click the Mail Merge Recipients button on the Mail Merge toolbar and then click the Edit button.
- To add a record, click the New Field button and then type a new record.
- To delete a record, display it and then click the Delete button.
- To add or remove fields from the data source, click the Customize button, make any changes, and then click the OK button. Remember that if you remove a field, you will delete any data already entered into that field.
- Click the Close button.

You'll try the second method now as you add some new records to Maria's data source. After you complete a merge using the Mail Merge Wizard, it's usually easiest to change the merge documents by using the Mail Merge toolbar, rather than the Task Pane. (Note that you only have to perform Step 1 if you took a break from the last session.)

To add records to Maria's data source:

1. If you took a break after the last session, start Word, open the document named **Club Letter with Field Codes**, display the Mail Merge toolbar (if necessary), click the **Open Data Source** button 📧 on the Mail Merge toolbar, and then use the Select Data Source dialog box to open the data source file named **Club Data** (from the Tutorial subfolder in the Tutorial.06 folder on your Data Disk). Next, click the **View Merged Data** button 《》 on the Mail Merge Toolbar to display the data for Ruth Jorgenson (just as you saw it earlier in Figure 6-21).

2. If the Mail Merge Task Pane is open, close it and verify that the Mail Merge toolbar is still visible. The main document still displays the data for Ruth Jorgenson, which first appeared when you previewed the merged document. You can redisplay the merge fields using a button on the toolbar.

3. Click 《》 on the Mail Merge Task Pane. The merge field codes are displayed in the main document.

4. Click the **Mail Merge Recipients** button 📇 on the Mail Merge toolbar. The Mail Merge Recipients dialog box opens. You saw this dialog box earlier, when you first selected the data source to use for the mail merge.

5. Click the **Edit** button. The Club Data.mdb dialog box opens. Note that this dialog box looks similar to the New Address List dialog box, which you used earlier when you first entered information into the data source.

6. Use the New Entry button to enter the information shown in Figure 6-24 into the data source. When you are finished, you should have added three new records, for a total of six.

Figure 6-24						
NEW DATA						

First Name	Last Name	Address Line 1	City	ZIP Code	Favorite Equipment	Favorite Class
Violette	Wolfgramm	3004 Falcon Parkway	Tampa	30902	cardiovascular	low-impact aerobics
Kathy	Armstrong	19284 White Sands	Tampa	30902	strength training	Pilates
Pablo	Orozco	248 North River Road	Aurora	30010	strength training	yoga

7. After you finish entering the data for Pablo Orozco, use the buttons in the View Entries section of the dialog box to review your work and make any necessary corrections.

8. Click the **Close** button. The Club Data.mdb dialog box closes, and you return to the Mail Merge Recipients dialog box, as shown in Figure 6-25. If your records look different from those in Figure 6-25, click the Edit button, edit the data source, and then click the Close button.

Figure 6-25	
NEW RECORDS ADDED TO DATA SOURCE	

new records

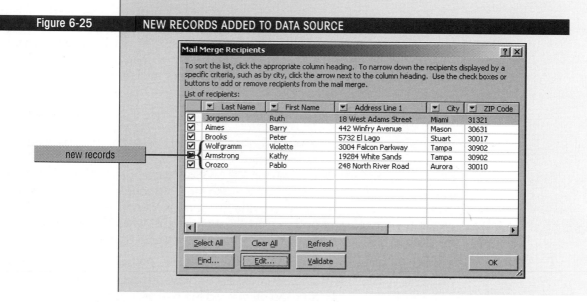

You'll leave the Mail Merge Recipients dialog box open so you can use it to make other changes to the data source.

Sorting Records

As Maria looks through the letters to Palm Tree Athletic Club members in the merged document, she notices one problem—the letters are not grouped by ZIP codes. Currently, the letters are in the order in which members were added to the data source file. She plans to use bulk mailing rates to send her letters, and the U.S. Postal Service requires bulk mailings to be separated into groups according to ZIP code. She asks you to sort the data file by ZIP code and perform another merge, this time merging the main document with the sorted data source.

You can sort information in a data source table just as you sort information in any other table. Recall that to **sort** means to rearrange a list or a document in alphabetical, numerical, or chronological order. You can sort information in ascending order (A to Z, lowest to highest, or earliest to latest) or in descending order (Z to A, highest to lowest, or latest to earliest) by clicking a column heading in the Mail Merge Recipients dialog box. The first time you click the heading, the records are sorted in ascending order. If you click it twice, the records are sorted in descending order.

REFERENCE WINDOW **RW**

Sorting a Data Source

■ Click the Mail Merge Recipients button on the Mail Merge toolbar to display the Mail Merge Recipients dialog box.

■ To sort data in ascending order, click the heading for the column you want to sort by. For example, if you want to arrange the records alphabetically according to the contents of the First Name column, click the First Name column heading.

■ To sort data in descending order, click the column heading a second time.

Currently, the records in the data source appear in the order you entered them, with the information for Ruth Jorgenson first. You'll sort the records in an ascending order, based on the contents of the ZIP Code column.

To sort the data source by zip code:

1. Verify that the Mail Merge Recipients dialog box is still open. If it is not, click the **Mail Merge Recipients** button 🗒 on the Mail Merge toolbar.

2. Click the **ZIP Code** column heading. Word sorts the rows of the data table from lowest zip code number to highest. The information for Pablo Orozco is now at the top of the list. See Figure 6-26.

| Figure 6-26 | RECORDS SORTED IN ASCENDING ORDER BY ZIP CODE |

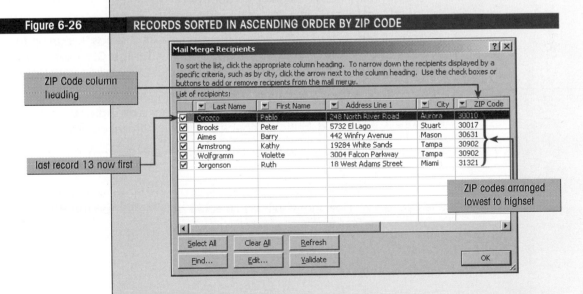

When you merge the data source with the form letter, the letters will appear in the merged document in the same order.

3. Click the **OK** button. The Mail Merge Recipients dialog box closes.

4. Click the **Merge to New Document** button on the Mail Merge toolbar, and then click the **OK** button in the Merge to New Document dialog box. Word generates the new merged document with six letters, one letter per page as before, but this time the first letter is to Pablo Orozco, who has the lowest ZIP code (30010).

5. Scroll through the letters in the newly merged document to see that they are arranged in ascending order by ZIP code.

6. Save the new merged document in the Tutorial subfolder in the Tutorial.06 folder, using the filename **Club Merged Letters2**, and then close it. You return to the main document.

As Maria requested, you've created a merged document with the letters to Palm Tree Athletic Club members sorted by zip code. She then tells you that the letters to members who frequent the Tampa club need additional information.

Selecting Records to Merge

Maria plans to offer an extra hour of personal trainer time to members of the Tampa club, because renovations at that branch caused the most inconvenience. Maria wants to modify the form letter slightly, and then merge it with only those records of Palm Tree Athletic Club members who live in Tampa. To select specific records in a data source, you need to use the Mail Merge Recipients dialog box.

To select specific records for a merge:

1. Make sure the document named Club Letter with Field Codes is displayed in the Document window. Use the Find command on the Edit menu to find the sentence that begins "As a sign of our gratitude."

2. Change "three" to **four** in the part of the sentence that reads "...sign up for three free hours," and then save the document as **Tampa Club Letter with Field Codes** in the Tutorial subfolder in the Tutorial.06 folder on your Data Disk.

3. Click the **Mail Merge Recipients** button on the Mail Merge toolbar. The Mail Merge Recipients dialog box opens. To remove an individual record from the merge, you can deselect its check box in the leftmost column.

4. Click the check box next to the first record (for Pablo Orozco). The check mark is removed.

5. Remove the check marks for all the records *except* those for Tampa residents. See Figure 6-27. Now that you have selected only the Tampa records, you can complete the Merge.

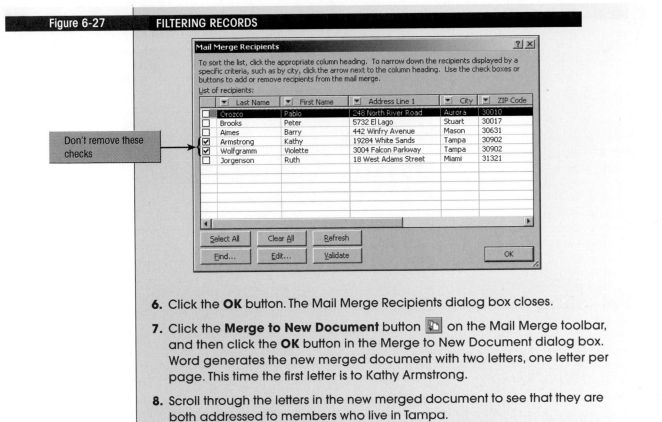

Figure 6-27 FILTERING RECORDS

Don't remove these checks

6. Click the **OK** button. The Mail Merge Recipients dialog box closes.

7. Click the **Merge to New Document** button on the Mail Merge toolbar, and then click the **OK** button in the Merge to New Document dialog box. Word generates the new merged document with two letters, one letter per page. This time the first letter is to Kathy Armstrong.

8. Scroll through the letters in the new merged document to see that they are both addressed to members who live in Tampa.

9. Save the new merged document in the Tutorial subfolder in the Tutorial.06 folder, using the filename **Club Merged Letters3**, close it, save your changes to the document named Tampa Club Letter with Field Codes, and then close it.

You give the completed file to Maria, who will print the letters on the company stationery. Next you'll create and print mailing labels for the form letter envelopes and also create a telephone list—both using the Mail Merge Wizard.

Creating Mailing Labels

Now that you've created and printed the personalized sales letters, Maria is ready to prepare envelopes in which to mail the letters. She could print the names and addresses directly onto envelopes, or she could create mailing labels to stick on the envelopes. The latter method is easier because she can print 14 labels at one time; by comparison, printing envelopes is far too time-consuming. Maria asks you to create the mailing labels.

She has purchased AveryLaser Printer labels, product number 5162 Address. These labels, which are available in most office-supply stores, come in 8½ × 11-inch sheets designed to feed through a laser printer. Each label measures 4 × 1.33 inches; each sheet has seven rows of labels with two labels in each row, for a total of 14 labels per sheet, as shown in Figure 6-28. Word supports most of the Avery label formats.

Figure 6-28 **LAYOUT OF A SHEET OF AVERY 5162 LABELS**

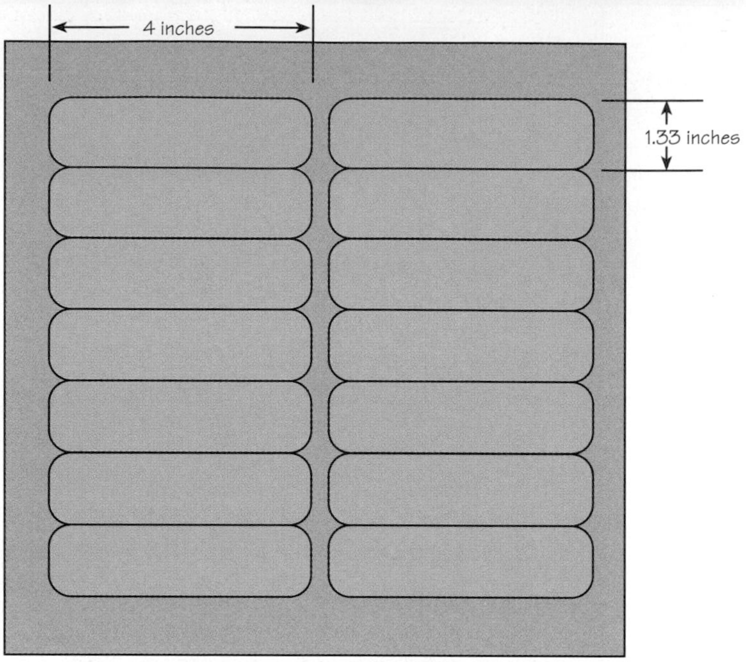

Creating mailing labels is similar to creating form letters, and the Mail Merge Wizard walks you through all six steps. You'll begin creating the mailing labels by starting the Mail Merge Wizard. You can use the same data source file (Club Data) as you used earlier.

To specify the main document and data source for creating mailing labels:

1. Open a new, blank document.

2. Click **Tools** on the menu bar, point to **Letters and Mailings**, and then, click **Mail Merge Wizard.** Next you will change the document view so you can see the entire document.

3. If necessary, switch to **Print Layout** view and change the zoom setting to **Whole Page**.

4. Under "Select Document Type" click the **Labels** option button, and then click **Next: Starting document**. The Task Pane displays information and options relating to setting up the document layout for labels. (Note: If Maria wanted you to print envelopes instead of mailing labels, you would have selected Envelopes as the type of main document.)

5. Under "Select starting document" click the **Change document layout** option button to select it (if necessary), and then, under "Change document layout," click **Label options**. The Label Options dialog box opens.

6. If necessary, click the **Label products list arrow** and select **Avery standard**.

7. Scroll the Product number list box, and then click **5162 - Address**. Your Label Options dialog box should look like Figure 6-29.

TROUBLE? If your printer is a dot matrix printer, select the Dot matrix option button rather than the Laser and ink jet option button.

Figure 6-29	LABEL OPTIONS DIALOG BOX

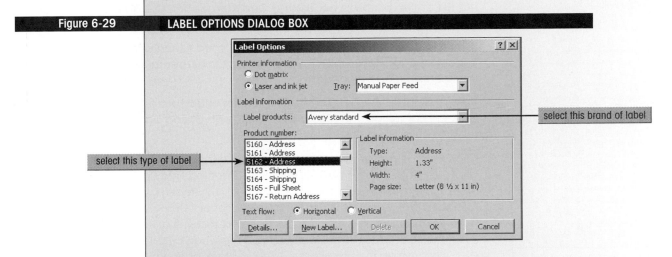

8. Click the **OK** button. The Label Options dialog box closes.

9. Click **Tools** on the menu bar, click **Options**, click the **View** tab, click the **Text boundaries** check box (in the lower-left corner) to select it, and then click the **OK** button. The document is now subdivided into label-sized rectangles, as shown in Figure 6-30.

Figure 6-30	DOCUMENT SETUP FOR LABELS

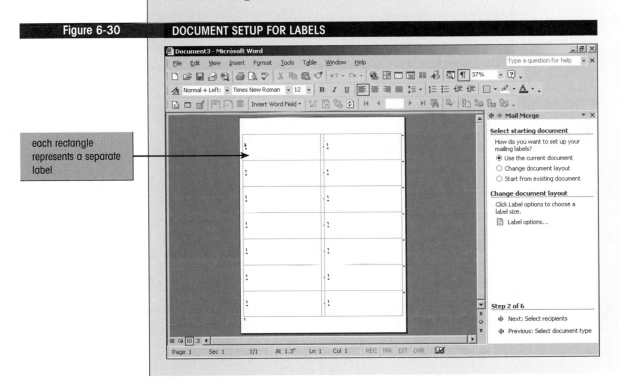

You are finished setting up the document. Next you need to select the data source you created earlier.

To continue the mail merge:

1. Click **Next: Select recipients**. Under "Select recipients," click the **Use an existing list** option button (if necessary), and then, under "Use an existing list," click **Browse**. The Select Data Source dialog box opens.

2. Use the Look in list arrow to select the file named **Club Data** in the Tutorial subfolder in the Tutorial.06 folder, and then click the **Open** button. The Mail Merge Recipients dialog box opens.

3. Verify that all the records are displayed with check boxes selected and then click the **OK** button. The Mail Merge Recipients dialog box closes. Now you are ready to insert field codes into the document.

4. Click **Next: Arrange your labels**, and then change the Zoom setting to **100%**. The Task Pane displays options related to inserting field codes into the document. Note that if the data source included a State field, you could use the Address block option to insert a complete set of fields for a single address. However, because the data source does not include a State field, you need to insert the field codes individually, as you did when creating the form letter. (You'll have a chance to use the Address block option in the Review Assignments and Case Problems at the end of this tutorial.)

5. Verify that the insertion point is located in the upper-left label in the document, click **More Items** in the Task Pane, and then use the Insert Merge Field dialog box to insert the First Name field into the document. Click the **Close** button. The First Name field code is inserted into the document.

6. Press the **spacebar** to add a space after the First Name field code, insert the **Last Name** field code, press **Enter**, insert the **Address Line 1** field code, press **Enter**, insert the **City** field code, type **,** (a comma), press the **spacebar** to insert a space, type **FL**, press the **spacebar**, and then insert the **ZIP Code** field code. You are finished inserting the field codes for the first label. Now you can copy your work to the remaining labels.

7. Click the **Update all labels** button, near the bottom of the Task Pane. (You may have to scroll down to see it, using the scroll button at the bottom of the Task Pane.) The address field codes are inserted into all the labels in the document, as shown in Figure 6-31. Note that the Next Record code is a special code that tells Word how to insert the data into the document. You can ignore it. You are now ready to preview the labels and complete the merge.

Figure 6-31	FIELD CODES INSERTED INTO DOCUMENT

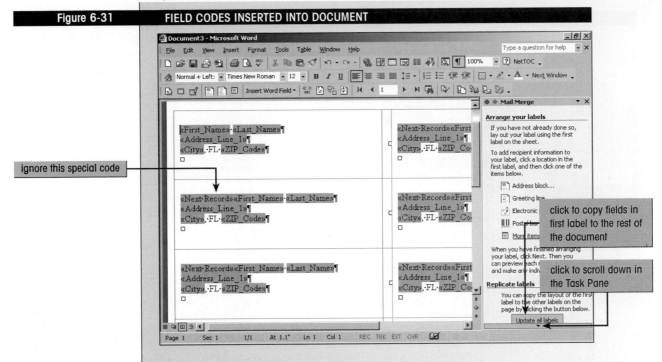

8. Click **Next: Preview your labels** in the Task Pane. (You may have to scroll down to display this option, again using the scroll button at the bottom of the Task Pane.) The data for the club members is displayed in the labels. (If you see some extra text in labels that would otherwise be blank, ignore it for now.) You are ready to merge to a new document.

9. Click **Next: Complete the merge** in the Task Pane, click **Edit individual labels** in the Task Pane, and then click the **OK** button in the Merge to New Document dialog box. The finished labels are displayed in a new document.

The labels are almost finished. All you need to do is edit the document to remove any extra text, save the document, and print the labels. For now, you'll just print the labels on an 8½ × 11-inch sheet of paper so you can see what they look like. Later, Maria will print them on the sheet of labels.

To save and print the labels:

1. Scroll through the document. Note that the document contains space for 14 labels, but that the data source only contained six records. However, when you clicked the Update Labels button in the Task Pane earlier, the comma and the state abbreviation (FL) were copied to all the labels, including those that don't contain any address information. See Figure 6-32. You can solve this problem by deleting the extra text in the bottom four rows of labels. (As you'll see in the Review Assignments at the end of this tutorial, you can avoid this issue entirely by using the Address block option for inserting field codes. However, as mentioned earlier, the Address block option is only useful when your data source contains all the necessary address fields.)

| Figure 6-32 | **EXTRA TEXT IN LABELS DOCUMENT** |

comma and state abbreviation in labels that would otherwise be blank

2. Change the Zoom setting to **Whole Page**, drag the mouse pointer to select the bottom four rows of labels, and then press the **Delete** key. The extra text is deleted.

3. Save the merged document in the Tutorial subfolder in the Tutorial.06 folder using the filename **Club Labels**.

4. Print the labels on a sheet of paper, just as you would print any other document.

   TROUBLE? If you want to print on a sheet of labels, ask your instructor or technical support person how to feed the sheet into the printer. If you're using a shared printer, you may need to make special arrangements so other users' documents aren't accidentally printed on your label sheet.

5. Close the merged document.

6. Save the main document to the Tutorial subfolder in the Tutorial.06 folder using the filename **Club Labels with Field Codes**, and then close the document.

Creating a Telephone Directory

As your final task, Maria wants you to create a list of telephone numbers for all the branches of Palm Tree Athletic Club. Maria has already created a Word document containing the phone numbers for each branch. She asks you to use that document as the data source for the merge. You'll set up a mail merge as before, except this time you'll select Directory as the main document type. You'll start by examining the Word document that Maria wants you to use as the data source.

To prepare for creating the telephone list:

1. Open the document named **Phone** from the Tutorial subfolder in the Tutorial.06 folder on your Data Disk, and review the document. Note that the information is arranged in a table, with two column headings, "Branch" and "Number." Maria wants the telephone directory in alphabetical order by branch. She asks you to sort the table before using it as the data source in the Mail Merge Wizard.

2. Display the Tables and Borders toolbar, use the Sort Ascending button ⬛ on the Tables and Borders toolbar to sort the table alphabetically by branch, close the Tables and Borders toolbar, and then save the document as **Sorted Phone List** in the Tutorial subfolder in the Tutorial.06 folder on your Data Disk.

3. Close the Sorted Phone List document, open a new, blank document, start the Mail Merge Wizard, and then display the blank document in Print Layout view.

4. If you see a gray border on the page margins, click **Tools** on the menu bar, click **Options**, click the **View** tab, click the **Text boundaries** check box to deselect it, and then click the **OK** button.

5. Display the rulers, and change the zoom setting to **85%** (or a setting that will let you see the 6-inch mark on the horizontal ruler).

6. In the Mail Merge Task Pane, under "Select document type" click the **Directory** option button, click **Next: Starting document**, verify that the **Use the current document** option button is selected, click **Next: Select recipients**, verify that the **Use an existing list** option button is selected, and then click **Browse**. The Select Data Source dialog box opens.

7. Select the file named **Sorted Phone List** (in the Tutorial subfolder in the Tutorial.06 folder on your Data Disk) as the data source, click the **Open** button, review the records in the Mail Merge Recipients dialog box, and then click the **OK** button.

8. In the Task Pane, click **Next: Arrange your directory**.

You're ready to insert the field codes in the main document and merge the main document with the data source. Maria wants the telephone list to include the name of the club branch at the left margin of the page and the phone number at the right margin. You'll set up the main document so that the phone number is preceded by a dot leader. A **dot leader** is a dotted line that extends from the last letter of text on the left margin to the beginning of text aligned at a tab stop.

To create the main document:

1. With the insertion point at the top of the blank document, insert the **Branch** merge field. Now you'll set a tab stop at the right margin (at the 6-inch mark on the ruler) with a dot leader.

2. Click **Format** on the menu bar, and then click **Tabs**. The Tabs dialog box opens.

3. Type **6** in the Tab stop position text box, click the **Right** option button in the Alignment section, and then click the **2 ....** option button in the Leader section to create a dot leader. See Figure 6-33.

Figure 6-33 | **CREATING A TAB WITH A DOT LEADER**

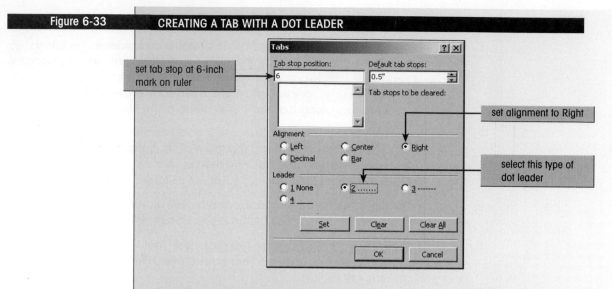

set tab stop at 6-inch mark on ruler

set alignment to Right

select this type of dot leader

4. Click the **OK** button. Word clears the current tab stops and inserts a right-aligned tab stop at the 6-inch mark on the horizontal ruler.

5. Press the **Tab** key to move the insertion point to the new tab stop. A dotted line stretches across the page, from the Branch field code to the right margin.

6. Insert the **Number** merge field at the location of the insertion point, and then press the **Enter** key. You must insert a hard return here so that each name and telephone number will appear on a separate line. Notice that the dot leader shortened to accommodate the inserted field code. The completed main document should look like Figure 6-34.

Figure 6-34 | **COMPLETED MAIN DOCUMENT FOR TELEPHONE DIRECTORY**

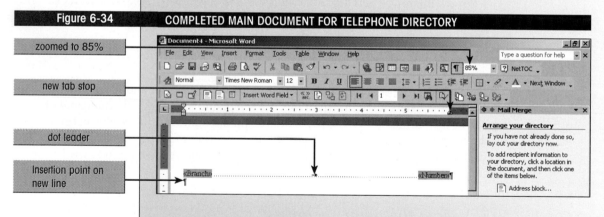

zoomed to 85%

new tab stop

dot leader

Insertion point on new line

7. Save the main document in the Tutorial subfolder in the Tutorial.06 folder using the filename **Club Phone Directory with Field Codes**.

You are now ready to merge this file with the data source.

To merge the files:

1. In the Task Pane, click **Next: Preview your directory**, review the data in the document, click **Next: Complete the Merge** in the Task Pane, click **To New Document** in the Task Pane, verify that the All option button is selected in the Merge to New Document dialog box, and then click the **OK** button. Word creates a new document that contains the completed telephone list. See Figure 6-35.

Figure 6-35	COMPLETED TELEPHONE DIRECTORY

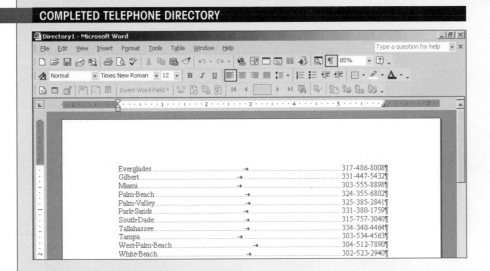

2. Save the document as **Club Phone Directory** in the Tutorial subfolder in the Tutorial.06 folder on your Data Disk and then close it.

3. Save and then close the document named Club Phone Directory with Field Codes.

   TROUBLE? If you see a dialog box asking if you want to save changes to the data source, click the Yes button.

4. Exit Word.

You have created the telephone list. Maria will have it printed and distributed to each branch of the club. Now that you are familiar with the many types of documents you can create using Word's Mail Merge Features, you can use them whenever you need to distribute customized information to a group of people. As you will learn in the Case Problems at the end of this tutorial, you can even use the Mail Merge Wizard to send out mass e-mail messages.

Session 6.2 QUICK CHECK

1. True or False: To create mailing labels, you can use the same data source file you used for a form letter.

2. Explain how to create mailing labels.

3. What is a dot leader? (The telephone directory you created in this tutorial used a dot leader.)

4. Explain how to filter a data source to display only the records with Iowa entered in the State field.

5. Explain how to alphabetize a data source by last name.

REVIEW ASSIGNMENTS

The club's free personal training offer was a great success, and Maria was pleased with how convenient it was to send out form letters with the Word Mail Merge feature. Now Radine Robbins, the club's special events coordinator, wants to use the Mail Merge Wizard to send out a letter inviting members to sign up for their annual health assessments. Members will be invited for either a cardiovascular screening or a strength training screening, depending on what type of assessment they chose when they first joined the club. Radine asks you to help her with the mailing.

1. If necessary, start Word and make sure your Data Disk is in the appropriate drive. Open the file **Assess** from the Review folder for Tutorial 6 on your Data Disk, and then save it with the filename **Health Assessment** in the Review folder for Tutorial 6 on your Data Disk.

2. With the Health Assessment document open, start the Mail Merge Wizard, select Letters as the type of main document, and then select the current document as the main document.

3. In Step 3 of the Mail Merge Wizard, create a new data source with the following fields: First Name, Last Name, Address Line 1, City, ZIP Code, and Type. Remove any extra fields so that the data source contains only six fields.

4. Create records using the following information:
   - Sandy Martinez, 2483 Anderson Ferry Drive, Tampa, 30307, cardiovascular
   - April Matthews, 471 S. Valley View, Flambeau, 31321, strength
   - Thomas Peacemaker, 372 Wildwood Avenue, Greeley, 30631, strength
   - David Menaker, 988 Heather Circle #32, Tampa, 30204, cardiovascular

5. Save the data source as **Assessment Data** in the Review folder for Tutorial 6 on your Data Disk.

6. Sort the data source by zip code from the lowest to the highest zip code.

7. In Step 4 of the Mail Merge Wizard, replace the field names in brackets with actual merge fields. Remember to replace [Date] with a Word date field.

8. Save your changes to the main document, and then preview the merged document. Correct any formatting problems or extra spaces.

9. In Step 6 of the Mail Merge Wizard, click Edit individual letters to merge to a new document. Save the merged document as **Merged Health Assessment Letters**, and then close it.

10. Return to Step 5 in the Mail Merge Wizard, edit the data source to select only records for members interested in cardiovascular assessments, and then complete a second merge. Save the new merged document as **Cardio Health Assessment Letters**, and then print the first letter. Close all documents, saving changes as needed.

Next Radine wants you to create envelopes to use for mailing the form letters. She wants you to use the Address block option in the Mail Merge Wizard to insert the address fields, so you will have to edit the data source to insert a State field. To learn how, complete these steps:

11. Open a new, blank document, start the Mail Merge Wizard, and select Envelopes as the type of main document.

Explore ▶ 12. In Step 2 of the Mail Merge Wizard, verify that the Change document layout button is selected, and then click Envelope Options. In the Envelope Options dialog box, verify that Size 10 (4⅛ × 9 inches) is selected in the Size box, and then click the OK button.

Explore ▶ 13. In Step 3 of the Mail Merge Wizard, select the **Assessment Data** file you created earlier as the data source. Edit the data source to add a State field after the City field, and then add "FL" to the state field in each record.

Explore ▶ 14. In Step 4 of the Mail Merge Wizard, click the recipient address area of the envelope, and click Address block in the Task Pane to open the Insert Address Block dialog box. Select the "Joshua Randall Jr." name format, and deselect the Insert company name check box. Verify that the Insert postal address check box is selected and then click the OK button. The Address Block merge field codes are inserted into the main document. Save the main document as **Envelopes with Field Codes** in the Review folder for Tutorial 6.

15. Preview the merged envelopes, merge to a new document, save the document as **Merged Envelopes**, print the first envelope, and then close all open documents, saving changes as necessary.

As you learned in the tutorial, you can use many types of files as your data source. For example, right now Sam Lee, the club's human resources manager, needs to send a memo to all club employees regarding their health insurance plans. The data you'll need for this mail merge is stored in a Microsoft Excel worksheet named Insurance Data. This file contains the following field names: First Name, Last Name, Address Line 1, Work Phone, and Number. To merge this alternate data source with a Word document, complete the following:

16. Open the document named **Memo** from the Review folder in the Tutorial.06 folder on your Data Disk, and then save it as **Insurance Memo** in the same folder.

17. With the Insurance Memo document open, start the Mail Merge Wizard, and complete the first two steps. Select Letters as the document type, and use the current document (the Insurance Memo document) as the main document.

Explore ▶ 18. In Step 3 of the Mail Merge Wizard, select the Use an existing list option button, click Browse, navigate to the Review folder for Tutorial 6, click the file named **Insurance Data** and then click Open. In the Select Table dialog box, click the OK button, and then review the records in the Mail Merge Recipients dialog box. Click the OK button.

19. In Step 4 of the Mail Merge Wizard, insert the merge field codes into the main document. Move the insertion point after the colon(:) in TO:, press the Tab key, insert the First Name field (for the employee's first name), press the spacebar, and then insert the Last Name field (for the employee's last name).

20. To the right of DATE: in the memo, press the Tab key, and insert the Word date field in a format that matches "April 26, 2003."

Explore ▶ 21. Select the Word date field and the name fields, and then toggle off the Bold button. Notice that character formatting can be applied to fields just as to regular text.

22. In the body of the memo, immediately before the word individual(s), insert the Number field followed by a space.

23. Save the main document with the changes. Then preview the merged document and check each record for any mistakes.

24. Merge to a new document. Scroll through the new document to verify that the information has been correctly inserted into the memos, and then save the new merged document as **Merged Insurance Memos.**

25. Print the memo for Minh Lien, and then close all documents, saving any changes.

26. Create an e-mail directory using the same format as the telephone directory you created in the tutorial. Use the Insurance Data file as the data source. The directory should include the first name, last name, and e-mail address for each employee in the Insurance Data Excel file. Set a right tab at six inches, and use a dot leader to separate the names from the e-mail addresses. Be sure to press Enter after you insert the merge field for the e-mail addresses. Save the main document as **Directory with Field Codes** and the merged document as **Merged Directory.** When you are finished, close all documents and exit Word.

CASE PROBLEMS

Case 1. Friends of Sugar Creek Justin Chambers is chair of The Friends of Sugar Creek, an organization working to prevent a convenience store from being built on a wetlands area in northern Wisconsin. He is sending a letter to community leaders, asking for their support. He asks you to help with the mail merge.

1. If you are working from a floppy disk, verify that you have copied the Cases folder for Tutorial 6 to a new, blank floppy disk. (This will ensure that you can fit all the solution files for all the case problems on one disk.) If necessary, start Word and make sure your Data Disk is in the appropriate drive. Open the file **Creek** from the Cases folder for Tutorial 6 on your Data Disk, and then save it as **Sugar Creek Letter.**

2. Start the Mail Merge Wizard and create a form letter main document using the **Sugar Creek Letter** file.

3. Create a data source with the following field names: Last Name, First Name, Nickname, Title, Company, Address Line1, and E-mail Address. Arrange the field names in the order given in this step.

4. Enter the following four records into the data source. (Don't include the commas in the records.)

   ■ Joliet, Pierre, Picrre, Chief Medical Officer, Peshtigo Medical Center, 1577 Cooperville Drive, joliet@pmc.org

   ■ Regenbogen, David, Dave, President, Regenbogen and Associates, 633 Wentworth, d_regenbogen@world.net

   ■ Suyemoto, Mae, Mae, Chief Engineer, Taylor and Culkins Engineering Services, 4424 Bedford, m_suyemoto@TaylorCulkins.com

   ■ James, Theodore, Tad, Principal, Peshtigo High School, 844 Tiger Way, tad_james@peshtigo-high-school.peshtigo.edu

5. Save the data source as **Sugar Creek Data** in the Cases folder for Tutorial 6, and then sort the records alphabetically by last name.

6. Change the Zoom setting to 100%. In Step 4 of the Mail Merge Wizard, insert the merge field codes into the document. Replace the field names in brackets with the actual merge field codes. Remember to insert the merge field code for Nickname in the body of the letter.

7. Save your changes to the main document.

8. Preview the merged document, and then complete the merge.

9. Save the merged letters document as **Merged Sugar Creek Letters** in the Cases folder for Tutorial 6.

10. Print the first letter and then close all open documents, saving any changes.

11. Open a new blank document, save it as **Sugar Creek Envelopes** in the Cases folder for Tutorial 6, and then start the Mail Merge Wizard.

Explore ▶ 12. In Step 1 of the Mail Merge Wizard, select Envelopes as the type of main document. In Step 2 of the Mail Merge Wizard, verify that the Change document layout button is selected, and then click Envelope Options. In the Envelope Options dialog box, verify that Size 10 (4⅛ × 9 inches) is selected in the Size box, and then click the OK button. In Step 3 of the Mail Merge Wizard, select the **Sugar Creek Data** file you created earlier as the data source. In Step 4 of the Mail Merge Wizard, click the recipient address area of the envelope, and then insert the necessary merge field codes to print a first name, last name, company name, and street address on each envelope. For the last line of the address, type "Peshtigo, WI 53734".

13. Preview the merged envelopes, merge to a new document, and then save the document as **Merged Sugar Creek Envelopes**.

14. Print the first envelope and then close all open documents, saving changes as necessary.

15. Create an e-mail directory of prospective contributors. Use the file named **Sugar Creek Data** (which you created earlier) as the data source. Use a dot leader to separate the name on the left from the e-mail address on the right.

16. Save the main document for the e-mail directory as **Sugar Creek E-mail Directory** in the Cases folder for Tutorial 6.

17. Save the merged document as **Merged Sugar Creek E-mail Directory**.

18. Print the e-mail directory and then save and close all open documents. Exit Word.

Case 2. Joseph's Gems   Joseph Brennan owns a small jewelry store in Dubuque, Iowa. Frequently, he notifies regular customers (who live in nearby communities in Iowa, Wisconsin, and Illinois) of upcoming sales. He decides to prepare personalized form letters to mail to all his regular customers one month before their birthdays. He'll mail the letters along with a two-page color catalog and a gift certificate. He asks you to help perform a mail merge using Word.

1. If you are working from a floppy disk, verify that you have copied the Cases folder for Tutorial 6 to a new, blank floppy disk. (This will ensure that you can fit all the solution files for all the case problems on one disk.) If necessary, start Word and make sure your Data Disk is in the appropriate drive. Open the file **Gems** from the Cases folder for Tutorial 6, and then save it as **Gems Letters** in the Cases folder for Tutorial 6.

2. Start the Mail Merge Wizard and create a form letter main document using the Gems Letter document.

3. Create a data source with the following field names: First Name, Last Name, Address Line 1, City, State, ZIP Code, Birthday, Birth Month, Birthstone.

4. Enter the following five records into the data source. (Don't include the commas in the records.) Enter months by numbers (1, 2, 3), not names (January, February, March), so you can sort in chronological order.

   ■ Kayleen, Mitchell, 882 River Way, Dubuque, IA, 52001, 23, 1, garnet
   ■ Tammy, Minervini, 8244 Westbrook Way, Platteville, WI, 52143, 31, 9, sapphire
   ■ Susan, Gardner, 804 Derby Road, Dubuque, IA, 52001, 14, 6, pearl

- Garth, Poduska, 77 Catskill Circle, Rockford, IL, 51345, 7, 1, garnet
- Oscar, Pike, 402 Waverly Avenue, Waterloo, IA, 53400, 22, 9, sapphire

5. Save the data source as **Gems Data** in the Cases folder for Tutorial 6.

6. At the beginning of the main document, insert a date field and merge fields for the inside address and salutation, in a proper business-letter format. Remember to include the state field in the inside address. Use the member's first name in the salutation.

7. In the body of the letter, insert the Birth Month, Birthday, and Birthstone fields at the locations indicated by the bracketed words. Put a slash (/) between the Birthday and Birth Month fields. Save your changes to the main document.

8. Use the Mail Merge Recipients button on the Mail Merge toolbar to display the data source and sort records alphabetically by last name. Then select only the records for customers with January birthdays.

9. Preview the merged document, and then merge to a new document. Save the merged document as **Merged Gems Letters** in the Cases folder for Tutorial 6.

10. Print the letters that result from the merge.

11. Create a main document for generating mailing labels on sheets of Avery 5162 Address labels, using the **Gems Data** file as your data source. Save the main document as **Gems Labels** in the Cases folder for Tutorial 6. (*Note:* In the tutorial, you used the Options command on the Tools menu to display the rectangular outlines of the labels, but that is not strictly necessary. If you do not see the label outlines now, do *not* display them.).

Explore 12. In Step 4 of the Mail Merge Wizard, click the label in the upper-left corner of the main document, and then click Address block in the Task Pane to open the Address Block dialog box. Select the "Joshua Randall Jr." name format, and deselect the Insert company name check box. Verify that the Insert postal address check box is selected and then click the OK button. The Address block merge field code is inserted into the main document. Click Update all labels to insert the Address block field in all the labels. Save your changes to the main document.

13. Preview the merged document and then merge to a new document.

14. Print the labels on an 8½ × 11-inch sheet of paper, and save the merged document as **Merged Gems Labels** in the Cases folder for Tutorial 6. Close all open documents, saving any changes.

15. Open a new, blank document, save it as **Gems Customer Directory** in the Cases folder for Tutorial 6, start the Mail Merge Wizard, select Directory as the main document type, and then select the **Gems Data** file as your data source. Close the Mail Merge Recipients dialog box.

Explore 16. In Step 4 of the Mail Merge Wizard, insert merge fields into the main document to create a directory entry that looks like the example below. Use the Address block option (as described above in Step 12) to insert the complete address, and the More items option to insert the birthday, birth month, and birthstone.

Garth Poduska
77 Catskill Circle
Rockford IL 51345
1/7
garnet

17. Insert two blank lines after the last line of merge field codes, and then save your work.

Explore ▶ 18. In the tutorial you learned how to select specific records in a data source by using the checkboxes to the left of each record. You can also filter a data source to display only records that meet certain conditions, Filtering is a good option for a data source containing numerous records; however, you may find that this feature doesn't work as reliably as the checkbox method. To filter the Gems Data data source: Open the data source, click the list arrow at the top of the City column, and then click Dubuque. The data source displays only the records for Dubuque residents. (Note that to redisplay all the records in the data source, you can click the list arrow at the top of the City column and then click All.)

19. Preview the merged document, and then complete the merge to a new document. Save the merged document as **Merged Gems Dubuque Directory** in the Cases folder for Tutorial 6, and then print the directory.

20. Close all open documents, saving any changes, and then exit Word.

Case 3. Liberty Auto Sales   Tom Reynolds is the customer relations manager for Liberty Auto Sales in Cadillac, Michigan. After a customer purchases a new car, Tom sends out a Sales Satisfaction Survey accompanied by a personalized letter. He wants you to help him use the Word Mail Merge feature to perform this task.

1. If you are working from a floppy disk, verify that you have copied the Cases folder for Tutorial 6 to a new, blank floppy disk. (This will ensure that you can fit all the solution files for all the case problems on one disk.) If necessary, start Word and make sure your Data Disk is in the appropriate drive.

2. In a new, blank document, create a Word table with six rows and eight columns. Insert the following labels in the heading row: First Name, Last Name, Address Line 1, City, ZIP Code, Car Make, Car Model, Sales Rep.

3. Enter the following five records into the Word table. Don't include the commas in the records.
   - Donald, Meyers, 344 Spartan Avenue, Detroit, 48235, Honda, Civic, Bruce
   - Arlene, Snow, 46 North Alberta Road, Ecorse, 48229, Toyota, Camry, Lillie
   - Lance, Nakagawa, 4211 Livonia Drive, Kentwood, 49508, Honda, Accord, Martin
   - Peter, Siskel, 92 Waterford Place, Walker, 49504, Toyota, Corolla, Bruce
   - Marilee, Peterson, 8211 University Drive, Detroit, 48238, Honda, Civic, Lillie

4. Save the file as **Auto Sales Data** in the Cases folder for Tutorial 6 and then close it.

5. Open the file **Auto** from the Cases folder for Tutorial 6, and then save it as **Auto Sales Letters**.

6. Create a letter main document using the current document.

7. Select the **Auto Sales Data** document that you created earlier as the data source.

8. Edit the main document to include the following in the letter, using a proper letter format: date, inside address, and salutation. You'll need to add the state (MI) as text.

9. Edit the body of the form letter to replace words in brackets with their corresponding merge field names.

10. Save your changes to the main document.

11. Preview the merged document and merge to a new document. Save the merged document as **Merged Auto Sales Letters** in the Cases folder for Tutorial 6.

12. Print the first letter in the merged document.

13. Create a directory that lists the make of car purchased by each customer. Use a dot leader to separate the name from the make of car. Save the main document as **Auto Sales Directory** in the Cases folder for Tutorial 6. Use the **Auto Sales Data** file as the data source.

14. Preview the merged document, merge to a new document, and then save the merged document as **Merged Auto Sales Directory** in the Cases folder for Tutorial 6.

15. Print the directory, and then close all open documents, saving any changes as needed.

Explore
16. Open a new blank document, start the Mail Merge Wizard, select Letters as the document type, use the current document as the main document, select the **Auto Sales Data** document that you created earlier as the data source, close the Mail Merge Recipients dialog box, and then, in Step 4 of the Mail Merge Wizard, experiment with the Greeting line, which you can use to insert a salutation in a letter. Use the Greeting line link to insert a salutation that includes the customer's first name, followed by a colon. Keep in mind that you can use the Greeting line link to personalize form letters. Close all documents without saving any changes. Exit Word.

Case 4. E-Mail Merge for DataTech Software You are an associate product manager for DataTech, a software firm that sells a popular line of database products. Your manager asked you to learn how to use the Mail Merge Wizard to send out mass e-mails to the company's sales representatives. To learn how to use the Mail Merge Wizard, follow these steps:

1. If you are working from a floppy disk, verify that you have copied the Cases folder for Tutorial 6 to a new, blank floppy disk. (This will ensure that you can fit all the solution files for all the case problems on one disk.) If necessary, start Word and make sure your Data Disk is in the appropriate drive.

2. Open a new, blank document, and save it as **E-mail Message**.

3. Start the Mail Merge Wizard, and, in Step 1, select E-mail messages as the main document type. In Step 2, select the current document as the main document.

4. In Step 3, create a new data source that contains three fields: First Name, Last Name, and E-mail Address. Add four records to the data source, using the names and e-mail addresses of your friends, fellow students, or colleagues. One of the records should include your name and e-mail address, so you can verify that the e-mail message is sent as planned.

5. Save the data source as **E-mail Data** in the Cases folder for Tutorial 6.

6. Type a message in the main document indicating that you are sending an e-mail in order to test Word's E-mail Merge option. Ask the recipient to reply to your message, so you can confirm that the messages were sent to the correct address. The message should begin with a brief salutation that includes the First Name field.

7. Save your changes to the main document.

8. Preview the merged document.

Explore
9. In Step 6 of the Mail Merge Wizard, click Electronic mail. In the Merge to E-mail dialog box, verify that the E-mail Address field is selected in the To text box. Type "Testing Word E-mail Merge" in the Subject text box and verify that the All option button is selected.

10. If you have Outlook Express or Outlook selected as your default e-mail program, and your computer is already connected to the Internet, Word will send your e-mail messages when you click the OK button. If you do not have Outlook or Outlook Express installed on your computer, or if your computer is not connected to the Internet, the Merge to E-mail dialog box will close without any visible change to the E-mail Message main document. Click the OK button.

11. If you see a new, merged document, save the merged document as **Merged E-mail Message** in the Cases folder for Tutorial 6.

12. If your computer was set up to send the e-mail messages, check your e-mail account to see if you received the message. Watch for replies from the other recipients.

13. Create an e-mail directory using the **E-mail Data** file as the data source. Save the main document as **My E-mail Directory** in the Cases folder for Tutorial 6, and save the merged document as **My Merged E-mail Directory** in the Cases folder for Tutorial 6.

14. Print the merged directory, and then close all open documents, saving any changes.

Explore ▷ 15. If you have Outlook installed on your computer and have selected Outlook as your default e-mail client, you can use your Outlook address book as the data source for a mail merge. To learn how: Open a new blank document, and start the Mail Merge wizard. In Step 1 of the Mail Merge wizard, select e-mail message. In Step 2 use the current document. In Step 3, click the Select from outlook contacts option button and then click Choose contacts folder. (If you see the Choose Profile dialog box, select your user profile. If you don't have the option of selecting a specific user profile, accept the default setting. Click the OK button.) In the Select Contact List folder dialog box, double-click your address book. Your Outlook contacts are displayed in the Mail Merge Recipients dialog box. Use the checkboxes to deselect all of the records except the records for three friends, fellow students, or colleagues to whom who can send a test e-mail message.

16. In Step 4 of the Mail Merge Wizard, type an e-mail message indicating that you are testing Word's e-mail merge feature. Use the Insert Merge Fields button on the Mail Merge toolbar to insert a first name field in the document, just as you would for an ordinary mail merge. Complete the e-mail merge as described in Steps 7 through 10 of this case problem. If you see a new, merged document, save it as **Merged Outlook E-mail** document in the Cases folder for Tutorial 6.

17. Close all open documents, saving any changes, and exit Word.

QUICK CHECK ANSWERS

Session 6.1

1. **a.** A form letter is a document containing general information to be sent to many recipients, and to which you can add personalized data, such as name, and address.

   b. A main document is a document (such as a letter or a contract) that, in addition to text, contains placeholder text to mark where variable information from the data source (such as a name or an address) will be inserted.

   c. A data source is a document (often in the form of a table) that contains information, such as members' names and addresses, which can be merged with the main document.

   d. A merge field is placeholder text in a main document. When the main document and the data source are merged, merge fields are replaced by specific information from each record in the data source.

   e. A record is a collection of information about one individual or object in a data source. For example, a record might include the first name, last name, address and phone number for a member.

2. record

3. True

4. From within the New Address List dialog box, click Customize, click Add, type the Gender, click OK, and then click OK again.

5. Microsoft Office Address Lists

6. Click More Items in the Mail Merge Task Pane, or click the Insert Merge Fields button on the Mail Merge toolbar. In the Insert Merge Field dialog box, click the field you want to insert, click Insert, and then click Close. Adjust the spacing or formatting around the merge field code as necessary.

7. Click Edit individual letters in the Mail Merge Task Pane (or click the Merge to New Document button on the Mail Merge toolbar) and then click OK. Save the merged document.

Session 6.2

1. True.

2. In Step 1 of the Mail Merge Wizard, select the Labels as the main document type; in Step 2 click Label options to select a label type, in Step 3 select a data source, in Step 4 insert merge field codes in the main document, click Update Labels, and then preview the merged document and the merge to a new document. Delete unnecessary text from labels that would otherwise be blank.

3. A dot leader is a dotted line extending from text on the left margin to text at the tab stop.

4. Open the Mail Merge Recipients dialog box, click the list arrow in the State column, and then click Iowa..

5. Open the Mail Merge Recipients dialog box, and then click the Last Name column heading.

LABS

The Internet:
World Wide
Web

COLLABORATING WITH OTHERS AND CREATING WEB PAGES

Writing a Grant Proposal for Space Station Education

CASE

Space Station Education

Nalani Tui is assistant principal of Thoreau Elementary and Middle School. For the past six months she has been developing a new sci-ence program inspired by the International Space Station (ISS), a per-manent laboratory orbiting the earth. Requiring the collaboration of 16 nations and costing over $60 million, the ISS will take at least eight years and 46 separate space flights to complete. Scientists aboard the space station will perform experiments that could lead to impor-tant breakthroughs in technology.

Nalani's program, called Space Station Education, will allow stu-dents to communicate directly with the astronauts at the space sta-tion via the Internet. At the same time, students will use data generated by the space station scientists in their own research pro-jects. Nalani hopes that a combination of speakers, field trips, and hands-on activities will encourage students to learn about the link between space travel and technology. In the process, she hopes her students will become more confident computer users.

Nalani has finished planning the Space Station Education curricu-lum. Now she needs to apply for a grant from the U.S. Department of Education to fund the program. Nalani has completed part of a grant proposal—a document that outlines the scope of the program and provides details on its implementation. Because Nalani has applied for other grants in the past, she knows that writing a grant proposal is a group process. In particular, she understands the value of having a grant proposal reviewed by colleagues, professional editors, and other qualified readers. As a first step, she asked Tom Jenkins and Karen Goldberg, principals at neighboring schools, to review a draft of her proposal. Both Tom and Karen edited the proposal document in Word, made some grammatical corrections, and inserted com-ments. Now Nalani has to merge the two edited versions of the pro-posal into one document.

After Nalani creates a new version of the document, she wants to add budget figures compiled by her assistant, Jeremy Woods. She also has to add a pie chart created by Margarita Lopez, an administrator for the county school district. Finally, she wants several teachers at Thoreau School and other colleagues scattered throughout the state's school districts to review her proposal. Nalani can simply hand deliver printed copies of her proposal to the teachers at Thoreau School. However, to make the proposal available to teachers throughout the state, she plans to publish it on her school's Web site.

SESSION 7.1

In this session, you will merge two edited copies of the proposal with Nalani's original document. Then you'll see how Nalani planned the proposal. Next, you'll embed an Excel workbook in the proposal, modify the workbook within Word, and insert a link to an Excel chart. You'll use Excel to modify the chart, and then update it in Word.

Comparing and Merging Documents

Nalani asks you to help her combine, or **merge**, three copies of the grant proposal. The first document, named Grant, contains Nalani's original draft of the proposal. The second document, named Tom, contains Tom Jenkins' edited copy of the proposal. The third document, named Karen, contains Karen Goldberg's edited copy. Nalani asks you to use the Compare and Merge Documents command on the Tools menu to merge these three documents into a new document. In the new document, Tom and Karen's changes will be underlined and highlighted in color. In addition, a vertical line will appear in the left margin next to every edited line of text. In Word, these special underlines, font colors, and vertical lines are known as **revision marks**.

Once you have merged two documents into one new document, you can merge that new document with a third document. When you have merged all the documents you want to compare, you can use the buttons on the Reviewing toolbar to accept or reject individual editing changes.

REFERENCE WINDOW   **RW**

Comparing and Merging Documents
- Open the original document.
- Click Tools on the menu bar, and then click Compare and Merge Documents.
- Select an edited version of the original document.
- Click the Merge list arrow, and then click Merge into new document.
- To merge an additional document, click Tools on the menu bar, click Compare and Merge Documents, select a document, click the Merge list arrow, and then click Merge into current document.
- Use the Next button on the Reviewing toolbar to move the insertion point from one edit to the next.
- Click the Accept Change or Reject Change buttons on the Reviewing toolbar to accept or reject changes.

In the following sections you will practice comparing documents that contain some simple edits. The steps in this tutorial are designed to give you a general idea of how to compare and merge documents. Keep in mind, however, that Word's Compare document feature can sometimes produce unexpected results, especially with heavily edited documents.

Merging Changes in a New Document

You'll start by opening Nalani's original draft of the grant proposal. Then you will merge it with Tom's edited copy of the proposal. Before you begin, you will verify that you have copied the Tutorial.07 folder to your computer's hard drive. The files you'll create in this tutorial are fairly large. Storing them on the hard drive allows Word to save and update files more quickly than if they were stored on a floppy disk.

To merge Nalani's proposal with Tom's edited copy:

1. Verify that you have copied the Tutorial.07 folder to your computer's hard drive, and then start Word.

2. Open the document named **Grant** from the Tutorial subfolder in the Tutorial.07 folder on your hard drive.

3. Switch to Print Layout view (if necessary), and quickly read through the proposal. Notice the photograph in the last section, which like any graphic, is not visible in Normal view.

4. Click **Tools** on the menu bar, and then click **Compare and Merge Documents**. The Compare and Merge Documents dialog box opens. First you must select the document you want to compare to the Grant document.

5. If necessary, use the **Look in** list arrow to select the Tutorial subfolder in the Tutorial.07 folder on your hard drive.

6. In the file list, click **Tom**. Next, you need to indicate where you want the revision marks to appear.

7. Click the **Merge** list arrow, as shown in Figure 7-1. A menu with three options appears. If you click Merge, Word will open the document selected in the file list (in this case, Tom), and highlight with revision marks any differences between the Tom document and the Grant document. Clicking Merge into current document will insert revision marks into the current document (Grant), leaving the document selected in the file list (Tom) unopened. However, to avoid confusion between the original document and edited copies, use the Merge into new document option.

Figure 7-1	SELECTING A LOCATION FOR REVISION MARKS

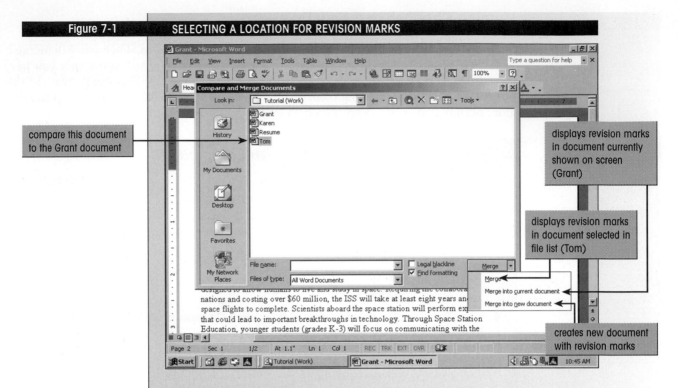

compare this document to the Grant document

displays revision marks in document currently shown on screen (Grant)

displays revision marks in document selected in file list (Tom)

creates new document with revision marks

TROUBLE? If the document named Tom opens, you accidentally clicked the Merge button, rather than the Merge button list arrow. Close the Tom document without saving any changes, and begin again with Step 4.

8. Click **Merge into new document**. A new document opens and the Reviewing toolbar appears.

   TROUBLE? If a new document does not open, or if the document named Tom opens, close all open Word documents without saving changes, and start again with Step 2.

9. Scroll down to review the revision marks shown in Figure 7-2. (The revision marks on your computer might be a different color from the ones in Figure 7-2.) A note in the right margin indicates that Tom deleted the text "fully functional." Notice that Tom added a comment to the words "National Radio Astronomy Observatory." (You might have to scroll right to read the text of this comment.)

Figure 7-2 **REVISION MARKS IN NEW DOCUMENT**

edited lines marked with vertical bars

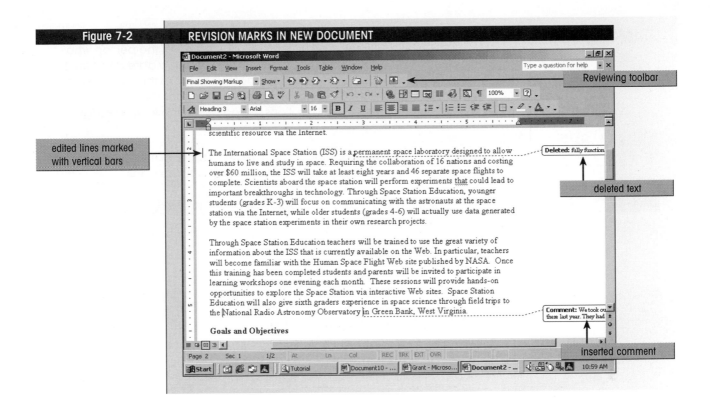

Merging Changes in the Current Document

The revision marks in Document2 show you Tom's edits to the original grant proposal. Next, you need to merge Karen's edits with Tom's. To do this, you can merge the document named Karen with the Tom's current document. When you merge, Karen's edits will be added to Document2. However, the original document named Karen will remain unchanged.

To merge Karen's edits with the current document:

1. Click **Tools** on the menu bar, and then click **Compare and Merge Documents**. The Compare and Merge Documents dialog box opens.

2. If necessary, use the **Look in** list arrow to select the Tutorial subfolder in the Tutorial07 folder on your hard drive, and then click **Karen** in the file list.

3. Click the **Merge** list arrow, and then click **Merge into current document**. Additional revision marks are added to Document2, reflecting Karen's changes to the original grant proposal.

4. Scroll through the Document2 text and review the edits. Notice that, at the beginning of the document, Karen added a comment to the title. She also replaced the passive verb "be trained" with the active verb "learn" in the beginning of the third paragraph of the Project Abstract section. Also notice that Tom and Karen's changes appear in different colors. (Exactly what colors you see depends on how your computer is set up.)

5. Place the mouse pointer over the box containing the text "Deleted: be trained" in the right margin. A ScreenTip appears with the name of the person who made the change (in this case, Karen Goldberg), and the date and time the change was made. See Figure 7-3. (Note that the name in this ScreenTip is the name specified in the User Information tab of the Options dialog box on Karen's computer. You'll see the Options dialog box in the Review Assignments at the end of this tutorial.)

TROUBLE? If you see a name other than Karen Goldberg in the ScreenTip (for instance, your own name), ignore it and continue with the steps.

Figure 7-3   SCREENTIP WITH NAME OF EDITOR

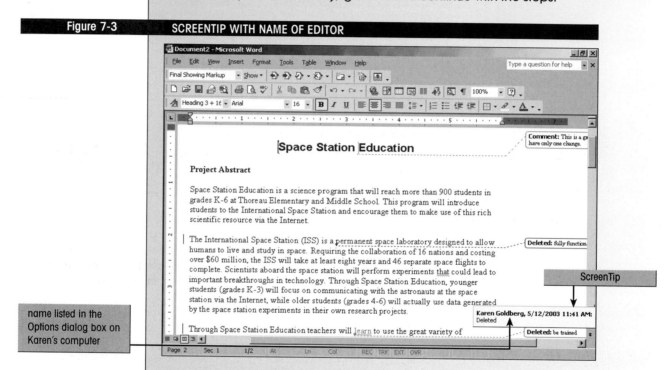

name listed in the Options dialog box on Karen's computer

6. Place the mouse pointer over the box containing the text "Deleted: fully functional," in the right margin. A box appears indicating that Tom Jenkins made this change.

TROUBLE? If you see a name other than Tom Jenkins in the ScreenTip (for instance, your own name), ignore it and continue with the steps.

7. Place the mouse pointer over Tom's comment (just before the Goals heading). Again, a box appears indicating the author of the comment (in this case, Tom Jenkins).

8. Switch to Normal view and notice that the boxes are no longer visible in the right margin. Now, instead of a note indicating that "fully functional" was deleted, the words are crossed out in the paragraph.

9. Switch back to Print Layout view.

Accepting and Rejecting Changes

After you merge documents, you must decide which changes you want to accept. To do this, you can use the buttons on the Reviewing toolbar. To simply accept an individual change (including the addition of a comment), you click the Accept Change button. To reject a change (or to delete a comment), you click the Reject Change/Delete Comment button. You can also use the list arrows on these buttons to make decisions about all the changes in a document. For example, you can accept all the edits in a document by clicking the Accept Change list arrow, and then clicking Accept All Changes in Document. Likewise, you can reject all the edits in a document by clicking the Reject Change/Delete Comment buttons, and then clicking Reject All Changes in Document.

To accept and reject changes in Document2:

1. Press **Ctrl+Home** to move the insertion point to the beginning of the document.

2. Click the **Next** button on the Reviewing toolbar. The insertion point moves to the first change—Karen's comment at the beginning of the document. You've read this comment, so there's no reason to keep it.

3. Click the **Reject Change/Delete Comment** button in the Reviewing toolbar. The comment is deleted.

4. Click . The deleted text "fully functional," is highlighted in the right margin. You will accept this change.

5. Click the **Accept Change** button in the Reviewing toolbar. You could continue to accept and reject individual changes, but Nalani wants to accept all the remaining changes. The only exception is Tom's comment (just before the Goals heading), which she has already read, and wants to delete.

6. Click the **Reject Change/Delete Comment** list arrow on the Reviewing toolbar. A menu of options appears, as shown in Figure 7-4.

Figure 7-4	REJECTING CHANGES IN A DOCUMENT

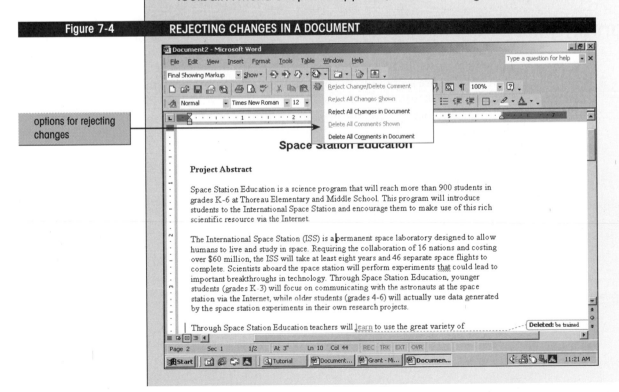

options for rejecting changes

7. Click **Delete All Comments in Document**, and then scroll down to verify that Tom's comment has been deleted. Now you will accept the remaining changes.

8. Click the **Accept Change** list arrow [icon] on the Reviewing toolbar, and then click **Accept All Changes in Document**. The remaining revision has been incorporated into the document, and the revision marks disappear. Now you will save this new copy of the grant proposal.

9. Save the document as **Grant Proposal** in the Tutorial subfolder in the Tutorial.07 folder on your hard drive.

You are finished reviewing Tom and Karen's edits to the original grant proposal. Finally, you need to close Nalani's original draft of the document.

To close the Grant document:

1. Click the taskbar button for the document named **Grant**.

2. Close the document named **Grant** without saving any changes.

3. If necessary, redisplay the document named **Grant Proposal**.

4. Close the Reviewing toolbar.

Revision marks allow you to see any changes in a document, and they simplify the process of combining multiple copies of a document. As you become an experienced Word user, you will learn how to use revision marks even more extensively.

Now that you have incorporated Karen and Tom's suggestions, you are ready to add Jeremy's budget and Margarita's pie chart. This is a good time to plan your work on the grant proposal.

Planning the Document

Nalani's proposal follows the format required by the agency offering the grant. She will ultimately add more sections to the proposal, including a project timeline and detailed explanations about the program curriculum. The current draft, however, begins with a Project Abstract, and then reviews the main goals of the program. The Budget section explains how the grant money will be used, and the last section introduces Peter Brooks, the teacher who will coordinate the program.

Nalani gives you two Microsoft Excel workbooks to combine with the Word document. One workbook contains Jeremy's budget projections. The other contains Margarita's pie chart illustrating computer ownership data in the Thoreau school district. Figure 7-5 shows how Nalani wants to combine these elements into a complete proposal.

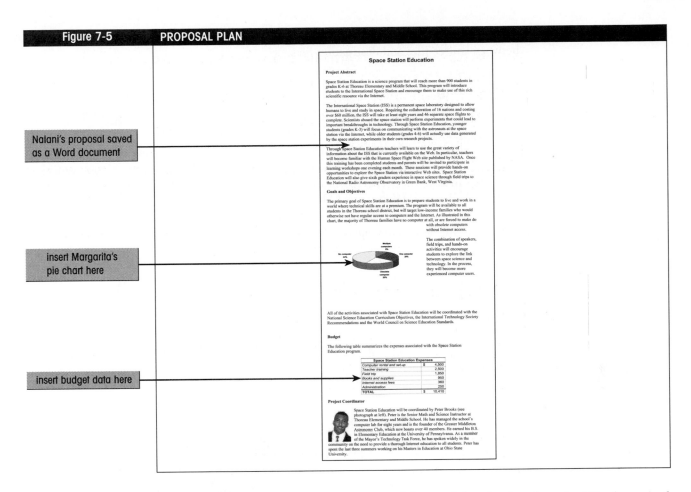

Figure 7-5 PROPOSAL PLAN

Your immediate task is to place the Excel data and the pie chart into the Word proposal document.

Integrating Objects from Other Programs

Every software program is designed to accomplish a set of specific tasks. As you've seen with Microsoft Word, you can use a word-processing program to create, edit, and format documents such as letters, reports, newsletters, and proposals. A **spreadsheet program**, on the other hand, allows you to organize, calculate, and analyze numerical data. A spreadsheet created in Microsoft Excel is known as a **worksheet**. An Excel file typically consists of multiple worksheets, and is called a **workbook**. Jeremy Woods created the budget for Space Station Education in an Excel worksheet. Margarita also used Excel to create her chart.

Both the worksheet and the chart are Excel objects. An **object** is an item such as a graphic image, clip art, WordArt image, chart, or section of text that you can modify and move from one document to another. Nalani asks you to place the worksheet and chart objects into her proposal, but she also wants to be able to modify the Excel objects after they are inserted into the document. A technology called **object linking and embedding**, or **OLE** (pronounced "oh-lay"), allows you to integrate information created in one program (such as Excel), into a document created in another program (such as Word), and then to modify that information using the tools originally used to create it, such as the Excel menus and toolbars for information created in Excel.

The program used to create the original version of the object is called the **source program** (in this case, Excel). The program into which the object is integrated is called the **destination program** (in this case, Word). Similarly, the original file is called the **source file**, and the file into which you insert the object is called the **destination file**.

The next two sections describe embedding and linking: two options for transferring data between source files and destination files.

Embedding

Embedding is a technique that allows you to insert a copy of an existing object into a destination document. In the destination document, you can double-click an embedded object to access the toolbar buttons and menus of the source program. This allows you to edit the object within the destination document. Because the embedded object is a copy, any changes you make to it are not reflected in the original source file, and vice versa. For instance, you could embed a workbook named "Itemized Expenses" in a Word document named "Travel Report." Later, if you change the Itemized Expenses workbook, those revisions will not appear in the embedded version of the workbook in the Travel Report document. The opposite is also true. If you edit the embedded version of the workbook, those changes will not show up in the original Itemized Expenses workbook. The embedded workbook retains a connection to the source program, Excel, but not to the source workbook.

Figure 7-6 illustrates the process of embedding Jeremy's Excel worksheet in Nalani's Word proposal.

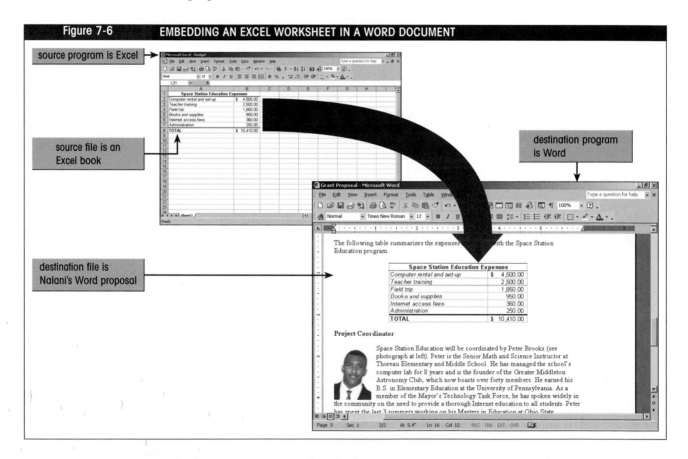

Figure 7-6   EMBEDDING AN EXCEL WORKSHEET IN A WORD DOCUMENT

source program is Excel

source file is an Excel book

destination file is Nalani's Word proposal

destination program is Word

Linking

Linking is similar to embedding, except that the object inserted into the destination file maintains a two-way connection between the source file and the destination file. Just as with an embedded object, you can double-click a linked object to access the toolbar buttons and menus of the source program. However, any changes you make to a linked object within the destination program also appear in the original source file. Likewise, if you edit the original file in the source program, those changes appear in the linked object. The linked object in the destination document is not a copy; it is a representation of the original object in the source file. As a result, a document that contains a linked object usually takes up less space on a disk than does a document containing an embedded version of the same object. Figure 7-7 illustrates how you can use linking to place Margarita's Excel chart into Nalani's Word document proposal.

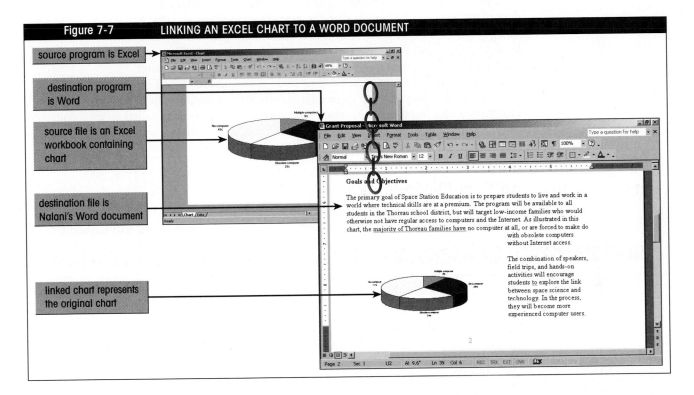

| Figure 7-7 | LINKING AN EXCEL CHART TO A WORD DOCUMENT |

One drawback to linking is that by moving files or folders, you can accidentally disrupt the connection between the source file and the document containing the linked object. For example, suppose you insert a linked workbook in a document, and then close the document and go home. Later that evening, a colleague moves the source file (the workbook) to a different folder, or deletes the workbook. As a result, the next time you open the document containing the linked object, you might get an error message, or find that you can't update the linked object.

Choosing Between Embedding and Linking

Embedding and linking are useful when you know you must edit an object after inserting it into Word. (If you don't need to edit the object, you can consider a simpler option: pasting a copy of the object into a Word document, similar to the way you paste a selection of copied text. You'll practice this technique in the Case Problems at the end of this tutorial.) Before you can use either embedding or linking, you must verify that you have the source program installed on your computer. Then you can decide if you want to embed or link the object.

Embedding is best if you won't have access to the original source file in the future, or if you don't need to maintain the connection between the source file and the document containing the linked object. In general, embedding is simpler than linking because you can change the embedded object without changing any other file. The source file is unaffected by any editing in the destination document. You could even delete the source file from your disk without affecting the copy embedded in your Word document.

Link a file whenever you have data that is likely to change over time, or if someone else updates your data regularly. For example, suppose you created a Word document called "Refinancing Options" into which you want to insert an Excel workbook containing the latest interest rates for home mortgages. Suppose also that your assistant updates the Excel workbook daily to make sure it reflects current rates. By linking the workbook to the Refinancing Options document, you can be certain that the mortgage rates are updated every time your assistant updates the Excel workbook. The advantage to linking is that the data in both the Excel workbook and the Word document can reflect recent revisions. A disadvantage to linking is that you must have access both to Excel and to the linked file on your computer.

Keep in mind that files containing embedded and linked objects can be very large. For that reason, you'll usually want to store such files on your computer's hard drive or network drive rather than on a floppy disk. Also note that you must have Excel installed on your computer to perform the steps in the rest of this session. If Excel is not installed on your computer, read the remainder of this session, but do not attempt to perform the steps.

Embedding an Excel Workbook

Nalani asks you to insert Jeremy's worksheet in the document. You will embed the entire Excel workbook into the Budget section of the proposal, replacing the "[Insert Excel worksheet]" placeholder. You'll use the Object command on the Insert menu to embed the existing Excel workbook in the proposal. Then you can use Excel commands to modify the expense workbook within Word.

To embed the Excel workbook:

1. Click **Edit** on the menu bar, click **Find**, find the placeholder **(Insert Excel worksheet)**, click **Cancel** to close the Find and Replace dialog box, and then press **Delete**. The placeholder (Insert Excel worksheet) is deleted. The insertion point should be located on a blank line, two lines above the heading "Project Coordinator." This is where you will embed the Excel workbook.

2. Click **Insert** on the menu bar, and then click **Object** to open the Object dialog box, which has two tabs—Create New and Create from File.

3. Click the **Create from File** tab. You'll use the Browse feature to find the Excel worksheet file in the Tutorial folder for Tutorial 7 on your hard drive.

4. Click the **Browse** button. The Browse dialog box opens.

5. If necessary, use the **Look in** list arrow to select the Tutorial folder for Tutorial 7, click **Budget** in the file list, and then click the **Insert** button. The Browse dialog box closes, and you return to the Object dialog box. The name of the selected file (Budget.xls), and the names of the folders in which it is stored, appear in the File name text box. See Figure 7-8. Make sure the Link to file check box is not selected. You don't want to link the worksheet—only embed it.

Figure 7-8	EMBEDDING A FILE

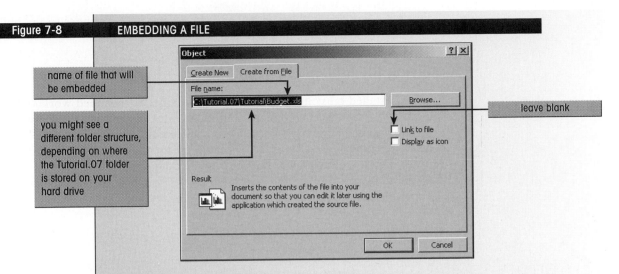

name of file that will be embedded

you might see a different folder structure, depending on where the Tutorial.07 folder is stored on your hard drive

leave blank

6. Click the **OK** button. The Excel worksheet appears in the document. It would look better, however, if it were centered between the left and right margins.

7. Click the **worksheet** to select it. Black selection handles appear around the outside of the worksheet.

8. Click the **Center** button on the Formatting toolbar. The Excel worksheet is centered horizontally in Nalani's proposal document. See Figure 7-9.

Figure 7-9	EMBEDDED WORKSHEET CENTERED HORIZONTALLY

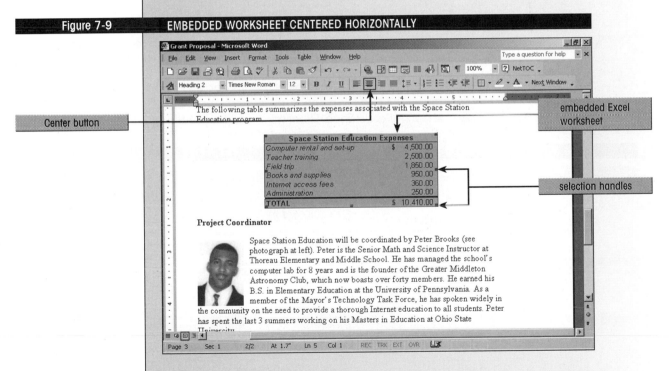

Center button

embedded Excel worksheet

selection handles

TROUBLE? Depending on how your computer is set up, you may see the embedded worksheet on a white background, rather than on a gray background (as in Figure 7-9). To display the worksheet on a gray background, click Tools on the menu bar, click Options, click the View tab, click the Field Shading list box, and then click Always. Note, however, that displaying the gray background is optional, and that the background will not be visible in the printed document.

9. Click anywhere in the document outside the worksheet to deselect the embedded object.

Because the workbook object is embedded, you can make changes to the object within Word, which you'll do in the next section.

Modifying the Embedded Workbook

If Excel is installed on your computer, you can edit the embedded workbook by double-clicking it and using Excel commands and tools. After you modify the workbook, you can click anywhere else in the Word document to deselect the workbook and redisplay the usual Word editing commands and tools. Any changes that you make in the embedded workbook affect only the copy in Word and not the original Budget file.

Because all the cost figures are large and rounded to the nearest $100 increment, Nalani wants you to remove the decimal points and trailing zeroes.

To eliminate the decimal places in the embedded workbook:

1. Double-click the workbook. After a moment, the workbook opens in an Excel window. See Figure 7-10. Depending on how your computer is set up, the Excel toolbars may appear one on top of the other, as in Figure 7-10, or side by side on one row.

   Notice that an Excel worksheet is arranged in rows and columns, just like a Word table. The intersection between a row and column is called a **cell** and takes its name from its column letter and the row number. For example, the intersection of column B and row 2 is "cell B2." To remove the decimal places from the cells containing dollar signs (cell B2 and cell B8), you can use a toolbar button. First, you must select these two cells.

   TROUBLE? If you see the Excel menus and toolbars displayed in the Word window (rather than in a separate window), just continue with these steps.

   TROUBLE? If you don't see the Excel menus and toolbar, or a message indicates that Word can't find the source program, ask your instructor or technical support person for assistance. Excel might not be installed on your computer.

| Figure 7-10 | EDITING THE EMBEDDED WORKSHEET |

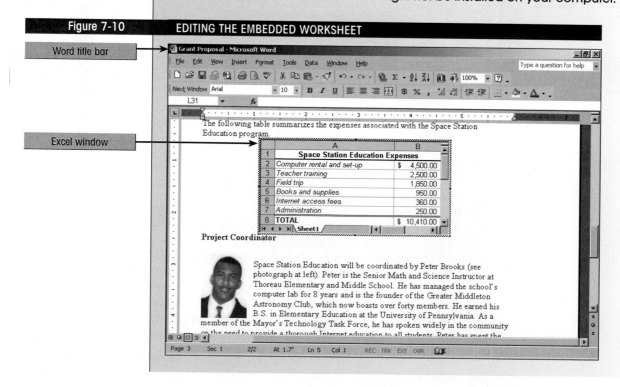

Word title bar

Excel window

2. Click cell **B2**, which contains the figure $4,500.00, press and hold the Ctrl button, click cell **B8** (which contains the figure $10,410.00), and then release Ctrl. Cell B2 is highlighted, and cell B8 is outlined by a thin black line, indicating that the two cells are highlighted.

3. Click the **Decrease Decimal** button on the Excel Formatting toolbar twice. The numbers in the selected cells change to whole dollar amounts. Next, you'll use the Format Cells dialog box to remove the decimal places from cells B3 through B7.

   TROUBLE? If you don't see the Decrease Decimal button on your screen, click Format on the menu bar, and then click Cells. The Format Cells dialog box opens. Click the Number tab, if necessary, click Currency in the Category list box, change the setting in the Decimal places box to 0, click the Symbol list box, click $, and then click the OK button.

4. Click cell **B3** (which contains the number 2,500.00), and then drag the mouse down to cell **B7** (which contains the number 250.00). Cells B3 through B7 are selected. See Figure 7-11.

Figure 7-11   **SELECTING CELLS IN A WORKSHEET**

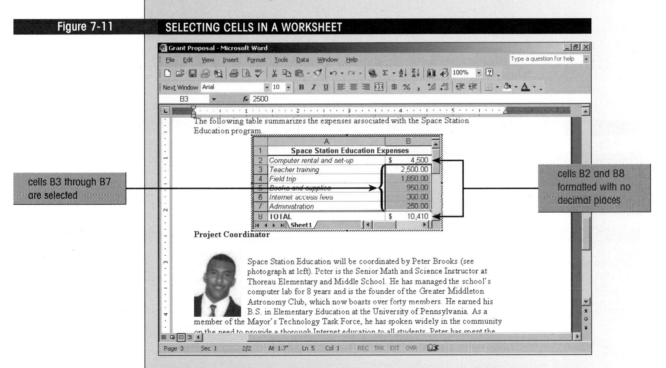

cells B3 through B7 are selected

cells B2 and B8 formatted with no decimal places

5. Click **Format** on the Excel menu bar, and then click **Cells**. The Format Cells dialog box opens.

6. Click the **Number** tab, if necessary, click **Currency** in the Category list box, change the setting in the Decimal places box to **0**, and verify that the entry in the Symbol box is **None**. Your Format Cells dialog box should look like Figure 7-12.

Figure 7-12   **SELECTING A CURRENCY FORMAT**

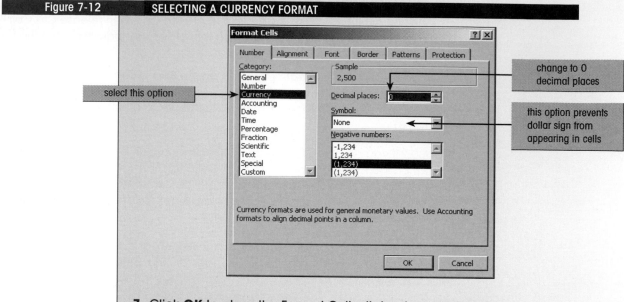

select this option

change to 0 decimal places

this option prevents dollar sign from appearing in cells

7. Click **OK** to close the Format Cells dialog box, and then click outside the worksheet. You return to the Grant Proposal document, where the embedded worksheet displays the newly formatted budget figures.

8. Click anywhere outside the Excel worksheet in the proposal to deselect it, if necessary. See Figure 7-13.

Figure 7-13   **EDITED WORKSHEET EMBEDDED IN PROPOSAL**

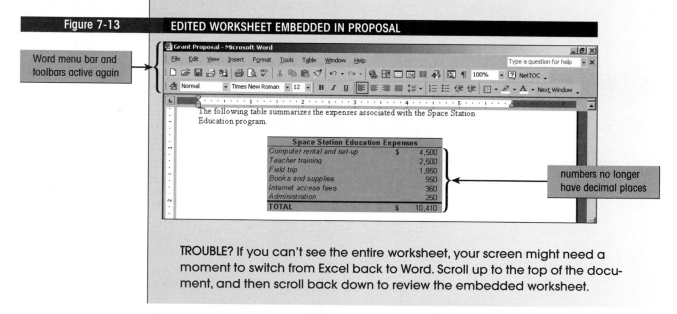

Word menu bar and toolbars active again

numbers no longer have decimal places

TROUBLE? If you can't see the entire worksheet, your screen might need a moment to switch from Excel back to Word. Scroll up to the top of the document, and then scroll back down to review the embedded worksheet.

The Excel workbook, Budget, remains in its original form on your disk, with the two decimal places. You have modified only the embedded copy in Nalani's proposal.

Linking an Excel Chart

Next, Nalani wants you to incorporate the chart that illustrates data on computer ownership in the Thoreau school district. Because Margarita plans to revise her data soon, Nalani decides to insert a linked version of the chart rather than embedding it. That way, once Margarita updates the chart, the latest version will appear in Nalani's proposal.

You'll link to the Chart file in the Tutorial folder the proposal document. Because you'll make changes to the chart after you link it, you'll make a copy of the chart as you link it. This leaves the original file in the Tutorial folder unchanged in case you want to repeat the tutorial steps later. Note that you don't always have to copy a file before you link it to a Word document.

To link an Excel chart to the proposal document:

1. Click **Edit** on the menu bar, click **Find**, find the placeholder **(Insert Excel chart)**, click **Cancel** to close the Find and Replace dialog box, and then press **Delete** to delete the placeholder (Insert Excel chart). Make sure the insertion point is positioned on a blank line between two paragraphs of text.

2. Click **Insert** on the menu bar, and then click **Object** to open the Object dialog box. You used this dialog box earlier to embed the Excel workbook in the proposal. This time, you'll use it to insert a linked object.

3. Click the **Create from File** tab.

4. Click the **Browse** button to open the Browse dialog box, and then, if necessary, use the **Look in** list arrow to open the Tutorial subfolder in the Tutorial.07 folder. The Browse dialog box lists the files in the Tutorial folder for Tutorial 7. Because you want to leave the original file unchanged in your Tutorial folder, you'll make a copy of it now.

5. Right-click the filename **Chart**. A shortcut menu opens.

6. Click **Copy** and then press **Ctrl+V**. A new file, Copy of Chart, appears in the file list.

7. Click **Copy of Chart** and then click the **Insert** button. The name of the selected file appears in the File name text box. Now you must specify that you want the chart file linked to, not embedded in, the proposal document.

8. Click the **Link to file** check box to select it. See Figure 7-14.

Figure 7-14	INSERTING A LINKED OBJECT

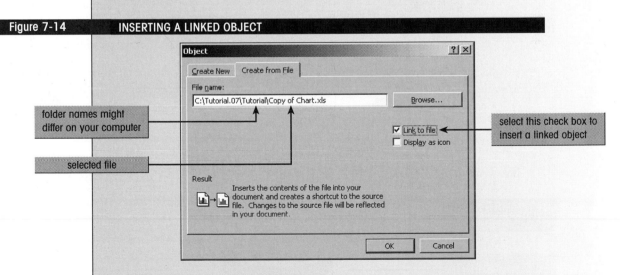

9. Click the **OK** button. After a moment, the chart image appears in the proposal.

The chart is far too large for the document. You can change its size easily, just as you would change the size of any graphic in a Word document. You can either drag its resize handles, or use a command on the Format menu.

To resize the chart and wrap text around it:

1. Click the chart. Black resize handles appear around its border.

2. Click **Format** on the menu bar, and then click **Object**.

3. Click the **Size** tab, and in the Scale section, use the **Height** down arrow to decrease the Height and Width settings to **40%**. Both the height and width of the selected object will be reduced to 40% because the Lock aspect ratio check box is selected. (If it is not selected, select it now.)

4. Click the **OK** button.

5. Scroll up, if necessary, to display the chart. After a pause, the chart appears in the Word document in a smaller size. Next, you'll wrap text around the chart.

   TROUBLE? If the chart is no longer located below the first paragraph after the heading "Goals," just continue with the steps. You will have a chance to adjust its position later.

   TROUBLE? Don't be concerned if it takes a few moments for the chart to appear. Some computers need extra time to display graphics. You might notice similar delays throughout this tutorial. You also might observe that the colors of your graphics change slightly.

6. If necessary, click the **chart** to select it, click **Format** on the menu bar, click **Object**, and then click the **Layout** tab in the Format Object dialog box.

7. Click the **Square** icon, click the **Left** option button to align the chart on the left margin, and then click the **OK** button. After a pause, the document text wraps to the right of the chart.

8. If necessary, drag the chart to position it on the second page, as shown in Figure 7-15.

Figure 7-15	LINKED EXCEL CHART IN WORD PROPOSAL

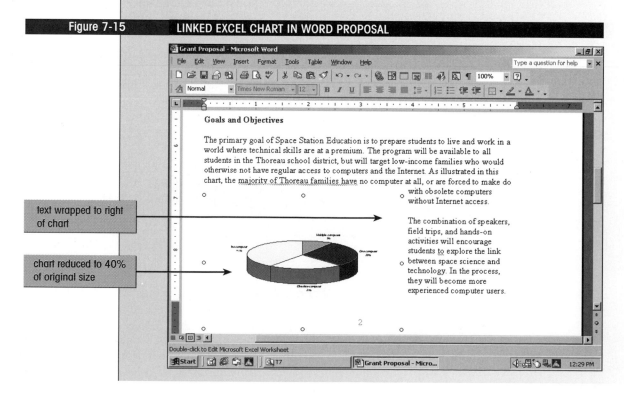

> **9.** Click anywhere in the **document** to deselect the chart, and then save the document. Review the percentages in the chart. (You might need to temporarily increase Word's Zoom setting to read the percentages easily. When you are finished, remember to return the zoom setting to 100%.)

Because you linked the file, you did not insert a copy of the file in the proposal, but merely a visual reference to the original. The size of the proposal file on disk has not increased significantly as a result of the link. If you double-click the chart, Excel will start and display the original source file. Instead of seeing the Word title bar at the top of the screen, you would see the Excel title bar, along with the Excel menus and toolbars, just as you did earlier when you edited the embedded workbook.

Modifying the Linked Chart

The advantage of linking a file over embedding it is that the destination file is updated whenever you modify the source file. Furthermore, you can update the source file either within the source program or within the destination program. In the following steps, you'll simulate what would happen if Margarita modified the source file in Excel. You'll open the file named Copy of Chart in Excel, change some values, and then view the updated information in the Word proposal.

> *To modify the chart in the source program:*
>
> **1.** Click the **Start** button [Start] on the taskbar, point to **Programs**, and then click **Microsoft Excel**. The Excel program window opens.
>
> TROUBLE? You must have Microsoft Excel version 2002 installed on your computer to complete this section. If you do not see Microsoft Excel on your Programs menu, ask your instructor or technical support person for help.
>
> TROUBLE? If the Office Assistant opens asking if you want help, click the Start Using Excel button.
>
> **2.** Click the **Open** button [icon] on the Excel Standard toolbar to display the Open dialog box.
>
> **3.** Use the **Look in** list arrow to open the Tutorial folder for Tutorial 7.
>
> **4.** Double-click **Copy of Chart**. The Excel workbook with the computer ownership chart opens. If necessary, maximize the Excel window. Notice that 41% of students in the Thoreau school district have no computer at home, and 21% have only an obsolete computer at home. See Figure 7-16.

Figure 7-16   CHART DISPLAYED IN THE SOURCE PROGRAM—EXCEL

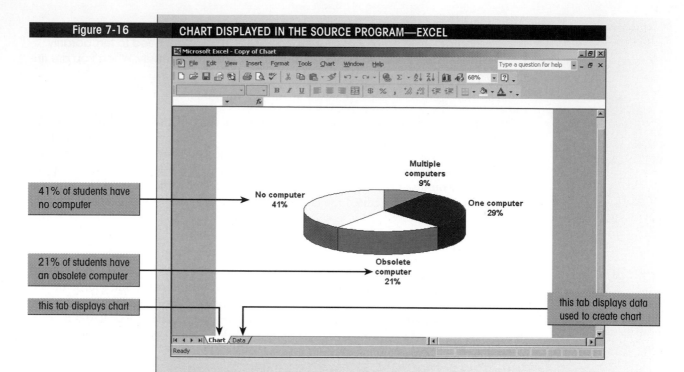

At the bottom of the window are two tabs. The Chart tab contains the chart, and the Data tab contains the data Margarita used to create the chart. Any changes made to the data on the Data tab will automatically be reflected in the chart. Assume Margarita has audited her data and found that the number of students with no computer at home is actually higher than she had originally thought. You'll enter that revised data next.

5. Click the **Data** tab. The worksheet containing the computer ownership data appears.

6. Click cell **B7**, which currently contains the value "350."

7. Type **400**, and press the **Enter** key. Now you'll look at the chart in Excel and see the effect of this change.

8. Click the **Chart** tab, and note that the "No computer" percentage changed from 41% to 44%, reflecting the new value you entered. See Figure 7-17.

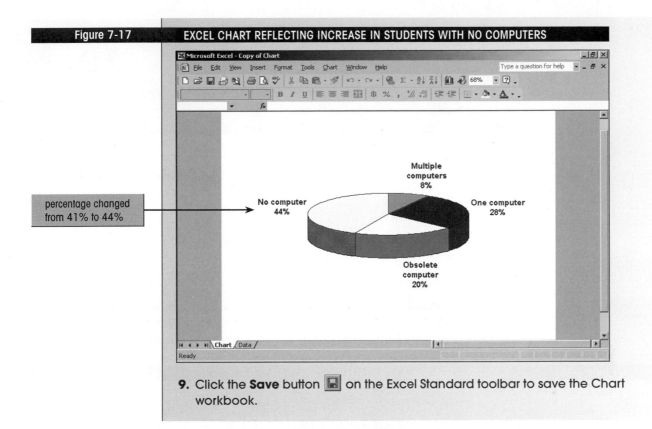

Figure 7-17   EXCEL CHART REFLECTING INCREASE IN STUDENTS WITH NO COMPUTERS

9. Click the **Save** button 🖫 on the Excel Standard toolbar to save the Chart workbook.

Now you'll return to the proposal and view the linked version.

To view the linked chart in the proposal:

1. Close **Excel**. The Word program window reappears, with the linked version of the chart displayed in the Grant Proposal document.

Notice that in the linked version of the chart, the "No computer" value is still 41%. Why doesn't it reflect the change you made in the source program? To make sure the changes are carried over to the linked version, you must perform one more step: updating the link.

Updating the Link

When you **update** a link, you ensure that the linked object in the destination file reflects the latest version of the source file. If you modify a linked object in the source program while the Word document to which it's linked is closed, Word will automatically update the link the next time you open the document. (In some cases, Word might ask if you want to update the link before you open the document.) But if you modify a linked object in the source program while the Word document is open, you have to tell Word to update the link.

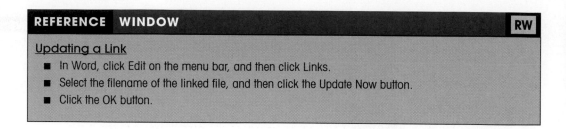

REFERENCE WINDOW | **RW**

Updating a Link
- In Word, click Edit on the menu bar, and then click Links.
- Select the filename of the linked file, and then click the Update Now button.
- Click the OK button.

Once the linked chart in Word is updated, it will reflect the change you made in Excel.

To update a linked file:

1. Make sure Microsoft Word appears in the title bar, and that you still see the linked chart in the Document window.

2. Click anywhere in the Microsoft Word window to activate it if necessary.

3. Click **Edit** on the menu bar, and then click **Links**. The Links dialog box opens. See Figure 7-18. A list of linked objects appears; in this case it consists of only one file named Copy of Chart. (You probably can't see the entire filename, however.)

Figure 7-18 | **UPDATING LINKS IN A DOCUMENT**

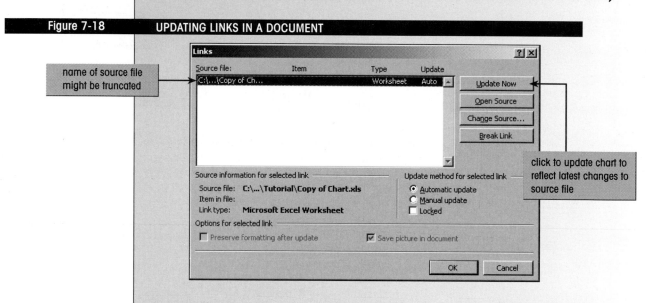

4. Click **Copy of Ch...**, if necessary to select it, and then click the **Update Now** button. Word updates the linked object to reflect the latest changes to the source file.

5. Click the **OK** button in the Links dialog box. The Links dialog box closes.

6. If necessary, deselect the chart. The updated version of the chart appears in Word.

7. Change Word's Zoom setting to 175%, scroll to display the chart in the Word window, and review the percentages. The "No computer" percentage is now 44%. See Figure 7-19.

   TROUBLE? If the percentage has not changed in your chart, save the Grant Proposal document and close Word. Then start Word again and re-open the Grant Proposal document.

Figure 7-19	UPDATED CHART IN PROPOSAL DOCUMENT

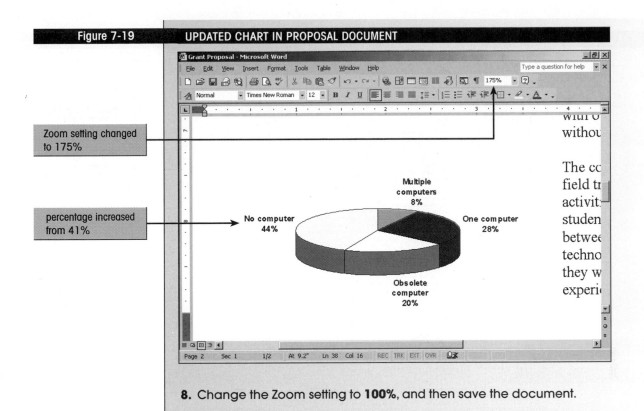

Zoom setting changed to 175%

percentage increased from 41%

8. Change the Zoom setting to **100%**, and then save the document.

Now you can be assured that any updates Margarita makes to the chart will be reflected whenever the proposal is opened.

Keep in mind that although you just edited the source file by opening it in the source program (Excel), you can just as easily edit the source file in the destination program. You would double-click the linked object in the destination document window. The source program would start, and the source file would open. After editing the source file, you would simply close the source program. The linked object in the destination file would update automatically.

Your grant proposal document is finished. You are ready to print it for distribution to the teachers at Thoreau School.

To print and then close the document:

1. Switch to Header and Footer view, and then click the **Format Page Number** button.

3. Preview the document. Don't be concerned if one line of the Goals section appears by itself at the top of the second page. Nalani will add additional text to the proposal after her colleagues review it, so at this point she isn't concerned about adjusting page breaks in the document.

3. Print the document. Your two-page document should look similar to Figure 7-20, although the exact layout of the text and graphics might differ.

Figure 7-20   **PRINTED DOCUMENT READY FOR DISTRIBUTION**

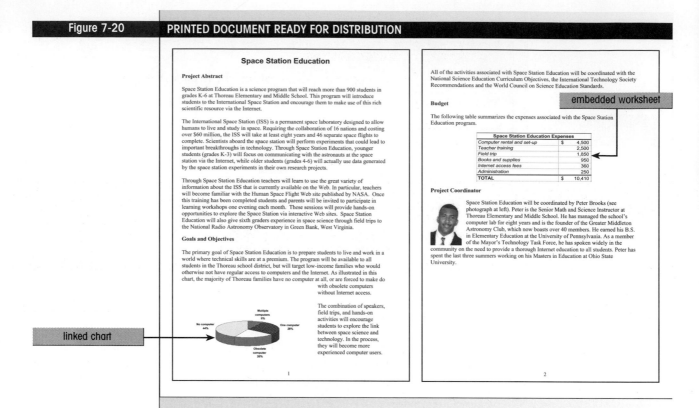

3. Close the Grant Proposal document, saving any changes.

You give the completed proposal to Nalani, who then distributes it to the teachers at Thoreau School. She asks them to mark their suggestions directly on the printed document with a brightly colored pen. Now she wants you to focus on the task of distributing the document electronically, which you'll do in the next session.

Session 7.1 QUICK CHECK

1. Explain how to merge two edited copies of a document with the original document.

2. Define the following in your own words:

   a. source file

   b. object

   c. source program

   d. destination file

3. What is the difference between embedding and linking?

4. In what situations would you choose linking over embedding?

5. How do you embed an Excel workbook into a Word document? How do you link an Excel chart to a Word document?

6. Explain how to create a copy of a file within the Browse dialog box.

7. How do you modify an embedded object from the destination program?

8. True or False: When you modify an embedded object, your changes are also made to the source file.

SESSION 7.2

In this session, you will modify the proposal so that it is easier for Nalani's statewide colleagues to read online. You'll begin by creating hyperlinks that allow users to navigate through the document more easily and to access additional information. Then you'll see how the document looks in Web Layout view. Finally, you'll modify the document's appearance to make it more interesting.

Distributing Word Documents Online

In addition to printing the proposal for teachers at Thoreau, Nalani wants to make the proposal available to other colleagues **online**, which means they will read it on the computer screen rather than on a printed page. You can make a document available online in one of two ways—you can either e-mail the document to specific people, or you can make it available as a Web page.

Whichever online option you choose (Web page or e-mail), keep in mind that reading a document online is different from reading it in printed form. If you are certain a document will only be read online (and therefore don't have to worry about how the document will look when printed on a black and white printer), you can sometimes use more interesting formatting options, such as a fancy background or colored fonts. Because it is difficult to "flip through pages" online, you might also need to organize online information for easy access, or provide a quick method (such as a hyperlink) for opening related files. (You'll learn more about hyperlinks later in this tutorial.) Finally, remember that when distributing documents online, large document files can be problematic.

The following section provides information on e-mailing Word documents. After that, you'll learn more about working with Web pages.

E-Mailing Word Documents

Nalani plans to e-mail copies of the proposal to Tom Jenkins and Karen Goldberg so they can review the revised proposal. To e-mail a Word document, you need to use an e-mail program such as Microsoft Outlook. First you create an e-mail message, type the recipient's e-mail address, and then type the text of the e-mail. Finally, you need to attach the Word document to the e-mail message. The exact steps to attach a document to an e-mail message vary from one e-mail program to another, but they are similar to opening a document in Word: you need to find and then select the file you want to attach.

When you e-mail documents you should know a few basic rules:

■ Many e-mail programs have difficulty handling large attachments. Consider using a compression program (such as WinZip) to reduce a large file to a more manageable size before e-mailing it. Alternately, you could convert the Word document to a Web page (as described later in this tutorial).

A Web page is usually much smaller than a Word document containing the same amount of text.

- You might find that early versions of Word cannot open files created in the most recent versions of Word. Before e-mailing a file, ask the recipient which version of Word he or she is using. To avoid problems with conflicting versions, save the Word document as a rich text file (using the Rich Text File document type in the Save As dialog box) before e-mailing it.

- If you plan to e-mail a document that contains links to other files, remember to e-mail all the linked documents.

- E-mail attachments, including Word documents, are sometimes used maliciously to spread computer viruses. Remember to include an explanatory note with any e-mail attachment so that the recipient can be certain the attachment is legitimate. If you plan to send and receive e-mail attachments, install a reliable virus checker program on your computer.

E-mailing Word documents is especially useful when you are collaborating with a group. You can exchange documents with colleagues in the office or around the world with just a click of the mouse. In Nalani's case, e-mailing documents enabled her to get Tom and Karen's comments on her proposal in the space of a few hours.

To make a document available to a wider audience, however, it's easier to publish it as a Web page, because then you don't have to take time to read and manage several e-mail messages. You'll learn more about working with Web pages in the next section.

Publishing Word Documents as Web Pages

Web pages are special documents designed to be viewed in a program called a **browser**. The two most popular browsers are **Microsoft Internet Explorer** and **Netscape Navigator**. You can create a Web page on just about any kind of computer, but if you want other people to open your Web page in a browser, you must store it on a special network computer called a **Web server**. Browsers send messages through a computer network to a Web server. The Web server responds by sending a file containing the Web page back to the browser, which then displays the Web page in the browser window. When you make a Web page available to others via a Web server, you are **publishing** the Web page.

Web servers are found on two different types of networks—intranets and the Internet. An **intranet** is a self-contained network, belonging to a single organization, which relies on Web servers and related technology. For example, the science and math teachers at Thoreau School recently created an intranet to connect all the computers in the school. Because Nalani's computer is connected to the Thoreau School intranet, she can use her browser to retrieve school-related Web pages from a Web server that is down the hall from her office.

At the same time, Nalani's computer is also connected to the largest, most widely used computer network in the world, the **Internet**. The part of the Internet that transfers and displays Web pages is called the **World Wide Web**, or simply, the **Web**. Each Web page has its own specific **address** (or **URL**), such as *www.microsoft.com* or *www.cnn.com*. A group of related Web pages is called a **Web site**. The main Web page within a Web site (the one that is usually displayed first) is called a **home page**. When her computer is connected to the Internet, Nalani can use her browser to access well-known Web sites such as *www.microsoft.com* or *www.cnn.com*.

You probably have experience using a browser to view Web pages. If so, you know that Web pages usually contain text and graphics, and also can contain audio and video. Web pages include **hyperlinks** (or **links**) which you can click to open, or "jump to," additional information. A hyperlink can be a word, a phrase, or a graphic. Text hyperlinks are usually underlined and appear in a different color from the rest of the document.

While hyperlinks are widely used in Web pages, you can also use them in ordinary Word documents that are intended for online reading. (You already have some experience using hyperlinks in Word documents.) In the next section, you will learn more about using hyperlinks in online Word documents and Web pages.

Using Hyperlinks in Word

As you know, you can include a hyperlink to a Web page in a Word document. You can also include e-mail links that you can click to type an e-mail message. In addition, you can include a link that opens another Word document, or that jumps to another part of the same document. If you have many Office XP documents that are related to each other, you can create a useful hyperlink system that allows users to retrieve and view related material. For example, a business proposal might include links to a budget stored in an Excel workbook and to product photographs stored in a PowerPoint presentation. In fact, instead of using Margarita's chart as a linked object, you could have inserted a hyperlink that users click to open the chart in Excel. (You used a linked object because you wanted the chart to appear in the printed version of the proposal.)

Nalani wants you to add two hyperlinks to the proposal document—one hyperlink that targets a location within the proposal, and one that targets a different document.

Inserting a Hyperlink to a Bookmark in the Same Document

According to Nalani, one of the strengths of her proposed Education Space Station program is the project's coordinator, Peter Brooks. A teacher at Thoreau School, Peter is well known in the community for helping introduce students to new technology. Nalani decides to add to the Project Abstract a sentence that introduces Peter. She also wants to include a hyperlink that jumps to the "Project Coordinator" section at the end of the proposal.

Creating a hyperlink that jumps from one location to another in the same document requires two steps. First, you insert an electronic marker called a **bookmark** at the location you want the link to jump to. Second, you enter the text that you want users to click, and format it as a hyperlink. Figure 7-21 illustrates this process.

Figure 7-21   HYPERLINK THAT TARGETS A BOOKMARK

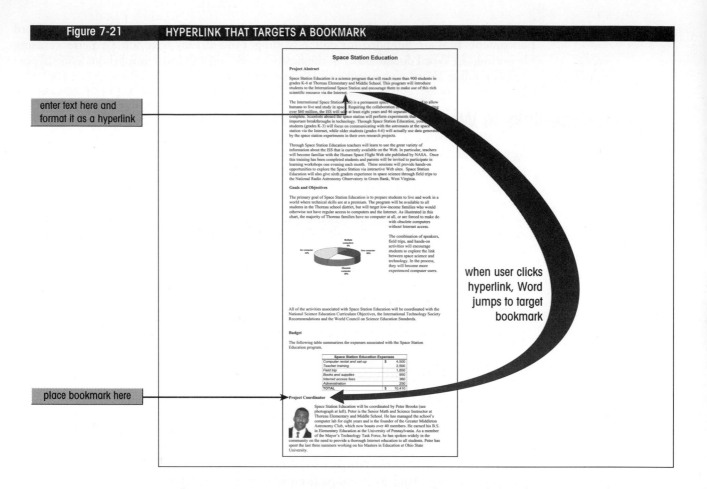

enter text here and format it as a hyperlink

when user clicks hyperlink, Word jumps to target bookmark

place bookmark here

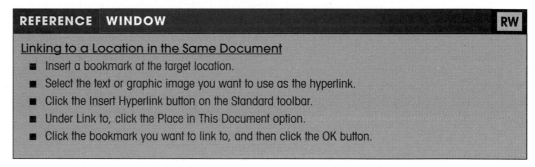

REFERENCE   WINDOW   **RW**

Linking to a Location in the Same Document

- Insert a bookmark at the target location.
- Select the text or graphic image you want to use as the hyperlink.
- Click the Insert Hyperlink button on the Standard toolbar.
- Under Link to, click the Place in This Document option.
- Click the bookmark you want to link to, and then click the OK button.

First you'll open the document you saved at the end of the previous session, and then insert a bookmark in the Project Coordinator section. Next, you'll insert the hyperlink in the Project Abstract section.

To insert a hyperlink to a location within the same document:

1. If you took a break after the last session, make sure Word is running, and then open the **Grant Proposal** document.

2. Use the **Find** command on the Edit menu to find the **Project Coordinator** heading, close the Find and Replace dialog box, and verify that the heading "Project Coordinator" is selected. This is where you'll insert a bookmark required for the hypertext link.

3. Click **Insert** on the menu bar, and then click **Bookmark**. The Bookmark dialog box opens. You can now type the bookmark name, which must be one word, without spaces.

4. Type **Coordinator**, and click the **Add** button. The Bookmark dialog box closes. Although you can't see it, a bookmark has been inserted before the heading. This bookmark will be the target of the hyperlink. When you click the hyperlink (which you will create next), the insertion point will jump to this bookmark.

5. Press **Ctrl+Home** to move the insertion point to the beginning of the document, and then click at the end of the first paragraph under the heading "Project Abstract." The insertion point should be positioned immediately following the phrase "...via the Internet."

6. Insert a space, if necessary, and then type: **The project coordinator is Peter Brooks, a Thoreau teacher who is well known in the community for introducing students to new technology.** (Include the period.) Next, you'll format part of this sentence as a hyperlink.

7. Select the name **Peter Brooks** in the sentence you just typed, and then click the **Insert Hyperlink** button 🔘 on the Standard toolbar. The Insert Hyperlink dialog box opens.

8. Under Link to, click **Place in This Document**. See Figure 7-22. The right side of the dialog box now lists the headings and bookmarks in the document. Here you can click the item you want the hyperlink to jump to. You can create a hyperlink that jumps to a specific document heading, rather than to a bookmark. However, notice that in this document Word considers the sentence that begins "Through Space Station Education..." to be a heading, even though it's really part of a paragraph. Because you can't always predict what text will appear in the heading list, it's usually easier to link to bookmarks rather than headings. (In the Review Assignments at the end of this tutorial you'll learn how to create hyperlinks that jump to document headings.)

Figure 7-22	INSERTING A HYPERLINK

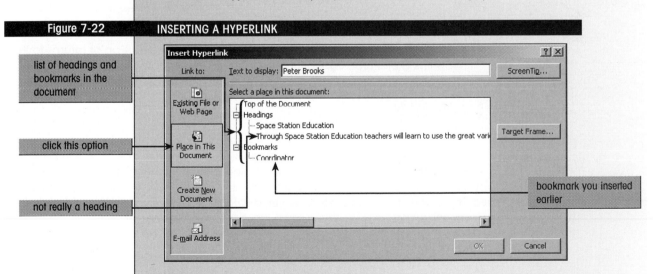

list of headings and bookmarks in the document

click this option

not really a heading

bookmark you inserted earlier

TROUBLE? If you see only three items in the right side of the dialog box, click the plus signs next to "Headings" and "Bookmarks."

9. Click **Coordinator**, and then click the **OK** button. The name "Peter Brooks" appears in underlined blue text. The hyperlink now targets the Coordinator bookmark.

> **TROUBLE?** If you formatted the wrong text as a hyperlink, click the Undo button and begin again with Step 7.

Now that you have inserted a hyperlink into the document, you should test it. When working with hyperlinks in a document, it's helpful to display the **Web toolbar**, which contains buttons that simplify the process of working with hyperlinks and Web pages. So before testing the hyperlink, you'll display the Web toolbar.

To test the hyperlink in your document:

1. Right-click the **Formatting toolbar**, and then click **Web** on the shortcut menu. The Web toolbar appears.

2. Move the mouse pointer over the blue underlined text (the hyperlink). After a moment, a ScreenTip (yellow rectangle) appears with the name of the bookmark (Coordinator) and instructions for following the link. See Figure 7-23.

Figure 7-23	DISPLAYING THE HYPERLINK SCREENTIP

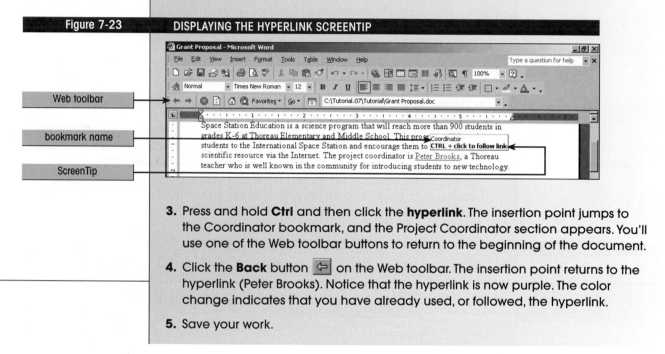

3. Press and hold **Ctrl** and then click the **hyperlink**. The insertion point jumps to the Coordinator bookmark, and the Project Coordinator section appears. You'll use one of the Web toolbar buttons to return to the beginning of the document.

4. Click the **Back** button on the Web toolbar. The insertion point returns to the hyperlink (Peter Brooks). Notice that the hyperlink is now purple. The color change indicates that you have already used, or followed, the hyperlink.

5. Save your work.

In this document it's not important that the hyperlink changes color after you use it. However, hyperlinks can also jump to other documents, including Web documents on the World Wide Web. In that environment, it's helpful to know which links you've already tried. If you were to close and then reopen the document, the hyperlink would again be blue until you clicked it.

Creating Hyperlinks to Other Documents

The greatest power of hyperlinks lies not in jumping to another location within the same document, but in jumping to other documents. These documents can be located on the World Wide Web, on your computer's hard drive, or on your company's network server. When you add a hyperlink to another document, you don't necessarily target a bookmark as you do for hyperlinks pointing to a location within the same document.

Instead, you target either the URL of a Web page, or the path and filename of a file on your computer or network.

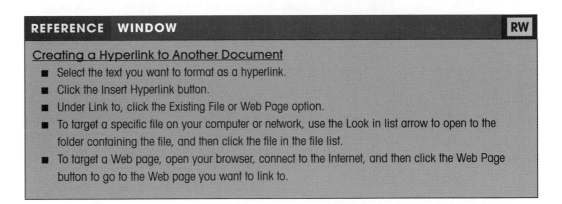

Creating a Hyperlink to Another Document
- Select the text you want to format as a hyperlink.
- Click the Insert Hyperlink button.
- Under Link to, click the Existing File or Web Page option.
- To target a specific file on your computer or network, use the Look in list arrow to open to the folder containing the file, and then click the file in the file list.
- To target a Web page, open your browser, connect to the Internet, and then click the Web Page button to go to the Web page you want to link to.

Nalani wants to insert a hyperlink that will open a Word document containing Peter's resume. Because this hyperlink will take users to a different document, you don't need to insert a bookmark. Instead, you use the name of the target document.

To create a hyperlink to another document:

1. Use the hyperlink again to jump to the Project Coordinator section.

2. Click at the end of the Project Coordinator section. The insertion point should be located immediately to the right of the phrase "at Ohio State University." This is where you'll insert text, some of which will become the hyperlink.

3. Press the **spacebar**, and type **(See his resume.)** making sure to include the parentheses.

4. Select the word **resume** in the text you just typed. See Figure 7-24.

Figure 7-24   **SELECTING TEXT TO FORMAT AS A HYPERLINK**

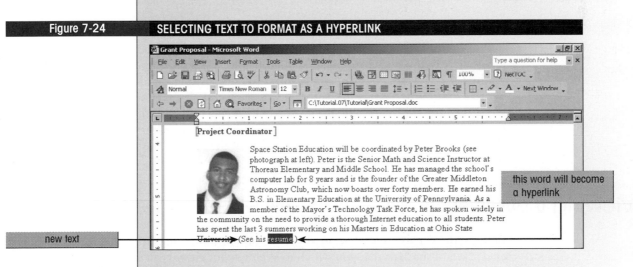

5. Click the **Insert Hyperlink** button 🔗 on the Standard toolbar. The Insert Hyperlink dialog box opens.

6. Under Link to, click the **Existing File or Web Page** option. The right side of the dialog box displays options related to selecting a file or a Web page.

7. If necessary, use the **Look in** list arrow to open the Tutorial subfolder in the Tutorial.07 folder on your hard drive.

8. Click **Resume** in the file list, and then click the **OK** button. The word "resume" is now formatted in blue with an underline, as a hyperlink.

When your documents include hyperlinks to other documents, you must keep track of where you store those target documents. If you move a target document to a different location, any hyperlinks to it contained in other documents might not function properly. In this case, you created a hyperlink in the Grant Proposal document that links to the Resume document. Both documents are stored in the Tutorial subfolder in the Tutorial.07 folder, which is most likely located on a hard disk. To ensure that the hyperlink in the Proposal document will continue to function, you must keep the two documents in the same folder.

Now you're ready to test the hyperlink you just created.

To use a hyperlink to jump to another file:

1. Move the pointer to the hyperlink **resume**.

2. Press and hold **Ctrl** and then click **resume**. Word opens the document named Resume.

3. Read through the resume, and then click the **Back** button ⟵ on the Web toolbar to return to the Proposal document. Notice that the hyperlink color has changed, indicating that you have used the hyperlink.

4. Use the hyperlink again to return to the Resume document, and then close the Resume document without saving any changes.

5. Save your changes to the Grant Proposal document.

As you can see, hyperlinks allow you to display information instantaneously. When used thoughtfully, hyperlinks make it possible to navigate a complicated document quickly and easily. If you don't want to include hyperlinks in your document, but still require an easy method for moving among sections while you are editing the document, you can use the **Word Document Map**. This feature displays a list of all the headings in the document. To move the insertion point to a specific section, you click that heading in the Document Map. For the Document Map to work, however, headings must be formatted with Word's default heading styles. (You'll use the Document Map in the Review Assignments at the end of this tutorial.)

Viewing a Document in Web Layout View

Because the version of the proposal you are now working on is intended for an online audience, Nalani suggests that you switch to Web Layout view. **Web Layout view** offers several advantages for online viewers:

- Text appears larger in Web Layout view.
- Text wraps to the window, not to the printed page. Each line of text spans the width of the document window.

- Documents can be displayed with different background effects.
- Page setup elements, such as footers, headers, and breaks, are not displayed. (Because users don't view the document as printed pages, these elements aren't necessary.)

Web Layout view is useful when you need to format a document for online viewing. Text wrapping doesn't always survive the conversion from a Word document to a Web page, and graphics often shift position when you save a document as a Web page. Web Layout view prepares you for this by showing you what the graphics look like in their new positions.

Keep in mind that, despite its name, Web Layout view does not show you exactly how a document will look when saved as a Web page. Some features you see in Web Layout view (such as the animation you will add in the next section) do not appear when you save the document as a Web page. (You will learn more about saving a document as a Web page later in this tutorial.)

If you switch to Web Layout view and then save the document in that view, it will open automatically in Web Layout view. Nalani asks you to display the Grant Proposal document in Web Layout view and then save it. Then when she e-mails the file to Karen and Tom, it will open for them in Web Layout view.

To display a document in Web Layout view:

1. Click the **Web Layout View** button [image] (next to the Normal View button, just above the status bar). Notice that paragraphs now span the width of the document window. The line widths are no longer constrained by the margin settings for the printed page. This makes the document easier to read online. See Figure 7-25.

Figure 7-25	DOCUMENT DISPLAYED IN WEB LAYOUT VIEW

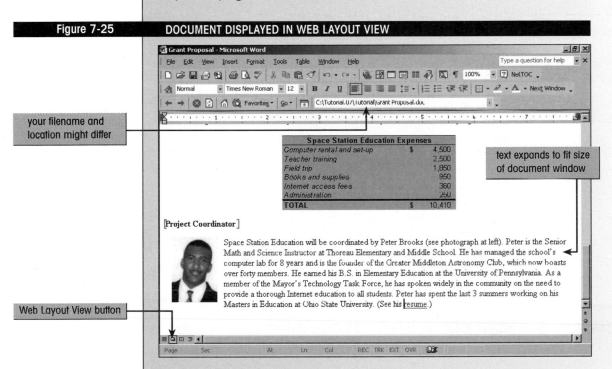

TROUBLE? Depending on the size of your monitor, the line breaks in your document may differ from those in Figure 7-25. This has to do with the fact the Web Layout View wraps text to fit the size of the screen, and is not a problem.

2. Scroll through the document to review its appearance in Web Layout View. Depending on the size of your computer screen, you might find that all the text in the first paragraph of the Goals and Objectives section has wrapped to the

right of the chart, leaving the heading "Goals and Objectives" floating over the chart. You could correct this problem now by dragging the chart down, until part of the first paragraph wraps over the top of the chart. However, if you move the chart, the text wrapping will not look right when you switch back to Print Layout view. Because Nalani wants Tom and Karen to be able to switch between Web Layout view and Print Layout view, she decides to leave the chart where it is for now. You'll have a chance to adjust its position later when you create a Web page version of the Grant Proposal.

3. Save your changes to the Grant Proposal document.

Next, you'll make some changes to the Grant Proposal document that will improve its online appearance.

Improving the Appearance of an Online Document

To make the online version of the proposal more visually interesting for online viewers, Nalani suggests you use two features—animated text and a colored background. You'll add these features now to improve the appearance of the document Nalani will e-mail to Karen and Tom. However, keep in mind that some features that appear in Web Layout view do not appear when you convert the document to a Web page. (You will learn more about converting a document to a Web page in the next session.)

Animating Text

Animated text is text that blinks, sparkles, shimmers, or displays a moving border. Most of these animations are not appropriate for official, professional documents, and Nalani would not consider using them in the final draft of her proposal, which she will submit to the U.S. Department of Education. But because she is acquainted with the people who will review her proposal, and because she knows they tend to be informal when reviewing each other's work, she thinks it's acceptable to use some animated text in this draft. Nalani suggests you try animating the proposal title, "Space Station Education," with sparkles.

To animate the title of the proposal:

1. Scroll to the beginning of the document.

2. Select the title **Space Station Education**.

3. Click **Format** on the menu bar, click **Font**, and then click the **Text Effects** tab.

4. In the Animations list, click **Sparkle Text**. Notice the Preview box shows a sample of this type of animation. See Figure 7-26.

Figure 7-26	PREVIEWING ANIMATED TEXT

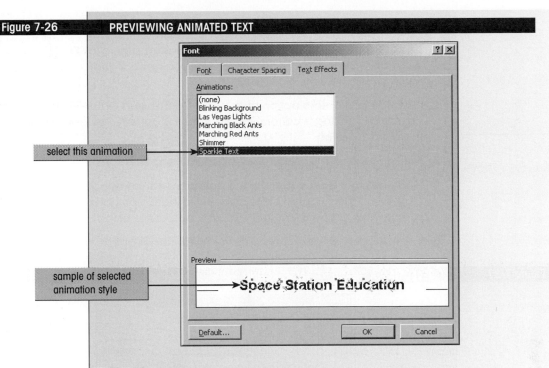

select this animation →

sample of selected animation style →

5. Click the **OK** button, and then click anywhere outside the title to deselect it. Rainbow colored sparkles have been added to the title.

Animation draws an online viewer's eyes immediately to the animated text, so use this feature only for your most important words or phrases. Overusing animated text makes your document difficult to view. Also keep in mind that animation effects don't appear in printed documents, nor will they survive the conversion to a Web page.

Applying a Background Effect

You also can make an online document more visually appealing by applying background effects. As with animated text, backgrounds do not appear in printed documents. You can apply one of the following background effects:

- Solid color
- Gradient—a single color or combination of colors that varies in intensity
- Texture—choose from a collection of textures
- Pattern—choose from a collection of interesting patterns; you designate the colors in the pattern
- Picture—a graphic image

When choosing a background color or texture, make sure your text is still readable. In poorly designed online documents, the background might be so dark or the pattern so obtrusive that the text is illegible. In addition, a background that contains a complicated pattern will increase the file size and take longer to appear on a user's screen. Nalani suggests you use a gradient background that ranges from white to pale blue.

To apply a background effect to a document:

1. Click **Format** on the menu bar, point to **Background**, click **Fill Effects**, and then click the **Gradient** tab, if necessary. First you need to indicate that you want to use two colors for the background.

2. Click the **Two colors** option button. The Color 1 and Color 2 list arrows appear. The Color 1 setting is currently white, which is correct. You only need to change the Color 2 setting.

3. Click the **Color 2** list arrow. A color palette appears.

4. Click the **pale blue square** in the bottom row, third from the right. The palette closes and the selected color appears in the Color 2 box. Finally, you need to specify how you want the color to vary across the page.

5. In the Shading styles section, click the **From corner** option button. See Figure 7-27.

Figure 7-27   **SELECTING A GRADIENT BACKGROUND**

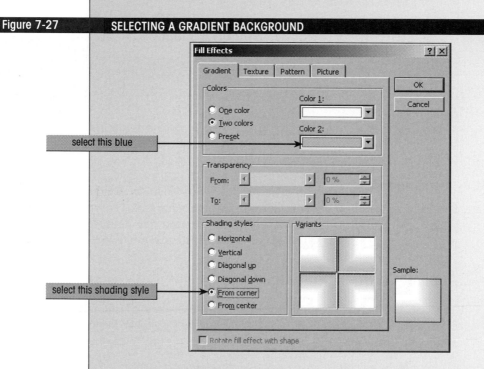

6. Click the **OK** button. The blue and white gradient fills the background of the Grant Proposal document.

7. Save the Grant Proposal document in Web Layout view, and then close it.

The gradient background is attractive and light enough to make the document text easy to read. The proposal is ready to be e-mailed to Karen and Tom. However, before Nalani e-mails the proposal, she will add a similar background to the Resume document. Then both of the linked documents will have a consistent look.

Session 7.2 Quick Check

1. What is a hyperlink?

2. What is a browser?

3. What's the difference between an intranet and the Internet?

4. Explain how to insert a hyperlink to a location in the same document containing the hyperlink.

5. Which name is an invalid bookmark name? a) Recommendations, b) Executive Summary, c) README

6. What does a change in the color of a hyperlink indicate?

7. True or False: Web Layout view shows you exactly what your document will look like when saved as a Web page.

SESSION 7.3

In this session, you will convert Nalani's proposal into a Web page for publication on the World Wide Web, and then format the Web page to make it easier to read in a Web browser. Finally, you'll insert and edit hyperlinks that link the Proposal and Resume documents, and then preview your Web page in a browser.

Saving a Word Document as a Web Page

So far, Nalani has created printed copies of her proposal to hand out to teachers at Thoreau School and an online version to e-mail to Karen and Tom. Next, she wants to convert the Grant Proposal document to a Web page so she can make it available on the World Wide Web. Another term for a Web page is **HTML document**. The letters HTML are short for **Hypertext Markup Language**, a special programming language that tells a Web browser how a Web page should look on the screen. When you save a Word document as a Web page, you are really inserting HTML codes that tell the browser exactly how to format the text and graphics. Fortunately, you don't have to learn the Hypertext Markup Language to create Web pages. When you save the document as a Web page, Word creates all the necessary HTML codes (called markings, or tags). This process is transparent to you, so you won't actually see the HTML codes in your Web pages.

The relatively small size of Web pages makes them easy to share on the Internet. For example, a Word document containing a moderate amount of formatting and a few graphics might be 500 KB in size. The same document saved as a Web page might be only 20 KB in size, along with about 50 KB of graphics files. To help keep your Web page file small, Word puts any graphics into a separate folder. This folder also contains other small files that your Web browser needs to display the Web page correctly. By default, this folder has the same name as your Web page, plus an underscore and the word "files." For instance, a Web page saved as "Finance Summary" would be accompanied by a folder named "Finance Summary_files."

Although saving a Word document as a Web page is easy, it's not foolproof, particularly when it comes to formatting. Some Word formatting features (such as paragraph borders or certain font effects) will not translate into HTML. When you save your document as a Web page, document formatting might be lost, or the formatting will look different. In some cases, the original document might contain special features, such as animation, that don't survive the translation to HTML. Sometimes you might need to reapply formatting after a document has been saved as a Web page. As a general rule, once you save a document as a Web page, you'll want to modify it to make it more attractive for users of the World Wide Web. At the very least, you will probably need to reposition graphics.

To create sophisticated Web pages (or entire Web sites), you'll probably want to use a dedicated HTML editor, such as Microsoft FrontPage. But to create a simple Web page from an existing document, you can save the document as a Web page.

REFERENCE WINDOW **RW**

Saving a Word Document as a Web Page
- Click File on the menu bar, and then click Save as Web Page.
- If desired, give the file a new filename. Word will add the file extension .htm at the end of the document, although this extension probably won't be visible in the Save As dialog box.
- Click the Save button.
- If Word warns you that the document has formatting not supported by Web browsers, click the Continue button.

You are ready to save the Grant Proposal document as a Web page.

To save the document as a Web page:

1. If you took a break after the last session, make sure Word is running. Close any Internet-related programs, such as e-mail editors or browsers, and then open the **Grant Proposal** document.

2. Click **File** on the menu bar, and then click **Save as Web Page**. The Save As dialog box, which you have used many times, opens. The only difference between this dialog box and the one you previously used is that the Save as type text box indicates that the document will be saved as a Web page.

3. Change the filename so it reads **Grant Proposal Web Page**.

4. Click the **Save** button. Word displays a warning message indicating that some elements of the document cannot be displayed in commonly used browsers (Microsoft Internet Explorer 4.0 and Netscape Navigator 4.0). The dialog box explains that animated text (the document heading, which is currently formatted with sparkles) will become italicized instead. Also, any pictures or objects with text wrapping will become left- or right-aligned. See Figure 7-28. You'll see exactly what this means after you finish saving the document as a Web page.

Figure 7-28	WARNING MESSAGE

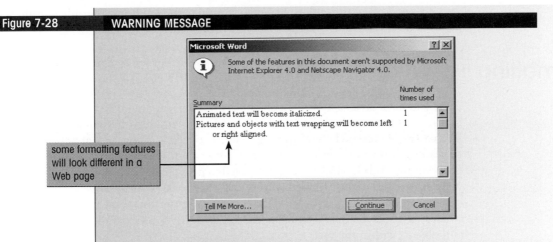

some formatting features will look different in a Web page

5. Click **Continue**. After a pause, the document is converted into a Web page.

TROUBLE? If you think that Word is taking a long time to convert and save the file in HTML format, don't worry. Depending on the speed of your system, it could take several minutes.

6. If necessary, display the Web toolbar. Your document should now look similar to Figure 7-29.

Figure 7-29	GRANT PROPOSAL WEB PAGE

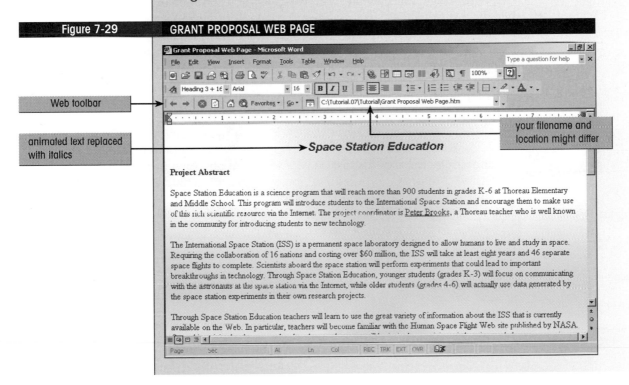

Web toolbar

animated text replaced with italics

your filename and location might differ

At first glance, the new Grant Proposal Web page might look identical to the Grant Proposal Word document when you displayed it in Web Layout View. But as you review the Web page, you'll notice at least one difference: the animated title is now formatted in italics. Another major difference is not actually apparent on the screen: The file size has decreased from about 66 KB to only about 17 KB (plus about 33 KB of related files). This reduced size is a tremendous advantage for Web pages that must be transferred electronically over long distances and often through slow network connections. The smaller file size allows the Web pages to appear as quickly as possible in a browser window.

Formatting a Web Page

After you have saved a Word document as a Web page, you need to format the Web page so that it is attractive when displayed in a browser—you need to format it for online viewing. You've already learned about the difference between reading a document online as opposed to reading it on the printed page. Recall that when you prepared an online version of the proposal (in Web Layout View), you added hyperlinks and a colored background. But when you created the earlier version of the grant proposal, your goal was to create a document suitable for e-mailing. Now you need to format the proposal to improve its appearance when it is displayed in a Web browser. You'll begin by correcting the placement of graphics and objects within the text.

Moving and Editing Text and Graphics

You can edit and format text and graphics in a Web page the same way you edit and format a normal Word document. First, Nalani asks you adjust the placement of the Excel chart. Depending on the size of your computer screen, this object (which had text wrapped around it) might have shifted to an awkward position when you first viewed the grant proposal in Web Layout view. Nalani didn't want you to adjust its position in Web Layout view, because then the text would have wrapped incorrectly in Print Layout view. However, now that you have converted the grant proposal to a Web document that is only meant to be viewed in a browser, you don't have to worry about how graphics will look in Print Layout view. You can position the chart for viewing in a browser.

To change the text wrapping around graphics:

1. Scroll down to display the Excel chart in the section below the "Goals and Objectives" heading, as shown in Figure 7-30. (Depending on the size of your computer monitor, the text on your screen might have wrapped around the chart differently). In Figure 7-30, the entire heading "Budget" (which used to be left-aligned) has wrapped to the right of the chart. You could adjust the position of the chart by adjusting settings in the Format Object dialog box, but it's easier to drag the chart up a few lines.

Figure 7-30	CHART WITH BUDGET HEADING WRAPPED TO THE RIGHT

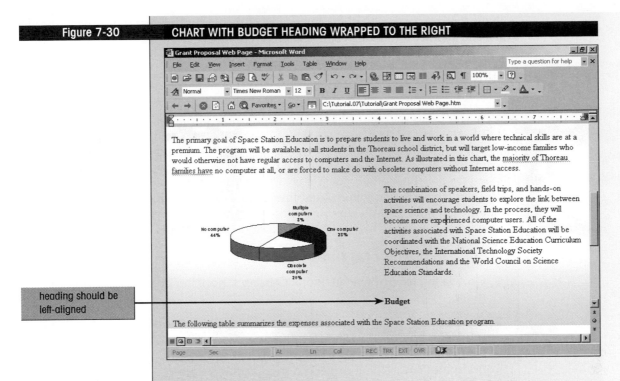

heading should be
left-aligned

2. If necessary, click the **chart** to select it, and then drag it up so that it is positioned similarly to the one in Figure 7-31, with the heading "Budget" left-aligned below the chart. Deselect the chart.

Figure 7-31	CHART WITH BUDGET HEADING IN PROPER POSITION

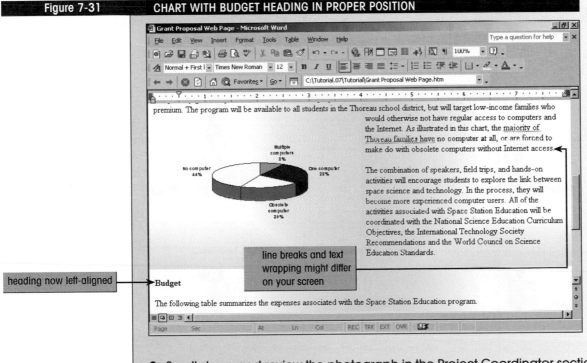

heading now left-aligned

line breaks and text wrapping might differ on your screen

3. Scroll down and review the photograph in the Project Coordinator section. Adjust its position, if necessary, so that the entire paragraph wraps to the right of the photograph. It's okay if the top of the photograph doesn't align perfectly with the top of the paragraph of text.

Now that you've corrected the placement of the text and graphics in Nalani's proposal, you'll add another formatting feature to the Web page.

Inserting Horizontal Lines

Many Web pages have horizontal lines that separate sections of a document. These lines make it easy to see at a glance where one section ends and another begins. You can also add horizontal lines to Word documents that you plan to read in Web Layout view, but they are more commonly used in Web pages. If you don't like a horizontal line after you insert one into a document, you can delete it by clicking the line and then pressing Delete.

Nalani wants you to add a horizontal line below the title and at the end of each section except the last one.

To insert horizontal lines into the Web page:

1. Click to the left of the "P" in "Project Abstract" near the beginning of the document.

2. Click **Format** on the menu bar, click **Borders and Shading**, click the **Borders** tab in the Borders and Shading dialog box, and then click the **Horizontal Line** button. The Horizontal Line dialog box opens, and lists many styles of horizontal lines. (There may be a short pause before you see the borders displayed within the dialog box.)

3. Scroll down until you see a red line in the left column.

4. Click the **red line**, as shown in Figure 7-32.

| Figure 7-32 | SELECTING A HORIZONTAL LINE STYLE |

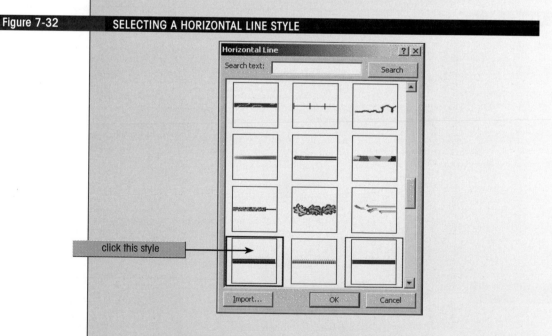

5. Click the **OK** button. A red line is inserted into the Web page below the title. Your Web page should look similar to Figure 7-33.

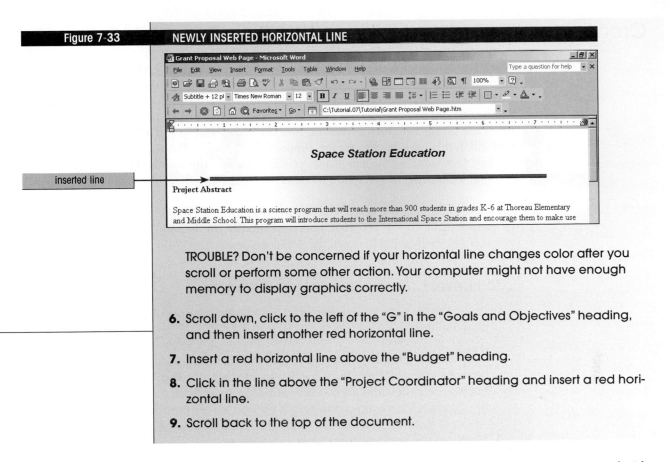

Figure 7-33 | **NEWLY INSERTED HORIZONTAL LINE**

inserted line

TROUBLE? Don't be concerned if your horizontal line changes color after you scroll or perform some other action. Your computer might not have enough memory to display graphics correctly.

6. Scroll down, click to the left of the "G" in the "Goals and Objectives" heading, and then insert another red horizontal line.

7. Insert a red horizontal line above the "Budget" heading.

8. Click in the line above the "Project Coordinator" heading and insert a red horizontal line.

9. Scroll back to the top of the document.

Now that you've used horizontal lines to give shape to the document, you decide to improve the appearance of the document's text.

Modifying Text Size and Color

Web pages use colored text to enhance the appearance of the page and to call attention to important information. You also can adjust text size on a Web page just as you would on a printed document. To improve the proposal's readability and appearance, Nalani wants you to increase the font size of the title text and change its color to red, to match the horizontal lines.

To change the size and color of text:

1. Select the title **Space Station Education** at the beginning of the Web page.

2. Use the **Font Size** list arrow on the Formatting toolbar to change the font size from 16-point to **24-point**.

3. Click the **Font Color** list arrow ▲▾ on the Formatting toolbar, click the **red square** (third row from the top, first column on the left), and then deselect the text. The title "Space Station Education" is formatted in red, to match the horizontal lines.

4. Save your work.

You've formatted Nalani's proposal document so that it will be visually appealing when displayed in a browser. Next, you'll create additional hypertext links and edit an existing link.

Creating and Editing Hyperlinks in a Web Page

As you looked through the HTML version of the proposal, you probably noticed that it still contains two hyperlinks. The Peter Brooks link jumps to the Project Coordinator section at the end of the Web page. The resume link jumps to a Word document containing Peter's resume. Nalani wants to save the Resume document as a Web page, and then format it to match the Grant Proposal document. She also wants you to add a hyperlink to the resume that will jump back to the Grant Proposal Web page. Finally, because you'll save the Resume document with a new name, you have to edit the resume hyperlink (in the Grant Proposal Web page) to make sure it opens the right file.

In the following steps, you will convert the resume to a Web page, create a new link from the resume back to the proposal, and then modify the hyperlink in the proposal so that browsers can easily jump between the two documents.

To convert the resume to a Web page:

1. Open the file named **Resume** from the Tutorial subfolder in the Tutorial.07 folder on your hard drive.

2. If necessary, switch to Print Layout View.

3. Save the document (in the Tutorial folder for Tutorial 7) as a Web page using the filename **Resume Web Page**. While the Save As dialog box is open, notice that Word has created a new folder, named "Grant Proposal Web Page_files," in which to store the files related to the proposal Web page. Note that you should never save any other documents in this folder.

4. Click the **Save** button to close the Save As dialog box. Word automatically switches to Web Layout view.

Next, you'll make some formatting changes to give the Resume Web page the same look as the proposal Web page. You'll use the procedures you learned earlier in this tutorial.

To format the Resume Web Page:

1. Click **Format** on the menu bar, point to **Background**, click **Fill Effects**, click the **Gradient** tab, and then apply a white and pale blue background to the Web page, using the From corner shading style.

2. Select the text **Peter Brooks** at the top of the page, and format it in red.

3. Save your work.

The resume and the proposal now have a similar appearance.

Inserting a Hyperlink to a Web Page

After users read Peter's resume they most likely will want to return to the proposal, so Nalani asks you to insert a hyperlink that jumps to the proposal. You insert hyperlinks into Web pages the same way as in Word documents.

To insert a hyperlink:

1. Press **Ctrl+End** to move the insertion point to the end of the Web page, and then type **Return to Grant Proposal**.

2. Select the text **Grant Proposal** in the phrase you just typed, click the **Insert Hyperlink** button 🖼 on the Standard toolbar and then, under Link to, click **Existing File or Web Page**.

3. If necessary, use the **Look in** list arrow to open the Tutorial subfolder in the Tutorial folder on your hard drive, click **Grant Proposal Web Page**, and then click the **OK** button. Word inserts the hyperlink to the proposal.

4. Save and close the Resume Web page. You return to the proposal.

The resume now contains a hyperlink that takes users back to the proposal.

Editing a Hyperlink

Recall that the proposal itself contains the hyperlink that targets a Word document containing the resume. You need to edit the hyperlink so that it targets the resume with its new Web page name. Rather than deleting the hyperlink and reinserting a new one, you can edit the existing hyperlink to target the Resume Web Page.

To edit a hyperlink:

1. Scroll to the end of the proposal, and position the pointer over the hyperlink. A ScreenTip appears indicating that the link will jump to a document named Resume.doc.

2. Right-click the **resume** hyperlink. A shortcut menu opens.

3. Click **Edit Hyperlink** in the shortcut menu. The Edit Hyperlink dialog box opens.

4. Verify that the Existing File or Web Page option is selected under "Link to."

5. If necessary, use the **Look in** list arrow to open the Tutorial folder for Tutorial 7.

6. Click **Resume Web Page** in the file list, and then click the **OK** button. You return to the proposal Web page.

7. Place the mouse pointer over the resume hyperlink. A ScreenTip appears, indicating that the link will now jump to a Web page named "Resume Web Page.htm."

8. Save your work.

The edited hyperlink in the proposal Web page correctly targets the Resume Web page. You're now ready to view the finished Web pages in a Web browser and to test the hyperlinks.

Viewing the Web Page in a Web Browser

While you're editing a Web page in Word, the document window shows how the document will look when viewed from a Web browser. However, it's always a good idea to view your Web pages with a Web browser to see exactly how they will look. This can help you discover unexpected formatting problems that you might not notice otherwise.

To view the Web page in a Web browser and test the links:

1. Click **File** on the menu bar, and then click **Web Page Preview**. Word opens your default Web browser and displays the Grant Proposal in its document window. See Figure 7-34. Regardless of your type of browser, your view of the Grant Proposal Web page should be similar to Figure 7-34. Maximize the browser window, if necessary.

Figure 7-34   PROPOSAL DISPLAYED IN BROWSER WINDOW

Internet Explorer title bar

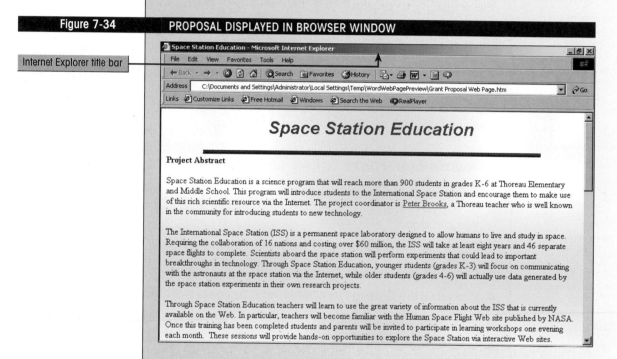

TROUBLE? If a message informs you that Internet Explorer is not your default browser and asks you if you want to make it your browser, click the No button.

2. Scroll through the document so you can see how it looks in the browser. (If you notice any formatting problems at this point, you will have to close the browser window, edit the document in Word, save your changes, and then preview it in the browser again). Next, you should check the hyperlinks to make sure they work properly. In a browser, you don't have to press the Ctrl key to use a hyperlink. Instead, you simply click the link.

3. Move the insertion point to the beginning of the document, and click the **Peter Brooks** hyperlink. The heading "Project Coordinator" is displayed in the browser window.

4. Click the **resume** hyperlink in the last paragraph of the document. The browser opens the Resume Web page.

5. Scroll through the document to view it. Notice that when you view the resume in the browser, the table format disappears and Peter's address information is

left-aligned. In this case, the format is still acceptable, so you don't have to make any additional changes in Word.

6. Click the **Grant Proposal** hyperlink. The browser now returns to the proposal Web page.

   TROUBLE? If any of the hyperlinks don't work properly, edit them so they link to the proper document.

7. Close the browser window. You return to the grant proposal in the Word window.

8. If necessary, press **Ctrl+End** to move the insertion point to the bottom of the Web page, press **Enter** twice, and insert the text **Prepared by** followed by your first and last name.

9. Print the document, save, and close the proposal. The printed Web page looks similar, but not identical, to the printed Word document.

You have now finished preparing two Web pages, the proposal and the resume, for online viewing. The Grant Proposal Web page contains an embedded Excel worksheet, as well as a linked Excel chart. As long as you keep the Excel file "Copy of Chart" and the Web page file "Grant Proposal Web Page" in the same folder (the Tutorial subfolder in the Tutorial.07 folder) the links between the two should be maintained.

In this tutorial you have integrated Word with two other programs—Excel and a browser. In doing so, you were able to progress far beyond simple word-processed text. In the Review Assignments and Case problems at the end of this tutorial, you will use other programs and features of Word to produce even more advanced documents. Among other things, you will create your own diagrams, charts, and graphics.

Session 7.3 QUICK CHECK

1. True or False: A Web page is the same thing as an HTML document.

2. Name two types of document formatting that will not survive the conversion to a Web page.

3. True or False: After you convert a Word document to a Web page, you need to re-create all hypertext links.

4. Explain how to insert a horizontal line into a Web page. What is the purpose of such a line?

5. List the various tasks you should perform after converting a Word document into a Web page.

6. Describe the steps necessary to preview a Web page in your default Web browser.

REVIEW ASSIGNMENTS

Nalani's grant proposal for the Space Station Education program was accepted. The school received the grant and the program was extremely successful. Now Nalani needs to submit a program evaluation report to the U.S. Department of Education, the agency that provided the funding. Nalani wrote the body of the report in Word, and then e-mailed it to Tom Jenkins and Karen Goldberg for their comments. Both Tom and Karen returned edited copies of the report document, and now Nalani wants you to merge their files with her original report document. She also wants you to embed a worksheet of actual budget figures and then link a graph illustrating ratings from student evaluation forms. Next, she wants you to create an online version of the report that she can e-mail back to Tom and Karen. This online version will include some hyperlinks. Finally, she asks you to save the report as a Web page for publication on the World Wide Web, and add a hyperlink to NASA's Human Space Flight Web site.

1. Verify that you have copied the Tutorial.07 folder to your hard drive.

2. Make sure that Word is running, and open the file named **Report** from the Review folder for Tutorial7.

3. Merge the Report document with Karen's edited copy (named **KGReport**). Merge these two documents to a new document. Then merge the new document with Tom's edited copy (named **TJReport**). Save the new document as **Evaluation Report** in the Review folder for Tutorial 7, and then close the original Report document without saving any changes.

4. Review all the edits in the Evaluation Report document, and read all the comments. If necessary, display the Reviewing toolbar.

5. Delete all the comments in the document, accept Karen's three edits (the insertion of "while", the insertion of "orbit around the earth", and the deletion of "space), and then reject Tom's three changes in the sentence that begins "Program volunteers participated in…" The end of the sentence should read "the Human Space Flight Web site published by NASA." Accept all remaining changes in the document, and then save your work.

Explore ▶ 6. Click Tools on the menu bar and then click Options. Click the User Information tab. Note the name in the Name box is the name that would appear in the revision mark ScreenTips if you used this computer to edit a document. Click Cancel to close the Options dialog box. Switch to Header and Footer view, click along the left margin of the Footer section, click Insert on the menu bar, click Field, in the Field Name list box scroll down and click User Name. The name you saw in the Options dialog box is inserted in the footer as field. If this is not your name, type a forward slash (/) to the right of the field and then type your own name. Use the Format Page Number button on the Header and Footer toolbar to make the page number field begin at 1 rather than 2, and then close Header and Footer view.

7. Delete the placeholder [Insert Excel chart], verify that the insertion point is positioned on a blank line between two paragraphs of text, and embed the Excel file named **EvalCht**. Use the Object command on the Format menu to reduce the chart's height and width to 30%, and then wrap text to the right of the chart, using the Square wrapping option (with the Left horizontal alignment option). Click at the beginning of the paragraph that begins "Space Station Education also gave sixth graders…" and insert a page break to move the chart and the related text to page 3. Nalani will eventually add more text to the first page, so you don't have to be concerned about the blank space at the bottom of page 1. Save your work.

8. Delete the placeholder [Insert Excel worksheet], verify that the insertion point is positioned on a blank line between two blank lines, and insert a linked copy of the workbook named **FinlBgt**. Remember to make a copy of the Excel file, so that the Excel file you actually link to the Word document is named **Copy of FinlBgt**. Also remember to click the Link to file check box to select it. Review the worksheet in the Word document, and notice that the figure for Computer rental and setup is 4.00. Center the worksheet in the page, save your work, and then close the Evaluation Report document.

9. Start Excel, open the workbook named **Copy of FinlBgt** from the Review subfolder in the Tutorial.07 folder, click cell B2 (the cell containing the number "4.00"), type 4000, press Enter, click the Save button on the Standard toolbar, and then close Excel. Open the Evaluation Report document in Word, and verify that the Computer rental and setup figure has been updated to $4,000. If it has not been updated automatically, right-click the worksheet, and then click Update Link in the shortcut menu. Save your work.

10. Print the proposal document.

11. Switch to Web Layout view, display the Web toolbar, if necessary, and then review the proposal and note any problems with text wrapping around the chart. You'll fix any text-wrapping problems later, when you save the proposal as a Web page.

12. Near the end of the document, select the phrase "Peter was assisted" and insert a book-mark named "Volunteers." In the paragraph following the "Introduction" heading, for-mat the phrase "Five teachers" as a hyperlink that targets the Volunteers bookmark. Test the hyperlink to make sure it works.

Explore ▶ 13. In documents that have been formatted using Word's default heading styles (Heading 1, Heading 2, and Heading 3), you can create hyperlinks that target specific headings. To try this now, select the phrase "International Space Station" in the paragraph under the "Introduction" heading, click the Insert Hyperlink button, click Place in This Document, and then review the list of headings in the Insert Hyperlink dialog box. (If you can't see the document headings, click the plus sign next to Headings.) Click "What is the International Space Station?" and then click OK. In the document window, test the International Space Station hyperlink to make sure it jumps to the heading "What is the International Space Station?"

Explore ▶ 14. In addition to using hyperlinks to move from one part of a document to another, you can use Word's Document Map feature. This feature is available in Normal, Page Layout, and Web Layout view. To learn how use the Document Map, click the Document Map button on the Standard toolbar. A Document Map window opens on the left side of the document window. Click Budget in the Document Map window to move the insertion point to the Budget section. Practice using the Document Map to move the insertion point to other sections of the document. Click the Document Map button again to close the Document Map window.

15. Format the report with a two-color gradient background, with pink as Color 1, and lavender as Color 2. Use the Horizontal shading style. Format the title and subtitle with animated text, using the Marching Black Ants animation style.

16. Switch to Print Layout view. Notice that the colored background is no longer visible. Switch back to Web Layout view and save your work.

17. Save the report as a Web page in the Review folder for Tutorial 7, using the name **Evaluation Report Web Page**.

18. Adjust the position of the Excel chart to make the text wrap around it properly. Make

sure the "Curriculum Objectives" heading is aligned on the left margin, below the chart.

19. Insert a horizontal line of your choice before each section heading (including the "Introduction" heading). Format the title, subtitle, and section headings using a font color of your choice. Save your work.

Explore

20. In the tutorial you inserted a hyperlink to another document stored on your computer. You can also insert hyperlinks to Internet Web sites. To learn how, use the Find command on the Edit menu to select the word "NASA," and then click the Insert Hyperlink button on the Standard toolbar. Click Existing File or Web Page, click in the Address text box, type "www.nasa.gov", and then click OK. Next, test the link. If your computer is already connected to the Internet, the NASA Web page will open in your browser. If your computer is not connected, your computer may attempt to connect and display the NASA Web page. (If necessary, click Connect in the Dial-up Connection dialog box.) If your computer cannot establish a connection, the browser might open and display a message indicating that the specified Web page could not be found. Close your browser and any dialog boxes. Save your changes to the report Web page.

21. Use the Web Page Preview command to view the report in your Web browser. Fix any formatting problems and test all the hyperlinks. (Don't test the NASA link if it didn't work for you earlier.)

22. Right-click the Start button, click Explore, and then use Windows Explorer to display the contents of the Evaluation Report Web Page_files folder (which you'll find in the Review folder for Tutorial 7). How many files does this folder contain? What is their total size? What size is the Evaluation Report Web Page file, in the Review folder?

23. Close your browser, save any changes to the report Web page, and then close Word.

24. Use your e-mail program to send the Evaluation Report Word document to a fellow student. In most e-mail programs, you need to create a new message, and then attach the file to the message. Ask the recipient of the file to open it, display it in Web Layout view, and test the various links. Can he or she access the source file for the Excel workbook? Why or why not? Do the other links in the document work? Why or why not?

Explore

25. Close all open files and programs.

CASE PROBLEMS

Case 1. Office Location for Vista Insurance Company Steven Woodhouse works for the Vista Insurance Company, a new, rapidly growing company. Emma Knightly, vice president of operations for the company, has proposed that Vista open a new downtown office, and has assigned Steven the responsibility of finding a good location. Steven has contacted local real estate agencies through the World Wide Web, and he has located an available office building that seems satisfactory. He has downloaded an image of the office building and asks you to prepare a memo to Emma describing the office site. He'd like you to include the image in the memo. When you've finished, he requests that you e-mail the memo to Emma for online viewing. Emma won't be viewing the memo in her browser; she'll just open it directly in Word.

1. If necessary, start Word. Open the file **Office** from the Cases folder for Tutorial 7 and then save it to the same folder as **Office Rental Memo**.

2. In the From: section of the memo, replace "Steve Woodhouse" with your name.

3. After the third paragraph, delete the bracketed phrase "[insert chart]," and embed the workbook called **Rates** from the Cases folder for Tutorial 7.

4. Reduce the size of the chart to 40% of its original size, and center it between the left and right margins.

5. Double-click the chart to display the Excel tools. Click the chart title, click before the "R" in "Rental," type "Monthly", and then press the spacebar so that the title reads "Monthly Rental Rates ($)." Click outside the chart to return to the Word menu and toolbars.

6. Click in the blank line above the heading "Interoffice Memo" and then insert "Vista Insurance" as a piece of WordArt, using the WordArt style with green letters and a shadow. Center the WordArt Logo.

7. Format the document with a solid, light green background. (*Hint:* Click Format on the menu bar, point to Background, then click the light green tile on the color palette.) Notice how Word switched automatically to Web Layout view, when you added the green background. Preview the Office Rental Memo document in Web Layout view, and note any problems with the formatting. Save your work.

8. Open the document named **Downtn** from the Cases folder for Tutorial 7, save it as **Downtown Development** in the Cases folder for Tutorial 7, switch to Web Layout view, and then format the document using the same background you used for the memo. Remove any SmartTags in the document, save your work, and close the document. (*Note:* that SmartTags can adversely affect the formatting when a Web page is viewed in a browser. For example, text with a SmartTag attached might appear on a white background, even though the rest of the document has a green background.)

9. In the Office Rental memo, in the paragraph above the photograph, just after the sentence that ends with "…in the heart of the downtown business district," insert the following text: See New Development Projects in the Downtown Area for a list of new renovations. Make "New Development Projects in the Downtown Area" a hyperlink, targeting the **Downtown Development** file in the Cases folder for Tutorial 7.

10. Test the hyperlink in the memo. When the Downtown Development document opens, insert a hyperlink at the end that takes users back to the memo. Test this new hyperlink.

11. Test all the links in the two documents one last time, and then close the Downtown Development document, saving your work, if necessary.

12. Print the Office Rental Memo document while it is displayed in Web Layout view. Save your work and close the document.

13. Use your e-mail program to send the Office Rental Memo document to a fellow student. (If you prefer, send the file to yourself.) In most e-mail programs, you need to create a new message, and then attach the file to the message. Ask the recipient of the file to open it, display it in Web Layout view, and test the various links. Do all the links in the document work? Why or why not?

Case 2. Mountain Time Web Page   Sophie Kurtz is a marketing manager for Mountain Time Inc., a company that offers guided tours to many popular tourist sites in the western United States. She recently prepared a flyer describing upcoming tours to selected western national parks. She asks you to help finish the project, and then convert it to a Web page so she can post it on the company's Web site and make it available to prospective tourists.

1. If necessary, start Word. Open the file **Parks** from the Cases folder for Tutorial 7, and then save it as **Mountain Time Parks Tour** in the same folder.

2. Position the photograph of the arch against the left margin, wrap text around it, and enlarge it so that the entire second paragraph wraps to the right of the photo.

Explore

3. In this tutorial you learned how to link and embed objects using the Object command on the Insert menu. If you prefer, you can also link or embed an object by copying it to the Clipboard, and then pasting it into the destination file using the Paste Special command on the Edit menu. To experiment using Paste Special now, press Ctrl+End to move the insertion point to the last line of the document, start Excel, and open the workbook named **TourInf** from the Cases folder for Tutorial 7. Click cell A1, and then drag down and to the right to cell E7. The worksheet data should now be selected. Click the Copy button on the Excel toolbar, click the Microsoft Word button on the taskbar, click Edit on the menu bar, and then click Paste Special. The Paste Special dialog box allows you to paste objects from the Clipboard in a variety of formats, including HTML, unformatted text, and formatted text. To embed the entire workbook, you could select the Microsoft Excel Worksheet Object option. To link the worksheet to the Word document, you could select the Paste link option button. In this case, you will experiment with pasting the worksheet data as formatted text. Click the Formatted Text (RTF) option in the As list box, verify that the Paste option button is selected, and then click OK. The worksheet is inserted into the document as a Word table.

4. If the Cost/person column is truncated by the right margin, move the mouse pointer over the table to display the Table move handle in the upper-left of the table, click the Table move handle, and then drag the entire table slightly left until you can see the entire Cost/person column. Add the heading "Accommodations" to the second-to-last column on the right. Delete the first row containing the text "Western Tours." Adjust column widths as necessary to make the table span the width of the current margins. Format the new table as necessary to make it attractive and easy to read.

Explore

5. When creating Web pages and online documents, you sometimes might need to create simple graphics. To learn how, open the Paint program from the Accessories submenu on the Start menu. Click Image on the menu bar, click Attributes, and then change the Width settings to 200 and the height setting to 50. Click View on the menu bar, point to Zoom, click Custom, click the 200% option button, and then click OK. Use the Brush button on the toolbar to draw some mountain peaks with a sun overhead. (If you don't like your first attempt, use the Erase button to erase your work.) Don't expect to produce a perfect work of art; your goal is just to get familiar with using Paint. Use the Rectangle tool to draw a rectangle the same size as the image, and then use the Fill tool to fill the rectangle with a lavender color. You also might need to click inside some of the shapes you drew to fill them with color. (*Hint:* Use the Undo command on the Edit menu to reverse any mistakes. Use the Magnifier tool to zoom in on the image, if necessary, to make it easier to edit.) Save the logo as a 24-bit bitmap file named **Logo** in the Cases folder for Tutorial 7, and then close Paint.

6. Insert a linked copy of the logo at the top of the Mountain Time Tours document, and then save your work. Open Paint, open the Logo file, change the background color to yellow, save your work, and then close Paint. Right-click the logo in the Word document, and then click Update Link to change the logo background to yellow.

7. At the bottom of the document type "Prepared by:" followed by your first and last name.

8. Save and print the document.

9. Switch to Web Layout view, and note any formatting problems.

10. Save the document as a Web page with the name **Mountain Time Parks Tour Web Page**. Adjust the placement of text and graphics as necessary. You might want to reduce the size of the photograph so that it doesn't extend below the two paragraphs of text. Add an appropriate background color, and one or two horizontal lines.

11. Open the file named **Comment** from the Cases folder for Tutorial 7, save it as a Web page named **Comment Web Page** in the Cases folder for Tutorial 7, format it to match the tour Web page, and then save and close the Comment Web Page. At the bottom of the tour Web page, insert the following text: "Click here to read comments about last year's tour!" Format this new text as a hyperlink that targets the file named **Comment Web Page**.

12. Place a hyperlink at the bottom of the Comment Web Page that takes the user back to the tour Web page. Test both links, save both files, and then close the Comment Web Page file.

13. Preview the Mountain Time Parks Tour Web Page in your browser. Fix any formatting problems in Word and test all links. (If your Web pages contain any SmartTags, you might want to delete them in Word, save your changes, and then preview the Web page in your browser again.) If you see the File Download dialog box when you click a link, click Open this file from its current location, and then click OK.

14. Print both Web pages from your browser, close your browser, and then close any open documents in Word and Excel, saving changes as necessary. Close Excel if it is still open.

Case 3. Bayside Health Web Page Susan Dague, publications director at Bayside Health Inc., is often asked to develop newsletters on a variety of topics related to health and fitness. To broaden the audience for these newsletters, she wants to transform them into Web pages and allow clients to read them over the World Wide Web. Susan asks you to open a blank Web page in Word, and then use it to create a Health News home page.

Explore

1. Click File on the menu bar, click New, and then click Blank Web Page in the New Document Task Pane. A blank document opens, similar to a regular Word document.

2. Save the Web page in the Cases folder for Tutorial 7 as **Health News Home Page**.

3. Type "Bayside Health Inc." and press Enter twice. Type "Welcome to Our Health News Home Page" and press Enter twice. Type "Our Health News reports give you quick updates on these important topics:" and press Enter twice. Click the Bullets button in the Formatting toolbar, and then type the following list:
    - Exercise
    - Pain management
    - Low-fat cooking

4. Select the heading "Bayside Health Inc." and the subheading "Welcome to our Health News Home Page," and then format them in 26-point Arial with a red font color. Finally, center the heading and subheading.

Explore

5. Now that you have formatted the text, you can transform the look of the Web page itself by selecting a collection of formatting options known as a theme. Click Format on the menu bar, and then click Theme to open the Theme dialog box. In the Choose a Theme list box, click Blends. If you see a message indicating that the Blends theme is not installed on your computer, select another theme. Otherwise, click OK. Save your work.

6. Open the document named **Exercise** in the Cases folder for Tutorial 7, and then display the document in Print Layout view, zoomed to Whole Page. Review the document's format, and then switch to Web Layout view. The two-column portion of the document changes to a single column and the border is hidden. The graphic (which was originally near the end of the document, in the bottom of the right column) moves to the top of the second section, under the heading "Excessive Hype over Exercise Type."

7. Save the document as a Web page named **Exercise Web Page**.

8. Drag the graphic down to position it in the paragraph below the heading "Stress on Stress Management." Format the Exercise Web Page using the Blends theme you used earlier for the home page. (You might have to re-format the list of exercise guidelines with bullets after you apply the Blends theme.) Also, delete the WordArt headline, and then format the "Excessive Hype over Exercise" heading and the "Stress on Stress Management" heading to match the main heading in the Health News home page.

9. Insert a hyperlink at the bottom of the page that returns the user to the Health News home page. Save and close the Exercise Web Page, and display the Health News home page.

10. Select the text "Exercise" in the first bullet, and format it as a hyperlink that targets the file named **Exercise Web Page**. Test the hyperlinks in both pages, and then close the Exercise Web Page file.

11. Preview the Health News Home page in your browser, review the formatting, and check all links.

12. Correct any problems in Word, save your work, and then close your browser and any open documents.

Case 4. Financial Aid FAQ Page Your local high school recently sponsored a workshop for parents of prospective college students. The goal of the workshop was to teach parents how to apply for financial aid. Now the program coordinator wants to provide some follow-up information on the Web. She asks you to create a FAQ (Frequently Asked Questions) page that answers questions raised at the seminar. In addition to the FAQ page, she asks you to create a Web page summarizing the cost of going to college. You will use a Word template to begin creating the FAQ page. Finally, she wants you to create a diagram illustrating the process of applying for financial aid, and which she can use as a handout in future workshops.

1. Click File on the menu bar, click New, and then click General Templates in the New Document Task Pane. In the Templates dialog box, click the Web Pages tab, click Frequently Asked Questions, and then click OK. A FAQ template opens, with placeholder text for questions and answers and a table of contents at the top. The document headings are already formatted as hyperlinks, as is the text "Back to top" which appears after each answer placeholder.

2. Save the template as a Word document named **Financial Aid FAQ** in the Cases folder for Tutorial 7.

3. Delete the ellipses in the heading "How do I...?", press the spacebar, and then type "apply for financial aid". When you are finished, the heading should read "How do I apply for financial aid?" Edit the hyperlink "How do I...?" in the table of contents (at the top of the page) so that it also reads "How do I apply for financial aid?"

4. After the "How do I apply for financial aid?" heading, replace the placeholder "This is the answer to the question" with a few sentences explaining how to apply for financial aid. For example, you might say: "You need to fill out a financial aid form for each college to which you apply. Typically these forms request detailed income and tax information."

5. Edit the heading "Where can I find...?" so that it reads, "Where can I find the necessary forms?" Edit the hyperlink in the table of contents to match, and then insert an answer to this question.

6. Delete the placeholder questions and answers for the "Why doesn't...?" heading, the "Who is..." heading, and the "When is...?" heading. Delete the corresponding links in the table of contents, as well as the extra "Back to top" links.

7. Edit the heading "What is...?" so that it reads "What are the costs associated with a college education?" Edit the hyperlink in the table of contents to match, and then insert an answer to this question. The last sentence in the answer should read: "For more information, click here."

8. At the bottom of the page, replace the word "Date" with the current date, followed by your first and last name. Edit the title on the FAQ page so that it describes the page's content. Save your work.

Explore

9. If you need to create a chart quickly, and you don't have access to Microsoft Excel, you can use Word's chart feature. To learn how, click the New Web Page button on the Standard toolbar (this button appears in place of the New Document button when you are working on a Web page), click Insert on the menu bar, point to Picture, and then click Chart. In the Datasheet window, replace the row labels "East," "West," and "North" with three major college expenses. Replace the column labels (1st Qtr, and so on) with the labels 1st Yr, 2nd Yr, 3rd Yr, and 4th Yr. Replace the existing numbers with expense data for four years of college, and then click outside the chart window to embed the completed chart in the Web page.

10. Save the Web page as **College Expense Chart** in the Cases folder for Tutorial 7.

11. On the FAQ page, format the text "For more information, click here" as a hyperlink that targets the College Expense Chart page. Insert the text "Back to FAQ" at the bottom of the chart page, and format it as a link that targets the FAQ page.

Explore

12. Format the FAQ and the chart Web pages with a textured background, using an option on the Texture tab on the Fill Effects dialog box. Be sure to pick a texture that is light enough to make the text easy to read.

13. Finish formatting the Web pages using the techniques you learned in this tutorial. Remember to make the pages look similar. Increase the size of the chart to make it easy to read. Save your work.

14. Close the Chart page.

15. Preview the FAQ document in your browser, and test all the links, including the link to the chart. Test the link in the chart that jumps back to the FAQ. Adjust any formatting problems in Word, and then save your work.

16. Print both pages from the browser window.

17. Close your browser, and then close any open documents.

Explore

18. You can create a variety of diagrams in Word using the tools on the Drawing toolbar. To learn how, open a new, blank document, and save it as **Application Process** in the Cases folder for Tutorial7. Switch to Print Layout view and display the rulers. In the Help box on the right side of the menu bar, type diagram, press Enter, and then click About diagrams. Read all the information Help provides about creating diagrams (including flowcharts) in Word, and then close the Help window. Click the Drawing button on the Standard toolbar to display the Drawing toolbar. In the Drawing toolbar, click the Insert Diagram or Organization Chart button to open the Diagram Gallery dialog box. Click the middle option in the top row (Cycle Diagram), and then click OK. A diagram opens with placeholder text. Click the leftmost instance of "Click to add text," press Enter twice, and then type: "Estimate costs for upcoming school year." Replace the placeholder text on the rightmost side with "Apply for financial aid". (Use extra paragraph marks to center the text vertically.) Replace the bottom placeholder text with "Compare aid received with actual costs". In the Diagram toolbar, click the AutoFormat button, and then select a format that appeals to you. Preview your diagram, make any changes using Word's editing tools, then save and print your diagram.

The Internet: World Wide Web

LAB ASSIGNMENTS

This Lab Assignment is designed to accompany the interactive Course Lab called Internet World Wide Web. To start the Lab, click the Start button on the taskbar, point to Programs, point to Course Labs, point to New Perspectives Applications, and click Internet World Wide Web. If you do not see Course Labs on your Programs menu, ask your instructor or technical support person for help.

The Internet: World Wide Web

One of the most popular services on the Internet is the World Wide Web. This lab is a Web simulator that teaches you how to use Web browser software to find information. You can use this lab whether or not your school provides you with Internet access.

1. Click the Steps button to learn how to use Web browser software. As you proceed through the steps, answer all of the Quick Check questions that appear. After you complete the steps, you'll see a Quick Check summary report. Follow the instructions on the screen to print this report.

2. Click the Explore button. Use the Web browser to locate a weather map of the Caribbean Virgin Islands. What is its URL?

3. Enter the URL **http://www.atour.com**. A SCUBA diver named Wadson Lachouffe has been searching for the fabled treasure of Greybeard the pirate. A link from the Adventure Travel Web site leads to Wadson's Web page called "Hidden Treasure." Locate the Hidden Treasure page, and answer the following questions:
   a. What was the name of Greybeard's ship?
   b. What was Greybeard's favorite food?
   c. What does Wadson think happened to Greybeard's ship?

4. In the steps, you found a graphic of Jupiter from the photo archives of the Jet Propulsion Laboratory. In the Explore section of the lab, you can also find a graphic of Saturn. Suppose one of your friends wants a picture of Saturn for an astronomy report. Make a list of the blue underlined links your friend must click to find the Saturn graphic. Assume that your friend begins at the Web Trainer home page.

5. Jump back to the Adventure Travel Web site. Write a one-page description of the information at the site. Include the number of pages the site contains, and diagram the links it contains.

6. Chris Thomson, a student at UVI, has his own Web page. In Explore, look at the information Chris included on his page. Suppose you could create your own Web page. What would you include? Use word-processing software to design your own Web page. Make sure to indicate the graphics and links you would use.

QUICK CHECK ANSWERS

Session 7.1

1. Open the original version of the document, click Tools on the menu bar, click Compare and Merge Documents, select the first edited copy of the document, click the Merge list arrow, and then click Merge into new document. Open the Compare and Merge dialog box again, select the second edited copy of the document, and this time select Merge into current document.

2. a. A source file is the file containing the original object.

   b. An object is an item such as a graphic image, clip art, a WordArt image, a chart, or a section of text that you can modify and move from one document to another.

   c. The source program is the program in which an object was originally created.

   d. A destination file is the file into which you want to insert an object.

3. With embedding, you place an object into a document and retain the ability to use the tools of the source program. With linking, you place a representation of an object into a document. With embedding, there is no connection maintained between the source file and the destination file; with linking there is.

4. Link a file whenever you have data that is likely to change over time, or if you are using data that is updated regularly by someone else.

5. To embed an existing workbook, click Insert on the menu bar, click Object, click the Create from File tab, select the file, click Insert, and then click OK without selecting the Link to file check box. To link an Excel chart, follow the same procedure, but select the Link to file check box.

6. To copy a file, right-click it, click Copy, and then press Ctrl+V.

7. To modify an embedded object from within the destination program, double-click the object, and then use the tools and menus of the source program.

8. false

Session 7.2

1. A hyperlink is a word, phrase, or graphic image that you can click to jump to another document or Web page.

2. A browser is a program designed to retrieve files from a Web server and display Web pages.

3. An intranet is a self-contained web-based network that is owned by a single organization. The Internet is a worldwide network incorporating many organizations. Part of the Internet, the World Wide Web is used to transfer Web pages between Web servers and browsers.

4. Insert a bookmark at the location you want the hyperlink to jump to. Select the text you want to format as a hyperlink, click the Insert Hyperlink button on the Standard toolbar, click Place in this Document, click the bookmark you want to link to, and then click the OK button.

5. "Executive Summary" (b) is an invalid bookmark name because it has a space.

6. A change in the color of hyperlink text indicates that the link has been used, or followed.

7. false

Session 7.3

1. true
2. text wrapping around graphics and animated text
3. false
4. Click Format on the menu bar, click Borders and Shading, click the Borders tab, click the Horizontal Line button, select a line style, and then click the OK button. A horizontal line separates sections of a document to make it easier to read and navigate.
5. After converting a Word document to a Web page, you should adjust the formatting to make it more suitable for online viewing and possibly add some special formatting features such as a background color, that are not always available in printed documents. In some cases, the original document might already contain special features, such as text wrapping, that don't translate to HTML. In that case, you might need to reapply the feature once the document has been saved as a Web page. At the very least, you will probably need to reposition graphics.
6. To preview a Web page in the default Web browser, click File on the menu bar, and then click Web Page Preview.

INDEX

TASK	PAGE #	RECOMMENDED METHOD
Action, redo most recent	WD 2.11	Click ⟳
Action, undo most recent	WD 2.11	Click ⟲
AutoCorrect, use	WD 1.25	Click AutoCorrect Options ⚡▾, click correct spelling
Background, apply textured	WD 7.32	Click Format, point to Background, click Fill Effects, click Gradient tab, select colors and shading style, click OK
Boldface, add to text	WD 2.32	Select text, click **B**
Bookmark, create	WD 7.29	Move insertion point to desired location, click Insert, click Bookmark, type bookmark name, click Add
Border, change in table	WD 3.28	See Reference Window: Altering Table Borders
Border, draw around page	WD 4.28	Click Format, click Borders and Shading, click Page Border tab, click Box, click apply to Whole Document
Bullets, add to paragraphs	WD 2.28	Select paragraphs, click ☰
Character spacing, adjust	WD 5.37	Select text, click Format, click Font, click Character Spacing tab, click Spacing list arrow, click spacing style, change number of points between characters, click OK
Character spacing, expand or condense	WD 5.36	See Reference Window: Expanding or Condensing Spacing Between Characters
Click and Type, enable	WD 5.32	Click Tools, click Options, click Edit tab, select the Enable click and type check box, click OK
Clip art, crop	WD 4.20	Click clip art, click ✂, drag picture border to crop
Clip art, find	WD 4.17	Click 🖼 on Drawing toolbar, type search criteria, click Search
Clip art, insert in document	WD 4.17	Click 🖼 on Drawing toolbar, click Clip Organizer, click picture, click Copy, click in document, click 📋
Clip art, resize	WD 4.20	Click clip art, drag resize handle
Clip art, rotate	WD 4.21	Click clip art, click ⟳ on the Picture toolbar
Clip art, wrap text around	WD 4.22	Click clip art, click 🖼 button on the Picture toolbar, click text wrapping option
Clipboard Task Pane, open	WD 2.15	Click Edit, click Office Clipboard
Column, insert in table	WD 3.22	Click Table, point to Insert, click Columns to the Right or Columns to the Left

TASK	PAGE #	RECOMMENDED METHOD
Column width, change in table	WD 3.25	Double-click or drag border between columns; to see measurements, press and hold Alt while dragging
Columns, balance	WD 4.27	Click the end of the right-most column, click Insert, click Break, click Continuous, click OK
Columns, format text in	WD 4.13	Click where you want to insert columns, or select text to divide into columns, click Format, click Columns, select options, click OK
Columns, newspaper-style, create	WD 4.13	Click where you want to insert columns, or select text to divide into columns, click Format, click Columns, select options, click OK
Comment, display	WD 2.35	Point to comment
Comment, insert	WD 2.34	Click Insert, click Comment
Data source, attach	WD 6.06-6.16	Click Tools, point to Letters and Mailings, click Mail Merge Wizard; in Step 3 of the wizard, click Use an existing list, click Browse, select data source, click Open
Data source, create	WD 6.08-6.10	Click Tools, point to Letters and Mailings, click Mail Merge Wizard; in Step 3 of the wizard, click Type a new list, click Create, enter information, click OK
Data source, sort	WD 6.27	See Reference Window: Sorting a Data Source
Date field, insert	WD 6.16	Click Insert, click Date and Time, click a date and time format, click OK
Date, insert with AutoComplete	WD 1.28	Start typing date, press Enter
Document, close	WD 1.33	Click ⊠
Document, open	WD 2.03	Click 🖿, select drive and folder, click filename, click Open
Document, open new	WD 1.15	Click ▢
Document, preview	WD 1.30	Click ▦
Document, print	WD 1.31	Click ▤
Document, save with new name	WD 2.04	Click File, click Save As, select drive and folder, enter new filename, click Save
Document, save with same name	WD 1.18	Click ▦

TASK	PAGE #	RECOMMENDED METHOD
Documents, compare and merge	WD 7.02	See Reference Window: Comparing and Merging Documents
Drawing toolbar, open	WD 4.07	Click 📷
Drop cap, insert	WD 4.24	Click in paragraph, click Format, click Drop Cap, select options, click OK
Embedded object, modify	WD 7.14	Double-click object, use commands and tools of source program to modify object, click outside embedded object
Envelope, print	WD 1.32	Click Tools, point to Letters and Mailings, click Envelopes and Labels, click Envelopes tab, type delivery and return addresses, click Print
Find and replace text	WD 2.18	See Reference Window: Finding and Replacing Text
Folder, create new	WD 5.04	Click File, click Save As, click 📁, type folder name, click OK
Font and font size, change	WD 2.30	See Reference Window: Changing the Font and Font Size
Font size, select	WD 1.12	Click Format, click Font, click font size
Font, select	WD 1.12	Click Format, click Font, click font name
Footer, add	WD 3.11	Click View, click Header and Footer, click 📄, type footer text, click Close
Footnote, add	WD 5.30	Switch to Normal view, click footnote reference location, click Insert, point to Reference, click Footnote, select note type and numbering method, set format, click Insert, type footnote, click Close
Format, copy	WD 2.27	Select text with desired format, double-click 🖌, click paragraphs to format, click 🖌
Graphic, crop	WD 4.20	Click graphic, click ┿, drag to crop
Graphic, find	WD 4.17	Click 📷 on Drawing toolbar, type search criteria, click Search
Graphic, resize	WD 4.20	Click graphic, drag resize handle
Graphic, rotate	WD 4.21	Click graphic, click 🔄 on the Picture toolbar
Graphic, wrap text around	WD 4.22	Click graphic, click 🖼 button on the Picture toolbar, click text wrapping option
Header, add	WD 3.11	Click View, click Header and Footer, type header text, click Close
Horizontal line, insert	WD 7.42	Click Format, click Borders and Shading, click Borders tab, click Horizontal Line button, click a line style, click OK

TASK	PAGE #	RECOMMENDED METHOD
Hyperlink, add to document	WD 4.05	Type e-mail address or URL, press spacebar or Enter
Hyperlink, edit	WD 7.45	Right-click the hyperlink, click Edit Hyperlink, edit filename or select a new file, click OK
Hyperlink, remove	WD 4.06	Right-click hyperlink, click Remove Hyperlink
Hyperlink to another document, create	WD 7.31	Select text, click 🖳, click Existing File or Web Page, locate target document, click OK
Hyperlink to same document, create	WD 7.28	Insert bookmark at target location, select hyperlink text or graphic, click 🖳, click Place in This Document, click bookmark name, click OK twice
Hyperlink, use	WD 7.30	Hold down Ctrl and then click the underlined hyperlink; click ⇐ to return to original location
Hyphenation, change	WD 5.28	Click Tools, point to Language, click Hyphenation, enter size of Hyphenation Zone, set limit for consecutive hyphens, click Automatically hyphenate document, click OK
Insertion point, position with Click and Type	WD 5.33	Point to location where you want to insert text, table, or graphic; double-click
Italics, add to text	WD 2.33	Select text, click 𝐼
Line spacing, change	WD 2.23	Select text, press Ctrl+1 for single spacing, Ctrl+5 for 1.5 line spacing, or Ctrl+2 for double spacing
Link, update	WD 7.22	Open destination file, click Edit, click Links, select filename, click Update Now, click OK
Mail Merge, perform	WD 6.06	Click Tools, point to Letters and Mailings, click Mail Merge Wizard, follow wizard Steps 1-6
Mailing labels, create	WD 6.30	Click Tools, point to Letters and Mailings, click Mail Merge Wizard, click Labels, click Next: Starting document, click Label options, select label type, click OK, click Next: Select Recipients,select or create data source, click Next: Arrange your labels, insert merge fields, click Update all labels, click Next: Preview your labels, click Next: Complete the merge
Main Document, select	WD 6.07	Click Tools, point to Letters and Mailings, click Mail Merge Wizard, select document type, click Next: Starting document, select document
Margins, change	WD 2.21	Click File, click Page Setup, click Margins tab, enter margin values, click OK

TASK	PAGE #	RECOMMENDED METHOD
Merge fields, insert in main document	WD 6.18	Click Tools, point to Letters and Mailings, click Mail Merge Wizard; in Step 4, click More Items, click field name, click Insert, click Close
Merged data, view in main document	WD 6.21	Click Tools, point to Letters and Mailings, click Mail Merge Wizard; on Step 5, click Next and Previous buttons in Task Panes, or click ⏮, ◀, ▶, and ⏭ the Mail Merge toolbar
Nonprinting characters, show	WD 1.13	Click ¶
Normal view, change to	WD 1.08	Click ▤
Numbered list, create	WD 2.28	Select paragraphs, click ▤
Object, embed	WD 7.12	Click destination location, click Insert, click Object, click Create from File tab, click Browse, select file, click Insert, click OK
Object, link	WD 7.17	Click destination location, click Insert, click Object, click Create from File tab, click Browse, select file, click Insert, click Link to File check box, click OK
Object, modify linked	WD 2.19	Double-click linked object, use source program tools to modify object, click outside linked object; or open object in source program, modify, save, open destination program, and update links
Outline, create	WD 5.24	See Reference Window: Creating and Editing Outlines
Outline, edit	WD 5.24	See Reference Window: Creating and Editing Outlines
Page, preview more than one	WD 3.09	Click 🔍, click ▦
Page, vertically align	WD 3.10	Click File, click Page Setup, click Layout tab, click Vertical alignment list arrow, click Center
Page, view whole	WD 4.14	Click Zoom list arrow, click Whole Page
Page break, insert	WD 3.15	Click where you want to break the page, press Ctrl+Enter
Page number, insert	WD 3.12	Open header or footer, click 🔢 on Header/Footer toolbar
Paragraph spacing, adjust	WD 5.38	See Reference Window: Adjusting Spacing Between Paragraphs
Paragraph, decrease indent	WD 2.26	Click ▤
Paragraph, indent	WD 2.26	Click ▤
Paste options, select	WD 2.13	Click 📋

TASK	PAGE #	RECOMMENDED METHOD
Picture, insert Clip Art	WD 4.17	Click ⬛ on Drawing toolbar, click Clip Organizer, click picture, click Copy, click in document, click Paste
Print layout view, change to	WD 3.16	Click ⬛
Replace text	WD 2.18	See Reference Window: Finding and Replacing Text
Reviewing pane, open or close	WD 2.35	Click ⬛ on Reviewing toolbar
Revisions, accept and reject	WD 7.07	Click ⬛ on Reviewing toolbar, click ⬛ to reject change or click ⬛ to accept change
Row, delete from table	WD 3.24	Select the rows you want to delete, click Table, point to Delete, click Rows
Row, insert in table	WD 3.23	Click bottom-right cell, press Tab
Row height, change in table	WD 3.26	Drag divider between rows; to see measurements, press and hold Alt while dragging
Ruler, display	WD 1.10	Click View, click Ruler
Section, insert in document	WD 3.08	Click where you want to insert a section break, click Insert, click Break, click Section break types option button, click OK
Section, vertically align	WD 3.09	Click File, click Page Setup, click Layout tab, click Vertical alignment list arrow, click Center, click OK
Shading, apply to table	WD 3.29	Select table area to shade, click Shading Color list arrow on Tables and Borders toolbar, click a color
Smart Tag, remove	WD 1.29	Click ⬛ , click Remove this Smart Tag
Special character, insert	WD 4.26	Click Insert, click Symbol, click Special Characters tab, click special character, click Insert, click Close
Spelling and grammar, check	WD 2.05	See Reference Window: Checking a Document for Spelling and Grammatical Errors
Spelling and grammar, check document	WD 2.05	Click ⬛, click Correction, click Change; click Ignore Once to skip an item
Spelling, correct individual words	WD 1.27	Right-click misspelled word (as indicated by a wavy red line), click correctly spelled word
Style, apply	WD 5.15	Select text, click Style list arrow, click style name
Style, define by example	WD 5.19	See Reference Window: Defining New Styles
Style, define new with style command	WD 5.19	See Reference Window: Defining New Styles
Style, modify	WD 5.16	See Reference Window: Modifying a Style

TASK	PAGE #	RECOMMENDED METHOD
Symbol, insert	WD 4.26	Click Insert, click Symbol, click desired symbol, click Insert, click Close
Tab stop, set	WD 3.04	Click tab alignment selector, click ruler
Table, center on page	WD 3.30	Click in table, click Table, click Table Properties, click Table tab, click Center alignment option, click OK
Table, create	WD 3.15	Click ▣, drag to select columns and rows; or click ✎ on Tables and Borders toolbar, draw columns and rows
Table, insert blank	WD 3.15	Click ▣
Table, sort	WD 3.20	Click in the column you want to sort, click ⬇ or ⬇ on Tables and Borders toolbar
Tables and Borders toolbar, display	WD 3.19	Click ▦
Table of Contents, create	WD 5.39	See Reference Window: Creating a Table of Contents
Task Pane, close	WD 1.08	Click ✕
Telephone List, create	WD 6.35	Click Tools, point to Letters and Mailings, click Mail Merge Wizard, click Directory, click Next: Starting document, select or create telephone list document, click Next: Select Recipients, select or create data source, click Next: Arrange your directory, insert merge fields, click Next: Preview your directory, click Next: Complete the merge
Template, create new	WD 5.22	See Reference Window: Creating and Using a New Template
Template, saved in any location, open	WD 5.13	Click Tools, click Templates and Add-ins, click Attach, select template, click Open, select the Automatically update document styles check box, click OK
Template, saved in Template folder, open	WD 5.12	Click File, click New, click General Templates on the New Document Task Pane, click icon for template in the General tab, click OK
Text, align	WD 2.24	Select text, click ▤, ▤, ▤, or ▤
Text, align in table	WD 3.27	Click Align list arrow on Tables and Borders toolbar, click alignment option
Text, animate	WD 7.34	Select text, click Format, click Font, click Text Effects tab, click animation style, click OK
Text, bold	WD 2.32	Select text, click **B**
Text, copy and paste	WD 2.15	Select text, click ▤, move to target location, click ▤

TASK	PAGE #	RECOMMENDED METHOD
Text, delete	WD 2.10	Press Backspace to delete character to left of insertion point; press Delete to delete character to the right; press Ctrl+Backspace to delete to beginning of word; press Ctrl+Delete to delete to end of word
Text, highlight	WD 5.35	Select text, click [icon]
Text, italicize	WD 2.33	Select text, click [I]
Text, move by cut and paste	WD 2.15	Select text, click [scissors], move to target location, click [paste]
Text, move by drag and drop	WD 2.12	Select text, drag pointer to target location, release mouse button
Text, select a block of	WD 2.09	Click at beginning of block, press and hold Shift and click at end of block
Text, select entire document	WD 2.09	Press Ctrl and click in selection bar
Text, select multiple adjacent lines	WD 2.09	Click and drag in selection bar
Text, select multiple nonadjacent lines	WD 2.09	Select text, press and hold Ctrl, and select next text
Text, select multiple paragraphs	WD 2.09	Double-click and drag in selection bar
Text, select paragraph	WD 2.09	Double-click in selection bar next to paragraph
Text, select sentence	WD 2.09	Press Ctrl and click in sentence
Text, underline	WD 2.33	Select text, click [U]
Text, wrap around WordArt	WD 4.22	Click WordArt, click [icon] on the WordArt toolbar, click text wrap option
Thesaurus, use	WD 5.05	See Reference Window: Using the Thesaurus
Toolbar, display	WD 1.09	Right-click any visible toolbar, click toolbar name
Underline, add to text	WD 2.33	Select text, click [U]
Web layout view, change to	WD 7.33	Open document, click [icon]
Web page, create	WD 7.38	See Reference Window: Saving a Word Document as a Web Page
Web page, view in Web browser	WD 7.46	Click File, click Web Page Preview
Word, exit	WD 1.34	Click [X]

TASK REFERENCE

TASK	PAGE #	RECOMMENDED METHOD
Word, start	WD 1.05	Click [Start], point to Programs, click Microsoft Word
WordArt, change shape	WD 4.10	Click WordArt, click [Abc] on the WordArt toolbar, click shape
WordArt, edit text	WD 4.09	Click WordArt, click Edit Text button on WordArt toolbar, edit text, click OK
WordArt, insert	WD 4.07	Click [icon], click WordArt style, click OK, type WordArt text, select font, size, and style, click OK
WordArt, wrap text	WD 4.22	Click WordArt, click [icon] on the WordArt toolbar, click text wrap option
Zoom setting, change	WD 1.11	Click Zoom list arrow, click zoom percentage

Standardized Coding Number	Certification Skill Activity — Activity	Courseware Reqs	Tutorial Pages	End-of-Tutorial Practice — End-of-Tutorial Pages	Exercise	Step Number
W2002-1	**Inserting and Modifying Text**					
W2002-1-1	Insert, modify and move text and symbols	Insert, cut, copy, paste and paste special	1.16–1.18 (insert)	1.35	RA	1–9, 11
				1.36	CP1	3–7
				1.36–1.37	CP2	3–8
				1.37	CP3	2
				1.38	CP4	5–8
			2.14–2.17 (cut, copy, paste)	2.40	RA	14
				2.44	CP4	6
				7.55 (Paste Special)	CP2	3
		Finding and replacing text	2.17–2.19	2.38	RA	7
				2.41	CP1	8
				2.42	CP2	4
				2.43	CP3	11
				2.44	CP4	12
		Using AutoCorrect to insert frequently used text	1.23–1.25	1.35	RA	10
				1.36	CP1	4
W2002-1-2	Apply and modify text formats	Applying and modifying character formats	2.31–2.34	2.38	RA	7
				2.41	CP1	6, 13, 15, 16
				2.42	CP2	9
				2.43	CP3	4, 11, 14, 15
				2.44–2.45	CP4	13, 15, 16
W2002-1-3	Correct spelling and grammar usage	Using Spelling and Grammar checks	1.24–1.26	1.35	RA	15
				1.36	CP1	10
			2.05–2.06	2.38	RA	3
				2.41	CP1	2
				2.42	CP2	2
				2.44	CP4	3
		Using the Thesaurus	5.05–5.06	5.45	RA	5
				5.48	CP1	8
				5.50	CP3	6

Standardized Coding Number	Certification Skill Activity — Activity	Courseware Reqs	Tutorial Pages	End-of-Tutorial Practice — End-of-Tutorial Pages	Exercise	Step Number
W2002-1-4	Apply font and text effects	Applying character effects (superscript, subscript, etc.) and text effects (animation)	5.36	5.45	RA	8, 10
				5.48	CP1	
			7.34–7.35 (animation)	7.49	RA	15
		Applying highlights	2.08–2.09 (select)	2.40	RA	13, 14
				2.41	CP1	13, 15
				2.43	CP3	15
				2.44	CP4	11
			5.35–5.36 (color)	5.46	RA	16
				5.47	CP1	6
				5.50	CP3	10
W2002-1-5	Enter and format Date and Time	Inserting date/time fields and modifying field formats	1.27–1.29 (Auto Complete)	1.35	RA	10
				1.36	CP1	4
			5.34–5.35	5.46	RA	17
				5.49	CP2	13
				5.51	CP4	8
W2002-1-6	Apply character styles	Applying character styles	5.15	5.45	RA	9
W2002-2	**Creating and Modifying Paragraphs**					
W2002-2-1	Modify paragraph formats	Applying paragraph formats	2.23–2.25 2.27–2.28	2.38	RA	7
				2.41	CP1	5, 10
				2.42	CP2	10
				2.43	CP3	14
				2.44	CP4	11
		Applying borders and shading to paragraphs	5.19 4.28–29	2.32	CP1	9
		Indenting paragraphs	2.25–2.26	2.38–2.40	RA	6, 13
				2.42	CP3	6
				2.44	CP4	10

Standardized Coding Number	Certification Skill Activity — Activity	Courseware Reqs	Tutorial Pages	End-of-Tutorial Practice — End-of-Tutorial Pages	Exercise	Step Number
W2002-2-2	Set and modify tabs	Setting and modifying tabs	3.04–3.07	3.33	RA	3
				3.35	CP1	7
W2002-2-3	Apply bullet, outline, and numbering format to paragraphs	Applying bullets and numbering	2.28–2.29	2.38	RA	7
				2.41	CP1	9
				2.42	CP2	7
				2.43	CP3	6
				2.44	CP4	7
		Creating outlines	5.24–5.27	5.46	RA	11–13
				5.47	CP1	2
				5.49	CP2	7
				5.50	CP3	3-4
				5.51	CP4	3-6
W2002-2-4	Apply paragraph styles	Applying paragraph styles (e.g.; Heading 1)	5.16	5.45	RA	7
				5.49	CP2	4, 6
W2002-3	**Formatting Documents**					
W2002-3-1	Create and modify a header and footer	Creating and modifying document headers and footers	3.11–3.13	3.33	RA	7, 8
				3.35	CP1	5, 6
				3.36	CP2	6, 7
W2002-3-2	Apply and modify column settings	Applying columns and modifying text alignment	4.13–4.14 4.27–4.28	4.31	RA	12, 21
				4.32	CP1	10
				4.34	CP2	8
				4.35	CP3	6
		Creating newsletter columns	4.13–4.14	4.31	RA	12
				4.32	CP1	10
		Revising column layout	4.27–4.28	4.31	RA	21
				4.34	CP2	8
				4.35	CP3	6
W2002-3-3	Modify document layout and Page Setup options	Inserting page breaks	3.14–3.15	3.34	RA	8
				3.35	CP1	8
		Inserting page numbers	3.12	3.33	RA	8
				3.35	CP1	6
		Modifying page margins, page orientation	2.20–2.22 (margins)	2.38	RA	5, 6
				2.41	CP1	4
				2.42	CP2	5
				2.43	CP3	12, 13
W2002-3-4	Create and modify tables	Creating and modifying tables	3.13–3.18 3.21–3.27	3.34	RA	8, 10–12
				3.35	CP1	10–12
				3.36	CP2	8, 9
				3.37	CP3	4, 7
				3.38	CP4	6, 7

Standardized Coding Number	Certification Skill Activity Activity	Courseware Reqs	Tutorial Pages	End-of-Tutorial Practice End-of-Tutorial Pages	Exercise	Step Number
		Applying AutoFormats to tables	3.24	3.37	CP3	5
		Modifying table borders and shading	3.27–3.30	3.34 3.35 3.36 3.38	RA CP1 CP2 CP4	12, 13 13 11 6
		Revise tables (insert and delete rows and columns, modify cell formats)	3.21–3.27 3.35 3.36 3.37	3.34	RA CP1 CP2 CP3	10–12, 17,18 12 10 4
W2002-3-5	Preview and Print documents, envelopes, and labels	Using Print Preview	1.30–1.31	1.35 1.36 1.37 1.37 1.38	RA CP1 CP2 CP3 CP4	18 14 11 4 12
		Printing documents, envelopes, and labels	1.31–1.32 (documents)	1.35 1.36 1.37 1.37 1.38	RA CP1 CP2 CP3 CP4	18 14 11 4 12
			1.32 (envelopes)	1.35 1.37 1.37	RA CP2 CP3	20 12 5
W2002-4	**Managing Documents**					
W2002-4-1	Manage files and folders for documents	Creating folders for document storage	5.04–5.05	5.45 5.50	RA CP3	3 2
W2002-4-2	Create documents using templates	Creating a document from a template	5.22 5.47	5.47	RA	24
W2002-4-3	Save documents using different names and file formats	Using Save, Save As	1.18–1.19 (Save)	1.35 1.36 1.37 1.37 1.38	RA CP1 CP2 CP3 CP4	13, 17, 21 8, 14 9, 13 3, 6 10, 12

Standardized Coding Number	Certification Skill Activity		Courseware Reqs	Tutorial Pages	End-of-Tutorial Practice		
	Activity				End-of-Tutorial Pages	Exercise	Step Number
				2.04 (Save As)	2.38	RA	2, 18
					2.41	CP1	1
					2.42	CP2	1
					2.43	CP3	2
					2.44	CP4	2
W2002-5	**Working with Graphics**						
W2002-5-1	Insert images and graphics		Adding images to document	4.16–4.19	4.31	RA	14
					4.33	CP1	11
					4.34	CP2	9
					4.36	CP4	9
W2002-5-2	Create and modify diagrams and charts		Creating and modifying charts and diagrams	7.17–7.23	7.48 (charts)	RA	8
						CP1	3–5
					7.55 (diagrams)	CP4	18
W2002-6	**Workgroup Collaboration**						
W2002-6-1	Compare and Merge documents		Compare and Merge documents	7.2–7.6	7.48	RA	3–5
W2002-6-2	Insert, view and edit comments		Insert, view and edit comments	2.34–2.35	2.40	RA	17
					2.42	CP2	11
	Convert documents into Web pages		Previewing as documents as web pages	7.46–7.47	7.49, 7.50	RA	11, 21
					7.51	CP1	7
					7.52	CP2	9
			Saving documents as web pages	7.38–7.39	7.49	RA	17
					7.52	CP2	10
					7.53	CP3	7
					7.55	CP4	10

Word 2002 Level I File Finder

Location in Tutorial	Name and Location of Data File	Student Saves File As...	Student Creates New File
Tutorial 1			
Session 1.1	(No file)		
Session 1.2			Tutorial.01\Tutorial\Web Time Contract Letter.doc
Review Assignments			Tutorial.01\Review\Conference Call Memo.doc Tutorial.01\Review\Web Time Envelope.doc
Case Problem 1			Tutorial.01\Cases\Water Park Information Letter.doc
Case Problem 2			Tutorial.01\Cases\Confirmation Letter.doc
Case Problem 3			Tutorial.01\Cases\Liza Morgan Letter.doc
Case Problem 4			Tutorial.01\Cases\Meeting Memo.doc
Tutorial 2			
Session 2.1	Tutorial.02\Tutorial\FAQ.doc	Tutorial.02\Tutorial\Tree FAQ.doc	
Session 2.2	(Continued from Session 2.1)		
Review Assignments	Tutorial.02\Review\Statmnt.doc	Tutorial.02\Review\Monthly Statement.doc	Tutorial.02\Review\LMG Contact Information.doc
Case Problem 1	Tutorial.02\Cases\Form.doc	Tutorial.02\Cases\Authorization Form.doc	
Case Problem 2	Tutorial.02\Cases\CCW.doc	Tutorial.02\Cases\CCW Brochure.doc	
Case Problem 3	Tutorial.02\Cases\UpTime.doc	Tutorial.02\Cases\UpTime Training Summary.doc	
Case Problem 4	Tutorial.02\Cases\Ridge.doc	Tutorial.02\Cases\Ridge Top Guide.doc	
Tutorial 3			
Session 3.1	Tutorial.03\Tutorial\WAN.doc	Tutorial.03\Tutorial\New Hope WAN Report.doc	
Session 3.2	(Continued from Session 3.1)		
Review Assignments	Tutorial.03\Review\Trouble.doc	Tutorial.03\Review\Troubleshooting Report.doc	Tutorial.03\Review\Equipment List.doc
Case Problem 1	Tutorial.03\Cases\SunRep.doc	Tutorial.03\Cases\Sun Porch Report.doc	
Case Problem 2	Tutorial.03\Cases\Tour.doc	Tutorial.03\Cases\Masterpiece Tour Report.doc	
Case Problem 3	Tutorial.03\Cases\Contacts.doc	Tutorial.03\Cases\Sales Contacts.doc	
Case Problem 4			Tutorial.03\Cases\Camp Winnemac.doc
Tutorial 4			
Session 4.1	Tutorial.04\Tutorial\Clothes.doc	Tutorial.04\Tutorial\Travel Clothes.doc	
Session 4.2	(Continued from Session 4.1)		
Review Assignments	Tutorial.04\Review\Travel.doc	Tutorial.04\Review\Travel Highlights.doc	
Case Problem 1	Tutorial.04\Cases\Convert.doc	Tutorial.04\Cases\Software Conversion.doc	
Case Problem 2	Tutorial.04\Cases\Movers.doc	Tutorial.04\Cases\Movers Newsletter.doc	
Case Problem 3	Tutorial.04\Cases\Grains.doc	Tutorial.04\Cases\Wild Grains Brochure.doc	
Case Problem 4			Tutorial.04\Cases\New Job.doc

Word 2002 Level II File Finder

Location in Tutorial	Name and Location of Data File	Student Saves File As...	Student Creates New File
Tutorial 5			
Session 5.1	Tutorial.05\Tutorial\SafeSite.doc Tutorial.05\Tutorial\Professional Report.dot	Tutorial.05\Tutorial\Business Plan\SafeSite Business Plan.doc	Tutorial.05\Tutorial\Business Plan\SafeSite Company Documents.dot
Session 5.2	(Continued from Session 5.1)		
Session 5.3	(Continued from Session 5.2)		
Review Assignments	Tutorial.05\Review\SafeDesign.doc	Tutorial.05\Review\SafeDesign Technical Support\SafeDesign Policies.doc	Tutorial.05\Review\SafeDesign Technical Support\Fax Cover Sheet.doc Tutorial.05\Review\SafeDesign Technical Support\Additional Policies.doc Tutorial.05\Review\SafeDesign Technical Support\SafeDesign Template.dot
Case Problem 1	Tutorial.05\Cases\Furniture.doc	Tutorial.05\Cases\Rosewood Traditional Furniture.doc	Tutorial.05\Cases\Store Address.doc
Case Problem 2	Tutorial.05\Cases\Meals.doc Tutorial.05\Cases\Menu Template.dot	Tutorial.05\Cases\Meals & Menus.doc	
Case Problem 3	Tutorial.05\Cases\Business.doc	Tutorial.05\Cases\Writing Project\Business of Basketball.doc	
Case Problem 4			Tutorial.05\Cases\Preliminary Budget Draft.doc Tutorial.05\Cases\Budget Template.dot
Tutorial 6			
Session 6.1	Tutorial.06\Tutorial\Club.doc	Tutorial.06\Tutorial\Club Letter with Field Codes.doc	Tutorial.06\Tutorial\Club Data.mdb Tutorial.06\Tutorial\Club Merged Letters1.doc Tutorial.06\Tutorial\Club Merged Letters2.doc
Session 6.2	(Continued from Session 6.1)	Tutorial.06\Tutorial\Tamp Club Letter with Field Codes.doc	Tutorial.06\Tutorial\Club Merged Letters3.doc Tutorial.06\Tutorial\Club Labels.doc Tutorial.06\Tutorial\Club Labels with Field Codes.doc
Session 6.3	Tutorial.06\Tutorial\Phone.doc	Tutorial.06\Tutorial\Sorted Phone List.doc	Tutorial.06\Tutorial\Club Phone Directory.doc Tutorial.06\Tutorial\Club Phone Directory with Field Codes.doc
Review Assignments	Tutorial.06\Review\Assess.doc	Tutorial.06\Review\Health Assessment.doc	Tutorial.06\Review\Assessment Data.mdb Tutorial.06\Review\Merged Health Assessment Letters.doc Tutorial.06\Review\Cardio Health Assessment Letters.doc Tutorial.06\Review\Assessment Envelopes.doc Tutorial.06\Review\Envelopes with Field Codes.doc Tutorial.06\Review\Merged Envelopes.doc

Location in Tutorial	Name and Location of Data File	Student Saves File As...	Student Creates New File
	Tutorial.06\Review\Memo.doc Tutorial.06\Review\Insurance Data.xls	Tutorial.06\Review\Insurance Memo.doc	Tutorial.06\Review\Merged Insurance Memos.doc Tutorial.06\Review\Directory with Field Codes.doc Tutorial.06\Review\Merged Directory.doc
Case Problem 1	Tutorial.06\Cases\Creek.doc	Tutorial.06\Cases\Sugar Creek Letter.doc	Tutorial.06\Cases\Sugar Creek Data.mdb Tutorial.06\Cases\Merged Sugar Creek Letters.doc Tutorial.06\Cases\Sugar Creek Envelopes.doc Tutorial.06\Cases\Merged Sugar Creek Envelopes.doc Tutorial.06\Cases\Sugar Creek E-mail Directory.doc Tutorial.06\Cases\Merged Sugar Creek E-mail Directory.doc
Case Problem 2	Tutorial.06\Cases\Gems.doc	Tutorial.06\Cases\Gems Letters.doc	Tutorial.06\Cases\Gems Data.mdb Tutorial.06\Cases\Merged Gems Letters.doc Tutorial.06\Cases\Gems Labels.doc Tutorial.06\Cases\Merged Gems Labels.doc Tutorial.06\Cases\Gems Customer Directory.doc Tutorial.06\Cases\Gems Customer Directory.doc
Case Problem 3	Tutorial.06\Cases\Auto.doc	Tutorial.06\Cases\Auto Sales Letter.doc	Tutorial.06\Cases\Auto Sales.mdb Tutorial.06\Cases\Merged Auto Sales Letters.doc Tutorial.06\Cases\Auto Sales Directory.doc Tutorial.06\Cases\Merged Auto Sales Directory.doc
Case Problem 4			Tutorial.06\Cases\E-mail Message.doc Tutorial.06\Cases\E-mail Data.mdb Tutorial.06\Cases\Merged E-mail Message.doc Tutorial.06\Cases\My E-mail Directory.doc Tutorial.06\Cases\My Merged E-mail Directory.doc
Tutorial 7 Session 7.1	Tutorial.07\Tutorial\Grant.doc Tutorial.07\Tutorial\Karen.doc Tutorial.07\Tutorial\Tom.doc Tutorial.07\Tutorial\Chart.xls	 Tutorial.07\Tutorial\Copy of Chart.xls	Tutorial.07\Tutorial\Grant Proposal.doc
Session 7.2	(Continued from Session 7.1) Tutorial.07\Tutorial\Resume.doc		

Word 2002 Level II File Finder (continued)

Location in Tutorial	Name and Location of Data File	Student Saves File As...	Student Creates New File
Session 7.3	(Continued from Session 7.2)	Tutorial.07\Tutorial\Grant Proposal Web Page.htm Tutorial.07\Tutorial\Resume Web Page.htm	
Review Assignments	Tutorial.07\Review\FinlBgt.doc	Tutorial.07\Review\Copy of FinlBgt.doc	Tutorial.07\Review\Evaluation Report.doc Tutorial.07\Review\Evaluation Report Web Page.htm
Case Problem 1	Tutorial.07\Cases\Office.doc Tutorial.07\Cases\Downtn.doc	Tutorial.07\Cases\Office Rental Memo.doc Tutorial.07\Cases\Downtown Development.doc	
Case Problem 2	Tutorial.07\Cases\Parks.doc Tutorial.07\Cases\Comment.doc	Tutorial.07\Cases\Mountain Time Parks Tour.doc Tutorial.07\Cases\Mountain Time Parks Tour Web Page.htm Tutorial.07\Cases\Comment Web Page.htm	
Case Problem 3	Tutorial.07\Cases\Exercise.doc	Tutorial.07\Cases\Exercise Web Page.htm	Tutorial.07\Cases\Health News Home Page.htm
Case Problem 4			Tutorial.07\Cases\Financial Aid FAQ.htm Tutorial.07\Cases\College Expense Chart.htm Tutorial.07\Cases\Application Process.doc